Trust in E-Services:
Technologies, Practices and Challenges

Ronggong Song, National Research Council Canada, Canada

Larry Korba, National Research Council Canada, Canada

George Yee, National Research Council Canada, Canada

IDEA GROUP PUBLISHING

Hershey • London • Melbourne • Singapore

Acquisition Editor:	Kristin Klinger
Senior Managing Editor:	Jennifer Neidig
Managing Editor:	Sara Reed
Assistant Managing Editor:	Sharon Berger
Development Editor:	Kristin Roth
Copy Editor:	Angela Thor
Typesetter:	Jamie Snavely
Cover Design:	Lisa Tosheff
Printed at:	Yurchak Printing Inc.

Published in the United States of America by
    Idea Group Publishing (an imprint of Idea Group Inc.)
    701 E. Chocolate Avenue
    Hershey PA 17033
    Tel: 717-533-8845
    Fax: 717-533-8661
    E-mail: cust@idea-group.com
    Web site: http://www.idea-group.com

and in the United Kingdom by
    Idea Group Publishing (an imprint of Idea Group Inc.)
    3 Henrietta Street
    Covent Garden
    London WC2E 8LU
    Tel: 44 20 7240 0856
    Fax: 44 20 7379 0609
    Web site: http://www.eurospanonline.com

    Library of Congress Cataloging-in-Publication Data

Trust in e-services : technologies, practices, and challenges / Ronggong Song, Larry Korba, and George Yee, editors.
    p. cm.
 Summary: "This book provides an overall view of trust for e-services including definitions, constructs, and relationships with other research topics such as security, privacy, reputation and risk. It offers contributions from real-life experience and practice on how to build a trust environment for e-government services"--Provided by publisher.
 Includes bibliographical references and index.
 ISBN 1-59904-207-X (hardcover) -- ISBN 1-59904-208-8 (softcover) -- ISBN 1-59904-209-6 (ebook)
 1. Electronic commerce--Security measures. 2. Web services. 3. Trust. 4. Computer systems--Reliability. I. Song, Ronggong. II. Korba, Larry. III. Yee, George.
 HF5548.32.T745 2007
 658.8'72028558--dc22
                   2006033663

British Cataloguing in Publication Data
A Cataloguing in Publication record for this book is available from the British Library.

All work contributed to this book is new, previously-unpublished material. The views expressed in this book are those of the authors, but not necessarily of the publisher.

Trust in E-Services:
Technologies, Practices and Challenges

Table of Contents

Preface

There has been a rapid increase of electronic services (e-services) with the explosive nature of the information technology development in the past decades. E-services like Web banking, Web shopping, Web auctions, e-government, e-healthcare, e-manufacturing, and e-learning, are available in most countries and becoming part of everyday life for citizens everywhere. However, as a basis for deciding to use a service (Michalakopoulos & Fasli, 2005), and a central and crucial component in the online transaction process and information exchanges (Ba, Whinston, & Zhang, 1999), trust is becoming a major impediment to the growth of e-services. E-services change the traditional face-to-face service model. Since consumers cannot touch or even see first hand the physical products in a Web store to assess their quality, it is difficult to build an intuitive level of trust. The entities involved in such e-services must use technologies such as credentials and reputation for assessing trust. Another challenge to trust and e-services is the fact that integral to human nature, trust is very difficult to specify (McKnight & Chervany, 1996). Based on the wide range of existing research and definitions from psychology, sociology, economics, business, law, politics, and science, McKnight and Cervany developed and refined a conceptual framework of trust with six constructs: trusting intention, trusting behavior, trusting beliefs, system trust, depositional trust, and situational decision. This wide scope of trust concepts is difficult to interpret and represent with practical technologies. Research on trust definitions, constructs, and models from a more technical view is vital and urgent for e-services. In addition, the inherent complexity (e.g., dynamic distributed systems) and issues such as fraud, identity theft, security, and privacy associated with e-services make trust problems even harder and more complex in practice. This requires research on methodologies to tackle the trust problems in the early stage of system development from a holistic point of view in order to ensure the trustworthiness of the whole system. These trust issues and challenges (including legal issues) in e-services are explored in depth in the first part of this book: *Trust Concepts and Challenges in E-Services*.

Today's trust technologies are mainly focused on trust management and reputation systems. They have been studied over the last decade. The known and important trust management solutions include OpenPGP (Callas, Donnerhacke, Finney, & Thayer, 1998), KeyNote (Blaze, Feigenbaum, & Lacy, 1998), REFEREE (Chu, Feigenbaum, LaMacchia, Resnick, & Strauss, 1997), W3C PICS (PICS, 2006), IBM Trust Policy Language (TPL, 2006), SULTAN (Grandison & Sloman, 2002), Poblano (Chen & Yeager, 2000), Trusted Computing (TC, 2006), and so forth. These technologies provide trust-related services such as trust establishment, analysis, monitoring, and evidence collection. However, each of them has its limitations in practice, especially when applied to e-services. For instance, as Grandison mentioned (2006), PGP may not be suited for e-services due to its lack of official mechanisms to create, acquire, and distribute certificates. In addition, the issues and challenges of identities, privacy, and attacks require in-depth research when these technologies are deployed for real e-services. The detailed information for each trust management technology is reviewed and discussed in the "Trust Management Tools" chapter of this book. The challenges around the application of these tools in current real systems are discussed in the chapter "A Survey on Trust Use and Modeling in Real Online Systems." As a popular trust mechanism, reputation systems have been researched and used in many e-services for trust evaluation. One of the best known of these applications is eBay. Two serious problems related to reputation systems are fraud and defamation. The legal issues and challenges related to these require further exploration.

This book aims to provide the latest research and practice in trust management, evaluation approaches, and mechanisms for building trust in e-services. It also introduces research into the conceptions and constructs of trust, and discusses associated topics such as factors, requirements, challenges, and issues for building trusted e-services from the following three aspects:

- **Trust concepts** (definition, constructs, models, and taxonomy), issues, and challenges in e-services
- **Trust technologies** in e-services including holistic trust design for e-services and a review of trust management technologies
- **Trust practices** in e-services that describe the trust issues, challenges, and methods for e-health and the ambient world, including methods for building trust in e-services

The Challenges and Opportunities

Trust has been researched in multiple dimensions in computer systems for many years, but most trust technologies focus only on the evaluation and establishment of trust relationships (Grandison & Sloman, 2000), and less on studying the problem from the perspective of the broader e-services environment to include definitions, as well as legal, and trust design issues. The challenges for trust in e-services can be classified into the following categories:

- The challenges of establishing correct trust definitions, structures, and models for e-services, and a unified taxonomy framework that can be used for various distributed e-services environments. These challenges focus on answering the following questions:
  - ➢ What is trust? And what is trust for the e-services space?
  - ➢ How do you model and build trust relationships in e-service environments?
  - ➢ How do you provide a unified taxonomy framework that can be used as powerful tools in the analysis and design of trust in e-service systems?

- The challenges of developing trust design methodologies that help system designers identify trust issues and provide guidelines on the various facets of trust in e-services development. The questions to be answered here include:
  - ➢ How do you tackle trust issues in the early stage of e-service system development from a holistic point of view?
  - ➢ How do you analyze trust during the design of an e-service system?
- The challenges of establishing identity trust with security and privacy protection for the next generation of distributed e-services. Questions to be answered for these challenges include:
  - ➢ How do you fill the gap between identities and their level of trust?
  - ➢ How do you create and manage credentials or virtual identities in e-service systems?
  - ➢ How do you establish and apply trust models with identity trust and reliability trust for e-services?
- The challenges of developing trust practices for e-health, e-learning, pervasive computing and ambient world systems. Questions to be answered in these areas include:
  - ➢ How do you exploit trust for real e-services?
  - ➢ How do you apply trust technologies to real e-service systems?
- The challenges of examining the legal issues of trust in e-service systems, including fraud, misrepresentation, and defamation from the system operators and consumers.

Organization of the Book

This book reports on the latest research related to trust in e-services. It is organized into 3 sections and 12 chapters. A brief description of each chapter follows:

Section I: Trust Concepts and Challenges in E-Services

Chapter I discusses the fundamental concepts of trust with an emphasis on their applicability to e-services. It provides the prevailing perspectives and introduces a unifying definition on trust that can be used for e-services. The chapter also discusses the foundation of the trust construct: building blocks of a trust relationship and trust relationships in e-service environments. Current trust models, mechanisms employed today, and future research directions are highlighted.

Chapter II proposes a unified taxonomy framework of trust based on a formal definition of trust relationships with a strict mathematical structure. It discusses classification of trust under the taxonomy framework and properties of trust direction and symmetry. The chapter provides a set of definitions, propositions, and operations based on the trust relationships. The authors believe that this taxonomy framework of trust will provide accurate terms and useful tools for enabling the analysis, design, and implementation of trust.

Chapter III discusses the concept of trust and how trust is used and modeled in online systems currently available on the Web. It provides a classification of the systems that currently use trust and presents the most representative examples for each category. It also summarizes the open and interesting challenges for online systems that use and model trust information.

Chapter IV discusses the legal challenges of online reputation systems, which have become important tools for supporting commercial as well as noncommercial online interactions. It takes the example of eBay's Feedback Forum to review the potential legal liabilities facing the operators of online reputation systems. The chapter discusses the applicability of Canadian laws in the areas of negligent misrepresentation and defamation, indicating that lawsuits against the operators of online reputation systems have already emerged in the United States.

Section II: Trust Technologies in E-Services

Chapter V describes a holistic trust design methodology that builds upon the current understanding of trust and combines useful aspects encountered in existing works. It is based on a systematic analysis of scenarios that describe the typical use of e-services by employing a trust analysis grid composed of 11 trust issue categories that cover various aspects of trust. This approach is intended to be used to guide the design of computing systems by analyzing and refining the scenarios, and providing suggestions for appropriate technologies. It also illustrates the methodology via examples in the areas of e-health and e-learning.

Chapter VI proposes a common conceptual framework of two-layer models for managing authenticity and trust as an important security prerequisite. It discusses the key notions of entities, identities, authenticity, and trustworthiness, and classifies existing systems in terms of these layered models. The chapter proposes and defends the two-layer requirements for e-services, and describes the credential network model as an existing, general two-layer model.

Chapter VII discusses information valuation policies to effect a trustworthiness assessment for e-services. It presents an information selection algorithm based on intuitive policies for information valuation, and provides justification and analysis for the derived and calculated trust estimate. The chapter identifies five policies for valuing source information based on the different priorities. The authors believe that this research will make a major contribution toward assisting e-service users to obtain accurate information from online sources.

Chapter VIII discusses trust management tools researched and developed through the last decade. It presents their strengths, domain of application, and scope for improvement, providing a holistic view of the trust management problem. It outlines the evolution of these trust technologies and presents the catalyst(s) for each phase in its metamorphosis.

Section III: Trust Practices in E-Services

Chapter IX presents a literature survey of recent contributions related to trust in e-commerce. It points out that all studies arrive at the conclusion that trust plays a key role in consumers' decisions to adopt e-commerce. As well, it identifies some remarkable conclusions from the authors surveyed. The chapter then describes seven practical methods that can be employed by a B2C Internet service provider to increase consumer trust in the use of its services.

Chapter X presents a brief overview of e-health and describes how and why people are using the Internet for health advice and information. It proposes a staged model of trust in order to understand the trust processes behind this engagement, while exploring this model through a series of in-depth qualitative studies. The authors believe that this model will form the basis for a set of design guidelines for developing trust practices in e-health.

Chapter XI discusses how people will trust Ambient Intelligence and ubiquitous computing systems and ironically, at the same time achieve and maintain privacy. It describes recent research related to privacy and trust with regard to ambient technology.

Chapter XII discusses why authentication or the real-world identity is really necessary to use the human notion of trust. It proposes a user-centric identity management solution based on the consumer's ability to create and manage multiple virtual identities and presents different identities in different contexts, thereby limiting the ability to link transactions and users.

Conclusion

This book provides readers an overview of trust in e-services, including research on the conceptions and constructs of trust, and associated topics such as factors, requirements, challenges, methods, and issues for building trusted e-services. The editors have collected the latest research and practices in trust management, evaluation approaches, and trust design methodologies describing how to build trust in e-services.

The book is intended for educators, professionals, researchers, computer administrators, and software developers who are interested in trust research and development for e-services. Although there are other books on trust, no other book gives such a well-rounded view on trust for e-services, dealing with all the challenges of trustworthy e-services.

References

Ba, S., Whinston, A. B., & Zhang, H. (1999). Building trust in the electronic market using an economic incentive mechanism. In *Proceedings of the 1999 International Conference on Information Systems*, Charlotte, NC (pp. 208-213).

Blaze, M., Feigenbaum, J., & Lacy, J. (1996). Decentralized trust management. In *IEEE Conference on Security and Privacy*. Oakland, CA.

Callas, J., Donnerhacke, L., Finney, H., & Thayer, R. (1998). *OpenPGP message format*. IETF RFC 2440. Retrieved March 27, 2006, from http://www.ietf.org/ rfc/rfc2440.txt

Chen, R., & Yeager, W. (2000). Poblano: *A distributed trust model for peer-to-peer networks*. Sun Microsystems. Retrieved March 28, 2006, from http://www.jxta.org/docs/trust. pdf

Chu, Y. H., Feigenbaum, J., LaMacchia, B., Resnick, P., & Strauss, M. (1997). *REFEREE: Trust management for Web applications*. Retrieved March 28, 2006, from http://www. w3.org/PICS/TrustMgt/doc/referee-WWW6.html

Grandison, T. (2006). Trust management tools. In R. Song, L. Korba, & G. Yee (Eds.), *Trust in e-services: Technologies, practices and challenges*. Hershey, PA: Idea Group Inc.

Grandison, T., & Sloman, M. (2000). A survey of trust in Internet applications. *IEEE Communications Survey and Tutorials, 4*(4), 2-16.

Grandison, T., & Sloman, M. (2002). Specifying and analysing trust for Internet applications. In *Proceedings of 2nd IFIP Conference on E-Commerce, E-Business, E-Government (I3e2002)*, Lisbon, Portugal.

McKnight, D. H., & Chervany, N. L. (1996). *The meanings of trust* (Tech. Rep. No. WP9604). University of Minnesota, Management Information Systems Research Center.

Michalakopoulos, M., & Fasli, M. (2005). On deciding to trust. In *Proceedings of the 3rd International Conference on Trust Management (iTrust 2005)* (LNCS, 3477, pp. 61-67).

PICS. (2006). *Platform for Internet content selection.* Retrieved March 28, 2006, from http://www.w3.org/PICS/

TC. (2006). *Trusted computing.* Retrieved March 28, 2006, from http://en.wikipedia.org/wiki/Trusted_Computing_Group

TPL. (2006). *IBM trust establishment policy language.* Retrieved March 28, 2006, from http://www.haifa.ibm.com/projects/software/e-Business/TrustManager/Policy Language.html

Acknowledgments

We would like to thank all of the authors for their excellent contributions to this book.

Our deep appreciation and gratitude goes to all the reviewers who provided their insightful and constructive comments, in particular to Tyrone Grandison of IBM Almaden Research Centre, Weiliang Zhao of University of Western Sydney, Jennifer Chandler of University of Ottawa, Stéphane Lo Presti of University of London, Dimitar Christozov of American University in Bulgaria, Elizabeth Sillence of Northumbria University, Karen Fullam and Suzanne Barber of University of Texas at Austin, and last but not least, George Forester, our Business Development Office colleague.

Our thanks also go to all who were involved in the collation and review process of this book. Without their support, the project could not have been satisfactorily completed.

Special thanks also go to all of the staff at Idea Group Inc. Their contributions through the whole process, from inception of the initial idea to final publication, have been very helpful. In particular, we would like to thank Jan Travers, whose guidance through the initial contract formulation process made it all possible, Mehdi Khosrow-Pour, whose enthusiasm motivated us to initially accept the invitation to take on this project, and Kristin Roth, who continuously prodded via e-mail for keeping the project on schedule.

Finally, we are indebted to the Institute for Information Technology, National Research Council Canada, for providing us the resources for this project.

Ronggong Song, Larry Korba, and George Yee
National Research Council Canada
September 2006

Section I

Trust Concepts and Challenges in E-Services

Chapter I

Conceptions of Trust:
Definition, Constructs, and Models

Tyrone Grandison, IBM Almaden Research Center, USA

Abstract

This chapter introduces the fundamental concepts of trust, with emphasis on their applica-bility to the e-services platform. This sets the tone for this book and creates a platform from which the topics can be explored more deeply in the other chapters. This chapter presents a description of e-services and trust environments, provides the prevailing perspectives on trust, and introduces a unifying definition that can be used for e-services. Furthermore, the indicators that influence a trust decision when e-service invocation is desired, is specified, and the current trust models are highlighted. These models may be leveraged when designing the architecture for an e-service solution. In addition to being a resource during e-service system design, this chapter focuses on making the reader cognizant of the broader technical and management-related issues surrounding trust in e-services, and providing a common platform for discussion.

Introduction

The concept of trust has been widely studied in many fields, for example, psychology, sociology, business, political science, law, and economics. In computer sciences, trust research and technology is motivated by prior work in all these fields and has created a litany of perspectives and research directions. Research has focused on adapting psychological comprehension of trusting behavior (Castelfranchi & Falcone, 2001; Giorgini, Massacci, Mylopoulos, & Zannone, 2005; Grimsley, Meeham, Green, & Stafford, 2003; Riegelsberger, Sasse, & McCarthy, 2005), on modeling trust interactions using game theory and other economics tools (Fernandes, Kotsovinos, Ostring, & Dragovic, 2004; Kimbrough, 2005), on using logic to create models of trust (Demolombe, 2004; Jones & Firozabadi, 2000; Jøsang, 1997; Marsh, 1994; Millen & Wright, 2000; Simmons, 1993;) and on using definitions of trust to drive systems-based approaches to the management of trust relationships (Anderson, Matyas, & Peticolas, 1998; Blaze, Feigenbaum, & Lacy, 1996; Jøsang, 1999; Ketchpel & Garcia-Molina, 1996; Konrad, Fuchs, & Bathel, 1999; Su & Manchala, 1997; Viega, Kohno, & Potter, 2001; Yahalom, Klein, & Beth, 1993). Thus far, the majority of the efforts have been narrow in focus (Grandison & Sloman, 2000) and oblivious to the ecosystem that must exist for trust to be an integral part of the fabric of the Internet.

Examining the trust problem in the context of e-services is even harder than investigating trust in computer systems because solutions must take into account the dynamic nature of a distributed system, the fact that consumers may be prior strangers, the need to establish trust on both the service provider and consumer side, and the fact that there is a greater incentive to subvert valued, one-off services. These complications imply that there needs to a coordinated, dynamic infrastructure to create, foster, and maintain the delicate web of trust needed to spur the growth of e-services (Grandison, 2003). Current trust technologies focus primarily on only evaluating and establishing trust relationships (Grandison & Sloman, 2000). Our discussion will not only cover these better-known aspects of trust relations, but extend to the broader set of topics pertinent to the e-services environment.

In this chapter, the building blocks for discussion on trust in e-services are discussed. A presentation of the meanings of e-services and trust will be given, followed by a discussion of the elements and nature of a trust relationship and finally, there will be a presentation of trust models relevant to e-services.

Defining the E-Services Landscape

For this discourse, e-services will be defined as *functionality that is made available over the Internet*. For example, e-commerce transaction services for handling online orders, automatic bill payment services by banks, and application and document hosting by online service providers. Thus, e-services refer to any processing capability that is available online to a consumer.

Figure 1 shows that the concept can be generalized to apply to arbitrary electronic communication media without loss of the core tenet: leveraging network technology to enable

Figure 1. Typical e-services organization

Service Providers
NEWS
Communications Infrastructure
Service Consumers

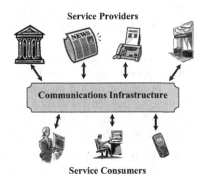

service provision through the communication channel(s). Thus, e-services applications can refer to technology constructed on devices connected through any (possibly proprietary) distributed network.

An important lesson from building trust technology for e-services (Van Dyke, 2004) is that the solution requires more than evaluation and analysis technology. Trust monitoring and evolution technology is often overlooked. The same is true for the nontechnical components that must be in place.

An e-services trust ecosystem that contains technology, legislative, business, and social components (Figure 2) must be in place before e-service provision is viewed as a natural way of doing business by the masses. Figure 2 is a refinement and extension of the require-

Figure 2. The four pillars of the e-services trust ecosystem

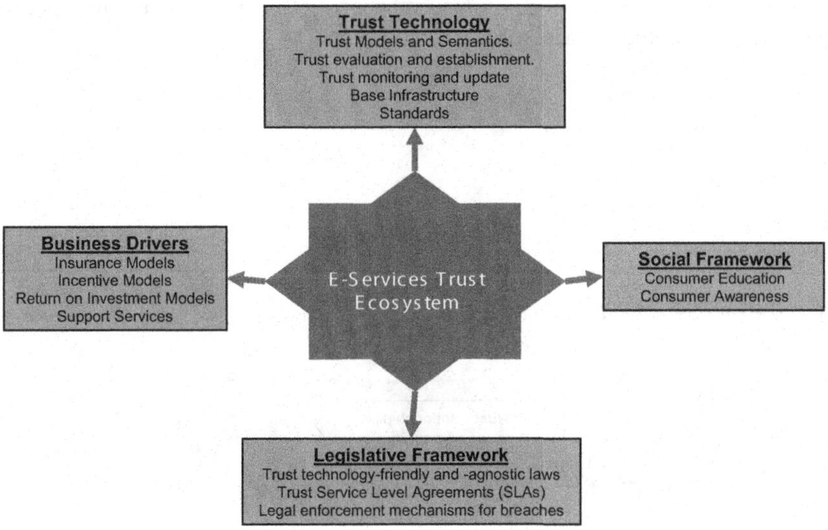

Trust Technology
Trust Models and Semantics.
Trust evaluation and establishment.
Trust monitoring and update
Base Infrastructure
Standards
Business Drivers
Insurance Models
Incentive Models
Return on Investment Models
Support Services
E-Services Trust Ecosystem
Social Framework
Consumer Education
Consumer Awareness
Legislative Framework
Trust technology-friendly and -agnostic laws
Trust Service Level Agreements (SLAs)
Legal enforcement mechanisms for breaches

ments for trust and e-commerce in Jones (1999) and an instantiation of the ecosystem that has been crucial for the Internet's success. For the Internet, a similar system of actors had to be in position and aligned before widespread acceptance and use was on the horizon. The same is true for e-services.

The technology component of the ecosystem should ensure the soundness and unambiguity of the trust models used, ensure the appropriate criteria are used to establish trust, and guarantee that relationships will evolve with service provision and use patterns. Two invariants for any trust technology developed for the e-services environment are that it should be interoperable (i.e., standards based) and not add considerable overhead to the user experience (i.e., integrated into the base infrastructure with minimal effect on system usability).

The business drivers ensure that there are compelling reasons for both the provider and the consumer to engage in an e-service transaction. On the consumer side, this means that there have to be models for insurance and incentive (which engender more trust) and clear indication from the provider that support services will be provided. From the provider's perspective, there needs to be a clear description of the return on investment or positive impact on total cost of ownership with regards to a service being made available online.

The legislative framework ensures that there are legal avenues for recourse in the event of the subversion of a service by either party. There may also be the need for legally binding contractual agreements on service provision and service use to foster client trust. These legal measures help to define the ramifications if something goes wrong.

The social framework makes sure that the public understands the technology and methods of protection available to them. Thus, a program of education on the tradeoffs of different trust technology is necessary. The level of education needed and the delivery mechanisms are still open issues. Thereafter, it is the client's responsibility to exercise good judgment in the trust tools and business and legislative safeguards that he/she chooses to use.

A more in-depth discussion on the components of the e-services trust ecosystem will be presented in other chapters. However, given an understanding of what an e-service is, and the ecosystem that needs to be in place for its deployment, we need to comprehend all the trust issues that impact the various ecosystem components. Our starting point should be the core concept in the problem space: trust.

Figure 3. A trust relationship

Defining the Trust Landscape

Trust is normally stated in terms of a relationship between a *trustor*, the subject that trusts a target entity, which is known as the *trustee*, that is, the entity that is trusted (Figure 3). It should be noted that though the trustor is assumed to be the service consumer and trustee the service provider, the opposite may also hold true.

After more than a decade into research on embedding trust into computing, there is still no consensus on the meaning of trust. This is due to the fact that trust is an integral part of human nature (Luhmann, 1982) and is normally treated as an intuitive and universally understood concept. A disparity arises when the realization is made that intuition is determined by people's experiences and when different individuals start to make varying interpretations. Thus, a viewpoint on trust will be different based on experiences.

What is Trust?

Many computer science researchers and practitioners have proposed definitions of trust because they realize that it is unwise to assume an intuitive, universal, and well-understood definition of trust. It is unwise to make this assumption because the landscape becomes unmanageable and may lead to the creation of solutions that are intractable or undecidable or that have no bearing on real-world systems. Definitions vary depending on the researcher's background, outlook on life, and the application domain of the problem being solved. In this chapter, an overview of the more popular definitions will be provided and a unifying definition proposed for the e-services platform.

The Webster dictionary defines trust as:

An assumed reliance on some person or thing. A confident dependence on the character, ability, strength or truth of someone or something., or *A charge or duty imposed in faith or confidence or as a condition of a relationship.* or *To place confidence (in an entity).*

These definitions demonstrate the common interpretations in the social context. The Oxford dictionary says that trust is:

The firm belief in the reliability or truth or strength of an entity.

This is a more general view of trust, but it would be difficult to interpret strength generally for the Internet.

Kini and Choobineh (1998), in their contemplations on the theoretical framework of trust, use the Webster dictionary's definition of trust, and examine trust from the perspectives of personality theorists, sociologists, economists, and social psychologists. They highlight the implications of these definitions and combine their results with the social psychological perspective of trust to create their definition of *trust in a system*—a belief that is influenced by the individual's opinion about certain critical system features.

This definition expresses only system trust, and excludes dimensions, such as trust in a transaction and trust in the attributes of the trustee, that are critical for e-service applications. The European Commission Joint Research Centre defines trust as:

The property of a business relationship, such that reliance can be placed on the business partners and the business transactions developed with them. (Jones, 1999)

This view of trust is from a business management perspective and neglects to highlight the reliance that is needed in the hardware and software infrastructure required to enable e-service transactions.

According to Lewis and Weigert (1985), trust is expressed as:

Observations that indicate that members of a system act according to and are secure in the expected futures constituted by the presence of each other for their symbolic representations.

Their perspective highlights the notion of system members having expectations. However, this approach assumes that expectations are positive (Lewis & Weigert, 1985). This is not always the case on the Internet. Mayer and Davis (1995) introduce an extra dimension in their definition. They define trust as:

The willingness of a party to be vulnerable to the actions of another party based on the expectation that the other will perform a particular action important to the trustor, irrespective of the ability to monitor or control that other.

This definition implies an element of being able to monitor trust and reevaluate a decision. Zand (1972) defines trust as:

The willingness to be vulnerable based on positive expectations about the actions of others.

However, this too is not always the case in real e-service scenarios. I may be willing to be vulnerable when there is a low-value product or service. However, high-valued services may require analysis of your past actions and the controls in place to ensure proper use.

In Curral and Judge (1995), trust is defined as:

An individual's reliance on another party under conditions of dependence and risk.

Dependence implies a strong degree of reliance by all parties involved. This implies that there is an equally weighted, reciprocal relationship between the trustor and trustee. This is not a suitable assumption to make for e-services. Mui, Mohtashemi, and Halberstadt (2002) define trust as:

A subjective expectation an agent has about another's future behaviour based on the history of their encounters.

This illustrates the subjective nature of trust. It also demonstrates the need to learn from past experiences. Their definition does not allow trust based on third parties' accounts of past interactions, like eBay. Even though, the description of their model (Mui et al., 2002) allows querying of the entire social network of past behavior.

The discussion of trust definitions in this section is an abridged one. However, it presents a sufficiently representative sample of the definitions in current literature. McKnight and Chervany (1996), Lamsal (2001), Gerck (1997), and Corritore, Kracher, and Wiedenbeck (2001) provide a more detailed discourse on trust definitions in philosophy, sociology, psychology, business management, marketing, ergonomics, and human-computer interaction (HCI). Thus far, each of the definitions presented can be easily justified as correct and appropriate. They highlight the fact that trust is multifaceted. However, there is a central theme that can be found in these definitions. This theme is that trust is a measurable, subjective belief about some action (or set of actions), that this belief expresses an expectation (Jones, 2002) and that this belief has implications on the features, properties, and attributes of a system. However, these definitions do not take into account the particular needs of a networked environment. Each definition is specific to its area of application, namely: business, logic, philosophy, social behaviour, and so forth. This limits their general use and applicability. For e-services, it is necessary to incorporate the notions relevant to commercial transactions, which include service provider dependability and honesty.

What is Trust for the E-Services Space?

For the reasons mentioned, trust, in the e-services context, is defined as:

The quantified belief by a trustor with respect to the competence, honesty, security and dependability of a trustee within a specified context.

Also distrust is defined as:

The quantified belief by a trustor that a trustee is incompetent, dishonest, not secure or not dependable within a specified context.

Both definitions are borrowed from Grandison and Sloman (2003), and are used because they merge the important aspects of the definitions previously discussed and also highlight the principles that are most appropriate for an e-service application, namely trust measurability, trust subjectivity, contextual trust belief, trust expectation, and the implications of trust on system attributes.

Quantification reflects that a trustor can have various degrees of trust (distrust) that could be expressed as a numerical range or as a simple classification such as low, medium, or high. A competent entity is capable of performing the functions expected of it or the services it is meant to provide correctly and within reasonable timescales. An honest entity is truthful and does not deceive or commit fraud. Truthfulness refers to the state where one consistently utters what one believes to be true. To deceive means to mislead or to cause to err (whether accidentally or not), while fraud refers to criminal deception done with intent to gain an advantage. A secure entity ensures the confidentiality and integrity of its valuable assets and prevents unauthorized access to them. Dependability is the measure in which reliance can justifiably be placed on the service delivered by a system (Verissimo & Rodrigues, 2001). Thus by definition, a dependable entity is also a reliable one. Timeliness is an implicit component of dependability, particularly with respect to real-time systems. Thus, the definition captures the basic set of attributes for comprehension of trust in the e-service environment.

Distrust diminishes the spectrum of possible present and future interactions, while trust does the opposite. Distrust is a useful concept to specify as a means of revoking previously agreed trust or for environments when entities are trusted, by default, and it is necessary to identify some entities that are not trusted.

The dominant attributes of trust and distrust relationships differ depending on the scenario in which they are used. Thus, particular patterns can be identified depending on the application context in which this technology is deployed. These patterns may be useful in deciding the correct combination of trust tools to be associated with an e-service.

Patterns of Service Provision Trust

In Grandison and Sloman (2000), a taxonomy of five trust-use cases was identified. One of these categories is *service provision trust*, where the trustor trusts the trustee to provide a service that does not involve access to the trustor's resources. Online services do not always follow this rule, as they may require applets and cookies to be downloaded (Morency, 1999), and so require access to resources owned by the trustor.

Service provision trust can be further categorized into scenarios emphasizing *confidence*, *competence*, or *integrity*. In the confidence trust scenario, trust maps into a form of access control that is subject-based, in that the subject is only permitted to access trusted services. Examples of *confidence-focused service provision trust* are:

- I trust eBay's recommendation service to only recommend products that are not defective or offensive to me.
- I trust American Express Financial Services Consultants to provide information that is accurate and sound.
- I distrust the sexy-eyes Web site to provide any services to me.

Examples of service trust that relate to the *competence* of the trustee are:

- I only trust Charles Swab consultants, whose investment portfolios exhibit double digit returns over the last three quarters, to manage my portfolio.
- I will only purchase PC support services from Company XYZ because they have proven in the past that they have capable and responsive staff.

A trustor's trust in the *competence* of the trustee's ability to provide a service differs from *confidence* trust in that *confidence* applies to entities the trustor will use and *competence* applies to entities that perform some action on behalf of the trustor.

In e-commerce and e-banking, the customer trusts the vendor or bank to support mechanisms that will ensure that passwords are not divulged, and to prevent transactions from being monitored. The vendor or bank is also trusted to maintain the *privacy* of any information such as name, address, and credit card details, which it holds about the customer. Thus, the trustor has concerns with respect to the *reliability* or *integrity* of the trustee. Examples of this type of trust are:

- I will store these critical files on MyVirtualPC.com, because it has a RAID file system and it is archived every 30 minutes. In this case, the trustee does have access to the trustor's resources.
- I trust the E-NewsAgent to e-mail me an electronic newspaper every morning before 8am.
- I trust my Internet bank not to divulge my name and address to companies for electronic marketing.

Breakdowns in the reliability or integrity of an e-service may lead to (1) privacy problems, (2) security problems, or (3) availability problems. All of which adversely affect the "brand" of the e-service and may lead to lowered levels of use by end-users and lower income levels for providers.

The discussion on the different categories or patterns of service provision trust highlights the significance of examining the driving factor behind a trust relationship. This impacts the technology measures that must be in place to create and maintain particular types of relationships.

Figure 4. Service provision rust with competence

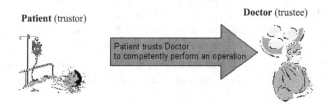

Figure 5. Service provision trust with honesty factor dominant

Chris (trustor)   **CarSalesman** (trustee)

Chris trusts CarSalesman
to honestly provide advice

The importance of competence, honesty, security, and dependability depends on the context in which they are used. However, it is near to impossible to definitively state that there is a particular combination of attributes that uniquely define a particular context. This is due to the fact that the example scenarios for each of these contexts are so varied that a different importance hierarchy may be found for examples within the same context. In Figure 4, it can be seen that the competence of the Doctor is the most important concern for the patient.

Figure 5 is another example of service provision trust. However, in this example, the primary concern of Chris is with the honesty of CarSalesman.

These two examples highlight the fact that it is hard to find a particular mix of attributes that can be used to characterize a particular context. More examples that substantiate this observation can be found in Grandison (2003). Despite this phenomenon, it is still possible to use the service provision trust patterns to guide the trust building blocks that are needed for a particular environment.

Building Blocks of a Trust Relationship

The essential components of a trust relationship are the trustor, the trustee, a specific context with associated level of trust, and the conditions under which this relationship becomes active. In this section, the base constructs of the trust relationship are explored and mapped to the e-service space.

Context

A trust relationship is never absolute, that is, X will never trust Y to do any possible action or provide any service it may choose. A trustor trusts a trustee with respect to its ability to provide a specific service within a *context*. For example, a Sure-Trade representative is only trusted to deal with my financial transactions that are less than $5,000.

A trust relationship is always defined with respect to a scenario, situation, or other contextual cues (Marsh, 1994). Even the service provider's trust in its ability to provide the service is not usually absolute. There may be a need to protect resources from mistakes or accidents.

For example, e-FileServer.com may have to protect files from accidental deletion by its subsystems.

Measurability

A relationship often has an associated *level* of trust (Mayer, 1990), which is a measure of belief in another entity. By our definition, this level is a measure of *belief* in the honesty, competence, security, and dependability of this entity, and not a measure of the *actual* competence, honesty, security, or dependability of an entity.

Some service providers may be trusted more than others. This measure can either be discrete or continuous. In either case, the reliable and consistent assignment of initial values and the representation of ignorance (or the uncertain) are currently unresolved concerns

Cardinality

Trust relationship can be *one*-to-*one*, *one*-to-*many*, or *many*-to-*many* (Grandison & Sloman, 2000), where *many* refers to either a group of providers or consumers. The assumption for the typical e-services transaction is that the relationship is *one*-to-*one* between two entities.

If trustees and trustors are considered to be from the same set (the set of all entities online), then the trust relation can be viewed as a mathematically defined binary relation, which seems to be a sensible assumption.

Mathematical Properties

If the trust relationship can be reduced to a mathematically defined binary relation, then this implies that there may be useful properties of this relation that would help in the comprehension and modeling of trust. It was shown in Grandison (2003) that the trust relation *cannot be said to possess any of the common mathematical properties that binary relations exhibit*. Thus, the trust relation does not universally adhere to any of the following properties: reflexivity, irreflexivity, nonreflexivity, symmetry, nonsymmetry, antisymmetry, asymmetry, transitivity, nontransivity, or intransitivity. However, there may be instances or scenarios where one of these properties is needed. For example, transitivity is useful in situations where subservice delegation is necessary (Agudo, Lopez, & Montenegro, 2005).

Influencing Factors

Trust mechanisms will be impacted by a multitude of factors, namely distrust (Grandison, 2001), mistrust (Marsh & Dibben, 2005), fraud (Falcone, Singh, & Tan, 2001), deception (Barber, Fullam, & Kim, 2002), risk (Braendeland & Stolen, 2004; Jøsang & Lo Presti, 2004), experience (Griffiths & Chao, 2005), diffidence (Castelfranchi & Falcone, 2001), confidence (Skevington, 1998), service level agreements (Kollingbaum & Norman, 2002), expectation (Jarvenpaa, Tractinsky, Saarinen, & Vitale, 1999), reputation (Jøsang, Hird, & Faccer, 2003; Mui et al., 2002; Patel, Teacy, Jennings, & Luck, 2005), recommendation (Massa & Bhattachargee, 2004; Pitsilis & Marshall, 2005;), privacy (Seigneur & Jensen, 2004), insurance (Millen & Wright, 2000), incentive (Salam, Rao, & Pegels, 1998) and legislation (Zanero, 2005). The purpose of this section is not to explain the connection between trust and all of these factors, but to introduce these concepts and to highlight the high-level interplay between trust and some of these concepts. Other chapters in this book will go into more detail on the relationships between trust notions in e-services.

Business Factors

Consumers may be willing to (repeatedly) trust an e-service provider, despite the fact that their goals and the goals of the providers are markedly different. For example, I know that Overstock.com is focused on profit maximization and I know that my personal philosophy is to buy the cheapest goods. However, I decide to trust Overstock.com, repeatedly, for extraneous factors, such as their excellent return policy or their AMEX-backed reward scheme. Thus, in this context, the trust relationship may be influenced by market forces, social and interaction cues, legislative mechanisms, assurance systems, insurance, and the lack of choice or effective alternatives. Sometimes a consumer's trust propensity may dictate that he/she sticks to companies, products, and services that he/she knows about, irrespective of all the other factors.

Some of these social devices are hard (and possibly unrealistic) to represent in a technological solution (Riegelsberger, Sasse, & McCarthy, 2003). However, Riegelsberger has demonstrated that some of these devices can be leveraged in user interface design and interaction. Similarly, there are other concepts, more amenable to computer science, that can be incorporated into trust frameworks, for example, experience and risk.

Experience

Experience with an entity determines the level of trust or distrust that will exist in a relationship. The better the experience that you have had with a business, the more likely you are to trust them. This implies that there is a direct relationship between experience and trust. In traditional commercial settings, the more experience that can be gained, over a longer period of time, will be a dominant factor in determining trusting behaviour. Suppose that I have been a customer of SecurityServices.com for 10 years and have had a majority of negative experiences with them (failures to deliver goods, defective products, etc.). When faced with an option to trust them or trust another more reliable (or even new) company, experience would lead to me to not use SecurityServices.com. There may be exceptions to this rule, for example, if there is a monopoly on a service that is routinely used, then the service may normally be accepted, in spite of experience information.

Risk

Risk is an intrinsic part of everyday life. It is normally expressed in terms of a monetary loss. For service transactions, the risk is dependent on a number of factors, such as the cost of the transaction and the capital loss or gain that could be incurred. A trust relationship is normally established between trustor and trustee when both can ascertain that the risk involved in performing the transaction is low. Thus, it becomes apparent that the basic relationship (or rule) between trust and risk is that the lower the risk, the more trust one is willing to place. There are also deviations from this rule of thumb, for example, Andrea may trust a high-risk venture of low value, but not a medium risk transaction of high value. High stakes gamblers in Las Vegas may trust highly valued, highly risky transactions. Thus, when the payoff is significant, the risk may be ignored. An analysis of the rules utilized during the formation of e-service trust relationships highlight similar trends.

Building Trust Relationships in E-Service Environments

Trust forms the basis for making a decision to use a service (Michalakopoulos & Fasli, 2005). When a consumer invokes an e-service, the initial question that is being asked is "*What criteria should we use to establish this relationship?*" The common mechanism to gather this information is to use security credentials (authentication tokens, attributes, etc.) to establish identity and determine the set of allowable trusted tasks. Both paths have their difficulties and both do not take into account the other facets of the trust decision-making process.

In a standard transaction e, where b wants to engage a, a must determine the level of trust or distrust and use this to determine whether to proceed. Apart from assurances on the competence, honesty, security, timeliness, and reliability of b (or the dominant attribute), a has other considerations to include in the trust decision. From a purely commercial standpoint, a favorable decision depends on the following factors:

1. Intrinsic properties of the transaction.
2. Assurances about respecting a's privacy.
3. a's experience with b with respect to the transaction.
4. b's past experience with others, with respect to the transaction.
5. b's reputation in the community of interest.
6. A recommendation on b's behalf.

At an abstract level, these points can be classified as either transaction-specific considerations or event-driven considerations.

Transaction-Specific Factors

These are the attributes that relate to the intrinsic properties of the transaction, namely its associated risk, its value, its insurance coverage, and any associated economic incentive (or disincentive) associated with performing the transaction (i.e., invoking the service). It is assumed that each consumer has a risk threshold value that may cross providers and service offerings. Transactions with values above this threshold are deemed risky, and those below not risky.

Value

Normally, a, who is rational, considers a low-valued transaction, service, or product trivial to her bottom line. She does not mind engaging with b, even if b is malicious and shatters her expectations. This is because she views low-valued transactions as having very little risk and thus, her risk thresholds for these transactions are low. Thus, a low-valued transaction will often lead to positive trust decisions.

Insurance

An insured transaction implies that the transaction value can be recovered (at the very least). Taking out insurance lowers the threshold for establishing a relationship for that transaction. Normally, decisions regarding insured transactions will not take the transaction's value into account. Instead, the other factors involved will contribute more to the outcome of the trust decision. If insurance is the only (or dominant) factor, then a will have propensity to make a favorable decision.

Economic Incentive

If b or a third party is willing to compensate a for engaging in e, such that the compensation is equal to or greater than the transaction's value, then a will view the transaction as being below her risk threshold and thus would be inclined to trust b. Similar reasoning can be applied for a disincentive where a third party pays a not to proceed with the transaction.

In the Real World

For a low-valued transaction, the cost of insurance may not be worth the investment. The same may be true for low-risk situations. However, a low-risk, high-value transaction may be insured depending on the service provider. Insurance and compensation are normally applied to high-valued transactions, products, or services. Value may be used as an indicator of the risk level, which indicates the mechanisms that need to be in place. Insurance and incentives are among the mechanisms that can be used. Other controls that can be employed relate to provider and consumer events and activity.

Event-Driven Factors

Event-driven factors relate to activity, agreements, arrangements, or information that occur either prior to or outside the scope of the current trust decision with consequences that extend beyond the existing decision. For example, a's body of knowledge concerning past encounters with b as it pertains to e constitutes information that occurred prior to the current decision and whose influence will extend beyond the decision. The effect of such factors is specified in Grandison (2003). In this section, the privacy-related and memory-related issues will be presented.

Privacy

The guarantees on the disclosure of sensitive information may be important for the provider or consumer or both. Assurances should be made on minimal sensitive information collection during communication, and on the use and exposure of confidential information during normal operation. The protection of a's privacy can be achieved in one of two ways:

1. a not releasing any private information. In this case, a ensures that she has the appropriate mandatory privacy controls in place to guarantee that her privacy policy is never violated. There may be instances where this is not feasible.

2. b asserting that it will not violate a's privacy, and a (and b) actively monitoring the disclosures and the activity of b. Remote monitoring may not be realistic (or desirable) for the real world.

If a privacy violation occurs, then it should negatively impact the trust relationship. If no violation happens, then the relationship remains intact. Negative impact would manifest itself as a decrease in the trust level for that relationship. The compromised party may choose to remember (or not) this event for future interactions.

Memory

An experience is an event that one has participated in. Trust interactions that are recorded and can be referenced in the future constitute one's experiences. The value of experience is that it can be used to enhance the quality of a decision. Experience is used to increase the probability of a favorable outcome and reduce the risk profile of a relationship. In essence, using experience to guide trust decisions makes life (and the trust decision process) simpler. A positive experience implies an increased confidence level, while a negative experience implies a lowered confidence level (even distrust). In other words, a positive experience is an event that positively impacts the trustor's trust level in the trustee, while a negative experience negatively impacts it. The trust level that a trustor has in a trustee with respect to some event is the result of the cumulative experiences that the trustor has had regarding the trustee with respect to the event. The experience that impacts the trustor's trust level in the trustee with respect to some transaction can be a purely cognitive experience, such as learning about an entity's reputation, or receiving a recommendation from a third party.

These concepts, which shape an e-service transaction, require a framework that allows them to be combined and incorporated into technology. They need to be embodied in a trust model.

Trust Models

Current trust models focus on particular functional aspects of the trust process, namely: trust establishment and trust reasoning. Trust establishment refers to the process of determining whether or not a trust relationship should be created. Trust reasoning involves using pre-defined trust information to gain insight into one's trusting behaviour. Though important, these processes do not model the entire trust in e-services process.

There is another focus area, trust monitoring, that has received little interest in the e-services community. Trust monitoring is the process of ensuring that the criteria and mechanisms to evolve trust relationships are in place. The rationale behind the need for monitoring, presented in Grandison and Sloman (2000), is that trust relationships are dynamic, and models should include mechanisms for both creating and evolving relationships. Current e-services frameworks still require work with respect to this issue.

The Web services infrastructure is becoming the platform of choice for e-services delivery. In current Web services literature (Platzer, 2004; Ratnasingam, 2002), it is normally assumed that a trust model is for the specification of the rules to be used to create a trust relationship. This represents only a small function of a trust model, which should also state how trust relationships change over time. There are efforts in the trust management domain that may be leveraged to create trust models that contain trust-monitoring elements, for example, Kinateder, Baschny, and Rothermel (2005).

In the following sections, an attempt is made to present the current set of trust models as they relate to their function (i.e., trust establishment or trust reasoning). There is commonality between the underlying techniques used in subcategories to be presented (Grandison, 2003). However, it is hoped that the functional demarcation is more appropriate for abstract comprehension of how these models may be used. It is beyond the scope of this section to discuss in detail all the models that have been created. Instead, the general characteristics of each category of model will be provided and at least one representative example presented. The list below is not purported to be exhaustive, but nearly a convenient start for further investigation.

Trust Establishment

Trust models directed at the establishment of trust relationships use the credential negotiation process, take a natural science-based approach, or leverage virtual cues as their founding construct.

Negotiation-Based Models

In negotiation-based models (Anderson et al., 2005; Platzer, 2004; Su & Manchala, 1997; Van Dyke, 2004; Winsborough, Seamons, & Jones, 1999), a challenge-response protocol is defined that allows both parties to gain sufficient information to decide if a relationship should be created and the service invoked.

The Web services trust model (Anderson et al., 2005) defines a protocol by which two participants can exchange security tokens to determine if trust should be established. The claims in the tokens are verified by each party to determine if they comply with the establishment policy. The system setup is reminiscent of the systems previously deployed in the trust management research community (Blaze, Feigenbaum, & Strauss, 1998). The Web service trust model may also be implemented in a brokered fashion, where a third party provides verification functionality.

Natural Science-Based Models

Some computational trust models, for example, Marsh (1994), take a natural science approach, that is, a phenomenon can always be examined by various methods. These models provide a mathematical framework with which trust can be examined. There are two categories of these models: numerical models and fuzzy logic-based models. Both model a typical scenario with a typical context and try to explain the trust each agent should have in each other. Thus, they try to evaluate whether trust should be established and, if it should be, then what is the appropriate initial trust value. Numerical models view the trust value as an arbitrary real number that can be used in further computation, while fuzzy logic models view the trust value as a linguistic label that represents a (range of) value(s). Fuzzy logic models also define a mathematical framework that allows the manipulation of these labels.

In Manchala (1998), a model for the measurement of trust variables and the fuzzy verification of e-commerce transactions is proposed. He highlights the fact that trust can be determined by evaluating the factors that influence it, namely risk. He defines cost of transaction, transaction history, customer loyalty, indemnity, and spending patterns as trust variables. Each variable is measured using semantic labels. His notation is focused on defining when two trust variables are related by an electronic commerce trust relationship (ECTR). Using this ECTR, a trust matrix is constructed between the two variables and a trust zone is established. He also describes a method for trust propagation and the construction of a single trust matrix between vendor and customer that governs the transaction. The problems with Manchala's model are that (1) it is unclear which variables should be used by default for the best results, (2) it is unclear if it is actually possible for a computer to automatically establish that two variables are related by an ECTR. In his definition, he mentions a semantic relationship between the variables, but neglects to mention how this fact will be specified to the computer so that evaluation can be automated and (3) it is unclear if ECTR merging will scale in the face of large trust matrices.

Human-Computer Interaction (HCI)-Based Models

People trust other individuals by using a set of social clues, such as a gaze, facial expression, and subtle details of their conversational style. The absence of similar cues online led the HCI community to investigate how such trust could be engendered using technology (Cassell & Bickmore, 2000; Shneiderman, 2000). HCI-based models are concerned with how trust is developed between two interacting individuals using computer-mediated communication (CMC) technology (chat, audio, e-mail, video). There are two dominant types of HCI-based models of trust, namely social models or economics-based models.

Social-Based HCI Models

The social models (Egger, 2001; Staples & Artnasingham, 1998) incorporate the use of CMC technology and human interaction cues to either assess the trustworthiness of entities or to help in the design of trustworthy interfaces. These models take into account the notions of the user's psychology (propensity to trust, trust in IT and the Internet, utility, usefulness, risk), reputation information (reputation of the industry, of the company and information from trusted third parties), interface properties (branding, usability), information quality, and pretransaction and posttransaction relationship management. The major concern with these models is that in their current states, they are essentially design methodologies with little or no tool support and too many abstractions of complex social notions that hinder their usability.

Economics-Based HCI Models

Economics-based models assume that individuals make trust choices based on rationally derived costs and benefits (Kim & Prabhakar, 2000). They are based on game theory, and firmly rooted in experiments and surveys to identify the action that should be taken by individuals embarking upon an interaction. A large proportion of economics-based models are founded on the prisoner's dilemna (PD) game, which is defined as follows: There are two men, *A* and *B*, who are charged with a joint law violation, being held separately by the police, and given three options. The first option is that someone confesses, say *A*, and *B* does not, then *A* will be rewarded and *B* fined. The second option is that if they both confess, each will be fined. The final option is that if neither confesses, both will go clear. So, should each man cooperate (keep quiet) or defect (confess)? The difference between the rewards when only one confesses and when both confess is significant.

Ideally, if all the parties are rational, then the best independent choice to make is defection. This may not lead to the optimal utility for each player, but a player will not find himself at a relative disadvantage. Researchers of economic-based HCI trust models use games to design experiments to evaluate the actions of participants engaging in cooperative task using various CMC technologies. The trust level is determined by the rate of cooperation, which is measured by the collective payoff. The problems with these models are that the games tend to be (1) synchronous and thus cannot be applied to all trust scenarios and (2) too simple to model an e-commerce application that includes many other factors such as experience, and so forth.

Hybrid HCI Models

There are models that combine both the social and economics perspectives (Patrick, 2001; Riegelsberger et al, 2003). These models tend to be based on very strict game theory models, which allows for better modeling in a wider range of situations. They also include specific social concepts that they consider pertinent to the trust problem and thus avoid the complexity of trying to model complex social ideas.

To gain insight into the trust process, it is possible to leverage trust-reasoning models either before or after the trust establishment process.

Trust Reasoning

In this section, trust models that are based on formal logic representations of the social process of trust will be presented. These models emphasize the specification of and reasoning about beliefs. Forms of first order predicate logic or (modified) modal logic have been used to represent trust and its associated concepts. As the distributed nature of the domain of application must be modeled, these models have representations for actions and interactions.

Predicate Logic-Based Models

Simple relational formalisms are used to model trust with statements of the form *Ta b*, which means "*a* trusts *b*." Each formalism extends this primitive construct with features such as temporal constraints and predicate arguments. Given these primitives, traditional conjunction, implication, negation, and disjunction operators, these logical frameworks express trust rules (such as trust is not transitive) in their language and reason about these properties. These simple formalisms are not capable of modeling e-service trust relationships. However, extensions on these simple concepts yield trust models that are usable in the distributed environment, for example, subjective logic.

Subjective logic (Jøsang, 1996, 1997, 1998) is a logic that operates on subjective beliefs about well-defined, uncertain propositions. The basic component of this logic is an opinion, which is the 4-tuple, consisting of b – belief in the proposition, d – the disbelief in the proposition, u – the uncertainty in the proposition, and a – the relative atomicity of the proposition. The four elements are related by the facts that $b + d + u = 1$ and the probability expectation value is $b + a * u$. The relative atomicity expresses the relative weighting of the proposition with respect to the other propositions defined. The probability expectation value represents the value obtained when an opinion is translated to a standard probability value. The logic builds on both a Shaferian belief model and probability calculus. In order to reason about uncertainty, six operators are defined: conjunction, disjunction, negation, consensus, discounting, and conditional inference. In situations characterized by high uncertainty and quick response times ("hard real time systems"), subjective logic produces better results than the classical Dempster-Shafer model. This model's strength lies in the ability to reason about the opinions on a mathematically sound basis by using its operators, which are based on probability density functions and standard logic. However, its major weakness is that it cannot be guaranteed that users will accurately assign values appropriately, which is a problem is experienced by most formalisms.

Modal Logic-Based Models

Modal logics can be used to express possibility, necessity, belief, knowledge, temporal progression, and other modalities (Firozabadi & Sergot, 1999; Jones & Firozabadi, 2000; Rangan, 1988). It is an extension of traditional logics (propositional and predicate). The □ (necessity) operator and the ◊ (possibility) operator are added to the traditional syntax. The notion of possible worlds (or multiple worlds) is fundamental to the interpretation of modal logics and simply states that a statement will have a different meaning depending on the world it is in. Kripke structures are used to represent possible worlds, where a Kripke structure consists of the set of all possible worlds and an accessibility relation (which may be referred to as a possibility relation depending on the modal logic). The accessibility relation states the conditions for which an agent can access a world. Let us discuss two of these models to show the difference in what is being modeled and the techniques used.

Jones and Firozabadi (2000) address the issue of the reliability of an agent's transmission. They use a modal logic of action developed by Kanger, Porn, and Lindahl to model agent's actions. For example, $E_i\, p$ means "agent i brings it about that p." They use a variant of a normal modal logic of type KD45 as the foundation for their belief system. For example, $B_i A$ means "agent i believes that A." The topic of institutional power is incorporated through the use of a *counts as* operator. Institutional power refers to the fact that a person performing an act in a particular institution will lead to the formation of an institutional fact. In a different institution, this fact cannot be established. For example, a minister performing a marriage ceremony at a church leads to the fact that two people are married; yet in a different church this fact will not exist. They adopt the relevant axiomatic schemas into their formalism and use their composite language to model various trust scenarios. For example, b's belief that a sees to it that m is expressed as $B_b\, E_a\, m$. They also use their language to model the concepts of deception and an entity's trust in another entity. In their own words: *We do not investigate the formal representations of procedures by means of which trust-relations between agents can be established. Assuming the existence of a trust-relation, we try to make explicit the reasoning patterns characteristic of a trusting agent.* Their focus is on understanding the behaviour of a trusting party.

Rangan (1988) views a distributed system as a collection of agents communicating with each other through message passing in which the state of an agent is its message history (all sent and received messages). The state of the system is the state of all the agents in the system. He then devises conditions that function as his accessibility relation (in this context, possibility relation is a more accurate term). His model consists of simple trust statements, for example, $B_i\, p$, which means "agent i believes proposition p," and properties such as transitivity, Euclidean property, and so forth, are defined. These constructs are then used to specify systems and analyze them with respect to the property (or properties) of interest. Rangan's model more fluently follows the traditional lines of modal logics of beliefs than does Jones and Firozabadi's, but the model is simpler in the sense of the nontreatment of actions and their effects.

All these models can be used in any synergistic combination possible dependent upon one's needs and priorities for trust establishment and trust reasoning. Models for trust monitoring and update are still open issues in the field.

Future Direction

Recognition of the fact that an e-services trust ecosystem must be in place in order to ensure widespread acceptance of e-services as a viable business channel raises some very interesting concerns that relate to *business models*, *legislative support*, *technology*, and a *social framework*.

Business models need to be defined that demonstrate to management that providing e-services helps to deliver business value for their firm or lower the total cost of ownership. Thus, the return on investment and contribution to profit increase must be quantifiable and explainable. This is still an open concern that requires a lot more work to be done before mature models can be produced.

Legislation is normally written to be ambiguous and open to interpretation. This is counter to the declarative programming environment that will be used to construct e-services. Thus, mechanism and tools need to be built that bridge this gap such that it is possible to create technology-components that clearly represent legal rules or that can be verified of instances of law.

In the area of *technology*, the current set of models needs to be augmented with those that address trust evolution. Also, trust establishment and reasoning models need to be deployed in real-world environments and hardened according to the lessons learned. Trust mechanisms must be embedded in the base infrastructure in order to ensure that all transactions have access to their functionality. Current trust technology must also be enhanced to address the following concerns:

- How should the notion of a trust measure (i.e., level) be included?
- How should one accurately and consistently assign and apply a trust measure?
- How does one include the influencing factors into the current trust models for e-services?
- How does one define policy that ensures that the correct concern (i.e., privacy, incentives, etc.) is being used in the establishment process?

These are the obvious initial questions. As each is explored, more will be uncovered.

Just as users became familiar with Internet technology, there needs to be a conscious program to create a *social network* that creates awareness around the proper use of trust technology and the safety nets around their use. Currently, such an effort does not exist. This effort would ensure that consumers are motivated to use e-service applications because they are cognizant of controls in place to protect them and the transaction.

There is still much more work to be done, and this chapter does not make any claims on completeness with regards to identifying all the issues.

Conclusion

The concept of building trust into computer systems is a relatively new one for computing practitioners. The underlying notions borrow from human intuition and prior work in a multitude of fields, particularly behavioral psychology. Central ideas to the trust concept, such as distrust, mistrust, expectation, diffidence, and so forth, are difficult for systems builders to incorporate into their solutions. Thus, initial attempts at infusing trust into systems approached the problem from a purely security engineering angle and abstracted away the more difficult components. The basic concern stems from specifying the problem space: What is trust?

Trust, in the e-services context, was defined as:

The quantified belief by a trustor with respect to the competence, honesty, security and dependability of a trustee within a specified context.

Distrust was defined as:

The quantified belief by a trustor that a trustee is incompetent, dishonest, not secure or not dependable within a specified context.

These definitions consolidate previous thought on the topic, make no assumptions about the nature of the entities involved (whether they are humans, software, hardware, etc.), emphasize the facts that trust is subjective and a belief, highlight that trust is context-specific and is related to a property (or group of properties), and illustrate that trust can be either positive or negative. After knowing the phenomenon of interest, it then becomes clear that there are other factors that influence trust that must be understood and incorporated.

These business- and event-related concepts include transaction value, insurance, incentive, privacy, experience, reputation, and recommendation. All of these techniques were presented, and then models that contained and leveraged these factors were discussed.

The aim of this chapter was to capitalize on the work done in the trust technology community, and provide fundamentals for *trust in e-services*, and avoid the pitfalls of work done in the trust computing field. For even though significant progress has been made in the comprehension of trust for computer systems, there is still tremendous discourse on the fundamentals, that is, "What is trust?" "What are the key components of trust that are relevant to computing?" "What trust models are pertinent?", and so forth.

This is a starting point, and the reader is encouraged to delve deeper into the discussion to further the state of the art in the e-services environment.

References

Agudo, I., Lopez, J., & Montenegro, J. A. (2005). A representation model of trust relationships with delegation extensions. In P. Herrmann, V. Issarny, & S. Shiu (Ed.), *Third International Conference on Trust Management (iTrust 2005)*, Paris (LNCS 3477, pp. 116-130).

Anderson, R. J., Matyas, V., Jr., & Petitcolas, F. A. P. (1998). The eternal resource locator: An alternative means of establishing trust on the World Wide Web. In *Proceedings of the 3rd USENIX Workshop on Electronic Commerce*, Boston (pp. 141-153).

Anderson, S., Bohren, J., Boubez, T., Chanliau, M., Della-Libera, G., Dixon, B., et al. (2005). *Web services trust language*. Retrieved January 14, 2006, from http://www.verisign.com/wss/ws-trust.pdf

Barber, K. S., Fullam, K., & Kim, J. (2002). Challenges for trust, fraud and deception research in multi-agent systems. In R. Falcone, K. S. Barber, L. Korba, & M. P. Singh. (Ed.), *First International Conference on Autonomous Agents and Multi-Agent Systems (AAMAS 2002)*, Bologna, Italy (LNCS 2631, pp. 8-14).

Blaze, M., Feigenbaum, J., & Lacy, J. (1996). *Managing trust in medical information systems* (Tech Rep. No. 96.14.1). Murray Hill, NJ: AT&T. Retrieved January 20, 2006, from http://research.att.com/resources/trs/TRs/96/96.14/96.14.1.body.ps

Blaze, M., Feigenbaum, J., & Strauss, M. (1998). Compliance checking in the PolicyMaker trust management system. In *Financial Cryptography: Second International Conference* (pp. 251-265). Anguilla, British West Indies: Springer-Verlag.

Braendeland, G., & Stolen, K. (2004). Using risk analysis to assess user trust-A net bank scenario. In C. Jensen, S. Poslad, & T. Dimitrakos (Ed.), *Second International Conference on Trust Management (iTrust 2004)*, Oxford, UK (LNCS 2995, pp. 146-160).

Cassell, J., & Bickmore, T. (2000). External manifestations of trustworthiness in the interface. *Communications of the ACM, 43*(12), 50-56.

Castelfranchi, C., & Falcone, R. (1998). Principles of trust for MAS: Cognitive anatomy, social importance, and quantification. In *Proceedings of the International Conference on Multi-Agent Systems* (pp. 72-79). Paris: IEEE Computer Society.

Castelfranchi, C., & Falcone, R. (2001). *Social trust: A cognitive approach*. Retrieved January 20, 2006, from http://www.istc.cnr.it/T3/download/Social-trust.pdf

Corritore, C. L., Kracher, B. J., & Wiedenbeck, S. (2001). *An overview of trust: Working document*. Retrieved January 16, 2006, from http://cobacourses.creighton.edu/trust/articles/trustpaper2-9-01_final.rtf

Curral, S., & Judge, T. (1995). Measuring trust between organizational boundary role persons. *Organizational Behaviour and Human Decision Processes, 65*, 601-620.

Demolombe, R. (2004). Reasoning about trust. In C. Jensen, S. Poslad, & T. Dimitrakos (Ed.), *Second International Conference on Trust Management (iTrust 2004)*, Oxford, UK (LNCS 2995, pp. 291-303).

Egger, F. N. (2001). *Affective design of e-commerce user interfaces: How to maximise perceived trustworthiness*. Retrieved January 16, 2006, from http://www.mis.coventry.ac.uk/~pevery/m81is/docs/trust.pdf.

Evans, C., Feather, C. D. W., Hopmann, A., Presler-Marshall, M., & Resnick, P. (1997). *PICSRules* 1.1. Retrieved May 8, 2000, from http://www.w3.org/TR/REC-PICSRules

Falcone, R., Singh, M. P., & Tan, Y.-H. (Eds.). (2001). *Trust in cyber-societies: Integrating the human and artificial perspectives* (LNCS/LNAI). Berlin, Germany: Springer-Verlag.

Fernandes, A., Kotsovinos, E., Ostring, S., & Dragovic, B. (2004). Pinocchio: Incentives for honest participation in distributed trust management. In C. Jensen, S. Poslad, & T. Dimitrakos (Ed.), *Second International Conference on Trust Management (iTrust 2004)*, Oxford, UK (LNCS 2995).

Firozabadi, B. S., & Sergot, M. (1999). *Power and permission in security systems*. Retrieved January 16, 2006, from http://www.sics.se/ps/pbr/papers/SecurityProtocol99.pdf.

Gerck, E. (1997). *Toward real-world models of trust: Reliance on received information*. Retrieved January 16, 2006, from http://mcwg.org/mcg-mirror/trustdef.htm

Giorgini, P., Massacci, F., Mylopoulos, & Zannone, N. (2005). Modeling social and individual trust in requirements engineering methodologies. In P. Herrmann, V. Issarny, & S. Shiu (Ed.), *Trust Management, Third International Conference (iTrust 2005)*, Paris (LNCS 3477, pp. 161).

Grandison, T. (2001). Trust specification and analysis for Internet applications. In *Proceedings of the 2nd IFIP Conference on E-Commerce, E-Business, E-Government (I3e 2002)*, Lisbon, Portugal. Retrieved January 16, 2006, from http://www.eyetap.org/~maali/trust-papers/I3e2002.pdf.

Grandison, T. (2003). *Trust management for Internet applications*. Unpublished doctoral dissertation, Imperial College - University of London, UK.

Grandison, T., & Sloman, M. (2000). A survey of trust in Internet applications. *IEEE Communications Surveys and Tutorials,* 4(4), 2-16.

Grandison, T., & Sloman, M. (2003). Trust management tools for Internet applications. In P. Nixon, & S. Terzis (Ed.), *First International Conference on Trust Management (iTrust 2003)*, Heraklion, Crete, Greece (LNCS 2692, pp. 91-107).

Griffiths, N., & Chao, K. M. (2005). Experience-based trust: Enabling effective resource selection in a grid environment. In P. Herrmann, V. Issarny, & S. Shiu (Ed.), *Third International Conference on Trust Management (iTrust 2005)*, Paris (LNCS 3477, pp. 240-255).

Grimsley, M., Meeham, A., Green, G., & Stafford, B. (2003). Social capital, community trust and e-government services. In P. Nixon, & S. Terzis (Ed.), *First International Conference on Trust Management (iTrust 2003)*, Heraklion, Crete, Greece (LNCS 2692, pp. 165-178).

Jarvenpaa, S. L., Tractinsky, N., Saarinen, L., & Vitale, M. (1999). Consumer trust in an Internet store: A cross-cultural validation. *Journal of Computer-Meditated Communication, 5*(2), 1-33.

Jones, A. J. I. (2002). On the concept of trust. *Decision Support Systems. Special issue: Formal modeling and electronic commerce, 33*(3), 225-232.

Jones, A. J. I. ,& Firozabadi, B. S. (2000). On the characterisation of a trusting agent—aspects of a formal approach. In *Proceedings of the Workshop on Deception, Trust and Fraud in Agent Societies* (pp. 157-168). Norwell, MA: Kluwer Academic Publishers.

Jones, S. (1999, April 8-9). *TRUST-EC: Requirements for Trust and Confidence in E-Commerce. TRUST-EC: Requirements for Trust and Confidence in E-Commerce: Report of the Workshop held in Luxembourg* (Tech. Rep. No. EUR 18749 EN). European Communities EUR Report, 1999. Issue 2.

Jøsang, A. (1996). The right type of trust for distributed systems. In *Proceedings of the ACM New Security Paradigms Workshop*. Retrieved from http://www.idt.ntnu. no/~ajos/papers.html

Jøsang, A. (1997). Artificial reasoning with subjective logic. In *Proceedings of the 2nd Australian Workshop on Commonsense Reasoning*. Retrieved January 17, 2006, from http://security.dstc.edu.au/staff/ajosang/papers/artreas.ps

Jøsang, A. (1998). A subjective metric of authentication. In *Proceedings of the 5th European Symposium on Research in Computer Security (ESORICS'98)*. Springer. Retrieved from http://www.idt.ntnu.no/~ajos/papers.html

Jøsang, A. (1999). Trust-based decision making for electronic transactions. In L. S. Yngström (Ed.), *The 4th Nordic Workshop on Secure IT Systems (NORDSEC'99)*, Stockholm, Sweden (Stockholm University Rep. No. 99-005). Retrieved January 20, 2006, from http://security.dstc.edu.au/staff/ajosang/papers/decimak.ps

Jøsang, A., Hird, S., & Faccer, E. (2003). Simulating the effect of reputation systems on e-markets. In P. Nixon, & S. Terzis (Ed.), *First International Conference on Trust Management (iTrust 2003)*, Heraklion, Crete, Greece (LNCS 2692, pp. 179-194).

Jøsang, A., & Lo Presti, S. (2004). Analysing the relationship between risk and trust. In C. Jensen, S. Poslad, & T. Dimitrakos (Ed.), *Second International Conference on Trust Management (iTrust 2004)*, Oxford, UK (LNCS 2995, pp. 135-145).

Ketchpel, S. P., & Garcia-Molina, H. (1996). Making trust explicit in distributed commerce transactions. In *Proceedings of the 16th International Conference on Distributed Computing Systems* (pp. 270-281).

Kim, K., & Prabhakar, B. (2000). Initial trust, perceived risk and the adoption of Internet banking. In *Proceedings of the International Conference on Information Systems*. Brisbane, Queensland, Australia (pp. 537-543). Atlanta, GA: Association for Information Systems Publishers.

Kimbrough, S. O. (2005). Foraging for trust: Exploring rationality and the stag hunt game. In P. Herrmann, V. Issarny, & S. Shiu (Ed.), *Third International Conference on Trust Management (iTrust 2005)*, Paris (LNCS 3477, pp. 1-16).

Kinateder, M., Baschny, E., & Rothermel, K. (2005). Towards a generic trust model—comparison of various trust update algorithms. In P. Herrmann, V. Issarny, & S. Shiu (Ed.), *Third International Conference on Trust Management (iTrust 2005)*, Paris (LNCS 3477, pp. 177-192).

Kini, A., & Choobineh, J. (1998). Trust in electronic commerce: Definition and theoretical considerations. In *Proceedings of the 31st Annual Hawaii International Conference on System Sciences,* HI (Vol. 4, pp. 51-61).

Kollingbaum, M. J., & Norman, T. J. (2002). Supervised interaction—a form of contract management to create trust between agents. In R. Falcone, K. S. Barber, L. Korba, & M. P. Singh (Ed.), *First International Conference on Autonomous Agents and Multi-Agent Systems (AAMAS 2002)*, Bologna, Italy (LNCS 2631, pp. 108-122).

Konrad, K., Fuchs, G., & Bathel, J. (1999). Trust and electronic commerce—more than a technical problem. In *Proceedings of the 18th Symposium on Reliable Distributed Systems*, Lausanne, Switzerland (pp. 360-365).

Krauskopf, T., Miller, J., Resnick, P., & Treesee, W. (1996). *PICS label distribution label syntax and communication protocols, Version 1.1.* Retrieved May 8, 2000, from http://www.w3.org/TR/REC-PICS-labels

Lamsal, P. (2001). *Understanding trust and security.* Retrieved from January 20, 2006, from http://citeseer.nj.nec.com/lamsal01understanding.html

Lewis, D., & Weigert, A. (1985). Social atomism, holism and trust. *Sociological Quaterly, 26*(4), 455-471.

Luhmann, N. (1982). *Trust and Power.* Chicester: John Wiley & Sons.

Manchala, D. W. (1998). Trust metrics, models and protocols for electronic commerce transactions. In *Proceedings of the 18th International Conference on Distributed Computing Systems* (pp. 312-321).

Marsh, S., & Dibben, M. R. (2005). Trust, untrust, distrust and mistrust—an exploration of the dark(er) side. In P. Herrmann, V. Issarny, & S. Shiu (Ed.), *Third International Conference on Trust Management (iTrust 2005)*, Paris (LNCS 3477, pp. 17-33).

Marsh, S. P. (1994). *Formalising trust as a computational concept.* Unpublished PhD dissertation, University of Stirling.

Massa, P., & Bhattachargee, B. (2004). Using trust in recommender systems: An experimental analysis. In C. Jensen, S. Poslad, & T. Dimitrakos (Ed.), *Second International Conference on Trust Management (iTrust 2004)*, Oxford, UK (LNCS 2995, pp. 221-235).

Mayer, F. L. (1990). A brief comparison of two different environmental guidelines for determining "levels of trust" (computer security). In *Proceedings of the Sixth Annual Computer Security Applications Conference* (pp. 244-250).

Mayer, R. C., & Davis, J. H. (1995). An integrative model of organizational trust. *Academy of Management Review, 20*(3), 709-734.

McKnight, D. H., & Chervany, N. (1996). *The meanings of trust.* Retrieved January 17, 2006, from http://misrc.umn.edu/wpaper/WorkingPapers/9604.pdf

Michalakopoulos, M., & Fasli, M. (2005). On deciding to trust. In P. Herrmann, V. Issarny, & S. Shiu (Ed.), *Third International Conference on Trust Management (iTrust 2005)*, Paris (LNCS 3477, pp. 61-76).

Millen, J. K., & Wright, R. N. (2000). Reasoning about trust and insurance in a public key infrastructure. In *Proceedings of the 13th IEEE Computer Security Foundations Workshop (CSFW'00)* (pp. 16-22).

Morency, J. (1999). *Application service providers and e-business*. Retrieved February 11, 2000, from http://www.nwfusion.com/newsletters/nsm/0705nm1.html?nf

Mui, L., Mohtashemi, M., & Halberstadt, A. (2002). A computational model of trust and reputation for e-businesses. In *Proceedings of the 35th Annual Hawaii International Conference on System Sciences (HICSS'02)*, Big Island, HI (p. 188). Washington, DC: IEE Computer Society.

Patel, J., Teacy, W. T. L., Jennings, N. R., & Luck, M. (2005). A probabilistic trust model for handling inaccurate reputation sources. In P. Herrmann, V. Issarny, & S. Shiu, (Ed.), *Third International Conference on Trust Management (iTrust 2005)*, Paris (LNCS 3477, pp. 193-209).

Patrick, A. (2001). *Privacy, trust, agents and users: A review of human-factors issues associated with building trustworthy software agents*. Retrieved January 18, 2006, from http://www.iit.nrc.ca/~patricka/agents/agents.pdf

Pitsilis, G., & Marshall, L. (2005). Trust as a key to improving recommendation systems. In P. Herrmann, V. Issarny, & S. Shiu (Ed.), *Third International Conference on Trust Management (iTrust 2005)*, Paris (LNCS 3477, pp. 210-223).

Platzer, C. (2004). *Trust-based security in Web services*. Unpublished MSc dissertation, Technical University of Vienna, Austria.

Rangan, P. V. (1988). An axiomatic basis of trust in distributed systems. In *Proceedings of the Symposium on Security and Privacy* (pp. 204-211). Washington, DC: IEEE Computer Society Press.

Ratnasingam, P. (2002). The importance of technology trust in Web services security. *Information Management & Computer Security, 10*(5), 255-260.

Riegelsberger, J., Sasse, A. M., & McCarthy, J. D. (2005). The mechanics of trust: A framework for research and design. *International Journal of Human-Computer Studies, 62*(3), 381-422.

Riegelsberger, J., Sasse, A. M., & McCarthy, J. (2003). The researcher's dilemma: Evaluating trust in computer mediated communications. *International Journal of Human Computer Studies, 58*(6), 759-781.

Salam, A. F., Rao, H. R., & Pegels, C. C. (1998). An investigation of consumer-perceived risk on electronic commerce transactions: The role of institutional trust and economic incentive in a social exchange framework. In *Proceedings of the 4th Americas Conference on Information Systems*. Baltimore, MD: Association of Information Systems.

Seigneur, J.-M., & Jensen, C. D. (2004). Trading privacy for trust. In C. Jensen, S. Poslad, & T. Dimitrakos (Ed.), *Second International Conference on Trust Management (iTrust 2004)*, Oxford, UK (LNCS 2995, pp. 93-107).

Shneiderman, B. (2000). Designing trust into online experiences. *Communications of the ACM, 43*(12), 57-59.

Simmons, G. J. (1993). An introduction to the mathematics of trust in security protocols. In *Proceedings of the Computer Security Foundations Workshop VI* (pp. 121-127).

Skevington, P. J. (1998). From security to trust-creating confidence to trade electronically. In *Proceedings of the IEE Colloquium on eCommerce—trading but not as we know it* (Tech. Rep. No. 1998/460, pp. 6/1-6/6).

Staples, S. D., & Artnasingham, P. (1998). Trust: The panacea of virtual management. In *Proceedings of the 19ᵗʰ International Conference on Information Systems*. Helsinki, Finland: Association for Information Systems. Retrieved January 20, 2006, from http://portal.acm.org/ft_gateway.cfm?id=353064&type=pdf.

Su, J., & Manchala, D. (1997). Building trust for distributed commerce transactions. In *Proceedings of the 17ᵗʰ International Conference on Distributed Computer Systems* (pp. 332-329). IEEE.

Van Dyke, J. (2004). *Establishing federated trust among web services*. Unpublished bachelors dissertation, University of Virginia, USA.

Verissimo, P. & Rodrigues, L. (2001) *Distributed Systems for System Architects*. Kluwer Academic Publishers.

Viega, J., Kohno, T., & Potter, B. (2001). Trust (and mistrust) in secure applications. *Communications of the ACM, 44*(2), 31-36.

Winsborough, W., Seamons, K., & Jones, V. (1999). *Automated trust negotiation: Managing disclosure of sensitive credentials*. IBM Transarc Research White Paper.

Yahalom, R., Klein, B., & Beth, T. (1993). Trust relationships in secure systems-a distributed authentication perspective. In *Proceedings of the IEEE Computer Society Symposium on Research in Security and Privacy* (pp. 150-164).

Zand, D. E. (1972). Trust and managerial problem solving. *Administrative Science Quarterly, 17*, 229-239.

Zanero, S. (2005). Security and trust in the Italian legal digital signature framework. In P. Herrmann, V. Issarny, & S. Shiu (Ed.), *Third International Conference on Trust Management (iTrust 2005)*, Paris (LNCS 3477, pp. 34-44).

Chapter II

A Unified Taxonomy Framework of Trust

Weiliang Zhao, University of Western Sydney, Australia

Vijay Varadharajan, Macquarie University, Australia

George Bryan, University of Western Sydney, Australia

Abstract

In this chapter, we provide a formal definition of trust relationship with a strict mathematical structure that can reflect many of the commonly used notions of trust. Based on this formal definition, we propose a unified taxonomy framework of trust. Under the taxonomy framework, we discuss classification of trust. In particular, we address the base level authentication trust at the lower layer and a hierarchy of trust relationships at a higher level. We provide a set of definitions, propositions, and operations based on the relations of trust relationships. Then we define and discuss properties of trust direction and trust symmetry. We define the trust scope label in order to describe the scope and diversity of trust relationship. All the definitions about the properties of trust become elements of the unified taxonomy framework of trust. Some example scenarios are provided to illustrate the concepts in the taxonomy framework. The taxonomy framework of trust will provide accurate terms and useful tools for enabling the analysis, design, and implementation of trust. The taxonomy framework of trust is first part of research for the overall methodology of trust relationships and trust management in distributed systems.

Introduction

Trust has been studied in multiple dimensions in the computing world. Trust management and trustworthy computing are becoming increasingly significant. Trust has been studied in trusted systems (U.S.A. National Computer Security Council, 1985) and trusted computing (Felten, 2003; Landauer, Redmond, & Benzel, 1989). Marsh has tried to formalize trust as a computational concept (Marsh, 1994). Multiple community-based reputation systems (Jøsang, 1999; Jøsang & Knapskog, 1998; Manchala, 2000; Mui, Mohtashemi, & Halberstadt, 2002; Wang & Vassileva, 2003; Xiong & Liu, 2003), trust negotiation systems (Huhns & Buell, 2002; Winsborough, Seamons, & Jones, 2000; Winslett et al., 2002) and trust management systems (Blaze, Feigenbaum, & Keromytis, 1999; Blaze, Feigenbaum, & Lacy, 1996; Chu, Feigenbaum, Lamacchia, Resnick, & Strauss, 1997) have been proposed. However, a clear and comprehensive definition that can be used to capture a range of commonly understood notions of trust is still lacking.

XML-based Web services technologies have been rapidly evolving since 1999. Web services technologies address the challenges of distributed computing and B2B integration. There is a huge number of service-oriented applications on the Internet and they are coupled loosely. Web services technologies target at loosely coupled, language-neutral and platform-independent way of linking applications for business process automation within organizations, across enterprises, and across the Internet. There is no centralized control, and the users are not all predetermined. Normally, the computing components involved in an e-service can belong to different security domains and there is no common trusted authority for the involved entities. The new technologies of Web services make the related issues about trust more important than ever before. The properties of trust and how to define/model trust relationships are important concerns in the analysis and design of Web services. The issues of trust are also broadly embedded in broad spectrums of Web services such as WS-trust (Della-Libera et al., 2002; Anderson et al., 2004), WS-security, WS-policy and WS-federation. Unfortunately, in all these documents, the details of classification and properties of trust have not been discussed.

Our main objective is to develop a unified taxonomy framework of trust that can provide accurate terms and can be used as enable tools to analyze and model trust relationships in distributed environments. This chapter is mainly based on the results of our previous research (Zhao, Varadharajan, & Bryan, 2004; Zhao, Varadharajan, & Bryan, 2005). We outlined a formal definition of trust relationship and provided a set of operations and definitions about the relations of trust relationships (Zhao et al., 2004). We discussed the classification of trust and provided a set of definitions for the properties of trust that include trust direction, trust symmetry, scope, and diversity of trust relationships (Zhao et al., 2005). The unified taxonomy framework of trust is composed of a series of definitions in Zhao et al. (2004) and Zhao et al. (2005) and it is illustrated in Figure 1.

Our current unified taxonomy framework of trust includes the formal definition of trust relationship, types of trust, relations of trust relationships, and properties of trust relationships. The formal definition of trust relationship will be described in section "Definition of Trust Relationships"; the types of trust will be described in section "Classification of Trust." The relations of trust relationships will be described in section "Relations of Trust Relationships." For the properties of trust relationships, the current unified taxonomy

Figure 1. Unified taxonomy framework of trust

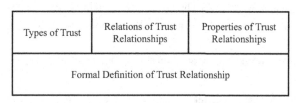

Types of Trust	Relations of Trust Relationships	Properties of Trust Relationships
Formal Definition of Trust Relationship		

framework of trust only includes properties for trust direction, trust symmetry, trust scope, and diversity. Trust direction and symmetry will be described in section "Trust Direction and Symmetry." Trust scope and diversity will be described in section "Trust Scope and Diversity." Some scenario examples will be provided to show readers how to understand and use the elements of the unified taxonomy framework of trust. The unified taxonomy framework of trust is an important part of the overall methodology of trust management in distributed environments.

This chapter will be organized as follows. In section "Definition of Trust Relationships," we provide the definition of trust relationship. In section "Classification of Trust," we discuss different forms of trust and the hierarchy of trust relationships under the unified taxonomy framework. In section "Relations of Trust Relationships," we describe a set of operations and definitions for the relations of trust relationships. In section "Trust Direction and Symmetry," we provide a set of definitions for trust direction and symmetric properties of trust relationships. In section "Trust Scope and Diversity," the scope and diversity of trust relationships are discussed. The definition of trust scope label and comparison rules between trust scope labels are defined. Section "Future Research Based on the Taxonomy Framework" provides some discussion about research based on the taxonomy framework of trust. Finally, the last section provides some concluding remarks.

Definition of Trust Relationship

In our previous work (Zhao et al., 2004), we have provided a formal definition of trust relationship with a strict mathematical structure. It is expressed as:

Definition 1: A trust relationship is a four-tuple $T = <R, E, C, P>$ where:

- R is the set of trustors. It contains all the involved trustors. It is a nonempty set.
- E is the set of trustees. It contains all the involved trustees. It is a nonempty set.
- C is the set of conditions. It contains all conditions (requirements) for the current trust relationship. Normally, a trust relationship has some specified conditions. If there is no condition, the condition set is empty.

- *P* is the set of properties. The property set describes the actions or attributes of the trustees. It is a nonempty set. The property set can be divided into two subsets:

  o **Action set:** the set of actions that the trustors trust that trustees will and can perform.

  o **Attribute set:** the set of attributes that trustors trust that trustees have.

When trust relationships are used, the full syntax (four-tuple <*R, E, C, P*> must be followed. Trust relationship *T* means that under the condition set *C*, trustor set *R* trust that trustee set *E* have the properties in set *P*. There are some extreme cases of the trust relationship when some involved sets included nothing (empty set) or anything (whole set of possible entities). The extreme cases have special meanings and are crucial in the understanding of the definition of trust relationship. These extreme cases will play important roles in the real world. The followings are the five extreme cases of trust relationship:

1.   *R* is ANY. trustor set includes all possible entities. All possible entities trust that the set of trustees *E* have the set of properties *P* under the set of conditions *C*.

2.   *E* is ANY. Trustee set includes all possible entities. All possible entities can be trusted to have the set of properties *P* by the set of trustors *R* under the set of conditions *C*.

3.   *C* is EMPTY. There is no condition in the trust relationship. The set of trustors *R* trust that the set of trustees *E* have the set of properties *P* without any condition.

4.   *P* is ANY. The property of the trustee can be anything. The set of trustors *R* trust that the set of trustees *E* have all possible properties under the set of conditions *C*.

5.   *C* is EMPTY and *P* is ANY. The set of trustors *R* trust that the set of trustees *E* have all possible properties without any condition. This case happens when the set of trustors *R* trust the set of trustees *E* by default.

In the definition of trust relationship, all the four tuples are defined as sets. It is straightforward to use set for conditions in the definition of trust relationship. In the formal definition of trust relationship, the trustors, trustees, and properties turn up as sets are based on the following concerns:

1.   The concept of security domain is broadly used and related technologies are quite mature. The role-based access control is broadly used and well understood by programmers and business people. When a set of trustors, a set of trustees, and a set of properties are used in the definition of trust relationship, the similar ideas in security domain and role-based access control can be employed easily. It is convenient to define some abstraction characteristics based on a group of trustors, a group of trustees, and a group of properties. We hope that a set of trustors, a set of trustees, and a set of properties in the definition of the trust relationship have better abstraction and it is easier to use the definition.

2.   The set theory can provide formal mathematical notion and handy tools to discuss the relationships of sets.

3.   An individual trustor (or trustee, or property) is a special case of the set of trustors (or trustees, or properties).

4.   It is convenient to discuss special cases of trust relationship when trustor (or trustee, or property) is anyone.

When a trust relationship is used in the real world, trustors, trustees, and properties are normally involved individually. The trust relationship can always be evaluated based on one trustor, one trustee, and one property. It is a runtime task to map individual trustor, trustee, and property to corresponding sets in a trust relationship. For system analysis and design, it is convenient to define trust relationship with trustor set, trustee set, condition set, and property set as four tuples. The evaluation or measurement of trust relationships will not be discussed here because they are not the main concern of this chapter.

We believe that the formal definition of trust relationship has a strict mathematical structure and a broad expressive power. The definition can be used for different computing purposes and it can reflect the commonly used notions of trust. It provides a solid foundation for discussing the properties of trust relationships in the following sections of this chapter. It provides the basis of all other definitions in the unified taxonomy framework of trust discussed in this chapter.

Classification of Trust

In this section, we will describe different types of trust. Grandison and Sloman (2000) have given a bottom-up classification and used the terms as resources access trust, service provision trust, certification trust, delegation trust, and infrastructure trust. Under our taxonomy framework, they are as follows:

- **Resources access trust:** Resources access trust relationship is a kind of trust relationship for the purpose of accessing resources. The access control has been the central concern of security for many decades. The trust relationship can be refined into authorization policies that specify actions the trustee can perform on the trustor's resources and constraints that apply, such as the time periods for which the access is permitted. With the syntax of formal definition of trust relationship, resource access trust will be like "the trustors trust trustees under some conditions that trustees have the right to get access to some of trustors' resources."

- **Services provision trust:** Services provision trust describes trustors' trust in provided services or resources of trustees. It is related to protection from maliciously or unreliably provided services or resources. With the syntax of formal definition of the trust relationship, service provision trust will be like "the trustors trust trustees under some conditions that trustees will provide the claimed services."

- **Certification trust:** Certification trust is based on certification of the trustworthiness of the trustee by a third party. Certification trust is related to a special form of service provision trust. Certification authority is, in fact, providing a trust certification service.

With the syntax of formal definition of trust relationship, certification trust will be like that "trustors trust trustees if trustees can provide certificates that trustees have a set of attributes or can do a set of actions according the certificates." The related service provision trust of certification trust will be like that "trustors trust certification authority under some conditions that the certification authority will only give certificates to suitable entities."

- **Delegation trust:** Delegation trust is a special form of service provision trust (Ding & Petersen, 1995). With the syntax of formal definition of trust relationship, delegation trust will be like that "trustors trust trustees under some conditions that trustees can make decisions on trustors' behalf, with respect to resources or services that the trustors own or control."

- **Infrastructure trust:** Infrastructure trust is a kind of trust that trustors trust some base infrastructure under some conditions (Abrams, 1995; Abrams & Joyce, 1995). With the syntax of formal definition of trust relationship, infrastructure trust will be like that "trustors trust base infrastructure under some conditions for a set of properties of the infrastructure (some actions and attributes)."

Under our taxonomy framework, we categorize the trust relationships into two layers and provide a new hierarchy of trust relationships. All of these trust types must build on a more basic trust relationship, that is, the authentication trust or identity trust. Authentication trust is "trustors trust trustees under some condition that trustees are what they are claimed." Authentication trust belongs to a separate layer and all other trust types belong to another layer above it. This is illustrated in Figure 2. Note that trust types of layer two may not be necessarily specified in terms of an identity. Anonymous authorization belongs to access trust, and it is an example that there is no specified identity. Anonymous authorization can be implemented using certificates with capabilities. The real identity of the involved trustee will not be revealed. For example, a customer has a certificate for accessing some resources on the Internet. The customer's behaviors of accessing the resources can be recorded. If it is desirable that the customer cannot be identified, the related access trust is a kind of anonymous access trust. Particularly for the resource access trust and service provision trust, the anonymous authentication is desirable in some cases. In such a situation, the layer of authentication still needs to provide a mechanism to deal with the same entity as the trustee in the whole scope of the trust process. Normally, there is a temporary and dynamic identification that will be uniquely connected with the involved trustee in the scope of the trust process.

Figure 2. Trust layers

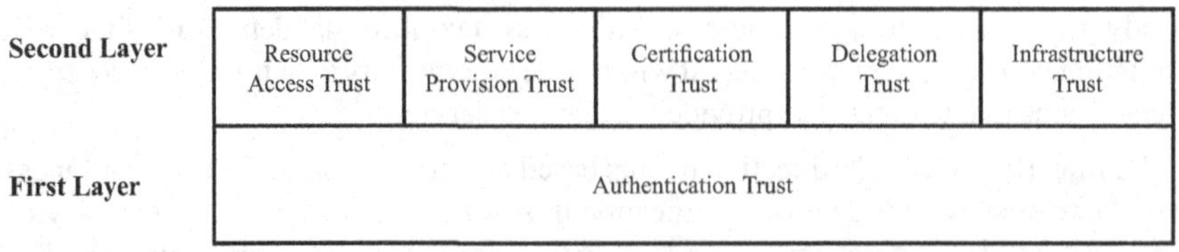

Second Layer	Resource Access Trust	Service Provision Trust	Certification Trust	Delegation Trust	Infrastructure Trust
First Layer	Authentication Trust				

Figure 3. Trust hierarchy

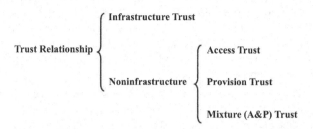

At layer two, trust relationships can be classified in different ways. In the following part of this section, we will give another kind of classification that is different from the bottom-up classification of Grandison and Sloman (2000). Based on strict definition of trust relationship, trust relationships at layer two can be classified according to the nature of the trustees in trust relationship $< R, E, C, P >$. If E is an infrastructure, the trust relationship belongs to infrastructure trust. If E is not an infrastructure, the trust relationship belongs to noninfrastructure trust. Noninfrastructure trust relationships can be classified based on the ownership of the property set. If the trustors have the ownership of the property set, the trust relationship belongs to access trust. If the trustees have the ownership of the property set, the trust relationship belongs to provision trust. If some properties are owned by trustees and some other properties are owned by trustors, then the trust relationship belongs to mixture ($A\&P$) trust. The hierarchy of trust relationships at layer two is illustrated in Figure 3. In such a classification, delegation trust and certification trust are not independent types. As we have discussed, the delegation trust is a special form of provision trust, trustees are the providers of delegated decisions on behalves of trustors. A certification trust can be any subtype of noninfrastructure trust based on the nature of its property set.

Relations of Trust Relationships

There are relations among existing and possible trust relationships in information systems. These relations are important in the analysis and modeling of trust relationships in information systems. In this section, we will describe some important operations and definitions based on the relations of trust relationships. All definitions about these relations are elements of the unified taxonomy framework. From the nature of trust relationship and its mathematical structure, some new trust relationships can be derived based on the existing trust relationships. We will define a set of operations to generate new trust relationships based on existing trust relationships. We will describe the definitions of equivalent, primitive, derived, direct redundant, and alternate trust relationships. Then we will classify direct redundant trust relationships into several subtypes.

In this section, we discuss the relations of trust relationships based on our strict definition of trust relationship. The trust relationship has a full syntax with trustor set, trustee set, condition set, and property set. It is incorrect to only talk about the trust relationship between trustors and trustees without mention of the condition set and property set. The discussions of properties of trust relationship are based on the full syntax of trust relationship in its definition. In the following part of this section, we will give some definitions, propositions, and operations related to trust relationships. The mathematical properties of trust relationships are embedded in these definitions, propositions, and operations. These mathematical properties focus on some relations of trust relationships and they will be used as tools in the analysis and design of trust relationships in real systems.

From the nature of trust relationship and its mathematical structure, some new trust relationships can be derived based on the existing trust relationships. In the following part of this section, we will define the operations of using two existing trust relationships to generate a new trust relationship under specific constraints and operations of decomposing one existing trust relationship into two new trust relationships under specific constraints.

Operation 1: Let $T_1 = (R_1, E_1, C_1, P_1)$ and $T_2 = (R_2, E_2, C_2, P_2)$. There is a set $T = (R_1 \cap R_2, E_1 \cap E_2, C_1 \cup C_2, P_1 \cup P_2)$. If $R_1 \cap R_2 = \Phi$ or $E_1 \cap E_2 = \Phi$, $T = \Phi$.

If $R_1 = R_2$ and $E_1 = E_2$, the operation becomes:

Operation 1A: Let $T_1 = (R, E, C_1, P_1)$ and $T_2 = (R, E, C_2, P_2)$. There is a set $T = (R, E, C_1 \cup C_2, P_1 \cup P_2)$.

If $R_1 = R_2$, $E_1 = E_2$ and $C_1 = C_2$, the operation becomes:

Operation 1B: Let $T_1 = (R, E, C, P_1)$ and $T_2 = (R, E, C, P_2)$. There is a set $T = (R, E, C, P_1 \cup P_2)$.

Operation 2: Let $T_1 = (R_1, E_1, C, P)$ and $T_2 = (R_2, E_2, C, P)$. There is a set $T = (R_1 \cup R_2, E_1 \cap E_2, C, P)$.

If $E_1 = E_2$, the operation becomes:

Operation 2A: Let $T_1 = (R_1, E, C, P)$ and $T_2 = (R_2, E, C, P)$. There is a set $T = (R_1 \cup R_2, E, C, P)$.

Operation 3: Let $T_1 = (R_1, E_1, C, P)$ and $T_2 = (R_2, E_2, C, P)$. There is a set $T = (R_1 \cap R_2, E_1 \cup E_2, C, P)$.

If $R_1 = R_2$, the operation becomes:

Operation 3A: Let $T_1 = (R, E_1, C, P)$ and $T_2 = (R, E_2, C, P)$. There is a set $T = (R, E_1 \cup E_2, C, P)$.

Operation 4: Let $T = <R, E, C, P>$. If there are R_1, R_2 and $R = R_1 \cup R_2$, there are trust relationships $T_1 = <R_1, E, C, P>$ and $T_2 = <R_2, E, C, P>$.

Operation 5: Let $T = <R, E, C, P>$. If there are E_1, E_2 and $E = E_1 \cup E_2$, there are trust relationships $T_1 = <R, E_1, C, P>$ and $T_2 = <R, E_2, C, P>$.

Operation 6: Let $T = <R, E, C, P>$. If there are P_1, P_2 and $P = P_1 \cup P_2$, there are trust relationships $T_1 = <R, E, C, P_1>$ and $T_2 = <R, E, C, P_2>$.

This operation has the following special case:

Operation 6A: Let $T = <R, E, C, P>$. If there are P_1, P_2, C_1, C_2 and $P = P_1 \cup P_2$, $C = C_1 \cup C_2$, C_1 is the condition set for P_1 and C_2 is the condition set for P_2, there are trust relationships $T_1 = <R, E, C_1, P_1>$ and $T_2 = <R, E, C_2, P_2>$.

The previous operations can be used to generate new trust relationships from the existing trust relationships under some specific constrains. The **Operation 1** deals with any two trust relationships, and a new trust relationship is possibly generated (if the result is not Φ). The **Operation 1A, 1B, 2A,** and **3A** deal with how to use two trust relationships to generate one trust relationship under some specific constraints. **Operation 4, 5, 6,** and **6A** deal with how to decompose one trust relationship into two trust relationships under some specific constraints. **Operation 1A** and **Operation 6A** are inverse operations. **Operation 1B** and **Operation 6** are inverse operations. **Operation 2A** and **Operation 4** are inverse operations. **Operation 3A** and **Operation 5** are inverse operations.

In the following part of this section, we will discuss and define the equivalent, primitive, derived, direct redundant, and alternate trust relationships. We will classify the direct redundant trust relationships into different types as well.

Definition 2: Let $T_1 = <R_1, E_1, C_1, P_1>$ and $T_2 = <R_2, E_2, C, P_2>$. If and only if $R_1 = R_2$ and $E_1 = E_2$ and $C_1 = C_2$ and $P_1 = P_2$, then T_1 and T_2 are equivalent, in symbols:

$$T_1 = T_2 \Leftrightarrow R_1 = R_2 \text{ and } E_1 = E_2 \text{ and } C_1 = C_2 \text{ and } P_1 = P_2$$

Definition 3: If a trust relationship cannot be derived from other existing trust relationships, the trust relationship is a primitive trust relationship.

Definition 4: If a trust relationship can be derived from other existing trust relationships, the trust relationship is a derived trust relationship.

Note: Trust relationships are predefined in information systems. A derived trust relationship is always related to one or more other trust relationships. For an independent trust relationship, it is meaningless to judge it as a derived trust relationship or not.

Proposition 1: If a derived trust relationship exists, there is information redundancy.

Proof: When the derived trust relationship is moved out of the system, the information of the derived trust relationship has not been lost. The derived trust relationship can be built when it is necessary. From the viewpoint of information, there is redundancy.

Definition 5: Let $T=<R, E, C, P>$. If there is trust relationship $T' = <R', E', C', P'>$ and $T \neq T', R \subseteq R', E \subseteq E', C \supseteq C', P \subseteq P'$. T is a direct redundant trust relationship.

In the following part of this section, we discuss several special cases of direct redundant trust relationships based on one special tuple of a trust relationship. We believe that these special cases play important roles in the analysis and design of trust relationships in information systems.

Direct Redundancy Type 1: DLR-Redundant Trust Relationship

Let $T = <R, E, C, P>$. If and only if there is a trust relationship $T' = <R', E, C, P>$ and $R' \supset R$, T is a DLR-redundant trust relationship.

Trust relationship T is DLR-redundant trust relationship means that there is another trust relationship with super set of trustors and all other tuples are same as peers in T.

Direct redundancy Type 2: DLE-Redundant Trust Relationship

Let $T=<R, E, C, P>$. If and only if there is a trust relationship $T'=<R, E', C, P>\$$ and $E' \supset E$, T is a DLE-redundant trust relationship.

Trust relationship T is DLE-redundant trust relationship means that there is another trust relationship with super set of trustees and all other tuples are same as peers in T.

Direct Redundancy Type 3: DMC-Redundant Trust Relationship

Let $T = <R, E, C, P>$. If and only if there is an alternate trust relationship $T' = <R, E, C', P>$ and $C' \subset C$, T is a DMC-redundant trust relationship.

Trust relationship T is DMC-redundant trust relationship means that there is another trust relationship with subset of conditions and all other tuples are same as peers in T.

Direct Redundancy Type 4: DLP-Redundant Trust Relationship

Let $T = <R, E, C, P>$. If and only if there is a trust relationship $T' = <R, E, C, P'>$ and $P' \supset P$, T is a DLP-redundant trust relationship.

Trust relationship T is DLP-redundant trust relationship means that there is another trust relationship with super set of properties and all other tuples are same as peers in T.

Definition 6: Let $T = <R, E, C, P>$, $T' = <R, E, C', P>$ and $C \neq C'$. T and T' are alternate trust relationships of each other.

An alternate trust relationship means that there is an alternate condition set for the same trustor set, trustee set, and property set. Perhaps, there are multiple alternate trust relationships. In distributed computing, multiple mechanisms and multiple choices are necessary in many situations and it is the main reason why we define and discuss alternate trust relationship here.

Proposition 2: If T is a DMC-redundant trust relationship, there is one or more than one alternate trust relationships that are not DMC-redundant trust relationship.

Proof: If T is a DMC-redundant trust relationship, there is $T' = <R, E, C', P>$ and $C' \subset C$. T' is an alternate trust relationship of T. If T' is not DMC-redundant trust relationship, the proposition is proved. If T' is a DMC-redundant trust relationship, the next T'' can be found, $T'' = <R, E, C'', P>$ with $C'' \subset C'$. Such a process will continue until the set of conditions includes minimum number of conditions. In every turn of the process, one or more conditions are removed from the condition set. Because C contains limited conditions, the process can finish when no condition can be removed from the condition set. The final set of conditions is C'. $T' = < R, E, C', P>$ is an alternate trust relationship with nonredundant conditions.

A DMC-redundant trust relationship may have multiple alternate trust relationships with different sets of nonredundant conditions.

In the following, we will make up two scenarios for discussing the relations of trust relationships in the real world. We hope that these examples can be helpful in understanding the definition of trust relationship and how to use the mathematical properties that focus on relations of trust relationships described above.

Scenario 1: When people want to change their names, they need to apply to a specific organization (In Australia, the organization is the Registry of Births Deaths & Marriages). The officers in the organization and the requesters are involved in this scenario. Using the full syntax of our definition of trust relationship, some trust relationships may be modeled as follows:

- **TS1-1:** Officers trust requesters if requesters have their Birth Certificate & Driver's License that requesters have the right for the change.
- **TS1-2:** Officers trust requesters if requesters have their Citizenship Certificate & Driver's License that requesters have the right for the change.
- **TS1-3:** Officers trust requesters if requesters have their Birth Certificate & Citizenship Certificate & Driver's License that requesters have the right for the change.

If **TS1-1**, **TS1-2** and **TS1-3** are all the trust relationships in this information system, based on the definitions and operations in section "Classification of Trust," we can have the following analysis:

- **TS1-1** and **TS1-2** are primitive trust relationships.
- **TS1-1** and **TS1-2** are alternate trust relationships of each other.
- **TS1-3** is a derived trust relationship which can be derived by **Operation 1A** with **TS1-1** and **TS1-2**.
- **TS1-3** is a DMC-redundant trust relationship and it should be removed out of the system.

Scenario 2: An online e-commerce service is called FlightServ, which can provide flight booking and travel deals. FlightServ is designed based on the new technologies of Web services. FlightServ connects with customers, airlines, hotels, and credit card services (some of them may be Web services). The whole system could be very complicated, but we only consider some of trust relationships in the system. In the system, customers are classified into normal flyers and frequent flyers. Originally, some trust relationships are modeled as:

- **TS2-1:** Airlines trust normal flyers if they have address details and confirmed credit card information that normal flyers can make their airline bookings.
- **TS2-2:** Airlines trust frequent flyers with no condition that frequent flyers can make their airline bookings.
- **TS2-3:** Hotels trust normal flyers if they have address details and confirmed credit card information that normal flyers can make their hotels booking.
- **TS2-4:** Hotels trust frequent flyers if they have address details and confirmed credit card information that frequent flyers can make their hotels booking.
- **TS2-5:** Credit card services are trusted by all possible entities without any condition that the credit card services will give the correct evaluation of credit card information.
- **TS2-6:** Credit card services are trusted by all possible entities without any condition that the credit card services will keep the privacy of credit card information.

For these trust relationships in the system, based on definitions and operations in section "Classification of Trust," we have the following analysis:

- All above trust relationships are primitive.
- Using the **Operation 3A**, trust relationships **TS2-3** and **TS2-4** can be merged to a new trust relationship **TS2-(3)(4)**: "Hotels trust customers if they have address details & confirmed credit card information that customers can make their hotel booking." If **TS2-(3)(4)** has been defined in the system, **TS2-3** and **TS2-4** becomes DLE-redundant trust relationships and will be removed out of the system.

- Using the **Operation 1B**, trust relationships **TS2-5** and **TS2-6** can be merged to a new trust relationship **TS2-(5)(6)**: "Credit card services are trusted by all possible entities without any condition that the credit card services will give the correct evaluation of credit card information & the credit card services will keep the privacy of credit card information." If **TS2-(5)(6)** has been defined in the system, **TS2-5** and **TS2-6** becomes DLP-redundant trust relationships and will be removed out of the system.

Here we employ these two examples to illustrate how to understand and use the definition of trust relationship in section "Definition of Trust Relationships" and the relations of trust relationships in this section. The definitions in section "Definition of Trust Relationships" and this section provide terms and helpful tools in the analysis of the above two scenarios. In the analysis of the two scenarios, we only employ some definitions, propositions, and operations expressed in this section, and we hope that readers can obtain a general picture from these scenarios. In these two scenarios, we only choose some trust relationships as examples and employ these examples to illustrate the operations and definitions about relations of trust relationships. The definitions and operations in this section are elements of unified taxonomy framework of trust and they can be used as enabling tools in the analysis and modeling of trust relationships in information systems.

Trust Direction and Symmetry

The properties of trust direction and trust symmetry play an important role in information systems. In this section, we will provide a general description of the properties of trust direction and trust symmetry by a set of definitions and a scenario example. These definitions about trust direction and symmetry are new elements of the unified taxonomy framework of trust. We believe that these definitions can cover most situations about trust direction and symmetry in the real world and these definitions can be used as standard scenarios for analyzing and modeling the trust direction and symmetric characteristics of trust. In real systems, one or multiple kinds of trust direction and trust symmetry can be chosen based on the specified requirements of the information systems.

The definitions about trust direction and trust symmetry are related to each other and they should be cooperatively used to analyze and model the properties of direction and symmetry of trust in information systems. We define one-way trust relationship, two-way trust relationship, and reflexive trust relationship for the properties of trust direction. For the properties of symmetry of trust relationships, we provide the definitions of symmetric trust relationships, symmetric two-way trust relationship, and the whole set of trust relationships.

The details of the definitions are described as follows:

Definition 7: One-way trust relationship is the trust relationship with a unique trust direction from the trustors to trustees.

One-way is the default feature of a trust relationship if there is no further description.

Two-way trust relationship can be defined and used in information systems such as Microsoft's domain trust. Actually, two-way trust relationship is the result of binding two one-way trust relationships together. We define two-way trust relationship as follows:

Definition 8: Two-way trust relationship TT' is the binding of two one-way trust relationships $T = <R, E, C, P>$ and $T' = <R', E', C', P'>$, with $R' = E$ and $E' = R$. T and T' are the reflective trust relationships with each other in the two-way trust relationship.

In this definition, "binding" is the key word. If there are two one-way trust relationships between R and E but they are not bound with each other, then they are only two one-way trust relationships and there is no two-way trust relationship. When two one-way trust relationships are bound together, there is a two-way trust relationship and these two one-way trust relationships can be called reflective trust relationships with each other. If the trustors and the trustees are the same, the trust relationship is reflexive. The reflexive trust relationship is defined as follows:

Definition 9: Trust relationships $T = <R, E, C, P>$ is a reflexive trust relationship when $R = E$.

The symmetry of two trust relationships could be an important concern in the analysis or modeling of trust relationships in distributed information systems. The symmetry of two trust relationships is defined as the follows:

Definition 10: If there is trust relationship $T' = <R', E', C', P'>$, which is the result of swapping trustors and trustees in another trust relationship $T = <R, E, C, P>$ (the swapping includes all possible ownerships in condition set and property set), there is symmetry between T and T'; T and T' are symmetric trust relationships with each other.

In the above definition, the swapping of trustors and trustees includes all possible ownerships in condition set and property set. The two trust relationships have the same condition set and property set except the possible ownerships in them. The symmetric/asymmetric two-way trust relationship is defined as follows:

Definition 11: A two-way trust relationship TT' is symmetric two-way trust relationship if there is symmetry between T and T'; otherwise TT' is an asymmetric two-way trust relationship.

Sometimes it is necessary to discuss the symmetry of all trust relationships between a trustor set and a trustee set, we have the following definition:

Definition 12: $WTR(R, E)$ is the whole set of trust relationships with same trustor set R and trustee set E.

Definition 13: If every trust relationship in $WTR(R,E)$ has a symmetric trust relationship in $WTR(E,R)$, and every trust relationship in $WTR(E,R)$ has a symmetric trust relationship in $WTR(R,E)$, the trust between R and E are symmetric.

Scenario example: Here we use Microsoft's domain trust as a regressive scenario example to discuss the properties of trust direction and trust symmetry defined in this section. Domain trust allows users to authenticate to resources in another domain. Also, an administrator is able to administer user rights for users in the other domain. Our general definitions for the properties of direction and symmetry of trust relationships have general expressive power and can cover broad range of commonly used notations. The related concepts in domain trust can be viewed as specific cases of these general definitions. In the following, we will use our terms defined in this paper to review some concepts in domain trust.

- Based on **definition 1** in section "Definition of Trust Relationships," the domain trust can be expressed as "entities in domain A trust entities in domain B without any condition that entities in domain B have the right to get access of the set of resources in domain A."

- From our viewpoint of trust classification in section "Classification of Trust," Microsoft's domain trust belongs to resources access trust. Domain trust binds the authentication and authorization together and has a standard two-layer structure described in section "Classification of Trust."

- Microsoft's domain trust includes both one-way trust and two-way trust. In Microsoft's domain trust, one-way trust is defined as a unidirectional authentication path created between two domains. This means that in a one-way trust between domain A and domain B, users in domain A can access resources in domain B. However, users in domain B cannot access resources in domain A. Microsoft's one-way trust is an example of one-way trust relationship in **definition 7**. In a two-way domain trust, authentication requests can be passed between the two domains in both directions. Two-way trust is an example of two-way trust relationship in **definition 8**.

- The entities in the same domain trust each other without any condition that entities have the right to get access of the set of resources in the same domain. This is an example of reflexive trust relationship in **definition 9**.

- There is symmetry in the two-way domain trust. The two one-way trust relationships bound in the two-way trust relationship are "entities in domain A trust entities in domain B without any condition that entities in domain B have the right to get access of the set of resources in domain A" and "entities in domain B trust entities in domain A without any condition that entities in domain A have the right to get access of the set of resources in domain B." These two one-way trust relationships are symmetric trust relationships with each other in **definition 10**. Microsoft's two-way trust is symmetric two-way trust relationship in **definition 11**.

- In domain trust, the $WTR(A,B)$ based on **definition 12** has only one trust relationship from trustor domain A to trustee domain B. For two-way domain trust, the trust between domain A and domain B is symmetric based on **definition 13**.

We use this scenario to illustrate the definitions about trust direction and symmetry. Beyond the Microsoft's domain trust, these definitions about trust direction and symmetry are general concepts of trust and they can be used in applications, networks, domains, and so forth.

Trust Scope and Diversity

Scope and diversity are two other aspects related to the trust relationship. The diversity of trust has been discussed by Jøsang (1996), who expresses trust in three diversity dimensions. The first dimension represents trustors or trust originators; the second dimension represents the trust purpose; and the third represents trustees. Jøsang uses the term trust purpose based on the observation that trust is relative to a domain of actions. In our formal definition of trust relationship, trustors and trustees are two tuples and they are similar to the terms of Jøsang. The origin diversity about trustors and target diversity about trustees are straightforward and have been described clearly by Jøsang (Jøsang, 1996). Jøsang's term of trust purpose is related to a domain of actions. In this section, we will define trust scope label to take the place of the trust purpose. The benefits of trust scope label will be discussed in this section. The trust scope label is based on the four tuples of a trust relationship and it is the binding of the condition set and property set. The trust scope label is a new element of our taxonomy framework defined as follows:

Definition 14: A trust scope label is a two-tuple $SL = <C, P>$ where C is a set of conditions and P is a set of properties.

The details of condition set C and property set P can be found in the formal definition of trust relationship in section "Definition of Trust Relationships." Actually, trust scope label provides a new layer of abstraction under the trust relationship and it defines the properties of the trust and its associated conditions. To compare two trust scope labels $TSL_1 = <C_1, P_1>$ and $TSL2 = <C2, P2>$, we have the following rules:

1. $C_1 \subseteq C_2$ and $P_1 \supseteq P_2$ <=> $TSL_1 \geq TSL_2$
2. $C_1 = C_2$ and $P_1 = P_2$ <=> $TSL_1 = TSL_2$
3. $C_1 \supseteq C_2$ and $P_1 \subseteq P_2$ <=> $TSL_1 \leq TSL_2$
4. In other cases, TSL_1 and TSL_2 cannot be compared with each other.

The trust scope label is beyond the trust purpose in several aspects. Trust scope label composes of a subspace of trust relationships (two tuples out of four tuples) and describes the characteristics of the combination of condition set C and property set P.

Trust scope labels could be treated as an independent subspace of trust relationships in the analysis and design of overall information systems. The property set in trust scope label covers not only actions but also attributes of trustees. Trust scope labels can be embedded in all the trust types described in section "Classification of Trust," and two trust scope labels could be compared with each other based on the rules given previously.

Scenario example: Consider an online software shop. We assume that anybody who wants to enter the online shop must register as a member of the online shop first. For describing the condition set and property set in possible trust relationships between the shop and possible customers, we use the following notations:

- P_1 stands for that customers can read the documentation of the software.
- P_2 stands for that customers can download the software.
- C_1 stands for certificate of membership.
- C_2 stands for the commitment of the payment for the software.
- C_3 stands for the payment for the software.

We have the following trust scope labels:

1. $TSL_1 =< \{C_1\}, \{P_1\}$
2. $TSL_2 =< \{C_1, C_2\}, \{P_1, P_2\}$
3. $TSL_3 =< \{C_1, C_2, C_3\}, \{P_1, P_2\}$

Based on the rules to compare two trust scope labels, we have:

- TSL_1 cannot be compared with TSL_2 (or TSL_3). There is no obvious relationship between TSL_1 and TSL_2 (or TSL_3).
- $TSL_2 > TSL_3$. It means that the trust scope of TSL_2 is less strict than that of TSL_3.

In the analysis and modeling of trust relationships, the trust scope label may be quite complicated and these comparison rules provide helpful tools in making judgments.

Future Research Based on the Taxonomy Framework

The unified taxonomy framework of trust is the first step of our research about trust. Related with the taxonomy framework, we are currently working on the life cycle of trust relationships and unified trust management architecture as an overall solution of trust issues in information systems. In this section, we will provide more details about our research ideas about life cycle of trust relationships and trust management architecture.

Life Cycle of Trust Relationships

We are currently working on a methodology for life cycle of trust relationships using the definition of trust relationship, classification of trust, relations of trust relationships, properties of trust direction and symmetry, and properties of trust scope and diversity. Trust relationships between possible entities play crucial roles in many information systems. The analysis and design of trust relationships are normally very complicated and challenging. Trust requirements are normally integrated with other requirements of the whole information system. The modeling, implementing, and maintaining of trust relationships is an incremental, iterative process. The whole life cycle of trust relationships includes several stages such as extracting trust requirements in system, identifying possible trust relationships from trust requirements, choosing and refining the whole set of trust relationships from possible trust relationships, implementing trust relationships in systems, and maintaining trust relationships in systems. The initial trust relationships will be refined in multiple life cycles. There are two ways to accommodate new business requirements. One way is to introduce new trust relationships and another way is to modify existing trust relationships. When new trust relationships are introduced, several things need to be considered such as the type of trust, the scope and diversity of these trust relationships, the properties of direction and symmetry of these trust relationships, and the relations between them and existing trust relationships. In previous sections, we have proposed a set of definitions to enable the analysis of the above properties. We have also given some example scenarios to illustrate them. All the definitions are under the unified taxonomy framework of trust. We believe that the taxonomy framework of trust is helpful in the analysis and design of trust relationships in a broad variety of information systems and it is the initial part of our overall methodology of life cycle of trust relationships.

Trust Management Architecture

The importance of trust management has been recognized by many researchers. Different notions of trust have been developed. There are many services and applications that must accommodate appropriate notions of trust and related elements of trust such as community reputation and security credentials. Reputation-based systems such as XREP (Damiani, Vimercati, Paraboschi, Samarati, & Violante, 2002), NICE (Lee, Sherwood, & Bhattacharjee, 2003) and PGrid (Aberer & Despotovic, 2001) provide facility to compute the reputation of an involved entity by aggregating the perception of other entities in the system. Some reputation systems like TrustNet (Schillo, Rovatsos, & Funk, 2000) and NodeRanking (Pujol, Sangüesa, & Delgado, 2002) utilize existing social relationships to compute reputations based on various parameters. Normally, these systems are limited in the sense that they did not enable the linkage to the purpose of reputation evaluation in the systems. For example, the reputation of an entity will determine the restriction of access to resources and services. On the other hand, there are many trust management systems based on credentials. Public key certificates X.509 and PGP have already used credentials to deal with trust management problem. As a further step, Blaze et al. firstly identified trust management as a distinct and important component of security in distributed environments and proposed PolicyMaker (1996). After that, several automated trust management systems have been proposed and implemented including PolicyMaker (Blaze et al., 1996), KeyNote (Blaze et al., 1999) and REFEREE (Chu et al., 1997) and IBM Trust Establishment Framework (IBM). All of these systems use credentials as evidence of required trust. Normally, there are credential verification and secure application policies to restrict access to resources and services. G. Suryanarayana et al. (Grandison & Sloman, 2000) have pointed out that these systems are limited in the sense that they did not enable an entity to aggregate the perception of other entities in the system in order to choose a suitable reputed service. We are currently working on a unified trust management architecture that can break these limitations of trust systems. The architecture covers a broad variety of trust mechanisms including reputations and credentials. The trust management architecture will leverage established standards of trust management, and it covers a broad variety of situations in different environments. The main aims of the architecture are to establish trust management infrastructure that can provide utilizing and enabling tools for applications in distributed environments. Different trust mechanisms can be assembled together when multiple mechanisms of trust are necessary. The unified taxonomy framework of trust is the basis of the unified architecture of trust management. Our trust management architecture is based on the following general principles:

- **Unified framework:** Existing systems treat different trust mechanisms separately. There is no architecture to handle trust-related issues in a comprehensive and consistent manner. Our approach allows multiple established trust mechanisms to cooperate with each other under the same unified architecture.

- **Flexibility:** Our trust management architecture can support complex situations of trust management. The architecture can cover commonly used extreme notions of trust, and it is based on unified taxonomy framework of trust where a range of useful trust relationships can be expressed and compared. The trust relationships can occur in any distributed application in the real world.

- **Locality of control:** The entity involved in the trust relationship can make trust decisions based on the specific circumstance. The framework supports local control of trust relationships and the local control can be based on different trust parameters such as credentials, community-based reputation, data from storage, and environment conditions.

- **Standard interfaces:** The trust management architecture should have standard interfaces to applications or application specific policies. The interfaces can provide unified mechanisms for requesting trust, evaluating trust, and consuming trust in the real world.

Concluding Remarks

In this chapter, we described the unified taxonomy framework of trust in distributed environments. We believe that the unified taxonomy framework of trust can provide suitable terms for trust management in information systems and they can be used as powerful tools in the analysis and design of trust in the real world. The current taxonomy framework is still on the stage of developing. More properties of trust are still being formulated and after they have been defined, they will become new elements of the taxonomy framework. For example, we are currently developing the notions of delegation, propagation, and transitivity of trust.

References

Aberer, K., & Despotovic, Z. (2001). Managing trust in a peer-2-peer information system, In *CIKM'01 Tenth International Conference on Information and Knowledge Management* (pp. 310–317). Atlanta, GA: ACM Press.

Abrams, M. D. (1995). Trusted system concepts. In M. V. Joyce (Ed.), *Computers and security* (pp 45-56).

Abrams, M. D., & Joyce, M. V. (1995). Trusted computing update. *Computers and Security*, *14*(1), 57–68.

Anderson, S., Bohren, J., Boubez, T., Chanliau, M., Della-Libera, G., Dixon, B., et al. (2004). *Web services trust language (ws-trust), Version 1.1*. Retrieved from http://www-106. ibm.com/developerworks/library/ws-trust/

Blaze, M., Feigenbaum, J., & Keromytis, A. D. (1999). *KeyNote: Trust management for public-key infrastructures* (LNCS 1550, pp. 59-63).

Blaze, M., Feigenbaum, J., & Lacy, J. (1996). Decentralized trust management. In *IEEE Symposium on Security and Privacy* (pp. 164-173).

Chu, Y. H., Feigenbaum, J., Lamacchia, B., Resnick, P., & Strauss, M. (1997). REFEREE: Trust management for Web applications. *Computer Networks and ISDN Systems*, *29*(8-13), 953-964.

Damiani, E., Vimercati, S., Paraboschi, S., Samarati, P., & Violante, F. (2002). A reputation-based approach for choosing reliable resources in peer-to-peer networks. In *CCS '02: 9th ACM conference on Computer and communications security* (pp. 207-216). Washington, DC: ACM Press.

Della-Libera, G., Della-Libera, G., Dixon, B., Garg, P., Hallam-Baker, P., Hondo, M., et al. (2002). *Web services trust language (ws-trust), Version 1.0*. Retrieved from http:// www-106.ibm.com/developerworks/library/ws-trust/

Ding, Y., & Petersen, H. (1995). *A new approach for delegation using hierarchical delegation tokens*. University of Technology Chemnitz-Zwickau, Department of Computer Science.

Felten, E. W. (2003). Understanding trusted computing: Will its benefits outweigh its draw-backs? *IEEE Security & Privacy*, *1*(3), 60-62.

Grandison, T., & Sloman, M. (2000 Fourth Quarter). A survey of trust in Internet application. *IEEE Communications Surveys, 3*(4), 1-30.

Huhns, M. N., & Buell, D. A. (2002). Trusted autonomy. *IEEE Internet Computing, 6*(3), 92-95.

IBM. (2001). *IBM trust establishment - policy language*. Retrieved from http://www.haifa. il.ibm.com/projects/software/e-Business/TrustManager/PolicyLanguage.html

Jøsang, A. (1996). The right type of trust for distributed systems. In *Proceedings of the 1996 New Security Paradigms Workshop*. ACM.

Jøsang, A. (1999). An algebra for assessing trust in certification chains. In *Proceedings of the Network and Distributed Systems Security (NDSS'99) Symposium*. The Internet Society.

Jøsang, A. & Knapskog, S. J. (1998). A metric for trusted systems. In *Proceedings of the 21ˢᵗ National Security Conference* (pp. 16-29). NSA.

Landauer, J., Redmond, T., & Benzel, T. (1989). Formal policies for trusted processes. In *Proceedings of the Computer Security Foundations Workshop II* (pp. 31-40).

Lee, S., Sherwood, R., & Bhattacharjee, B. (2003). Cooperative peer groups in nice. In *Proceedings of the INFOCOM 2003 Twenty-Second Annual Joint Conference of the IEEE Computer and Communications Societies* (Vol. 2, pp. 1272-1282).

Manchala, D. W. (2000). E-commerce trust metrics and models. *IEEE Internet Computing, 4*(2), 36-44.

Marsh, S. (1994). *Formalising trust as a computational concept*. Doctoral dissertation, University of Sterling, 1990.

Mui, L., Mohtashemi, M., & Halberstadt, A. (2002). A computational model of trust and reputation. In *Proceedings of the 35ᵗʰ Annual Hawaii International Conference on System sciences*, Big Island, HI (pp. 7-10).

Pujol, J. M., Sangüesa, R., Delgado, J. (2002). Extracting reputation in multiagent systems by means of social network topology. In *Proceedings of the AAMAS '02: First international Joint Conference on Autonomous Agents and Multi-Agent Systems*, Bologna, Italy (pp. 467-474). ACM Press.

Schillo, M., Rovatsos, M., & Funk, P. (2000). Using trust for detecting deceitful agents in artificial societies. In C. Castelfranchi, Y. Tan, R. Falcone, & B. Firozabadi, *Applied Artificial Intelligence Journal, Special Issue on Deception, Fraud and Trust in Agent Societies*, *14*, 825-848.

U.S.A. National Computer Security Council. (1985). *Trusted computer system evaluation criteria* (DOD standard 5200.28-STD).

Wang, Y, & Vassileva, J. (2003). Trust and reputation model in peer-to-peer networks. In *Proceedings of the Third International Conference on Peer-to-Peer Computing*.

Winsborough, W. H., Seamons, K. E., & Jones, V. E. (2000). Automated trust negotiation. In *Proceedings of the DARPA Information Survivability Conference and Exposition*.

Winslett, M., Yu, T., Seamons, K. E., Hess, A., Jacobson, J., Jarvis, R., et al. (2002). Negotiating trust in the Web. *IEEE Internet Computing*, *6*(6), 30-37.

Xiong, L., & Liu, L. (2003). A reputation-based trust model for peer-to-peer e commerce communities. In *Proceedings of the IEEE International Conference on E-Commerce.*

Zhao, W., Varadharajan, V., & Bryan, G. (2004). *Modelling trust relationships in distributed environments* (LNCS 3184, pp. 40-49).

Zhao, W., Varadharajan, V., & Bryan, G. (2005). *Analysis and modelling of trust in distributed information systems* (LNCS 3808, pp. 106-119).

Chapter III

A Survey of Trust Use and Modeling in Real Online Systems

Paolo Massa, ITC-IRST, Italy

Abstract

This chapter discusses the concept of trust and how trust is used and modeled in online systems currently available on the Web or on the Internet. It starts by describing the concept of information overload and introducing trust as a possible and powerful way to deal with it. It then provides a classification of the systems that currently use trust and, for each category, presents the most representative examples. In these systems, trust is considered as the judgment expressed by one user about another user, often directly and explicitly, sometimes indirectly through an evaluation of the artifacts produced by that user or his/her activity on the system. We hence use the term "trust" to indicate different types of social relationships between two users, such as friendship, appreciation, and interest. These trust relationships are used by the systems in order to infer some measure of importance about the different users and influence their visibility on the system. We conclude with an overview of the open and interesting challenges for online systems that use and model trust information.

Introduction

The Internet and the Web are pretty new creations in human history, but they have already produced a lot of changes in the lives of people who use them. One of the most visible effects of these two artifacts is that nowadays everyone with an Internet connection has the possibility to easily create content, put it online, and make it available to everyone else, possibly forever. If we are to compare this with the situation of some dozens of years ago, the difference is striking. In fact, until recently, only a tiny fraction of the world population had the possibility to "publish" content and distribute it to the public: for instance, few were the authors of books and few the musicians able to publish their music. Conversely, now everyone with an Internet connection can easily publish his/her thoughts on the Web: opening and keeping a blog, for instance, is both very easy and cheap today (actually it is offered for free by many Web sites, for example, blogger.com). Likewise, any band can record its songs in a garage, convert them to MP3 format, and create a Web site for the band to place their song files for the global audience. Moreover, in the future, we can only expect to have these capabilities extended, both on the axis of types of content that can easily be created and shared, and in terms of the range of people that are currently excluded for different reasons, such as location (many countries in the world still have to get the benefit of reliable and cheap Internet connections), age, education level, income.

This phenomenon has been described as the "The Mass Amateurisation of Everything" (Coates, 2003), and we believe this term describes effectively the new situation. However, the easy publishing situation creates a problem, namely "information overload," a term coined in 1970 by Alvin Toffler in his book *Future Shock*. Information overload refers to the state of having too much information to make a decision or keep up to date about a topic. In fact, while it is good to have as many points of view as possible on any topic, it is impossible for a single human being to check them all. So we are faced with the challenge of filtering out the vast majority of the flow of daily created information and experience just the small portion that our limited daily attention and time can manage.

At the present time, it is unreasonable (and luckily almost impossible) to have a centralized quality control authority that decides what is good content, and thus worth our attention, and what instead must be ignored. But of course not all the content has the same degree of worthiness and interestingness for a specific person. What can be done is to infer the quality and value of the content from the "quality" of the content creator. However there is a problem: it is impossible for anyone to have a first-hand opinion about every other single creator of content. Until a few years ago, before the widespread availability of Internet, it was normal for most of the people to interact just with the people who were living physically close by. Geography was used to shape communities, and a person was able to decide about the neighbors trustworthiness in a lifelong ongoing process based on direct evidence and judgments and opinions shared by trusted people, for example by parents. Physical clues like the dress or the perceived sincerity of the eyes were also used to make decisions about trusting someone or not. Moreover, local authorities had some real power to enforce law in case of unacceptable and illegal behavior.

Instead, nowadays, as an example, it is a realistic possibility for a man in Italy to buy a used guitar from a woman in Taiwan and they will never see each other in the eyes, nor even talk. Also, the fact they live in different countries with different law systems makes it very difficult to enter into a legal litigation unless for really huge problems. Thanks to the Internet, we live in the so-called "global village," and in this new and totally different context we need new tools. To date, the most promising solution to this new situation is to a have a decentralized collaborative assessment of the quality of the other unknown people, that is, to share the burden to evaluate them. It is in fact the case that most of the community Web sites nowadays let a user express her opinions about every other user, asking how much she finds her interesting and worth her attention. We call these expressed opinions trust statements. For example, on Epinions (http://epinions.com), a site where users can review products, users can also specify which other users they trust, that is, "reviewers whose reviews and ratings they have consistently found to be valuable" (Epinions.com web of trust FAQ, n.d.) and which ones they do not. Similar patterns can be found in online news communities (for example, on slashdot.org, on which millions of users post news and comments daily), in peer-to-peer networks (where peers can enter corrupted items), in e-marketplace sites (such as eBay.com) and in general, in many open publishing communities (Guha, 2003). Usually judgments entered about other users (trust statements) are used to personalize a specific user's experience on the system, for example by giving more prominence to content created by trusted users. These approaches mimic real-life situations in which it is common habit to rely on opinions of people we trust and value: for instance, it is pretty common to ask like-minded friends their opinions about a new movie while considering if it is worth to go watching it or not. But the Web and the Internet exhibit a huge advantage for information dissemination on a global scale: all the trust statements can be made publicly and permanently visible and fetchable, possibly by everyone or only by some specific users. In this way, it is possible to aggregate in one single graph all the trust statements issued by users. We call such a graph, trust network. Figure 1 shows an example of a simple trust network, containing al the trust statements such as, for instance, the one issued by Alice expressing she trusts Carol as 0.7. In fact, trust statements can be weighted so that it is possible to express different levels of trust on another user. We assume the range of trust weights is [0,1]: small values represent low trust expressed by the issuing user on the target user while large values represent high trust. Precisely, the extremes, 0 and 1, represent respectively total distrust and total trust. Modeling distrust and making explicit its meaning is undoubtedly an open point and will be discussed in section "Open Challenges." Note that the trust network is, by definition, directed, and hence not necessarily symmetric. It is totally normal that a user expresses a trust statement on another user and that this user does not reciprocate: for example, Bob Dylan will hardly reciprocate a trust statement by a fan of his on a music site. In the simple trust network of Figure 1, for example, Bob totally trusts Dave but Dave did not express a trust statement on Bob. We say that Bob is unknown to Dave. Even when users know each other, it can be that their subjective trust statements exhibit different scores, as in the case of Alice and Bob in Figure 1.

On a trust network, it is possible to run a trust metric (Golbeck, Hendler, & Parsia, 2003; Levien, n.d.; Massa & Avesani, 2004; Ziegler & Lausen, 2004). A trust metric is an algorithm that uses the information of the trust network in order to predict the trustworthiness of unknown users. Coming back to Figure 1, since user Alice does not have a direct opinion about user David, a trust metric can be used to predict how much Alice could trust David (represented by the dotted edge in Figure 1). Let us suppose that in Figure 1 the trust statements are expressed by the source user based on perceived reliability of the target user as seller of used products, and let us suppose that Alice wants to buy a used camera. She finds

Figure 1. Trust network. Nodes are users and edges are trust statements. The dotted edge is one of the undefined and predictable trust statements.

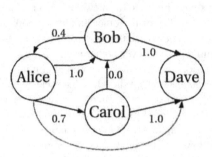

out that David is selling a camera but she does not know David and is not sure about his trustworthiness and reliability. However, Alice knows Bob and Carol, who both know and trust David. In this case, a trust metric can happen to suggest to Alice to trust (or not) David and, as a consequence, to buy (or not) the camera from him. Of course, more complex reasoning involving more users and longer trust paths can happen in more realistic examples. By using trust metrics, even if the users known on a first-hand basis are a small fraction, it is possible to exploit the judgments of other users and figure out how much a certain user (and indirectly the content she creates) is interesting for the active user. Trust metrics' common assumption is that trust can be propagated in some way, that is, if user A trusts user B and user B trusts user C, something can be said about the level of trust A could place in C.

The remaining of this chapter is organized as follows: Section "Categories of Online Systems in Which Trust is Modeled and Used" presents a classification of systems in which trust is modeled and used, along with a description of the most representative examples of real systems. For each of them, it describes what are the entities in the system (source and target of trust statement), which social and trust relationships they can express in the system, and how. It also analyzes how trust is used by the system for giving a better experience to the user. In section "Open Challenges," we discuss the challenges faced by online systems that model and use trust relationships.

Categories of Online Systems in Which Trust is Modeled and Used

This section presents a classification of the online systems in which the concept of trust is modeled and used, and some examples of online systems that fit into the different categories. Even if the listed systems span a large spectrum of purposes and designs, it is possible to recognize some common features, and these drove our classification. In these online systems, visitors are invited to create a user profile so that their online persona is made visible, in general within a "user profile" Web page. Usually this page shows a picture of the user and some information entered by himself/herself. Often it also shows a summary of the user's activity on the system. This page is very important in these systems since it completely represents the human being behind the online identity, and often users form their opinions about other users only based on this page. These systems also allow one user to express some level of relationship with the other users, for example, concerning friendship, professional appreciation, commercial satisfaction, or level of acquaintance. We use the term "trust" to represent many slightly different social relationships. Usually the list of expressed relationships with other users is public, but it might also be secret, as in the case of the distrust (or block) list in Epinions.

Trust is a very broad concept that has been investigated for centuries in fields as diverse as sociology, psychology, economics, philosophy, politics, and now computer science (see Mui, 2002 for a detailed summary of contributions from different research fields), and there are no commonly agreed definitions that fit all the purposes and all the investigation lines.

For the purpose of this chapter, we are going to provide an operational definition of trust.

Trust is defined as "the explicit opinion expressed by a user about another user regarding the perceived quality of a certain characteristic of this user." The term "trust statement" will be used as well with the same intended meaning. The user expressing trust (i.e., issuing the trust statement) is the "source user," while the evaluated user is the "target user." We will see in the following how trust is represented and modeled in different ways in the online systems we will explore. For example in some systems, quality refers to the ability to provide reliable and interesting product reviews (as in Epinions). In others systems, it refers to the ability of being a good friend for the user (as in Friendster.com), while in others it is the ability to find interesting new Web sites (as in Del.icio.us). This specificity is the "trust context," and it is the characteristic of the target user evaluated by the user who issues the trust statement. Of course, in different trust contexts, a user can express different trust statements about the same user. For example, the subjective trust expressed by Alice on Bob about his ability of writing an interesting story about computers (the trust context of Slashdot.org) is in general not correlated with the trust expressed by Alice on Bob about his quality of being an honest seller online (the trust context of eBay.com).

In the following we describe different online systems that use and model trust. We have identified few different categories in which the systems can be grouped based on the common features and properties the share. The categories we define are:

- E-marketplaces
- Opinions and activity sharing sites
- Business/job networking sites
- Social/entertainment sites
- News sites
- The Web, the Blogosphere, and the Semantic Web
- Peer-to-peer (P2P) networks

E-marketplaces are online systems in which a user can sell items owned and can buy offered items. In such a context, typically the buyer does not know the seller, and vice versa. So, in order to decide about a possible commercial exchange that involves the risk of not being paid or of not receiving the products already paid for, it is very important to be able to decide in a quick, reliable, and easy to understand way about the trustworthiness of the possible commercial partner. The success of eBay (http://ebay.com) is largely due to the fact it provides an easy way to do this.

Opinions and activity sharing sites on the other hand are Web sites where users can share with the other users their opinions on items and, in general, make their activities and preferences visible to and usable by other users. The best example of an opinions site is Epinions, in which users can write reviews about products. In activity sharing sites, the user activity is made visible to the other users who can in some way take advantage of it. Two examples of activity sharing sites are Del.icio.us, in which users can bookmark URLs they consider interesting, and Last.fm, in which users make visible which songs they listen to. Bookmarking a URL and listening to a song can be considered as the elicitation of a positive opinion about the considered item. However, a user might be more interested in following the reviews and activity of a certain other user, and trust statements can be used exactly for this purpose.

Business/job networking sites are Web sites where users post information about their job skills and ambitions so that other people can find them when they are looking for someone to hire for a specific job. Lately, many systems started to exploit the social (trust) network between users: users can explicitly state their connections, that is, professionals they have already worked with and found reliable and trustworthy. In this way, using the system, a user can enter in contact with the connections of his/her connections and discover potentially interesting new business partners. Linkedin.com and Ryze.com are two examples of such sites.

The idea behind the *social/entertainment sites* is similar to business/job networking sites. However, in this case, the context is more relaxed and informal, and sometimes involves dating and partner search. Here users are, in general, requested to list their friends so that, by browsing the social networks of them, it is possible to discover some friends of friends that might become friends. The first successful example was Friendster.com, soon followed by many other attempts.

News sites are centralized Web sites where users can submit news and stories and comment on them freely. The challenge is to keep the signal-to-noise ratio high. Usually, the users can rate other users' activities (posted news and comments) and these ratings are used to give more visibility to posts and comments the other users appreciate and value. Slashdot. org and Kuro5hin.org are two examples of this category.

The Web, the Blogosphere, and the Semantic Web can be viewed as decentralized news sites. They are systems in which anyone is free to publish whatever content at whatever time in whatever form. Different from the previous examples, in these systems, there is not a single, central point where content is submitted and stored, but the content is published in a decentralized way; for example, it is stored on different Web servers. The challenge in this case is to design a system able to collect all this content and find a suitable algorithm to quickly decide about its importance and value. Google.com was the first company able to achieve this and in fact, a large part of its initial success over search engines of the time is due to the PageRank algorithm (Brin & Page, 1998). PageRank's assumption is to consider a link from page *A* to page *B* as a vote of *A* to *B*, or, in our jargon, a trust statement. The number of received trust statements influences the authority value of every Web page. In the following, we will review also how the concept of trust can be used in the Blogosphere (the collections of all the Web logs) and research efforts for introducing and exploiting trust in the Semantic Web.

The last category of systems that use and model trust is *peer-to-peer (P2P) networks*. P2P networks can be used to share files. P2P networks are, in fact, a controversial technology: large copyright holders claim they are used mainly to violate the copyright of works they own and are fighting to shut down this technology all together. We will not comment on this issue, but present the technological challenges faced by P2P networks. The open, autonomous, and uncontrollable nature of P2P networks in fact opens new challenges: for example, there are peers that enter poisoned content (e.g., corrupted files, songs with annoying noise in the middle) into the network. It has been suggested that a possible way to spot these mali- cious peers is to let every peer client express their opinions about other peers and share this information using the P2P network in order to isolate them. On a more positive take, a peer can mark as interesting (i.e., trust) another peer when it makes available for download many files that are considered interesting by its human user, or P2P networks can be used to share files only with a controlled and limited community of trusted friends.

Before going on with the discussion, it is worth mentioning that one of the first uses of the concept of trust in computational settings was in PGP (pretty good privacy), a public key encryption program originally written by Phil Zimmermann in 1991. In fact, in order to communicate securely with someone using PGP, the sender needs to be sure that a certain cryptographic key really belongs to the human being he/she wants to communicate with. The sender can verify this by receiving it physically from that person's hands but sometimes this is hard, for example if they live in different continents. The idea of PGP for overcoming this problem was to build a "web of trust": the sender can ask someone whose key he/she already knows to send him/her a certificate confirming that the signed key belongs to that person. In this way, it is possible to validate keys based on the web of trust. The web of trust of course can be longer than two hops in the sense the sender can rely on the certificate received by someone who received it as well as from someone else, and so on. However, in this chapter, we are interested in the concept of trust from a more sociological point of view: trust here represents a social relationship between two entities, usually two users of an online system.

In the following, we present in more details different examples of online systems and, for each of them, what are the entities of the system and which social and trust relationships they can express in the system. We also analyze how trust is used by the system for provid- ing a better experience to the user.

E-Marketplaces

E-marketplaces are Web sites in which users can buy and sell items. The more widely adopted models for arranging a deal are the fixed price (first in first out) and the auction. While the fixed price sell is a fairly straightforward model we are all acquainted with, auctions can take several forms and indulge in a few variants, depending on variables such as visibility of the offer, duration in time, stock availability, start bid, and so on. In an auction, buyers will compete, over the stated period, to put the best bid and win the deal. For the purposes of this chapter, we do not need to go any further in detailing the difference between the types of deals that can be conducted on an e-marketplace, but rather focus on the trust issues between the two roles that users play in this environment: the buyer and the seller. The main complication in conducting a deal in a virtual marketplace is that, in general, the buyer and seller do not know each other, and they only know the information that the Web site is showing about the other user. It is clear that there is a risk involved in a commercial transaction with a total stranger and, in fact, it is not common to give our money to a stranger in the street who promises to send us, days later, a certain product. Akerlof, Nobel Prize in Economy, formalized this idea in his "The market for lemons: Quality uncertainty and the market mechanism" (Akerlof, 1970). He analyzes markets with asymmetry of information, that is, markets in which the seller knows the real quality of the goods for sale but the buyer does not have this information. Using the example of the market of used cars, he argues that people buying used cars do not know whether they are "lemons" (bad cars) or "cherries" (good ones), so they will be willing to pay a price that lies in between the price for lemons and cherries, a willingness based on the probability that a given car is a lemon or a cherry. The seller has incentives to sell bad cars since he/she gets a good price for them, and not good cars since he/she gets a too low price for them. But soon the buyer realizes this situation and that the seller is actually selling only or mainly bad cars. So the price will lower and even less good cars and more bad ones will be put for sale. In the extreme, the sellers of good cars are driven out of the market and only lemons are sold. This effect is the opposite of what a free market should achieve and the only reason for this is asymmetry of information: the buyer has less information about the quality of the goods than the seller. Here, trust metrics (Golbeck et al., 2003; Levien, n.d.; Massa & Avesani, 2004; Ziegler & Lausen, 2004) and reputation systems (Resnick, Zeckhauser, Friedman, & Kuwabara, 2000) come to provide an escape to this vicious circle by the means of removing or at least reducing asymmetry of information. Giving users the chance to declare their degree of trust in other users makes it possible for future interactions to be influenced by past misbehaviors or good conduct. From this point of view, we can thus say that trust metrics and reputation systems promise to "unsqueeze the bitter lemon" (Resnick et al., 2000) and are a means to even the "risk of prior performance" (Jøsang, 2005).

The prototype of e-marketplace is eBay (http://www.ebay.com), at present the most known and successful example. Let us go through a typical use case of an e-marketplace. Alice found a user whose nickname is CoolJohn12 who accepts bids for his own used guitar. Let us suppose the bid price is fine with Alice. How can Alice be sure that, after she sends the money, CoolJohn12 is going to send her the guitar? How can Alice be sure that the picture on the site is really the picture of the guitar for sale and she is not going to receive another, possibly older, guitar? Unless she finds some evidence reassuring her about these questions, she is probably not going to take the risk and start the commercial exchange. This phenomenon reduces the quantity of commercial exchanges and hence the creation of prosperity (Fukuyama, 1995). But what if the e-marketplace Web site shows Alice that the guitar seller has already sold 187 guitars and banjos, and 100% of the buyers were satisfied by the received product? Or vice versa, what if the site tells Alice that many of the buyers were reporting that seller did not ship the guitar? A simple bit of information shown on the site can make the difference between "It is too risky to buy the guitar" and "I'm going to buy it." This is precisely what eBay does and this is the reason for its worldwide huge success.

On eBay, users are allowed to rate other users after every transaction (provide "feedback" in eBay jargon or express trust statements in our jargon). The feedback can be positive, neutral, or negative (1, 0, -1). The main reason for the great success of eBay is due precisely to the idea of assigning a reputation score to every user and showing it. This simple bit of information is shown on the profile page of every eBay user and it is a summary of the judgments of the users who had in past a commercial transaction with that user. It represents what the whole community thinks about the specific user and corresponds to the definition of "reputation" found in Oram (2001). Thanks to this information, everyone can quickly form an opinion about every other user and decide if the risk of conducting a commercial exchange with this user is acceptable. Precisely, on eBay, the reputation score is the sum of positive ratings minus negative ratings. Moreover, the eBay user profile page also shows the total number of positive, negative, and neutral ratings for different time windows: past month, past 6 months, and past 12 months. The purpose is to show the evolution in time of the user's behavior, especially the most recent one.

EBay's feedback ecology is a large and realistic example of a technology-mediated market. The advantage of this is that a large amount of data about users' interactions and behaviors can be recorded in a digital format and can be studied. In fact, there have been many studies on eBay and in particular on how the feedback system influences the market (see for example Resnick & Zeckhauser, 2002). A very interesting observation is related to the distribution of feedback values: "Of feedback provided by buyers, 0.6% of comments were negative, 0.3% were neutral, and 99.1% were positive" (Resnick & Zeckhauser, 2002). This disproportion of positive feedback suggests two considerations: the first is actually a challenge and consists of verifying if these opinions are to be considered realistic or distorted by the interaction with the media and the interface. We will discuss this point later in section "Open Challenges." The second is about possible weaknesses of the eBay model. The main weakness of this approach is that it considers the feedback of every user with the same weight, and this could be exploited by the malicious user. Since on eBay there are so few negative feedbacks, a user with just a few negative feedbacks is seen as highly suspicious, and it is very likely nobody will risk engaging in a commercial transaction with him/her. Moreover, having an established and reputable identity helps the business activity. A controlled experiment on eBay (Resnick, Zeckhauser, Swanson, & Lockwood, 2003) found that a high reputation identity is able to get a selling price 7.6% higher than a newcomer identity with little reputa-tion. For this reason, there are users who threaten to leave negative feedback, and therefore destroy the other user's reputation, unless they get a discount on their purchase. This activity is called "feedback extortion" on eBay's help pages (EBay help: Feedback extortion, n.d.) and in a November 2004 survey (Steiner, 2004), 38% of the total respondents stated that they had "received retaliatory feedback within the prior 6 months, had been victimized by feedback extortion, or both."

These users are "attacking" the system: as eBay's help page puts it "Feedback is the foun-dation of trust on eBay. Using eBay feedback to attempt to extort goods or services from another member undermines the integrity of the feedback system" (EBay help: Feedback extortion, n.d.). The system could defend itself by weighting, in different ways, the feedback of different users. For example, if Alice has been directly threatened by CoolJohn12 and thinks the feedback provided by him is not reliable, his feedback about other users should not be taken into account when computing the trust Alice could place in the other users. In fact, a possible way to overcome this problem is to use a local trust metric (Massa & Avesani,

2005; Ziegler & Lausen, 2004), which considers only, or mainly, trust statements given by users trusted by the active user and not all the trust statements with the same, undifferentiated weight. In this way, receiving negative feedback from CoolJohn12 does not influence reputations as seen by the active user if the active user does not trust explicitly CoolJohn12. We will discuss global and local trust metrics, in section "Open Challenges." However, eBay at the moment uses the global trust metric we described before, which is very simple. This simplicity is surely an advantage because it is easy for users to understand it, and the big success of eBay is also due to the fact users easily understand how the system works and hence trust it (note that the meaning of "to trust" here means "to consider reliable and predictable an artifact" and not, as elsewhere in this chapter, "to put some degree of trust in another user"). Nevertheless, in November 2004, a survey on eBay's feedback system (Steiner, 2004) found that only 3% of the respondents found it excellent, 19% felt the system was very good, 39% thought it was adequate, and 39% thought eBay's feedback system was fair or poor. These results are even more interesting when compared with numbers from a January 2003 identical survey. The portion of "excellent" went from 7% to 3%, the "very good" from 29% to 19%, the "adequate" from 35% to 39%, the "fair or poor" from 29% to 39%. Moreover, the portion of total respondents who stated that they had received retaliatory feedback within the prior 6 months passed from 27% of the 2003 survey to 38% of the 2004 survey. These shifts seem to suggest that the time might have come for more sophisticated (and, as a consequence, more complicated to understand) trust metrics. EBay is not the only example of e-marketplace. Following the success of eBay, many other online communities spawned their e-marketplaces, notable examples are Amazon Auctions and Yahoo! Auctions.

Opinions and Activity Sharing Sites

Opinions and activity sharing sites are Web sites where users can share with the other users their opinions on items and, in general, make their activities and preferences visible to and usable by the other users. The best example of an opinion site is Epinions (http://epinions. com). On it, users can write reviews about products (such as books, movies, electronic appliances, and restaurants) and assign them a numeric rating from 1 to 5. The idea behind opinions sites is that every user can check, on the site, what are the opinions of other users about a certain product. In this way, he/she can form an informed opinion about the product in order to decide about buying it or not. However, different reviews have different degrees of interest and reliability for the active user. Reviews are based on subjective tastes and hence, what is judged a good review by a user might be judged as unuseful by another user. So, one goal of Epinions is to differentiate the importance and weight assigned to every single review based on the active user currently served. Epinions reaches this objective by letting users express which other users they trust and which they do not. Epinions' FAQ (Epinions.com web of trust FAQ, n.d.) suggests to place in a user's web of trust "reviewers whose reviews and ratings that user has consistently found to be valuable" and in its block list "authors whose reviews they find consistently offensive, inaccurate, or in general not valuable." Inserting a user in the web of trust is equal to issuing a trust statement in him/her while inserting a user in the block list equals to issuing a distrust statement in him/her. Note that Epinions is one of the few systems that model distrust explicitly. Trust information entered by the users is used to give more visibility and weight to reviews written by trusted users. Reviewers are paid royalties based on how many times their reviews are read. This gives a strong incentive to game the system and this is a serious challenge for Epinions use of trust. Challenges will be analyzed in section "Open Challenges." Epinions' use of trust has been analyzed in Guha (2003). Far from being the only example, other sites implementing metaphors very similar to Epinions are Dooyoo.com and Ciao.com. Note that their business models, heavily based on reviews generated by users, can be threatened by a controversial patent recently acquired by Amazon (Kuchinskas, 2005).

We decided to also place in this category those Web sites where users do not explicitly provide reviews and opinions, but their activity is made visible to the other users who can then take advantage of it. In fact, the activity performed by a user on a system can be seen as an expression of the opinions of that user on what are the most interesting actions to perform on the system, according to his/her personal tastes. Examples of these sites are Del.icio.us (http://del.icio.us), in which users can bookmark URLs they consider interesting, and Last. fm (http://last.fm), in which users make visible which songs they listen to. Bookmarking a URL and listening to a song can be considered as positive opinions about the considered item. On Del.icio.us, the act of trusting another user takes the form of subscribing to the feed of the URLs bookmarked by that user. In this way, it is possible for the active user to follow in a timely manner which URLs the trusted user considers interesting. Flickr (http://flickr.com) is defined by its founders as being part of "massive sharing of what we used to think of as private data" (Koman, 2005). In this scenario, of course, trust is something that really matters. On Flickr, users can upload their photos and comment on those uploaded by other users. Flickr users can then declare their relationship with other users on a role-based taxonomy as friend, family, or contact. Eventually, they can choose to make some photos only visible to or commentable by users of one of these categories. Similarly, Flickr makes use of this information by letting you see the pictures uploaded by your friends in a timely manner. Similar patterns can be seen in the realm of events sharing as well: Web sites such as Upcoming (http://upcoming.org), Rsscalendar (http://rsscalendar.com), and Evdb (http://evdb.org) allow one to submit to the system events the user considers interesting. It is also possible to add other users as friends (i.e., trusted users) in order to see all the public events they have entered. Then, if a user adds another user as a friend, the second also sees the private events entered by the first. In the domain of music, we already mentioned Last.fm: here the users can declare their friendship to other users by means of a free text sentence connecting user A with B (for example, Alice "goes to concerts with" Bob). Friends are then available to the user who can peek at their recently played tracks, or send and receive recommendations. On the other hand, the tracks played by Last.fm users are recorded in their profiles along with "favorites" (track the users especially likes) and "bans" (tracks the users does not want to listen to anymore). These are used by the system to evaluate a user's musical tastes and to identify his/her "neighbors" (members with interests in similar groups or musical genres). Last.fm members can then exploit their neighborhood by eavesdropping on casual or specific neighbor playlists. Many of these sites, including Del.icio.us, Last.fm, and Flickr and Upcoming, expose very useful application programming interfaces (API) so that the precious data users entered into the system can be used by independent programs and systems (see section "Open Challenges" on problems related to walled gardens). Obviously, by combining two or more dimensions of activity of a specific user, it is possible to aggregate a profile spanning more than one facet about activities of one identity, as the Firefox extension IdentityBurro tries to do (Massa, 2005). The challenge of keeping a single identity under which all users' activities can be tied is briefly addressed in section "Open Challenges." Interestingly enough, Flickr, Del.icio.us, and Upcoming were recently bought by Yahoo!, whose interest into this so-called "social software" seems huge.

Business/Job Networking Sites

On business/job networking sites, users can register and post information about their job skills and ambitions so that other people can find them when they are looking for someone to hire for a specific job. Lately, many systems started to exploit the social (trust) networks between users: users can explicitly state their connections, that is, professionals they have already worked with and found reliable and trustworthy. Notable examples of these sites are LinkedIn (http://linkedin.com) and Ryze (http://ryze.com). On these sites, a user can discover new possible business partners or employees, for example, by entering in contact with the connections of his/her connections. These sites invite users to keep their connections list very realistic and to add as connections only people they really have worked with and deem reliable and recommendable. In order to achieve this purpose, business/job networking sites rely on the fact that user's connections are shown in the profile page and that other users will judge on the basis of the connections (Donath & Boyd, 2004). It is intuitive to say that a user will be better judged as IT consultant if reciprocated connections include Richard Stallman and Steve Jobs than if they contain many random users.

A similar but more playful site is Advogato (http://www.advogato.org). Advogato is a community site of free and open source software developers. The site was designed by Raph Levien, who planned to use it for studying and evaluating his trust metric (Levien, n.d.). On Advogato, users can keep their journal and indicate which free-software projects they are contributing to. A user can also express a judgment on every other user based on their hacking skills by certifying him/her on a three-level basis: Master, Journeyer, and Apprentice. The Advogato trust metric is used to assign to every user a trust level. The trust metric is run once for every level on a trust network consisting only of the certificates not less than that level. Thus, Journeyer certification is computed using Master and Journeyer trust statements (certificates). The computation of the trust metric is based on a network flow operation, also called trust propagation. The trust flow starts from a "seed" of users representing the founders of the site, who are considered reliable ex-ante, and flows across the network with a decay factor at every hop. The computed certification level of a user (i.e., trust score) is the highest level of certification for which there was a flow who reached him/her; for example, if a user was reached both when propagating trust at level Journeyer and Apprentice, the certification is Journeyer. The trust metric is claimed to be attack-resistant, that is, malicious nodes are not reached by trust propagation (the topic is discussed in section "Open Challenges"). Some other community sites use Advogato's code and hence show similar features. Something notable about Advogato is that it is one of the few sites that let users express a relationship with other users on a weighted base, in this case 3 levels. As a consequence, it is one of the few trust networks with weighted edges. From a research point of view, the availability of the trust network data (at http://www.advogato. org/person/graph.dot) is surely a relevant fact.

On a similar line, Affero (http://www.affero.org) is a peer-based reputation system, combined with a commerce system. It enables individuals to rate other individuals (i.e., express trust statements) and make payments on their behalf. Its goal is to exploit trust elicitation in order to democratically and distributedly decide which projects and foundations are more promising for the community and worth funding. Also, the system does not come bundled with any particular forum or community platform, so any independent community host can integrate the services and individuals can share reputation across various communities. One possible use case is the following: messages written by a user on an independent forum (or via e-mail) are signed with a message such as "Was I helpful? Rate me on Affero." Any individual reading the message and feeling he/she was helped can click on this Affero link and express gratitude by offering ratings, comments, and financial gifts to worthy causes chosen by the helping user on his/her behalf. Affero did not seem to have gotten momentum and is currently used by very few users.

Social/Entertainment Sites

Friendster (http://friendster.com) (Boyd, 2004), founded in 2002, was the first successful site to reach a critical mass of users among the social networking sites. On these sites, every user can create an online identity by filling out a profile form and uploading one or more pictures, and can then express a list of friends. The friends list, along with the user's picture and details, is shown on the user profile page. The idea is that other users can search through the friends lists of their friends and, in this way, discover and be introduced to new people that might be more interesting than a random stranger. We have already called this intuition "trust propagation." In December 2005, Friendster homepage claimed that there were more than 21 millions users using the system; however, this is not verifiable. A similar system was Club Nexus (Adamic, Buyukkoten, & Adar, 2003), an online community site introduced at Stanford University in the fall of 2001. Creators were able to use the system to study the real world community structure of the student body. They observed and measured social network phenomena such as the small world effect, clustering, and the strength of weak ties (Adamic et al., 2003). A very interesting and almost unique aspect of Club Nexus was the ability of users to rate other users (express trust statements) on a number of different axis: precisely, based on how "trusty," "nice," "cool," and "sexy" they find their connections (called buddies). Instead, current real online systems in general let users express just a single kind of trust statement and not many facets of it, and we believe this is a strong limitation.

Social sites (and also the previously analyzed business/job networking sites) usually enjoy a rapid growth of their user base due to the viral nature of the invitation process. We have seen that when users register, they can express their trust statements, that is, indicate other users they are connected to. If those users are not on the system they usually receive an e-mail from the system containing an invitation to join the network. This viral invitation strategy is able to rapidly bootstrap the user base. However, one risk is that the social network quickly becomes not representative of the real world because users tend to compete in the game of having more connections than others. Moreover, since everyone can create an identity, fake identities, sometimes called "fakester" (Boyd, 2004), start to emerge and lead the online system even further from a representation of real-world relationships. We will discuss this challenge in section "Open Challenges"; however, let us briefly note how the creator of Club Nexus, Orkut Buyukkokten, later created Orkut (http://www.orkut.com), the social network of Google, and took a different approach. In fact, on Orkut site, it is not possible to create an identity without receiving an invitation from a user who already has an identity in the system. In this way, Orkut staff were able to control Orkut social network's growth, to keep it closer to reality and, as a by-product, to create a desire for users to be inside the system. In fact, the number of social networking sites counts at least in the hundreds, and there are less and less incentives for users to join and reenter their information in YASN (Yet Another Social Network).

Trust statements can be used also for making secure an otherwise risky activity such as hosting unknown people in one's personal house. CouchSurfing (http://couchsurfing.com) and HospitalityClub (http://hospitalityclub.org) are two Web sites in which registered users offer hospitality in their houses to other users, for free, with the goal to make their trips more enjoyable. In order to reduce the risk of unpleasant experiences, there is a trust system in place by which users can express their level of trust in other users (notably, on CouchSurfing the scale is based on 10 different levels ranging from "Only met online and exchanged emails" to "I would trust this person with my life"). The functioning is very similar to the other sites: users can create their profiles, filling in personal details and uploading photos of them. The system shows in the user profile the activity history (who that user hosted, by whom he/she was hosted, how the experiences were in the words and trust statements of the other users) so that, when receiving a request for hospitality from a user, anyone can check his/her history and what other users think about him/her and decide about hosting or denying the request. Additional security mechanisms are possible as well: for example, on CouchSurfing, a user can ask to have his/her physical location address certified by the system by a simple exchange of standard mail with the administrators of the site, and it is also possible to ask administrators to verify personal identity via a small credit card payment. In December 2005, CouchSurfing declared to have almost 44,000 users and HospitalityClub almost 98,000 users.

News Sites

News sites are Web sites where users can write and submit stories and news they want to share with the community. Two notable examples of news sites are Slashdot (http://slashdot.org) and Kuro5hin (http://kuro5hin.org). The most important requirement for such systems is the ability to keep the signal-to-noise ratio high. Slashdot was created in 1997 as a "news for nerds" site. It was a sort of forum in which users could freely post stories and comment on those stories. With popularity and an increased number of users, spam and low-quality stories started to appear and destroy the value of Slashdot. The first countermeasure was to introduce moderation: members of the staff had to approve every single comment before it was displayed. However, the number of users kept increasing and this moderation strategy did not scale. The next phase was the introduction of mass moderation: everyone could act as moderator of other users' posted stories. But in this way there was less control over unfair moderators and hence, metamoderation was introduced.

In December 2005, moderation on Slashdot consists of two levels: M1, moderation, serves for moderating comments, and M2, metamoderation, serves for moderating M1 moderators. Note that moderation is used only for comments; in fact, it is the staff of Slashdot editors who decide which stories appear on the homepage. Then, once a story is visible, anyone can comment on it. Every comment has an integer comment score from -1 to +5, and Slashdot users can set a personal threshold where no comments with a lesser score are displayed. M1 moderators can increase or decrease the score of a comment depending on the fact they appreciate it or not. Periodically, the system chooses some users among longtime regular logged-in ones and gives them some moderation points. A moderation point can be spent (during the next 3 days) for increasing the score of a comment by 1 point, choosing from a list of positive adjectives (insightful, interesting, informative, funny, underrated), or for decreasing the score of 1 point the score of a comment, choosing from a list of negative adjectives (offtopic, flamebait, troll, redundant, overrated). Moderation points added or subtracted to a comment are also added or subtracted to the reputation of the user who submitted it. User reputation on Slashdot is called Karma and assumes one of the following values: Terrible, Bad, Neutral, Positive, Good, and Excellent. Karma is important on Slashdot since a comment initial score depends on the Karma of its creator. Slashdot editors can moderate comments with no limits at all in order to cope with attacks or malfunctions in a timely fashion. So at M1 level, users rate other users (i.e., express trust statements on them) by rating their comments based on the perceived and subjectively judged ability to provide useful and interesting comments (the trust context of Slashdot M1 level). In fact, the ratings received by a comment directly influence its creator Karma.

Level M2 (called metamoderation) has the purpose to moderate M1 moderators and to help contain abuses by malicious or unreliable moderators. At M2 level, the trust context is related to how good a job a moderator did in moderating a specific comment. Only users whose account is one of the oldest 92.5% of accounts on the system can metamoderate, so that it is ineffective to create a new account just in order to metamoderate and possibly attack the system. Users can volunteer to metamoderate several times per day. They are then taken to a page that shows 10 randomly selected comments on posts along with the rating previously assigned by the M1 moderator. The metamoderator's task is to decide if the moderator's rating was fair, unfair, or neither. M2 is used to remove bad moderators from the M1 eligibility pool and reward good moderators with more moderation points. On Slashdot, there is also the possibility of expressing an explicit trust statement by indicating another user as friend (positive trust statement) or foe (negative trust statement). For every user in the system, it is possible to see friends, and foes (users at distance 1 in the trust network), friends of friends, and foes of friends (distance 2). For every user in the system it is also possible to see which users consider that user a friend (they are called fans) or a foe (called freaks). Every user can specify a comment score for every one of these categories so that, for example, he/she can increase the comment score of friends and be able to place their comments over the threshold, notwithstanding the comment score they received because of moderation.

Kuro5hin is a very similar system, but in December 2005, had a smaller community. However on Kuro5hin, users can directly rate stories and not only comments like on Slashdot. In this way, they influence which stories appear on the homepage, while on Slashdot this is done by editors. Kuro5hin users have the following options for rating a submitted story: "Post it to the Front Page! (+1)," "Post it to the Section Page Only (+1)," "I Don't Care (0)," "Dump It! (-1)." User reputation on Kuro5hin is called Mojo.

The goal of these systems is to keep the signal-to-noise ratio very high, even in the presence of thousands of daily comments, and in order to achieve this they rely on all the users rating other users' contributions and hence, indirectly expressing trust statements on them. The code running Slashdot and Kuro5hin is available as free software (GPL license). We will discuss, in section "Open Challenges," how the fact everyone can analyze and study the code is a positive fact for the overall security of the system and for the ability of the system to evolve continuously and to adapt to new situations and challenges.

The Web, the Blogosphere, and the Semantic Web

Different from the previous examples, in the systems presented in this section, there is not one single central point where content is submitted and stored, but the content is published in a decentralized way; for example, it is stored on different Web servers. The challenge here is to design a system able to collect this vast amount of content, and algorithms able to quickly decide about its relative importance and value. This section is about how the concept of trust can be used and modeled in the Web, the Blogosphere, and the Semantic Web, in order to make them more useful, so that, for example, users can search them and be informed about the quality of the different published information. This might mean either exploiting existing information such as the link structure of the Web or proposing new ways to represent trust information, for example, on the Semantic Web.

The World Wide Web (WWW, or in short simply the Web) is the collection of all the Web pages (or Web resources). It is an artifact created in a decentralized way by millions of different people who decided to publish a Web page written in Hypertext Markup Language (HTML). Web pages are published on billions of different Web servers and are tied together into a giant network by HTML links. Hence, the Web is not controlled in a single point by anybody: the Web can be considered as a giant, decentralized online system. Search engines try to index all the information published on the Web and make it available for searching. Typically, search engines return a list of Web page references that match a user query containing one or more words. Early search engines were using information retrieval (Salton & McGill, 1986) techniques and were considering all the pages published on the Web as equally relevant and worth. However, since search engines are the most used way to locate a page, Webmasters wanted to have their pages on top of the list returned by a search engine for specific keywords. This gave the rise in the mid-1990s to a practice called Spamdexing: some Webmasters were inserting into their Web pages chosen keywords in small-point font face the same color as the page background so that they are invisible to humans but not to search engine Web crawlers. In this way, performances of early search engines quickly degraded to very low levels since the returned pages were no more the most relevant ones but just the better manipulated. Note that there is not a single entity with control over the content published on the Web and hence, it was not possible to block this behavior. In 1998, Sergey Brin and Larry Page, at that time students at Stanford University, introduced a new algorithm called PageRank (Brin & Page, 1998) that was very successful for combating spamdexing and producing better search results. They founded a new search engine company, Google (http://google.com), that, thanks to PageRank, was able to quickly become the most used search engine. The simple and genial intuition of PageRank is the following: not all the pages have the same level of authority, and their level of authority can be derived by analyzing the link structure. PageRank assumption is that a link from page A to page B is a "vote" of A on B and that authoritative pages either received many incoming links (votes) or even few incoming links but from authoritative pages. As an example, it seems reasonable to assume that a page that received no links is a nonauthoritative page. Based on an iterative algorithm, PageRank is able to assign to every page a score value that represents its predicted authority. This score value can be used by the search engine in order to give more prominence to more authoritative pages in the results list. PageRank is reported in this chapter because links are essentially what we call "trust statements," and PageRank is performing what we called "trust propagation" over the link network representing the Web. Instead of asking trust statements in order to form the network as the previously introduced online systems did, PageRank's great intuition was to exploit a great amount of information that was already present, the links between Web pages, in a new and effective way.

Other even more explicit trust statements already available on the Web are represented by so-called blogrolls. Web logs (often contracted in blogs) are a very interesting recent phenomenon of the Web. A blog is a sort of online diary, a frequently updated Web page arranged chronologically, that is very easy to create and maintain and does not require knowing HTML or programming. It provides a very low barrier entry for personal Web publishing and so many millions of people in the world maintain their own blog and post on it daily thoughts (Coates, 2003). They pose new challenges and new opportunities for search engines and aggregators due to their continuously changing nature. In general, blogs contain a blogroll: a list of the blogs the blogger usually reads. With the blogroll the blogger is stating: "I trust these other blogs, so, if you like what I write, you will like what they write." What is relevant is that today there are millions of daily updated blogs and that blogs represent, in some sense, a human being identity. So the network of blogrolls really represents an updated, evolving social network of human beings who express their trust relationships via their blogrolls. There is an attempt to add some semantics to blogrolls: XFN (XHTML Friends Network, n.d.) is a microformat that allows representation of human relationships using hyperlinks. XFN enables Web authors to indicate their relationships to the people in their blogrolls simply by adding a rel attribute to their <a> tags. For example, <a href="http://alice.example.org" rel="met friend"> means that the author of the Web page in which the link is contained has met the person "represented" by http://alice.example.org and considers her a friend. There are also some Semantic Web proposals for expressing, in a semantic format, social relationships. Friend-of-a-friend (FOAF) (Golbeck et al., 2003) is an RDF format that allows anyone to express social relationships and place this file on the Web. There is also a trust extension that allows enrichment of an FOAF file by expressing a trust statement in other people on a 10 level basis (Golbeck et al., 2003). While preliminary research in this field hints its usefulness, the adoption of these semantic formats is slow and not straightforward.

Peer-to-Peer (P2P) Networks

Peer-to-peer (P2P) is "a class of applications that takes advantage of resources (storage, CPU cycles, content, human presence) available at the edges of the Internet" (Shirky, 2000), and has been defined as a disruptive technology (Oram, 2001). Three primary classes of P2P applications have emerged: distributed computing, content sharing, and collaboration. P2P networks are based on decentralized architectures and are composed by a large number of autonomous peers (nobody has control over the overall network) that join and leave the network continuously. In this sense, their open, autonomous, and evolving nature pushes the challenges of the Web to new and harder levels. Just as with Web pages, the reliability of other peers is not uniform. For example, in content-sharing networks, there are peers who insert poisoned content, such as songs with annoying noise in the middle, or files not corresponding to the textual description. And there are peers who share copyrighted content violating the law of some countries. The human controlling the peer, based on his/her subjective judgments, might not want to download files from peers of one of the two categories, that is, she distrusts them. So one possibility is that peers are allowed to express trust statements in other peers in order to communicate their level of desire of interacting in future with those peers. By sharing these trust statements (expressing both trust for appreciated peers and distrust for disliked peers), it is possible to use a trust metric to predict a trust score in unknown peers, before starting to download content from them or upload it to them. Trust metrics can also be used for individuating a close community of friends and share private files just with them.

There are some attempts to build trust-aware systems on top of current P2P networks: on the eDonkey network, it is possible for every peer to mark other peers as friends who are given more priority in downloading files, and a protocol for sharing trust statements has been proposed for the Gnutella P2P network (Cornelli, Damiani, DeCapitani di Vimercati, Paraboschi, & Samarati, 2002). A trust model called Poblano (Chen & Yeager, 2001) was introduced in JXTA, a Java-based P2P framework, and mechanisms based on trust and reputation are present in Free Haven (Oram, 2001) and in BitTorrent (Cohen, 2003).

There is also evidence that P2P networks suffer free riding (Adar & Huberman, 2000), that is, some peers only download files without letting their files available for downloads and in this way they reduce the value of the entire network. The same trust-aware techniques can be used to share information about which peers allow or not to download files and give priority to nonfree riding peers.

Research on reputation and trust in P2P networks is an ongoing effort and many proposals have been made lately. However, due to the autonomous and inherently uncontrollable nature of P2P networks, most of the research papers present results validated with simulations (Kamvar, Schlosser, & Garcia-Molina, 2003; Lee, Sherwood, & Bhattacharjee, 2003), while it is difficult to evaluate the real impact of these strategies on real and running systems.

Open Challenges

In this section, we will introduce what are the most interesting challenges related to the use and modeling of trust in online systems. They are divided into three subsections analyzing respectively: (1) differences in how trust relationships are modeled in real and virtual worlds, (2) how trust can be exploited in online systems, and (3) identity, privacy, and attacks in online systems.

Differences in How Trust Relationships are Modeled in Real and Virtual Worlds

It should come as no surprise that social relationships (particularly trust relationships) are different in the "real" world and in the "virtual" world. However, this fact is particularly relevant if the online systems designers want the trust statements expressed in their environment to resemble the real ones. The differences are especially evident with respect to the following issues: how trust relationships can be represented, how they begin and develop over time, and how their representation is perceived by the humans involved. What follows is a list of the most relevant issues.

Explicitness and visibility of trust statements. In a virtual environment, for example, on a community Web site, often trust relationships are explicit. And they are often publicly visible. This means that a user is in general able to check if there is a relationship between two users and, in this case, to see it and refer to it (Donath & Boyd, 2004). This is of course very different from the real world in which almost always interpersonal relationships and their levels are implicit and not publicly stated.

Trust statements realism and social spam. There is also a risk of creating what has been named "social spam" (Shirky, 2004). This happens when a new user in a social network site is allowed to invite, by e-mail, a large number of people into the system, for example, by uploading his/her entire address book. This has happened with at least two social network sites, ZeroDegrees (http://zerodegrees.com) and Multiply (http://multiply.com), and has generated a large vent of protests (Shirky, 2004). New users used this feature and, with a single click, sent an invitation e-mail to all the e-mail addresses in their uploaded contact list, often without realizing this would have resulted in thousands of sent e-mails. Exploiting the viral nature of social networks can be used for passing from zero members to millions, but designers should ask themselves if it is worthwhile to annoy so many users in the hope of retaining a small portion of them, or if this feature is just creating annoying "social spam." Instead, since the beginning, Orkut tried to exploit the same viral nature of sending invitations into the system but in an opposite and more creative way: it was possible to register on the Web site only by being invited by someone already inside the system. By manipulating the number of invitations members could use to invite other people who were still outside the system, Orkut staff was able to create a lot of expectation and a lot of requests for joining the network. In this way, they were also able to control the growth of the network, in order to check if their servers and code were able to handle the load. And another good side effect of this was that, at least at the beginning, the social network was resembling real-world relationships, since every user had a limited number of invitations he/she could use and could not easily engage in the activity of adding as many friends as possible, even if they are not real-world friends. The optimal situation would be the one in which the user remains the owner of his/her social network and trust statements and can export them to every social site instead of having to re-express them every time. We will comment on interoperability at the end of this section.

Disproportion in positive trust. The explicitness and visibility of social relationships represents a huge challenge especially for e-marketplaces. Some reports (see for example Resnick & Zeckhauser, 2002) have found there is high correlation between buyer and seller ratings on eBay, meaning that there is a degree of reciprocation of positive ratings and retaliation of negative ratings. This fact is probably a by-product of the site design and does not closely represent real-world opinions. We have also already commented on how feedbacks on eBay are disproportionately and unrealistically positive (almost 98% of feedback is positive) (Resnick & Zeckhauser, 2002). One explanation of this fact is that, for fear of retaliation, negative feedback is simply not provided in case of a negative experience. Gross and Acquisti (2003) suggest that "no feedback is a proxy for bad feedback," and one solution the authors propose is that the seller gives feedback first and then the buyer is free to give the "real" feedback without fear of retaliation. Anyway, it is easy to argue how often online trust statements do not represent real-world relationships; for example, on many social sites there is a run to have as many friends as possible, and on many e-marketplaces there is an incentive for not providing negative ratings. Psychological and sociological considerations must be taken into account when making available a system that allows one to express relationships online.

Modeling negative trust. Modeling negative relationships (i.e., distrust) is another serious challenge. Few systems attempt to do it: eBay allows users to give negative feedback, but we have seen how this is problematic and seldom used; Epinions allows the active user to place another user in the block list in order to communicate to the system his/her reviews are considered unreliable and should be hidden and not considered. However, Epinions clearly states that "the distrust list is kept private and only you can see your block list. Unlike the web of trust, there is no way you can display your block list to others. This feature was designed to prevent hard feelings or retaliation when you add members to your block list" (Epinions.com web of trust FAQ, n.d.). In a similar way, while in the real world it can happen, for example, that someone expresses, in private, doubts about the skills of the boss, it is very unlikely that he/she will state a negative trust statement on the boss on a professional site, if this is publicly visible. So surely, the visibility of trust statements changes how users express them and this is something that must be taken into account when designing an online system that models trust. Moreover, on a social site (like Friendster), there are few reasons for entering a negative concept like distrust, since people engaging in a community of friends are there for sharing experiences with people they like and not to punish people they do not appreciate. On the other hand, on P2P systems, trust statements are used both in a positive way in order to keep track of peers whose shared content is reliable and appreciated, but also in a regulative way in order to keep track of peers whose shared content is considered inappropriate and undesirable (for example, depending on the subjective desires, it is poisoned or it is illegally shared). So, in those systems, explicit modeling of negative relationships is necessary since one of the goals is to spot out what are the peers the active peer considers malicious and to warn other peers about them. In short, modeling negative trust statements must be dealt with even more care than positive trust statements, because of the perception humans can have of it and for its great potential of destroying the feeling of community users often look for in online systems. How to exploit negative trust statements, in case they are modeled, will be analyzed in the next section.

Rigidity of language for expressing trust statements. We have also seen in the examples of the previous section that online relationships are represented in a rigid way. For example, it is common to represent friendship as a binary relationship between two users: either it is there or not. Even the richest representations are just a set of numeric values or of predetermined text labels. Anyway, they are rigid. For instance, the evolution in time of a relationship in real life follows a smooth growth or decay and it is often unconscious, or at least not continuously explicitly represented and polled. On the other hand, in virtual environments, the representation is always explicit, and it grows or decays in discrete steps: a possible event on an online community is, for example: "today, I downgrade my friendship to you from level 7 to level 6" and this discreteness hardly models any real-world relationship evolutions. This is surely a challenge for a system that wants to model real-world trust relationships in a reasonable, human-acceptable way. On the other hand, it is possible to keep relationships implicit: for example, the strength of a relationship can be derived on the fly from the number of messages two users have exchanged and hence, this value would closely model changes in the relationship patterns. While this option partially solves the aforementioned issue, in this way the system would become a black box for the user who is not in the condition to know what the system thinks is his/her relationship with the other users and possibly to change it.

Keywords for trust statements conveying undesired meanings. Keywords used in the graphical user interface (GUI) of the system are very important as well. If the system uses the term "friend" for defining a relationship on the system, where a friend is someone who provides timely links to interesting pages (e.g., Del.icio.us), that could be misleading, since the term "friend" in real life means something else. For example, a non-Web savvy but real friend could be unhappy with not seeing himself/herself on the friend list. A reasonable suggestion is to avoid the term "friend" in online systems unless the social relationship really represents friendship, and to use less emotional terms such as "connection" (as LinkedIn and Ryze do) or to use a unique, made-up word with no predefined meaning in the real world (Allen, 2004). We believe this is a key issue for the representativeness of issued trust statements, but we are not aware of research analyzing, with controlled experiments, the impact of different chosen terms in the trust elicitation patterns.

Single-trust context. Moreover, real-world relationships are not embeddable into a single-trust context. A user might appreciate another user for his/her discussions on computer-related topics, but less for his/her always being late or for his/her political ideas. At the moment, it seems very unlikely that an online system that asks users to state trust statements for more than one trust context will be successful; the previously described Club Nexus (Adamic et al., 2003) was an exception in this sense. Even in this case, it is not easy to find the "right" categories for defining a relationship and, as already stated, rigid predefined categories are surely not optimal for representing ongoing real-world situations.

Incentives mechanism for trust elicitation. Another challenge is to find the correct incentives for providing trust statements. The basic assumption of economy, rationality, would suggest that users have the incentive to free ride. In this context, free riding means not providing trust statements and just relying on the trust statements provided by the other users. However, contrary to the basic assumption of economy, many eBay users do provide feedback after a transaction: Resnick and Zeckhauser (2002) found that on average 60.7% of the buyers and 51.7% of the sellers on eBay provided feedback about each other. However, in general, incentives must be envisioned by online-systems designers. On eBay, providing (positive) feedback after a transaction might be seen as an exchange of courtesies (Resnick & Zeckhauser, 2002), or it might be that users perceive the global value of the feedback system and that in order to keep the community healthy, they think they should contribute to it when they can by providing feedback.

On social and activity sharing sites, expressing a trust statement provides a direct benefit to the user since he/she is then able to spend more time on content created by trusted users and less time on not interesting content. In fact, the system in general gives more visibility to trusted users and the content they created. For example, Flickr shows to logged-in users the pictures uploaded by their friends and contacts in a timely manner, and the same happens on Upcoming, which gives visibility to events entered by friends; on Last.fm for songs recently played by friends and on Del.icio.us for URLs recently bookmarked by subscribed users. In a similar way, the Epinions "web of trust" and "block list" give an immediate benefit to the user: when an offensive or unreliable review is found, the user can simply add the reviewer into his/her "block list," telling the system he/she does not want to see his/her reviews again. On the opposite side, users who create interesting, useful reviews can be placed in the "web of trust" so that their reviews are given more prominence. An alternative way for using trust statements would be to exploit already existing information instead of asking it directly of the user. This was the path Google's founders followed when they created PageRank (Brin & Page, 1998). Links between Web pages were already there and PageRank intuition was to consider a link from page A to page B as a vote of A on B, or as a trust statement in our jargon.

How to Exploit Trust in Online Systems

In the previous subsection, we discussed challenges in modeling trust in online systems. In this one we assume the trust relationships information is available and concentrate on ways of exploiting it. Based on the subjective trust statements provided by users, we can in fact aggregate the complete trust network (see Figure 1). Trust metrics (Golbeck et al., 2003; Levien, n.d.; Massa & Avesani, 2004; Ziegler & Lausen, 2004) and reputation systems (Resnick et al., 2000) can then be used in order to predict a trust value for every other user based on the opinions of all the users. An important classification of trust metrics (TM) is in local and global (Massa & Avesani, 2004; Ziegler & Lausen, 2004). Global TMs predict the same value of trustworthiness of A for every user. PageRank (Brin & Page, 1998) is a global trust metric: the PageRank of the Web page Microsoft.com is, for example, 9/10 for everyone, notwithstanding what the active user querying Google likes and dislikes. Sometimes this identical value for all the members of the community is called reputation: "reputation is what is generally said or believed about a person's or thing's character or standing" (Oxford Dictionary). On the other hand, local TMs are personalized: they predict the trustworthiness of other users from the point of view of every single different user. A personalized PageRank (Haveliwala, Kamvar, & Jeh, 2003) would predict different trust values for the Web page Microsoft.com for a user who appreciates (trusts) GNU/Linux and a user who appreciates Windows. In fact, a trust statement is personal and subjective: it is absolutely possible for user Bob to be trusted by user Alice and distrusted by Carol, as it is the case in the simple trust network depicted in Figure 1. Actually, it is normal to have, in a real community, controversial users: users trusted by many other users and distrusted by many other ones (Massa & Avesani, 2005). We have seen that reputation is a global, collective measure of trustworthiness (in the sense of reliability) based on trust statements from all the members of the community. Surely, in many situations, it is important to compute an average value. For example, different people can have different opinions on who is the best physicist of the year and nominate different ones. However, only one physicist can get the Nobel Prize and it should be the one that is more appreciated by the community as a whole. The same happens when someone might be elected president of a country: different people would have different preferences but they must be averaged using a global metric in order to identify just one person who will become president. Actually, most of the system we reviewed in section 1 uses a global metric: eBay, Slashdot (on which reputation is called Karma), Kuro5hin (on which it is called Mojo), PageRank, and many others. Reputation is a sort of status that gives additional powers and capabilities in the online system, and it can even be considered a sort of currency. In fact, Cory Doctorow, in his science-fiction novel *Down and Out in the Magic Kingdom* (Doctorow, 2003) already envisioned a postscarcity economy in which all the necessities of life are free for the taking, and what people compete for is whuffie, an ephemeral, reputation-based currency. A person's current whuffie is instantly viewable to anyone, as everybody has a brain-implant giving them an interface with the Net. The usual economic incentives have disappeared from the book's world. Whuffie has replaced money, providing a motivation for people to do useful and creative things. A person's whuffie is a general measurement of his or her overall reputation, and whuffie is lost and gained according to a person's favorable or unfavorable actions. Note that Doctorow also acknowledges that a personalized and subjective whuffie can be useful as well, weighting opinions of other people differently depending on one's subjective trust in them. Even if this does not refer to how trust is used and modeled by current online systems, it is an interesting speculation into one of the possible futures and the central role trust would play in it. Coming back to current online systems, Epinions provides personalized results and filtering and hence, exploits a local trust metric, even if precise details about how it is implemented and used are not public (Guha, 2003).

It is worthwhile noting that the largest portion of research papers studying reputation and trust often run simulations on synthesized data representing online systems, and often assume that there are "malicious" peers and "good" peers in the system, and that the goal of the system is just to allow good peers to spot out and isolate malicious peers. In this sense, they also often assume there are "correct" trust statements (a good peer must be trusted) and "wrong" or "unfair" trust statements (if a peer does not trust a good peer, he/she is providing a wrong rating). We would like to point out how these synthesized communities are unrealistic and how reality is more complicated than this; see, for example, a study on controversial users on Epinions (Massa & Avesani, 2005). Assuming that there are globally agreed good peers and that peers who think differently from the average are malicious encourages herd behavior and penalizes creative thinkers, black sheep, and original, unexpected opinions. This is in essence the "tyranny of the majority" risk, a term coined by Alexis de Tocqueville in his book, *Democracy in America* (1835) (de Tocqueville, 1840). The 19th century philosopher John Stuart Mill, in his philosophical book *On Liberty* (Mill, 1859), analyzes this concept with respect to social conformity. Tyranny of the majority refers to the fact that the opinions of the majority within society contributes to create all the rules valid in that society. On a specific topic, people will express themselves for or against it and the largest subset will overcome, but this does not mean that people in the other subset are wrong. So for one minority, which by definition has opinions that are different from the ones of the majority, there is no way to be protected "against the tyranny of the prevailing opinion and feeling" (Mill, 1859). However, we believe the minority's opinions should be seen as an opportunity and as a point of discussion and not as "wrong" or "unfair" ratings, as often they are modeled in research simulations. However, there is a risk on the opposite extreme as well and it is called "echo chamber" or "daily me" (Sunstein, 1999). Sunstein notes how "technology has greatly increased people's ability to filter what they want to read, see, and hear" (Sunstein, 1999). He warns how in this way, everyone has the ability to just listen and watch what he/she wants to hear and see, to encounter only opinions of like-minded people and never again be confronted with people with different ideas and opinions. In this way, there is a risk of segmentation of society into microgroups who tend to extremize their views, develop their own culture and language, and not be able to communicate with people outside their group anymore. He argues that "people should be exposed to materials that they would not have chosen in advance. Unplanned, unanticipated encounters are central to democracy itself ," and that "many or most citizens should have a range of common experiences. Without shared experiences, ... people may even find it hard to understand one another" (Sunstein, 1999). Finding the correct balance between these two extremes is surely not an easy task, but something that must be taken into account both for systems designers and researchers.

Creating scalable trust metrics. A challenge for local trust metrics is to be time efficient, that is, to predict trustworthiness of unknown peers in a short time. In fact, in general, local trust metrics must be run one time for every single user propagating trust from his/her point of view, while global ones are just run once for the entire community. In this sense, the load placed on a centralized system (for example, on Google) for predicting the trust scores for every user as seen by every other user seems to be too large to be handled. We believe a much more meaningful situation is the following: every single user predicts the trust scores he/she should place in other users from his/her personal point of view and on his/her behalf. In this way, every user is in charge of aggregating all the trust statements he/she deems relevant (and in this way, he/she can, for example, limit himself/herself to just fetch information expressed by friends of friends) and run the local trust metric on this data just for himself/herself on his/her local device, his/her server or, in the short future, his/her mobile.

Exploiting negative trust statements. We mentioned earlier the challenges in modeling negative trust statements and how few systems attempt to do it. For this reason, research about how to exploit distrust statements is really in its infancy. The lines of early inquiry at the moment are limited to the already cited studies on eBay's feedback system (Resnick & Zeckhauser, 2002), to propagation of distrust (Guha, Kumar, Raghavan, & Tomkins, 2004), and analysis on controversial users (Massa & Avesani, 2005).

Visualization of trust network for explanation. Another open challenge is related to visualization and explanation of how the system used trust information, especially if this affects the user experience. For example, it is important that the user is aware of the reason a certain review is shown, especially if the system's goal is to let to the user be able to master and guide the process and provide additional information. Visualizing the social network, for example showing to the user a picture similar to Figure 1, might be a powerful option to give awareness to the user of his/her position in the network, and to let him/her navigate it. Surely this kind of interface promises to be useful and enjoyable (see for example, a study on visualization of Friendster network in Heer & Boyd, 2005). However, we note that none of the online systems we introduced earlier use them: the reasons might be that these interfaces are not easily doable with standard HTML, but at the moment require the browser to use external plugins (for example, supporting Java applets, Flash, or SVG), and in this way they also break standard browsing metaphors and linking patterns. Moreover, creating a visualization tool easily understandable and usable is a very difficult task.

Public details of the used algorithms. Another challenge we think should be overcome is related to "security through obscurity" principle. Security through obscurity refers to a situation in which the internal functioning of an artifact is kept secret with the goal to ensure its security. However, if a system's security depends mainly on keeping an exploitable weakness hidden, then, when that weakness is discovered, the security of the system is compromised.

In some sense, the system is not secure; it is just temporarily not compromised. This flaw is well acknowledged in cryptography: Kerckoffs' law states that: "a cryptosystem should be secure even if everything about the system, except the key, is public knowledge." Most of the systems we reviewed adopt the security through obscurity principle in the sense that the precise details of how they exploit trust information are kept secret. For example, PageRank is left intentionally obscure. There are early reports about its functioning (Brin & Page, 1998), but Google does not disclose the used algorithm (probably different from the original one) and in particular the parameters used to fine-tune it. Epinions follows the same "security through obscurity" principle: "Income Share is determined by an objective formula that automatically distributes the bonuses. The exact details of the formula must remain vague, however, in order to limit gaming or other attempts to defraud the system" (Epinions.com earnings FAQ, n.d.). Interesting exceptions are Slashdot and Kuro5hin, whose code is free software released under the GNU General Public License and available respectively at SlashCode (http://slashcode.org) and Scoop (http://scoop.kuro5hin.org). In a similar way, Advogato trust metric is described in detail (Levien, n.d.), and the code is available on the Advogato Web site as well. Of course, one problem is related to the fact that commercial companies do not want to disclose their secret algorithms because this would allow any competing company to copy them. Luckily this is not a problem for noncommercial online systems and for systems that do not rely on a central server. However, we believe that a user should be able to know how recommendations are generated (for example, for checking if the system introduces undesired biases) and, in case she desires it, to use trust information as she prefers. We will touch this topic briefly in the following section on walled gardens.

Identities, Privacy, and Attacks

Identity, privacy, and attacks are huge topics by themselves and in this subsection, we are just going to scrape the surface and touch on challenges related to online systems that model and use trust. In general, on these systems, users act under pseudonyms (also called nicknames or usernames). Seldom, the real-world identity of the person using the online system is verified by the system because this would create a huge access barrier, cause great costs, and slow down the process of creating an identity, in a significant way. Unless there is a great need for the user to enter the system, this will drive him/her away and to the next easier-to-enter online system.

Pseudonymity. As long as a user has some way to decide if another user (as represented by their nickname) is trustworthy, this is often enough. A partial exception in this is represented by eBay. An eBay user can enter credit card details and in this way, eBay can tie the pseudonym with that credit card so that it can be possible to find the person in the real world in case this is needed for some reason, for example, an accusation of fraud or a law suit. Pseudonymity is of course a situation that marks a striking difference between online systems and real world. In real-world interactions, almost always the identity of the other person is known, while this is really the exception in online systems, where it is often possible to interact, communicate, and make business with other users who will never be met in person. In general, users can enter some details that describe themselves, and the system shows this information in their profile page. Note that users can lie in providing this information; for example, a survey found that 24% of interviewed teens that have used instant messaging services and e-mail or been to chat rooms have pretended to be a different person when they were communicating online (Lenhart, Rainie, & Lewis, 2001). The profile page of a user often shows a summary of recent activity in the system and social relationships with other users (Donath & Boyd, 2004), and usually this is the only information available and other users will form an opinion of that user based on this information. The effect of pseudonymity is well captured in the popular cartoon depicting two dogs in front of a computer with one dog saying to the other dog "On the Internet, nobody knows you're a dog." Of course, this situation works until there are no problems, but in case something goes wrong (accusation of fraud, molestation, or any accusation of illegal activity), it is required to identify the real-world identity, and this is not always easy. Moreover, different legal systems make it hard to have justice for crimes perpetuated in the virtual world.

Multiple identities. It is also common for a person to have more than one identity in an online system (Friedman & Resnick, 2001). A recent survey (Aschbacher, 2003) found that users of an informal science learning Web site have more than one identity (60% of girls vs. 41% of boys) on the site. Respondents gave various reasons for the multiple identities including sharing them with school friends, using them to earn more points on the site, and just trying out different identities from day to day. This behavior is quite common in social sites.

Fake identities and attacks. Moreover, sometimes humans create fake identities (also known as fakester) (Boyd, 2004) such as identities representing famous people. However, besides playful reasons, often these multiple identities in control of a single human being are used to game the system. This behavior is often called "pseudospoofing" (a term first coined by L. Detweiler on the Cypherpunks mailing list) or "sybil attack" (Douceur, 2002). Usually these fake identities are used in a concerted way and collaborate with each other in order to achieve a certain result on the system. For example, a person might use them to submit many positive ratings for a friend in order to boost his/her reputation (positive shilling), or negative ratings for the competition in order to nuke his/her reputation (negative shilling) (Oram, 2001).

These multiple identities can also be used, for example, by a book's author for writing many positive reviews of his/her own book. At least an occurrence of this behavior has been revealed publicly because of a computer "glitch" that occurred in February 2004 on the Canadian Amazon site. This mistake revealed for several days the real names of thousands of people who had posted customer reviews of books under pseudonyms (Amazon glitch out, 2004), and it was possible to note that many reviews made about a certain book were in reality created by the author of that book using many different pseudonyms. This possibility seriously mines at the basis the functioning of opinion-sharing sites. Another similar attack occurs on the Web: a link farm is a large group of Web pages that contain hyperlinks to one another or a specific other page. Link farms are normally created by programs, rather than by human beings, and are controlled by a single principal. The purpose of a link farm is to fool search engines into believing that the promoted page is hugely popular, and hence the goal is to maliciously increase its PageRank. A considerable amount of research is devoted to designing methods to spot out these attacks. For example, TrustRank (Gyongyi, Molina, & Pedersen, 2004) is a technique proposed by researchers from Stanford University and Yahoo! to semiautomatically separate reputable, good pages from spam.

Another possible way to deal with link farms is to enrich the language for expressing links, that is HTML (hypertext markup language). In fact, a common practice for increasing the score of a certain page is to use programs that automatically insert links to that page on blogs (in the form of comments) and wikis available on the Web. In order to counter this practice, in early 2005, Google proposed a new solution suggesting that blog and wiki engines should add to every link not directly created by the blog and wiki author a rel="nofollow" attribute. This attribute of the <a> HTML element is a explicit way to tell search engines that the corresponding link should not be considered as a "vote" for the linked page, or a trust statement in our jargon. A related initiative is VoteLinks Microformat (Technorati.com, n.d.), which enriches HTML by proposing a set of three new values for the rev attribute of the <a> HTML element. The values are vote-for, vote-abstain, and vote-against, and represent agreement, abstention or indifference, and disagreement respectively. In fact, as already noted, PageRank's assumption is that a link from page A to page B is a vote of A on B. However, this means that a link created with the purpose of critiquing the linked resource is increasing its PageRank score, and this might induce the author to not link to the criticized page. In short, attention is not necessarily appreciation (Massa & Hayes, 2005). With VoteLinks, it would be possible to tell search engines the reason behind a link so that they could create more useful services. Considering these proposals from a trust point of view, nofollow would express "this is not a trust statement, do not consider it" and VoteLinks would allow authors to express weighted trust statements in a linked page: vote-for is trust, vote-against is distrust, vote-abstain is similar to nofollow. It is interesting to note that Google's nofollow proposal was adopted by most search engines and blog and wiki programs in a few weeks, while VoteLinks proposal seems very little used. This has to do a lot with the authority of the proponent and a little with the proposal itself.

As we already said, local trust metrics can be effective in not letting untrusted nodes influence trust scores (Levien, n.d.; Massa & Avesani, 2004; Ziegler & Lausen, 2004) and in fact, there is research into personalizing PageRank (Haveliwala, Kamvar, & Jeh, 2003) as well. OutFoxed (James, 2005) is exploring ways for a user to use his/her network of trusted friends to determine what is good, bad, and dangerous on the Web. This is done by adding functionality to the Firefox Web browser who is able to predict the trust score of Web pages based on opinions of trusted friends.

Another possible attack is the following. A user could "play" the good behaviored role for a while with an identity and gain a good trust and reputation through a series of perfectly good deals, then try to complete a fraud and eventually drop the identity to start again with a new one. This has been reported at least once in a mid-2000 eBay fraud in which the user "turned evil and cashed out" (Wolverton, 2000). Friedman and Resnick (2001) analyze the phenomenon of multiple pseudonyms and conclude that, in systems in which new pseudonyms can be acquired for free, since new logins could be malicious users who just dropped an identity, the starting reputation of newcomers should be as low as possible. They prove that "there is no way to achieve substantially more cooperation in equilibrium than that achieved by distrusting all newcomers. Thus, the distrust of newcomers is an inherent social cost of easy identity changes."

Local trust metrics (Massa & Avesani, 2004'Ziegler & Lausen, 2004) can solve the problem introduced by multiple identities. Since with local trust metrics only trusted users (or users trusted by trusted users) are considered, the activity of fake identities not reached by the trust propagation does not influence the active user. In fact, attack resistance of trust metrics and reputation systems is a very important topic that is starting to receive great attention only recently, probably because of the complexity of the problem itself. Some trust metrics are claimed to be resistant to some attacks, for example Advogato (Levien, n.d.): "If a bunch of attackers were to create lots of accounts and mutually certify each other, only a very few would be accepted by the trust metric, assuming there were only a few certificates from legitimate members to the hackers." On the other hand, eBay metric (Resnick et al., 2003) is a very simple one, and we have seen that many attacks can be easily mounted against it. However, it seems to work well in practice, and surely one of the reasons is that, because of its simplicity, every user can understand how it works and get some confidence in the functioning of the system: more complicated metrics would be harder to understand and the user would probably lose confidence in the system altogether. In fact, Resnick and Zeckhauser (2002) consider two explanations related to the success of eBay's feedback system: (1) "The system may still work, even if it is unreliable or unsound, if its participants think it is working. (...) It is the perception of how the system operates, not the facts, that matters" and (2) "Even though the system may not work well in the statistical tabulation sense, it may function successfully if it swiftly turns against undesirable sellers (...), and if it imposes costs for a seller to get established." They also argue that: "on the other hand, making dissatisfaction more visible might destroy people's overall faith in eBay as a generally safe marketplace." This seems confirmed by a message posted on eBay by its founder in 1996: "Most people are honest. And they mean well. Some people go out of their way to make things right. I've heard great stories about the honesty of people here. But some people are dishonest: or deceptive. This is true here, in the newsgroups, in the classifieds, and right next door. It's a fact of life. But here, those people can't hide. We'll drive them away. Protect others from them. This grand hope depends on your active participation" (Omidyar, 1996). On eBay, whose goal, after all, is to allow a large number of commercial transactions to happen, it seems that positive feelings and perceptions can create a successful and active community more than a sound trust metric and reputation system. This means that the fact that a trust metric or reputation system is proved to be attack resistant does not have an immediate effect on how users perceive it and hence, on how this helps in keeping the community healthy and working.

Another problem with online identities is represented by "identity theft." This refers to the ability of someone to get in control of someone elses identity on an online system. We have seen already how a reputable identity on eBay is valuable by an average 7.6% increase of selling price (Resnick et al,, 2003), and this gives a reason for trying to get into control of them. This phenomenon is also called "account hijacking" and usually happens by phishing or by password guessing. Since online identities have an economic value, they are also sold for real money, often on e-marketplaces.

Privacy. Privacy is another huge issue for online systems, and here we are just going to discuss its main implications. Who can access information users express in an online system undoubtedly modifies which kind of information they will be willing to express and how they express it. As we have already seen, fear of retaliation for a negative trust statement has the consequence of very few negative ratings on eBay and, for this reason for example, Epinions distrust list (block list) is kept secret and not visible. Moreover, trust statements can also be used to model access permission to published information. For example, on Flickr it is possible to make some photo visible only to contacts, friends, or family members. The topic of privacy is very large and has huge psychological implications we cannot address here for reasons of space. Also note that private information a user expresses in an online system can be disclosed by error, as the previously cited example of Amazon Canada showed. The best possible situation for users would be to remain in total control and possession of their information (not only trust statements), and to upload it and show it to who the user wants, when he/she wants.

Portability and interoperability. And in fact, the next challenge we are going to comment about is related to portability of trust and reputation scores across walled gardens. Let us consider the following situation. A person utilizes eBay for some years, provides a lot of trust statements and, even more importantly from his/her point of view, receives a lot of trust statements: he/she built up a good reputation and is recognized by the community. If then, for some reason, he/she would like to change e-marketplaces (for example, eBay could close its operations or the user could prefer a new system that applies smaller fees), he/she has no choice but to start from scratch: there is no way he/she can migrate with his/her activity history (the information he/she entered in the system) and his/her reputation. This is because his/her information is not under his/her control, but under the control of the online system: he/she does not own the information. Clearly, the value of an online system is in the network of users that are using it, and companies prefer to not allow interoperability because competitors would use this information to bootstrap their networks. For example, eBay started a law suit against another e-marketplace who was copying the information about users and their feedback from the eBay Web site or that was, according to eBay, "engaging in the wholesale copying of our content and then using that content without our permission" (Sandoval & Wolverton, 1999). We believe that the content is the users' content and not eBay's content and in fact, users would have all the advantages letting different online systems compete to provide useful and cheap services with the information they expressed. We already discussed about semantic formats for letting users express, on their servers and under their control in a decentralized way, information (for example about the people they know using FOAF or XFN). These attempts have still to gain momentum, and it is surely easier to manage information about millions of users on a centralized server (as eBay, Epinions, Amazon, and almost all the systems we reviewed do at the moment) because there are no problems with formats, retrieval, and update. An attempt to achieve portability of trust and reputation across communities was Affero (see description in section "Categories of Online Systems in Which Trust is Modeled and Used"), but it seems it did not reach a critical mass and has very few users. However, we note how many of the online systems we reviewed in the previous section are starting to expose application programming interfaces (API) so that the precious data users entered into the system can be extracted by them for backups and for migration and, even more interestingly, can be used by independent programs and systems. Flickr, Del.icio.us, Upcoming, and many more systems have already done this or are in the process of doing it and this fact, instead of endangering their existence, has favored a plethora of independent services that are adding value to the original systems.

We believe users are starting to understand that the data they inserted into an online system really belong to them and not to the system, and they will be requiring more and more possibility of directly managing these data and getting them back. When all the systems will export this information, it will be possible to aggregate all the different domains in which a user is acting and get an overall perception of his/her activity in the online world, as the Firefox extension IdentityBurro tries to do (Massa, 2005).

Conclusion

In this chapter, we have presented a classification and prototypical examples of online systems that model and use trust information. We have also discussed what are the most important challenges for these systems and some possible solutions. This domain is very active and new initiatives, both commercial startups and research studies, are proposed continuously. New service metaphors and algorithms are invented daily, also based on feedback from users who are becoming more and more aware of their needs. It seems unreasonable to claim that a single approach might fit all the different scenarios we presented in this chapter, and the ones that will emerge in future. Instead, the designers of the online communities will have to continuously rethink basic mechanisms and readapt them to the different needs that emerge. Nevertheless, learning from past experiences, successes, and failures is an important activity, and this is what we tried to do with this chapter. Modeling and exploiting trust in online systems is and will remain an exciting, ongoing challenge.

Acknowledgments

We would like to thank Riccardo Cambiassi for helpful feedback on this chapter and discussions. We would like to thank Jennifer Golbeck for compiling and making public a list of trust-enabled platforms (Golbeck, 2005) that was a good starting point for this chapter. We would also like to thank the creators of the online systems and Web sites we reviewed and commented. Without them, this chapter would have not been, and the Web would have been a less interesting place.

References

Adamic, L. A., Buyukkokten, O., & Adar, E. (2003). A social network caught in the web. *First Monday, 8*(6). Retrieved December 28, 2005, from http://www.firstmonday. rog/issues/issues8_6/adamic/

Adar, E., & Huberman, B. (2000). *Free riding on Gnutella*. Technical report, Xerox PARC.

Akerlof, G. A. (1970). The market for lemons: Quality uncertainty and the market mechanism. *The Quarterly Journal of Economics, 84*(3), 488-500.

Allen, C. (2004). *My advice to social networking services*. Retrieved December 28, 2005, from http://www.lifewithalacrity.com/2004/02/my_advice_to_so.html

Amazon glitch outs authors reviewing own books. (2004). Retrieved December 28, 2005, from http://www.ctv.ca/servlet/ArticleNews/story/CTVNews/1076990577460_35

Aschbacher, P. R. (2003). Gender differences in the perception and use of an informal science learning Web site. *Journal of the Learning Sciences, 9*.

Boyd, D. (2004). Friendster and publicly articulated social networking. In *CHI '04: CHI '04 extended abstracts on human factors in computing systems* (pp. 1279-1282). New York: ACM Press.

Brin, S., & Page, L. (1998). The anatomy of a largescale hypertextual Web search engine. In *WWW7: Proceedings of the Seventh International Conference on World Wide Web 7*. Elsevier Science Publishers.

Chen, R., & Yeager, W. (2001). *Poblano: A distributed trust model for peer-to-peer networks*. Technical report, Sun Microsystems.

Coates, T. (2003). *(Weblogs and) the mass amateurisation of (nearly) everything*. Retrieved December 28, 2005, from http://www.plasticbag.org/archives/2003/09/weblogs_and_the_mass_amateurisation_of_nearly_everything.shtml

Cohen, B. (2003). Incentives build robustness in BitTorrent. In *Proceedings of the Workshop on Economics of Peer-to-Peer Systems*, Berkeley, CA.

Cornelli, F., Damiani, E., De Capitani di Vimercati S., Paraboschi, S., & Samarati, P. (2002). Implementing a reputation-aware Gnutella servent. In *Proceedings of the International Workshop on Peer-to-Peer Computing*, Berkeley, CA.

de Tocqueville, A. (1840). *Democracy in America*. (G. Lawrence, Trans.). New York: Doubleday.

Doctorow, C. (2003). *Down and out in the Magic Kingdom*. Tor Books.

Donath, J. & Boyd, D. (2004). Public displays of connection. *BT Technology Journal, 22*(4), 71-82.

Douceur, J. (2002). The Sybil attack. In *Proceedings of the 1st International Peer-To-Peer Systems Workshop (IPTPS)*.

eBay help: Feedback extortion. (n.d.). Retrieved December 28, 2005, from http://pages.ebay.co.uk/help/policies/feedback-extortion.html

Epinions.com earnings FAQ. (n.d.). Retrieved December 28, 2005, from http://www.epinions.com/help/faq/show_faq_earnings

Epinions.com web of trust FAQ. (n.d.). Retrieved December 28, 2005, from http://www.epinions.com/help/faq/?show=faq_wot

Friedman, E. J., & Resnick, P. (2001). The social cost of cheap pseudonyms. *Journal of Economics and Management Strategy, 10*(2), 173-199.

Fukuyama, F. (1995). *Trust: The social virtues and the creation of prosperity*. New York: Free Press Paperbacks.

Golbeck, J. (2005). *Web-based social network survey*. Retrieved December 28, 2005, from http://trust.mindswap.org/cgibin/relationshipTable.cgi

Golbeck, J., Hendler, J., & Parsia, B. (2003). Trust networks on the semantic Web. In *Proceedings of Cooperative Intelligent Agents*.

Gross, B., & Acquisti, A. (2003). *Balances of power on eBay: Peers or unequals? The Berkeley Workshop on Economics of Peer-to-Peer Systems*, Berkeley, CA.

Guha, R. (2003). *Open rating systems*. Technical report, Stanford University, CA.

Guha, R., Kumar, R., Raghavan, P., & Tomkins, A. (2004). Propagation of trust and distrust. In *WWW '04: Proceedings of the 13th International Conference on World Wide Web* (pp. 403-412). ACM Press.

Gyongyi, Z., Molina, H. G., & Pedersen, J. (2004). Combating Web spam with TrustRank. In *Proceedings of the Thirtieth International Conference on Very Large Data Bases (VLDB)* (pp. 576-587). Toronto, Canada: Morgan Kaufmann.

Haveliwala, T., Kamvar, S., & Jeh, G. (2003). An analytical comparison of approaches to personalizing PageRank. In *WWW '02: Proceedings of the 11th International Conference on World Wide Web*. ACM Press.

Heer, J., & Boyd, D. (2005). Vizster: Visualizing online social networks. In *IEEE Symposium on Information Visualization (InfoViz)*.

James, S. (2005). *Outfoxed: Trusted metadata distribution using social networks*. Retrieved December 28, 2005, from http://getoutfoxed.com/about

Jøsang, A., Ismail, R., & Boyd, C. (2005). A survey of trust and reputation systems for online service provision. In *Decision support systems*.

Kamvar, S. D., Schlosser, M. T., & Garcia-Molina, H. (2003). The Eigentrust algorithm for reputation management in P2P Networks. In *WWW '03 Conference*.

Koman, R. (2005). *Stewart Butterfield on Flickr*. Retrieved December 28, 2005, from www.oreillynet.com/pub/a/network/2005/02/04/sb_flckr.html

Kuchinskas, S. (2005). *Amazon gets patents on consumer reviews*. Retrieved December 28, 2005, from http://www.internetnews.com/bus-news/article.php/3563396

Lee, S., Sherwood, R., & Bhattacharjee, B. (2003). Cooperative peer groups in NICE. In *IEEE Infocom*.

Lenhart, A., Rainie, L., & Lewis, O. (2001). *Teenage life online: The rise of the instant-message generation and the Internet's impact on friendships and family relationships*. Retrieved December 28, 2005, from http://www.pewinternet.org/report_display.asp?r=36

Levien R. (n.d.). *Attack resistant trust metrics*. Retrieved December 28, 2005, from http://www.advogato.org/trust-metric.html

Massa, P. (2005). *Identity burro: Making social sites more social*. Retrieved December 28, 2005, from http://moloko.itc.it/paoloblog/archives/2005/07/17/identity_burro_grease-monkey_extension_for_social_sites.html

Massa, P., & Avesani, P. (2004). Trust-aware collaborative filtering for recommender systems. In *Proceedings of Federated International Conference on the Move to Meaningful Internet: CoopIS, DOA, ODBASE*.

Massa, P., & Avesani, P. (2005). Controversial users demand local trust metrics: An experimental study on Epinions.com community. In *Proceedings of 25th AAAI Conference*.

Massa, P., & Hayes, C. (2005). Page-rerank: Using trusted links to re-rank authority. In *Proceedings of Web Intelligence Conference*.

Mill, J. S. (1859). *On liberty. History of economic thought books*. McMaster University Archive for the History of Economic Thought.

Mui, L. (2002). *Computational models of trust and reputation: Agents, evolutionary games, and social networks.* PhD thesis, Massachusetts Institute of Technology.

Omidyar, P. (1996). *eBay founders letter to eBay community.* Retrieved December 28, 2005, from http://pages.ebay.com/services/forum/feedback-foundersnote.html

Oram, A., editor (2001). *Peer-to-peer: Harnessing the power of disruptive technologies.* O'Reilly and Associates.

Resnick, P., & Zeckhauser, R. (2002). Trust among strangers in Internet transactions: Empirical analysis of eBay's reputation system. *The Economics of the Internet and eCommerce. Advances in Applied Microeconomics, 11* (pp. 127-157).

Resnick, P., Zeckhauser, R., Friedman, E., & Kuwabara, K. (2000). Reputation systems. *Communication of the ACM, 43*(12), 45-48.

Resnick, P., Zeckhauser, R., Swanson, J., & Lockwood, K. (2003). *The value of reputation on eBay: A controlled experiment.*

Salton, G., & McGill, M. J. (1986). *Introduction to modern information retrieval.* New York: McGraw-Hill, Inc.

Sandoval, G. & Wolverton, T. (1999). *eBay files suit against auction site bidder's edge.* Retrieved December 28, 2005, from http://news.com.com/2100-1017-234462.html

Shirky, C. (2000). *What is P2P ... and what isn't?* Retrieved December 28, 2005 from http://www.openp2p.com/pub/a/p2p/2000/11/24/shirky1-whatisp2p.html

Shirky, C. (2004). *Multiply and social spam: Time for a boycott.* Retrieved December 28, 2005, from http://many.corante.com/archives/2004/08/20/multiply_and_social_spam_time_for_a_boycott.php

Steiner, D. (2004). *Auctionbytes survey results: Your feedback on eBay's feedback system.* Retrieved December 28, 2005, from http://www.auctionbytes.com/cab/abu/y204/m11/abu0131/s02

Sunstein, C. (1999). *Republic.com.* Princeton, NJ: Princeton University Press.

Technorati.com. (n.d.). *VoteLinks.* Retrieved December 28, 2005, from http://microformats.org/wiki/votelinks

XHTML Friends Network. (n.d.). Retrieved December 28, 2005, from http://gmpg.org/xfn/

Wolverton, T. (2000). *EBay, authorities probe fraud allegations.* Retrieved December 28, 2005, from http://news.com.com/2100-1017_3-238489.html

Ziegler, C., & Lausen, G. (2004). Spreading activation models for trust propagation. In *Proceedings of the IEEE International Conference on E-Technology, E-Commerce, and E-Service (EEE'04).*

Chapter IV

Legal Challenges of Online Reputation Systems

Jennifer Chandler, University of Ottawa, Canada

Khalil el-Khatib, University of Ontario, Institute of Technology, Canada

Morad Benyoucef, University of Ottawa, Canada

Gregor von Bochmann, University of Ottawa, Canada

Carlisle Adams, University of Ottawa, Canada

Abstract

Online reputation systems have become important tools for supporting commercial as well as noncommercial online interactions. But as online users become more and more reliant on these systems, the question of whether the operators of online reputation systems may be legally liable for problems with these systems becomes both interesting and important. Indeed, lawsuits against the operators of online reputation systems have already emerged in the United States regarding errors in the information provided by such systems. In this chapter, we will take the example of eBay's Feedback Forum to review the potential legal liabilities facing the operators of online reputation systems. In particular, the applicability of the Canadian law of negligent misrepresentation and of defamation will be covered. Similar issues may be expected to arise in the other common law jurisdictions.

Introduction

Online reputation systems have become a significant feature of online behaviour in commercial as well as noncommercial contexts. These systems, also known as online rating systems, are "large-scale online word-of-mouth communities in which individuals share experiences on a wide range of topics, including companies, products, and services" (Dellarocas & Resnick, 2003). Recent evidence, based on a survey conducted in May and June of 2004, suggests that they are widely used.

The Pew Internet & American Life Project has found that 26% of adult internet users in the U.S., more than 33 million people, have rated a product, service, or person using an online rating system. (Hitlin & Rainie, 2004)

These systems, which enable the collective formation of reputation, represent a traditional social institution in a highly distributed electronic form. Given that other trust-building mechanisms, such as the law or established brands, are weakened or uncertain online, online reputation systems are a promising means of supporting online interactions. Indeed, they seem admirably suited to the formation of reputation because of the efficiency with which multiple far-flung experiences can be aggregated and distributed. On the other hand, although online reputation systems may be able to gather more information, the quality of this information is perhaps more questionable.

Online reputation systems are attracting increasing interest among researchers as well (Thompson, 2003, p. 4). An interdisciplinary symposium on online reputation systems in 2003 brought together specialists in economics, computer science, artificial intelligence, sociology, and psychology (Dellarocas & Resnick, 2003). So far a focus on the legal aspects of online reputation systems has been less developed, although several articles focusing on legal and regulatory issues in the American context have been published (Block-Lieb, 2002; Calkins, 2001; Gillette, 2002).

Lawyers can be expected to pay increasing attention to online reputation systems as the use of such systems increases. The formation and dissemination of information about reputation is surrounded by law and regulation in the off-line world, and the same difficulties that inspired the development of legal doctrine off-line have already emerged in the context of online reputation systems. The possibility of liability for an online reputation system that generates false or misleading results was raised in *Gentry v. eBay, Inc.* 99 Cal. App. 4th 816 (Cal. Ct. App. 2002).

Liability for the publication of defamatory comments within an online reputation system has also been raised: *Grace v. eBay* 120 Cal. App. 4th 984 (Cal. Ct. App. 2004), *Schneider v. Amazon.com, Inc.* 108 Wn. App. 454 (Wash. Ct. App. 2001). Defamation law imposes liability not just on the primary speaker of a defamatory comment, but also on subsequent publishers in certain circumstances.

Search engines are not recognized as a typical form of online reputation system, but those (such as Google) that rank Web sites in part according to the number of inbound links they attract make use of a type of distributed reputation formation. An inbound link may be interpreted in this case as a vote of approbation for a given Web site. It is accordingly instructive to note that several search engines were accused of misleading users contrary to the misleading advertising regulations when they failed to disclose clearly that a Web site's position within search results was purchased (Federal Trade Commission, 2002). It is possible that an online reputation system may fall afoul of regulations governing misleading advertising or other deceptive marketing practices where the system produces biased information.

This chapter takes the perspective that online reputation systems are a promising technology with wide potential applications of economic and political importance (Dellarocas & Resnick, 2003). The objective is to describe the most interesting potential legal pitfalls in order that they may be considered and avoided. As there are many different types of online reputation systems and a wide array of possible legal issues, it will be impossible to offer a comprehensive review. In addition, the law is unfortunately quite variable by jurisdiction, and readers should be aware that this chapter will address a selection of issues in the context of the Canadian common law jurisdictions only. The rules applicable in other jurisdictions may vary, although the issues identified will be shared.

Part I of this chapter will offer background on online reputation systems generally. Part II will discuss the effectiveness of online reputation systems, with a focus on eBay's Feedback Forum. This part will discuss the criticisms raised against the Feedback Forum as well as the results of empirical studies of whether the Feedback Forum appears to influence transaction behaviour. Part III will consider the law relating to misrepresentation and defamation as it might apply to online reputation systems.

Part I: Online Reputation Systems

The Role of Reputation in Building Trust

Trust is clearly an important objective in order to achieve the remarkable potential benefits of the Internet.

Trust is a key to the promise the online world holds for great and diverse benefits to humanity—its potential to enhance community, enliven politics, hasten scientific discovery, energize commerce, and more. Trust in the layered infrastructures of hardware, software, commercial and institutional presences, and its people is a necessary condition for benefits to be realized. People shy away from territories they distrust; even when they are prepared to engage voluntarily, they stay only as briefly as possible. Without people, without participants, many of the visions will be both literally and figuratively empty. (Nissenbaum, 2001)

Online commerce is risky for various reasons such as the inability to examine the items being sold and the nonsimultaneous nature of the transaction (which exposes the first mover to the risk that the other will not complete the transaction). In the context of online auctions between small players, other indicia of trustworthiness such as evidence of investment in an established brand are not available. The institution of contract law provides little comfort because litigation is unreasonably expensive for small value transactions and the other party may be located in a foreign jurisdiction (Gillette, 2002, p. 1166).

Reputation, or the ascription of characteristics to a person based on observations of the person's prior behaviour (Kollock, 1999), is one of the social mechanisms used to produce trust. This information may arise through an individual's own direct experience, or through reports from third parties (Bailey, Gurak, & Konstan, 2003).

The approach of judging reputation based solely on one's own direct experience is unsatisfactory. One can gather useful experience from a single interaction with another party, as a person who behaves honestly once is likely to do so again. Greater assurance about another party may emerge through repeated interactions, where expectations of reciprocity and retaliation may emerge to deter bad behaviour (Resnick, Zeckhauser, Friedman, & Kuwabara, 2000, p. 46). However, an individual takes risks in transacting with a new partner. An individual would prefer to discover untrustworthy people not by becoming their victim, but by learning from the experiences of others (Kollock, 1999). An individual is also limited in the number of different people he or she can observe. In addition, an individual does not always engage in repeated transactions, and cannot rely on the disciplinary effect of potential retaliation (Resnick et al., 2000).

As a result, social mechanisms for sharing information about potential transaction partners offer great benefits. These mechanisms can take many forms, including informal gossip networks, institutionalized review systems, and specialists whose role is to consume and evaluate goods or services (Kellock, 1999). Electronic reputation systems offer modern versions of these social mechanisms. Different types of electronic reputation systems have recently been proposed to control access to system resources (Blaze, Feigenbaum, Ioannidis, & Keromytis, 1999; Kagal, Finin, & Joshi, 2001), to secure peer-to-peer file-sharing (Tran, Hitchens, Varadharagan, & Watters, 2005; Wang & Vassileva, 2004;), to make optimal choices in differentiating between multiple services (Shi, von Bochmann, & Adams, 2004; Shi, von Bochmann, & Adams, 2005), and to build trust in electronic marketplaces (e.g., eBay, Yahoo Auction, Amazon).

In assessing the utility of reputation systems (including online reputation systems), it is necessary to recall that the link between reputation and trust depends on the assumption that past conduct is a reliable predictor of future conduct (Kollock, 1999). If it is not, a good reputation (which is based on past conduct) is not useful for making a decision on whether to trust in the present or future. A reputation for honesty may have predictive value in itself as an honest person may be expected to behave honestly in the future. Apart from this conclusion about the moral nature of the person in question, one can also imagine that a person will protect his or her reputation where it is valuable. In other words, reputation may provide a reliable predictor of behaviour where (1) reputation is valuable to the subject (e.g., because others are more willing to transact or offer good prices) and (2) bad behaviour is punished through damage to reputation. In these cases, one may presume that a person is likely to protect his good and valuable reputation by acting in a manner consistent with that reputation. Accordingly, where an online reputation system does not provide to the subject of the reputation something of value that is plausibly threatened by bad behaviour, it is unlikely to have much utility.

A serious constraint on reputation systems in the physical world has to do with the relative difficulty and expense of gathering and disseminating the reputation information. For example, it is costly to find and speak with all purchasers of product "X." However, if we were to do so, we could use our normal social and cognitive processes to assess the trustworthiness of each purchaser's review of product "X." In the online context, the costs of finding and speaking with the purchasers is potentially greatly reduced (Resnick, Zeckhauser, Swanson, & Lockwood, 2004), but we are less able to judge the quality and disinterestedness of the reviews (Calkins, 2001; Gillette, 2002). Some systems have attempted to address this problem by having a secondary trust mechanism in which users of a particular review will assess the accuracy of individual reviews or reviewers (see, for example, the Web of Trust system used by Epinions.com). In addition to the problem of understanding the quality of individual reviews, online reputation systems introduce another concern from the possibility that the system itself is inherently biased. For example, those purchasers who had positive (or negative) interactions may be disproportionately more likely to volunteer their reviews. These problems will be discussed at some length in the context of the eBay Feedback Forum in Part II of this chapter.

Types of Online Reputation Systems

There are many types of online reputation systems. They vary according to three main characteristics: (1) the subject of the ratings (individuals, products or services), (2) the providers of the ratings (open to the public or restricted) and (3) the business model (revenue derived from an associated online auction, retail channel, advertising, or a public service).

One might possibly add a fourth variation, namely, whether the review being provided relates to attributes about which there is legitimate variation because individual tastes vary (e.g., this book is too long, this retailer doesn't offer enough product choice), or attributes that are generally treated as objective facts (e.g., this book is 400 pages long rather than the 500 claimed, this retailer claims to offer more choice than it really does offer because it is always out of stock). Jøsang et al. would exclude systems that offer subjective reviews from the definition of a reputation system, instead calling systems consisting of subjective reviews "collaborative filtering" systems (Jøsang, Ismail, & Boyd, 2005). Whether or not the term "reputation system" should be limited in this way, it is useful from a legal perspective to note the distinction between expressions of fact and opinion as the two often fare differently at law. As a result, online reputation systems that contain reviews of the "opinion" variety may be treated differently by the law than those that purport to make more factual assertions.

The subject of the ratings might be an individual (e.g., eBay or Amazon's feedback systems, Ratemyprofessors.com, Allexperts.com), a business (e.g., BizRate.com), products and services (e.g., Epinions.com), or articles or postings (e.g., Kuro5hin.org, Slashdot.com).

The submission of ratings may be open to anyone who registers for a free account (e.g., epinions.com, kuro5hin.org, Amazon.com book reviews), open to those who complete a transaction (e.g., eBay.com), or restricted to a selected group of reviewers (e.g., Slashdot.com).

The reputation forum itself may serve various business models. First, in the case of market makers such as electronic auctions, the reputation system is used to encourage the trust necessary for transactions to take place (and transaction fees to be paid). Second, a retail site may offer product reviews to support sales (e.g., Amazon.com). Third, various sites provide reputation systems and derive their revenue from selling advertising. A Web site may adopt several of these strategies, for example, by selling products as well as advertising.

If one broadens the definition of a "reputation system," it is possible to identify other types. For example, certain systems deduce reputation indirectly from behaviour rather than directly from users' statements about their experiences. One might view the behaviour of creating a hyperlink to a Web page as evidence of the quality, reliability, and so forth, of that Web page. As a result, search engines, such as Google, that rank a Web page within search results in part according to the number and quality of inbound links to the Web page may be viewed as a form of reputation system that relies on the behaviour of Web page owners.

One may also broaden the definition of a "reputation system" to include a greater degree of automation than is typically understood by a collection of user-submitted reviews that are open to review by other users. For example, reputation software, also known as business intelligence software, is used to mine the Web or databases for useful data in the business-to-business commercial context (see, for example, Biz360.com).

The potential legal questions will necessarily vary according to the particular model being considered. This paper will consider the online reputation system model offered by eBay's Feedback Forum, addressing some of the legal issues raised by a reputation system designed to encourage online auction transactions.

Part II: Effectiveness of eBay's Online Reputation System

Introduction

Online auction transactions ought to be viewed as highly risky propositions for multiple reasons. Most transactions take place between strangers who are unlikely to deal with one another again (Resnick & Zeckhauser, 2001, p. 9). The strangers are relatively anonymous. The buyer does not have the opportunity to examine the product before purchasing. The transactions are nonsimultaneous, with the buyer running the risk that the seller will not complete the transaction. Finally, the reassurance offered by judicial enforcement of contracts is weakened by the high costs of litigation and enforcement against the other party (who may be in another jurisdiction).

Despite this, online auctions such as eBay have demonstrated remarkable success, with millions of users and billions of dollars worth of transactions (eBay, 2005a). Numerous observers have marvelled at the relatively small number of transactions that do go bad given the inherent risks in online trades (e.g., Kollock, 1999; Resnick & Zeckhauser, 2001). Nevertheless, online auction fraud is clearly a considerable problem (Gilbert, 2003; National White Collar Crime Center, 2004), although eBay has maintained that confirmed cases of fraud amount to 0.01% to 0.1% of auctions (Wolverton, 2002b).

Sellers in online auctions run some risks, including the most common risk that the winning bidder will refuse to complete the transaction (Resnick & Zeckhauser, 2001, p. 11). However, the focus of this chapter will be on the risks facing buyers. Buyers face greater risks because payment precedes delivery of the product. The buyer faces several key risks: (1) the seller may fail to send the product, (2) the product received may not be as described, (3) the seller may fail to deliver the product in a timely manner, and (4) the seller may fail to disclose all relevant information about a product or the terms of sale (Resnick & Zeckhauser, 2001, p. 12; U.S. Federal Trade Commission, 2005).

In order to address some of these risks, eBay has created its Feedback Forum. In the current version, the parties to a completed transaction have a window of time within which to provide feedback about the other party. Each party may leave a positive (+1), negative (-1) or neutral (0) rating, along with a short text comment.

When deciding on whether to bid on an item, a potential buyer may view the Feedback Score (the number of unique parties leaving a positive rating minus the number of unique parties leaving a negative rating), the percentage positive feedback, the number of unique members leaving positives and negatives, and certain other information. A breakdown of positive, neutral, and negative feedback over time is also provided. A buyer can also review the comments left about the seller, as well as comments left by the seller about others. eBay encourages users to use the feedback in making decisions about transactions, suggesting, for example, that "[b]efore you bid or buy on eBay, it's important to know your seller. Always look at your seller's feedback ratings, score and comments first to get an idea of their reputation within the eBay marketplace" (eBay, 2005f).

eBay has instituted limited insurance coverage to further reassure buyers. Eligibility for this coverage is usually dependent on a good feedback reputation. eBay offers a "Standard Purchase Protection Program" designed to reimburse buyers for transactions where an item is not received or is received but does not satisfy the requirements of the transaction (eBay, 2006a). To qualify for this protection, both parties to the transaction must have, among several other conditions, a feedback rating of zero or above at the time of the transaction.

Another protection program is offered by PayPal (http://www.paypal.com/) to eBay users. It is called "PayPal Buyer Protection" and is designed to protect those who use the PayPal services to pay for items purchased on the eBay marketplace. The program aims to reward those sellers who have accumulated a strong reputation by providing buyers another reason to purchase from them. The protection provides up to 1,250 CAD of coverage for the buyer at no additional charge for nondelivery of items and for items that are received significantly not as described (eBay, 2006b). Again, to qualify for this protection, both parties must satisfy several requirements, one of which states that the seller must have a 98% positive feedback and a feedback score of 50 or more on eBay.

Problems with Online Reputation Systems Such as eBay's Feedback Forum

Online reputation systems face some design challenges. First, users may not have sufficient incentives to provide any feedback. Second, the incentives that do exist may not be such as would lead individuals to provide useful and unbiased feedback. Third, the online reputation system may suffer from systematic faults that lead to the over- or underrepresentation of certain types of feedback. For example, the system may systematically discourage negative feedback, although the positive feedback may be accurate. These possibilities will be addressed in the context of eBay's Feedback Forum.

Users may not have sufficient incentives to take the time to prepare a review. Accurate and reliable reputation information is a public good and is thus prone to being underproduced (Gillette, 2002, p. 1182). Despite the intuition that most users would not spend their own time producing reviews to benefit the public, users of eBay rate each other surprisingly frequently. Buyers rate sellers 51.7% of the time, and sellers rate buyers 60.6% of the time (Resnick & Zeckhauser, 2001, p. 11). One explanation for this is that eBay users recognize a "quasi-civic duty" to provide comments (Resnick & Zeckhauser, 2001, p. 5), although this has been questioned given the rote and uninformative nature of the comments usually provided (Gillette, 2002, p. 1185). Another possibility is that users feel that it is courteous and fair to provide a small positive comment where a means to do so is provided through a feedback forum (Gillette, 2002 p. 1185; Resnick & Zeckhauser, 2002, p. 18).

However, the incentives that do exist may not be such as would lead users to provide useful and accurate reputation information. Instead, they have incentives to provide false information. There is reason to question the accuracy of reviews on eBay, where about 99% of ratings are positive (Resnick & Zeckhauser, 2001, p. 11). Users may be providing positive reviews hoping to elicit reciprocal positive reviews from their transaction partners, thereby building their own good reputations (Gillette, 2002, p. 1185; Jøsang et al., 2005). Cameron and Galloway (2005) report the practice of "feedback auctions" in which parties agree to exchange good feedback rather than goods and money.

A reputation system may also systematically suppress negative ratings, either in a good faith attempt to encourage parties to settle disputes amicably or because a system like eBay benefits from the aura of security created when there are only very few negative comments. As noted above, eBay contains about 99% positive ratings. This may be, in part, because eBay discourages negative feedback. Gillette points out that eBay's instructions on the Feedback Forum discourage negative feedback (Gillette, 2002, p. 1187-1189). Users are warned that negative comments cannot be removed once posted (eBay, 2005h) and should only be left after making efforts to resolve the problem with the other party (eBay, 2005i). Users are also warned that they are responsible for their own comments, and may be liable if a court finds that their remarks constitute libel or defamation (eBay, 2005h). Gillette suggests that such warnings will further discourage the posting of negative feedback.

Users may also be reluctant to post negative feedback for fear of retaliatory feedback from the other party (Resnick & Zeckhauser, 2002, p. 19). Indeed, sellers are more likely to post a negative comment about a buyer who has left a negative comment than a buyer who has left a neutral comment (Cabral & Hortacsu, 2005). Gillette suggests that where a negative comment is met with a retaliatory response, third parties will find it difficult to determine whose complaint is justified, and are likely to view both parties as untrustworthy (Gillette, 2002, p. 1187). In addition, since eBay permits one to view all of the feedback left *by* a person (and not just *about* a person), users may fear that they will develop a negative reputation if they leave negative feedback too frequently about others (Calkin, 2001). A user with a justified complaint may prefer to keep quiet and thereby avoid these risks rather than benefit unknown parties who might, in the future, transact with the bad actor. If justified complaints are suppressed, a falsely positive impression will be left regarding a bad actor.

The risk of retaliation, and its power to suppress negative feedback, is discussed on eBay's discussion forums (see, e.g., Rapscallion22, 2005). It appears that the fear of retaliation does suppress negative feedback, particularly by sellers whose reputation appears to matter more than buyers. An unhappy trader is advised in this discussion thread to set up a separate, presumably more disposable, buyer account in order to be able to leave negative feedback. This would, however, reduce the amount of feedback that the seller could accumulate since the feedback score is a sum of feedback received from both buyers and sellers. The concern that buyers would be deterred from leaving negative feedback by the risk of retaliation is weakened by the observation that it is relatively easy for a buyer to set up a new account and thereby shed a negative reputation. To the extent that buyers are nonetheless deterred, one suggestion is that only buyers be permitted to rate sellers and not vice versa (Jøsang et al., 2005).

Another systematic problem arises if it is easy for a user with a bad reputation to discard the reputation and start anew. As noted earlier, a reputation system is effective where the reputation has value to its subject. If it is easy to begin again, there is little to fear from behaving badly in a transaction. There are some costs to beginning again, although whether these costs are sufficient to deter bad behaviour is uncertain. A new seller is usually treated as less reliable than those with established reputations. In addition, eBay now requires that sellers register for a seller's account and verify their identities using a credit card, debit card, or through eBay's "ID Verify" system (eBay, 2005b). Buyers are required to verify their identities in this way only when registering using an anonymous email address such as a hotmail or yahoo email address. The requirement that sellers authenticate themselves makes it somewhat more difficult for them to shed a bad reputation. However, it may be worthwhile for a bad actor to invest in a good reputation by completing a series of legitimate transactions and then to "cash in" the reputation with a fraudulent high-value transaction. Calkins notes the case of one eBay user who was eventually convicted of fraud after adopting this strategy (Calkins, 2001). Even if the seller is not "cashing in" on the investment in a good reputation, others may do so. There is evidence that hackers are taking over the accounts of sellers with good reputations in order to defraud buyers (Wolverton, 2002).

Another problem emerges where reputation systems permit "ballot-stuffing" or repeated submission of reviews to skew the overall reputation. An earlier version of the eBay Feedback Forum permitted anyone to leave comments unrelated to a particular transaction, which led to "feedback padding" (Calkins, 2001). Groups of users colluded to exchange positive feedback to build up their ratings without actually going through any transactions. The Feedback Forum now permits comments to be left only by the parties to a completed transaction. Nevertheless, users may still hold sham auctions in order to pad their feedback files if they are willing to pay eBay the transaction fees for the fake auctions (Calkins, 2001; Cameron & Galloway, 2005, p. 188; Jøsang et al., 2005).

Empirical Assessments of eBay's Feedback Forum

Since eBay is one of the best known and most used online auction sites, it offers a rich data source for empirical study of various aspects of online auctions. Two key questions about the effect of eBay's Feedback Forum are relevant to our inquiry into the legalities of online reputation systems. First, do users rely on the reputation information? Second, is the reputation information correct? The empirical studies published so far have generated data useful, to some extent, in answering both of these questions. These studies inquire into whether sellers with high feedback scores are (1) more likely to conclude transactions, and (2) obtain higher prices. Evidence of this type would suggest that buyers do rely on feedback.

Over 15 observational studies of data from eBay auctions for particular products have been published in recent years. Resnick et al. (2004) offer a review and analysis of the accumulated results. The studies focus on particular items (e.g., specific coins, guitars, palm pilot PDAs, dolls, stamps, etc.) sold by sets of sellers with varying reputations. While most studies found that positive feedback was rewarded with higher prices and negative feedback was penalized by lower prices, a number of studies observed no effects or, in some cases, the opposite effects (Resnick et al., 2004, p. 9-10). In general, the studies suggested that reputation also affects the probability of sale (Resnick et al., 2004, p. 11). Resnick et al. warn that the observational studies run the danger of attributing these effects to reputation when they are properly to be attributed to covariates of reputation not visible to researchers such as whether the seller is responsive to email queries (2004, p. 12).

Nevertheless, some of these results have been confirmed using other experimental methods. Cameron and Galloway's (2005) interviews with eBay users confirmed the importance of reputation in willingness to bid.

The second question relevant to our inquiry is whether the feedback, which we have found is relied upon by users according to some of the studies mentioned, is actually reliable.

As a preliminary point, some might argue that buyers' reliance on feedback suggests that the feedback is accurate because rational actors would disregard or discount the value of the feedback if it were inaccurate. This might be so if buyers were experienced and well-informed about weaknesses of the feedback system. However, this assumption is questionable, and those who are most likely to be misled by the feedback (due to inexperience or other reason) are most likely to offer a higher bid and win the auction (Gillette, 2002, p. 1189-1190). In other words, the evidence of reliance may show only that some users are being misled, and not that the feedback is accurate. The information available to new users tends to support the use and reliability of the feedback system more than to explain its limitations.

Resnick and Zeckhauser (2001) made two observations relevant to the question of whether feedback is accurate. First, they noted that the percentage of negative and neutral feedback decreases as the number of positive ratings increases (2001, p. 12). This makes sense given that sellers with a large number of ratings are likely to have significant experience and so be better sellers. One might also expect sellers who have accumulated a lot of ratings to be more careful to protect their reputation than a newcomer whose costs of starting anew are lower. One might conclude from this that a high number of positive ratings is a good indicator of a lower probability of a problematic transaction. However, it is not possible to deduce anything from this observation about the actual likelihood of a problematic transaction, because we do not know how many negative reviews have been suppressed. It is also necessary to consider the possibility that users are increasingly reluctant to post negative feedback as a seller's reputation improves. Resnick and Zeckhauser (2001) suggest that there is a "stoning" phenomenon, according to which participants are more willing to post negative comments about those with poorer reputations and less willing to post them about those with better reputations. Explanations of this phenomenon may be that there is a natural tendency to attribute bad behaviour to a person with a bad reputation when something goes wrong with the transaction (Gillette, 2002), that a dissatisfied user may be more apt to doubt his or her own judgment if the other party has a good reputation (Resnick & Zeckhauser, 2001, p. 12), that there is a reputation cost in posting a negative comment about someone with a good reputation (i.e., the party complaining may appear to be "difficult" where everyone else has had a good interaction), or that there is a reputation cost in retaliating against a criticism made by a person with a good reputation.

Resnick and Zeckhauser (2001, pp. 13-15) also approach the issue of the accuracy of feedback by looking for a relationship between a buyer's feedback about a seller and the seller's previous feedback profile. Although they find that the previous feedback profile has some predictive value, this does not permit the conclusion that the feedback offers an accurate measure of the real probability of a problematic transaction given the reasons to suspect underreporting of negative feedback. In other words, we know that sellers with poor reputations may have a slightly higher chance of receiving additional negative feedback, which may suggest that a poor reputation is a useful predictor of future problems, but we do not know whether this chance is close to the real frequency of problematic transactions. Furthermore, the hypothesized "stoning" phenomenon would also be consistent with this observation.

Part III: Legal Issues Relating to Online Reputation Systems in the Context of Online Auctions

Introduction

Although online reputation systems, such as eBay's Feedback Forum, are remarkable for having apparently made possible a market under highly adverse conditions (i.e., anonymous, nonsimultaneous, nonrepeated transactions), they have given rise to some difficulties.

As noted above, serious difficulties remain with fraud in online auctions despite the use of reputation systems. If it is true that users are invited to rely and are relying to their detriment on an unreliable online reputation system, the provider of the online reputation system might face legal responsibility both under the common law as well as under certain statutes. In particular, the common law action in negligent misrepresentation is worth considering. Statutes that contain rules relating to misleading advertising may also be relevant. These concerns are not merely hypothetical, as eBay has already been sued in California for negligently misleading consumers about the reliability of the feedback system (*Gentry v. eBay*, 2002), and has already been criticized by a UK judge about the protection it offers to its users (Wearden, 2004).

It is also possible that an online auction might be responsible for disseminating defamatory content through its online reputation system. Although the original defamation is submitted by another user, defamation law holds publishers and republishers responsible for circulating defamatory content under certain circumstances. Once again, eBay has been sued for allegedly defamatory statements posted by one user about another in its online reputation system (*Grace v. eBay*, 2004).

The enforceability of contractual disclaimers of liability in the relevant user agreements is particularly important in the context of online auctions. User agreements may successfully disclaim liability arising out of online reputation systems associated with online auctions, as was the case in *Grace v. eBay* (2004). Although beyond the scope of the present chapter, it is important to recall that not all reputation systems will be able to rely on a user agreement to avoid liability. For example, individuals or businesses reviewed on sites such as Ratemyprofessors.com or BadBusinessBureau.com may not have agreed to submit to the online reputation system and to release the operator of the system from liability for harms caused by the system.

To our knowledge, there are no Canadian court decisions addressing online reputation systems. The following analysis will consider the U.S. decisions mentioned above, as well as the Canadian law that would likely apply if cases of this type were brought in Canada.

Liability for Negligent Misrepresentation

The U.S. Case of Gentry v. eBay, Inc.

The California case of *Gentry v. eBay, Inc.* (2002) 99 Cal. App. 4th 816 (Calif. C.A.) considered the argument that eBay's Feedback Forum was misleading and that eBay had negligently misrepresented its worth to users.

In this case, the plaintiffs bought forged autographed sports memorabilia along with forged certificates of authenticity in eBay auctions. Among other arguments, the plaintiffs claimed that the Feedback Forum was misleading because it permitted anyone to rate a dealer, and that most of the positive feedback ratings were self-generated or provided by coconspiring dealers. The Court of Appeal refused to hold eBay liable for the misleading content provided by third parties. In so doing, the Court relied upon a U.S. statutory provision that states that providers or users of interactive computer services are not to be treated as the publisher or speaker of any information provided by another information provider (47 U.S.C. 230(c)(1), introduced as the *Communications Decency Act of 1996* Pub.L. No.104-104 § 501, 509 (Feb. 8, 1996)). The Court characterized the plaintiffs' argument as an attempt to hold eBay responsible for the information provided by third parties, contrary to s.230. The broad interpretation of s.230 has been subject to some criticism in the U.S. for providing overly broad immunity contrary to the interests of consumers (Mann & Belzley, 2005; Rustad & Koenig, 2005).

However, it seems reasonable to draw a distinction between the information provided by others and eBay's own implicit and explicit representations as to the reliability of this information. Indeed, the plaintiffs referred to such representations as eBay's statement that "a positive eBay rating is worth its weight in gold" (*Gentry v. eBay, Inc.,*, 2002, at p. 835), as well as eBay's "star" system and "Power Sellers" endorsement. These are arguably statements made by eBay rather than information provided by third parties.

With respect to eBay's statement about the worth of a positive eBay rating, the Court held that it was a statement of opinion that, under the U.S. law of negligent misrepresentation, would not give rise to liability. Although the line between fact and opinion can be unclear, the Court held that "[t]his kind of vague, highly subjective statement as to the significance of a positive rating is not the sort of statement that a consumer would interpret as factual or upon which he or she could reasonably rely" (p. 835). In light of the empirical studies of eBay behaviour, which suggest that users do rely to some extent on feedback, there may be reason to question the presumption that consumers do not treat feedback as a valuable and reliable source of information.

With respect to the "star" system and "Power Sellers" endorsements, the Court held that they were no more than an indication of the amount of positive information provided by third parties, and so eBay was not responsible by virtue of s.230. This analysis seems to ignore the reasonable argument that eBay's various endorsements of the feedback clearly suggested that the feedback scores were reliable, and could thus be viewed as an independent statement by eBay rather than as merely the neutral dissemination of information provided by third parties for which eBay was not liable under s.230.

The *Gentry* case illustrates the approach taken by a U.S. court to the issue of liability for misrepresentation due to the unreliability of eBay's feedback system. Canadian law does not contain an all-purpose statutory immunity provision akin to s.230 of the U.S. *Communications Decency Act*. It is, accordingly, worthwhile to consider how a similar claim of negligent misrepresentation would fare under the Canadian law.

The Canadian Law of Negligent Misrepresentation

The Canadian common law provides a cause of action for recovery of economic losses caused by negligent misrepresentation (Fridman, 2002, p. 354-373, 609-620; Klar, 2003, p. 204-235; Linden, 2001, p. 405-432). In order for a plaintiff to succeed in this type of claim, it is necessary to establish that (1) there was a duty of care owed by the defendant to the plaintiff, which is based upon a special relationship between the parties, (2) the statement was untrue, inaccurate, or misleading, (3) the defendant acted negligently in making the misrepresentation, (4) the plaintiff reasonably relied on the misrepresentation, and (5) the reliance resulted in harm to the plaintiff (*Hercules Management*, 1997; *Queen v. Cognos*, 1993, p. 110).

Duty of Care

The determination of whether there is a duty of care takes place in two steps. In the first step, a *prima facie* duty of care will be found where "(a) the defendant ought reasonably to foresee that the plaintiff will rely on his or her representation; and (b) reliance by the plaintiff would, in the particular circumstances of the case, be reasonable" (*Hercules Management*, 1997, para.24). The Supreme Court of Canada has endorsed five factors that, while not a strict test, would suggest that a plaintiff's reliance on a defendant's representation was reasonable: (a) the defendant had a direct or indirect financial interest in the transaction in respect of which the representation was made, (b) the defendant was a professional or someone who possessed special skill, judgment, or knowledge, (c) the advice or information was provided in the course of the defendant's business, (d) the information or advice was given deliberately, and not on a social occasion, and (e) the information or advice was given in response to a specific enquiry or request (*Hercules Management*, 1997, para. 43).

The second step of the duty of care inquiry addresses the question of whether the *prima facie* duty of care ought to be negated or limited due to policy considerations (*Hercules Management,* 1997, para.31). One of the chief concerns at this stage is that the judicial recognition of a duty of care may expose defendants to potentially unlimited and indeterminate liability. The danger was clear to the Court in the *Hercules Management* case, which dealt with auditors' liability for negligent audit reports. It would be quite foreseeable to auditors that many parties might rely on the reports for a wide range of purposes, and that the reliance would be reasonable given the professional qualifications of the auditors. This would expose auditors to indeterminate liability whose harmful consequences would, in the Court's view, outweigh the benefits of deterring negligent behaviour. However, where indeterminate liability does not exist on the particular facts of the case, the *prima facie* duty of care need not be negated. The Court stated that "in cases where the defendant knows the identity of the plaintiff (or of a class of plaintiffs) and where the defendant's statements are used for the specific purpose or transaction for which they were made, policy considerations surrounding indeterminate liability will not be of any concern since the scope of liability can readily be circumscribed" (*Hercules Management,* 1997, para. 37).

There seems to be a reasonable argument that eBay would owe a duty of care to its customers not to mislead them with respect to the utility of the feedback system in making their transaction decisions. eBay should foresee that users will rely on it, particularly given eBay's suggestions that they do so. Users are informed that "[t]he feedback score represents the number of eBay members that are satisfied doing business with a particular member" (eBay, 2005c), that "[f]eedback is a valuable indicator of a buyer or seller's reputation on eBay" (eBay, 2005d), that "[f]eedback is each member's reputation on eBay and is the foundation of trust on eBay" (eBay, 2005e), that they may "[b]uy with confidence by reviewing a seller's eBay feedback" (eBay, 2005f), and that "[b]efore you bid or buy on eBay, it's important to know your seller. Always look at your seller's feedback ratings, score and comments first to get an idea of their reputation within the eBay marketplace" (eBay, 2005f).

In addition to being foreseeable, user reliance is arguably reasonable according to the factors mentioned by the Court in *Hercules Management* (1997). The representations about the Feedback Forum are made by eBay, which must be presumed to be best placed to understand the reliability of the system since it created and maintained it and gathers data about fraud. eBay provides the representations deliberately in the course of its own business and to promote its own business. Undoubtedly, experienced users may understand the limitations of the system. However, newer users may arguably be behaving reasonably when they take eBay's assertions at face value. A counterargument to the suggestion that user reliance is reasonable might be that users are also invited to take additional steps to protect themselves, which might suggest that feedback has some use, but ought to be supplemented with other safety measures. These additional measures include verifying a seller's contact information and location by contacting eBay, taking advantage of purchase protection programs available (subject to limits and deductibles) through eBay or PayPal, and by contacting sellers to learn about item return policies (eBay, 2005g). Nevertheless, given the representations about the usefulness of the feedback, the existence of other additional measures may not render reliance on the feedback unreasonable.

With respect to the risk of indeterminate liability, both the class of plaintiffs is known and eBay's statements about the Feedback Forum are being used exactly for the purpose for which they were made. Although the numbers of users and transactions are large, they are neither indeterminate nor unlimited. In summary, then, a reasonable argument can be advanced that there is a duty of care owed by eBay to its customers in relation to the reasonable accuracy of its statements about transaction safety and the utility of feedback in this respect.

An Untrue, Inaccurate or Misleading Statement

Having established a duty of care, the second element in a negligent misrepresentation case is an inaccurate or misleading statement. A literally false statement will qualify, but statements may also mislead by implication or by omission (Linden, 2001, p. 428). The distinction between statements of fact and opinion, which was at issue in the *Gentry* case, is also important in Canadian common law of negligent misrepresentation (Fridman, 2002 p. 612-613; Klar, 2003, p. 221;). The cases are, unfortunately, inconsistent. Some courts reject claims based on statements that they characterize as opinions or predictions, while others are willing to consider such claims (Klar, 2003, p. 222). The difficulty is that statements of opinion or prediction are often based on assertions of fact, or they imply certain facts. Some courts and commentators hold that an opinion or prediction that negligently misstates or implies an existing fact may give rise to liability for negligent misrepresentation (Fridman, 2002, p. 613; Klar, 2003, p. 221). The more obviously speculative a statement, however, the less reasonable will it be for a plaintiff to rely upon it (Klar, 2003, p. 222).

eBay's suggestion that "[t]he feedback score represents the number of eBay members that are satisfied doing business with a particular member" (eBay, 2005c), is a factual assertion that is likely inaccurate and misleading given the empirical evidence. The score is perhaps more accurately described as a combination of satisfied users, users attempting to induce reciprocal positive feedback in order to boost their own reputations, and dissatisfied users who fear retaliatory feedback and so leave a positive report. The assertion also misleads by omission since it makes no reference to the dissatisfied users who leave no feedback at all out of fear of retaliation.

eBay's suggestions that feedback is a valuable indicator of reputation and that buyers may buy with confidence by reviewing feedback are closer to statements of opinion, but arguably contain the implicit assertion of fact that feedback is a reasonably reliable predictor of a seller's actual rate of problematic transactions. This assertion of fact is suspect. It appears from the empirical research into eBay's auctions that there is some limited predictive value to the feedback. More experienced sellers are less likely to attract negative feedback, and there is some relationship between prior reputation and the likelihood of a subsequent negative feedback. However, since the evidence suggests that negative reviews are being suppressed, this evidence says nothing about the absolute likelihood of a problematic transaction. The evidence may (possibly) permit an assessment of the relative riskiness of competing sellers. Since material omissions may be misleading, the failure to explain that negative feedback may be missing might amount to a misleading misrepresentation for the purposes of liability.

A Negligent Statement

The third element in a negligent misrepresentation case is that the defendant was negligent in making the statement. The defendant is not held to a standard of perfection, but is held to a standard of reasonable care to ensure that a statement is neither inaccurate nor misleading. The standard of care varies from case to case, and depends upon such factors as the context within which the statement is made, the purpose for which the statement is made, the foreseeable uses of the statement, the probable damage that will result from the inaccuracy, the skill and knowledge of the defendant and of others similarly placed, and so forth. (Klar, 2003, pp. 224-225).

Thus far, we have been focusing on the explicit and implicit representations of reliability made by eBay about the Feedback system, rather than on the improvement of the system itself. The misleading quality of these representations may be cured by (a) modifying the representations so that users are made aware of the limitations of the system, and/or by (b) improving the Feedback system so that it is in fact as reliable as it is represented to be.

Given the suspicion that eBay's interest lies in creating the impression that online auctions are safe, and that the feedback is useful in avoiding problematic transactions (Calkins, 2001; Gillette, 2002, p. 1190), eBay is vulnerable to the further suspicion that it knowingly overstates the reliability of the feedback system. Given the body of commentary both on eBay discussion forums and in academic journals questioning the reliability of the feedback system, eBay cannot credibly claim lack of knowledge about its limitations. As a result, misleading representations that the feedback is a reliable predictor of the safety of transacting with a particular seller could be considered negligent by a court.

It is less likely that a court would find eBay negligent in operating a faulty feedback system, but this is also possible. Sookman cites numerous cases in which litigation has arisen over inaccurate information provided by a malfunctioning or improperly designed computerized system (Sookman, 2002). Various authors have suggested improvements to eBay's system (Dellarocas, 2001; Jøsang et al., 2005). For example, Jøsang et al. (2005) suggest that the problem that the eBay feedback system suppresses negative reviews might be addressed by permitting only buyers to rate sellers. Some of these solutions may be unworkable, and the standard of care required in negligence is that of reasonableness rather than perfection. It is possible that the quality demanded of an online reputation system will increase as experience and research accumulates.

Reasonable Reliance on the Misrepresentation

The fourth element is that the plaintiff must establish that he or she actually relied on the misrepresentation. If the plaintiff would have taken the same detrimental action even if the defendant had provided an accurate statement rather than the negligently inaccurate statement, the plaintiff's claim will fail. A court may be willing to infer reliance in situations where a statement would naturally tend to induce reliance (Klar, 2003, p. 225). In the eBay context, a plaintiff must be able to show that the feedback, and eBay's representations of its reliability, caused him or her to bid when he or she would not have done so if the limitations of the feedback system were known.

Harmful Reliance

The fifth element is that the plaintiff must have suffered damage as a result of his or her reliance on the defendant's negligent misrepresentation. In other words, even if the plaintiff can establish that he or she relied on the misrepresentation in taking a decision, there will be no liability unless the plaintiff's decision was financially detrimental.

Summary

In summary, it appears that there is a reasonable argument that eBay overstates the reliability of its Feedback Forum in enabling users to "buy with confidence" in a manner that amounts to negligent misrepresentation. This conclusion must be tempered by noting the difficulties facing a plaintiff in advancing such a claim. The plaintiff must show that reliance was reasonable under the circumstances. For example, reliance on feedback as the sole trust mechanism for a very expensive purchase might be regarded as unreasonable, perhaps even for an inexperienced user given the available payment escrow services. Another difficulty arises in proving that the system is inaccurate to an extent that eBay's representations about it are misleading. In addition, as will be discussed later in this chapter, eBay users face contractual exclusions of liability in the User Agreement.

The foregoing discussion has addressed the common law tort of negligent misrepresentation. However, the providers of online reputation systems should also consider the possible applicability of the statutory rules governing misleading advertising. For example, the federal *Competition Act*, R.S.C. 1985, c. C-34, and the Ontario *Consumer Protection Act 2002*, S.O. 2002, c.30, Sched.A, both contain rules regarding misleading advertising.

Liability for Defamation

Another legal problem that the providers of online reputation systems may possibly face is a defamation claim. Defamation law, which includes the law of libel and slander, is concerned with protecting reputation against unjustified and unfounded attacks.

The U.S. Case of Grace v. eBay Inc.

A claim in defamation by an individual against eBay for comments posted by a third party in the Feedback Forum was at issue in *Grace v. eBay Inc.* (2004) 120 Cal. App. 4th 984 (Cal. Ct. Appeal). The plaintiff asked eBay to remove the comments, and when eBay refused, the plaintiff sued eBay and the party who left the comment. The plaintiff's suit failed because the California Court of Appeal held that the User Agreement immunized eBay from liability. The User Agreement stated that the user released eBay from claims connected in any way to disputes with another user. Grace argued that his dispute was not just a dispute with another user but also a dispute with eBay directly. The Court rejected this argument, finding that the disclaimer clause covered claims against eBay that were based on its displaying or failing to remove the objectionable comments posted by another user.

Grace v. eBay is also notable for the Court's narrow interpretation of the statutory immunity provided in the United States by 47 U.S.C. section 230 in the context of defamation. The Court suggested that while s.230 might preclude liability for the publisher of defamatory statements, it did not preclude liability at common law for eBay as a distributor of defamatory statements where it knew or had reason to know a statement was defamatory. This ruling ran contrary to a number of other judicial decisions. Indeed, in an earlier case, the plaintiff's expectation that a court would find eBay immune from liability under s.230 deterred the plaintiff from suing eBay over allegedly defamatory postings by a competitor in the Feedback

Forum (Segal, 1999). The distinction between publishers and mere distributors is important in Canadian defamation law as well, as will be discussed later.

Defamation cases have been brought in the United States in relation to statements in other types of online reputation forums as well. For example, an author has sued Amazon.com and the reviewers of his books for their negative comments about him in Amazon.com's forum for book reviews (*Schneider v. Amazon.com, Inc.*, 2001). In *MCW, Inc. v. Badbusinessbureau. com* (2004), the plaintiff sued a consumer complaints forum for defamation.

The Canadian Law of Defamation

The Canadian law of defamation is a large and complex field and the following is a basic overview of the elements essential for our analysis of online reputation systems. The initial threshold of there being a defamatory statement is a low one, and most critical comment, whether in the form of fact or opinion will suffice (Klar, 2003, p. 673). The main argument in a defamation case takes place at the level of the relevant defences.

The defamatory statement must refer expressly, or by implication, to the plaintiff. This raises an interesting point in the context of online reputation systems in which users are known by pseudonyms. The essence of defamation is the protection of character and reputation against unjustified statements that would "lower a person in the estimation of right-thinking members of society, or [would] expose a person to hatred, contempt or ridicule" (*Botiuk v. Toronto Free Press Publications Ltd.*, 1995, para. 62). An action in defamation is also available to corporations and other entities with status as juridical persons. A corporation may sue for defamation that affects its property, or injures its trading or business reputation (Fridman, 2002, p. 650).

The law appears to be chiefly concerned with the harm to a real entity's social and economic interests. It is unclear whether a pseudonym that is not easily traceable to a real entity would attract similar solicitude. A name and a pseudonym are simply two different labels used to refer to a real entity. However, a name is generally known to more people, is less easy to change, and is linked to a greater range of dignitary, social, and economic interests of the real individual than a pseudonym. A pseudonym is usually adopted for specific purposes and so harm to the reputation associated with a pseudonym will have costs related to those purposes only. For example, damage to the reputation associated with an eBay user's pseudonym has economic costs, but does not affect other interests of that individual. Nevertheless, many people are increasingly engaging in social and economic behaviour of great personal importance online where the construction of identity around pseudonyms is common, and reputation within an online community may be of sufficient value to warrant protection. This issue was not mentioned by the California Court of Appeal in *Grace v. eBay*. eBay's Web site contemplates that feedback about members who are generally identifiable by pseudonym might be defamatory. It warns users that "[m]embers could be held legally responsible for damages to a member's reputation if a court were to find that the remarks constitute libel or defamation" (eBay, 2005h). It is probably safest to proceed on the expectation that defamatory comments that identify the plaintiff by his or her online pseudonym would satisfy this requirement.

Assuming that a defamatory statement has been made about a person in a manner that satisfies the requirements mentioned, another key issue in the eBay context is whether the online reputation system provider is responsible for the comments posted by third parties. Every publisher of a defamatory statement about the plaintiff is potentially liable to the plaintiff, and this may include many parties in the chain of distribution since each communication to a new person is viewed as a publication (see Fridman, 2002, p. 651; Klar, 2003, p. 682). However, special rules apply to so-called "innocent disseminators" of defamatory statements, such as vendors of books, librarians, and other such distributors who take on a subordinate role in the dissemination. The defence of innocent dissemination is available where a defendant distributed the content in the ordinary course of its business and (1) did not know of the defamatory content, (2) there was nothing in the material or the circumstances under which the defendant obtained or disseminated the material that ought to have led the defendant to suspect it was defamatory, and (3) the defendant's failure to be aware of the defamatory content was not due to any negligence on the defendant's part (*Vizetelly v. Mudie's Select Library Ltd.*, 1900).

The rationale underlying the defence of innocent dissemination is that such disseminators do not have the opportunity to read all of the material that passes through their hands and, further, that those whose contribution to dissemination is merely mechanical should not be liable for defamation (*Slack v. Ad-Rite Associates Ltd.*, 1998).

Although it is not an online reputation system case, the case of *Carter v. B.C. Federation of Foster Parent Associations* (2005) illustrates how Canadian courts may address the liability of the provider of an online forum for defamatory comments posted in that forum by third parties. This case involved a lawsuit against the defendant Federation for defamatory comments posted to one of its Internet chat rooms about the plaintiff. The plaintiff, upon becoming aware of defamatory comments in the chat room, asked the Federation to shut down the forum. The Board of the Federation directed that the offensive material be removed, and thought it had been removed. In fact, it had not and the plaintiff eventually sued. The trial judge found that the Federation was entitled to the defence of innocent dissemination. The Court of Appeal allowed an appeal of the decision, questioning whether the Federation was entitled to the defence given that it "did not take effective steps to remove the offending comment and there seem[ed] to have been no proper follow up to see that necessary action had been taken." (2005, para. 20-21). The Court of Appeal's decision seems to contemplate that the defence might have been available upon different facts.

The defence of innocent dissemination appears to be available to a defendant in the position of eBay, which would find it impossible to review all of the material posted in the Feedback Forum, and which maintains the Forum content in the ordinary course of its business. However, where the provider of an online reputation system is put on notice that a statement is defamatory, it risks a lawsuit in defamation if it does nothing to remove the statement. It is also worth noting that the operator of an online reputation system may also be drawn into a dispute between two users over defamatory content. In particular, the operator may be required to prevent a user from posting defamatory content about another user where a court issues an injunction to that effect (*Barrick Gold v. Lopehandia*, 2004, para. 76).

A range of other defences is available generally in defamation cases. For example, the truth of a statement is a defence to a civil defamation claim. In addition, the defence of fair comment may be available where a defendant expresses an opinion based on true facts about some matter of public interest. The defences to defamation will not be addressed further here, but additional detail is available in Canadian legal texts (Brown, 1994; Fridman, 2002; Klar, 2003).

The law in Canada extends a separate type of protection against false and injurious statements to businesses and products in the form of a cause of action for "slander of goods," which is sometimes referred to as "malicious falsehood" (see Fridman, 2002, p. 815). The cases in the U.S. against the publisher of the Consumer Reports suggest that providers of online reputation systems might also face claims based on slander of goods where they offer reviews of products (see, e.g., *Suzuki Motor Corp. v. Consumers Union*, 2003). The Consumers Union cases involve statements made by the defendant (Consumers Union) rather than third parties, as is the case with the online reputation systems under consideration here. Since the tort of slander of goods requires malice on the part of the defendant, it seems less likely that the provider of an online reputation system that contains the reviews of third parties would satisfy the requirements for liability.

In a Canadian case with interesting and unusual facts involving the statement that the plaintiff's rental property was haunted by a ghost, it was made clear that malice refers to a lack of good faith in the publication of a false statement, and that this can be inferred where the defendant knows a statement is false or recklessly disregards the truth of the statement (*Nagy v. Manitoba Free Press,* 1907). The requirement of malice suggests that slander of title cannot be committed negligently, as a greater level of fault is required (Fridman, 2002, pp. 826-827). It is possible that the continued inclusion of a product review after notice of its falsity has been delivered to an online reputation system provider may satisfy the requirement of malice. The potential claim in "slander of goods" will not be discussed further here, since the analysis aims at eBay's Feedback Forum, which generally concerns statements about individuals. Nevertheless, slander of goods may be an issue for certain types of online reputation or ratings systems that collect statements about goods.

In summary, it seems likely that an online reputation system provider would be able to take advantage of the defence of innocent dissemination to avoid liability for defamatory statements provided by third parties. However, this would depend upon its meeting the requirements of the defence. Where an aggrieved plaintiff gave notice of defamatory content, the online reputation system provider would likely lose this defence if it did nothing to remove the content. An online reputation system provider might, in the appropriate case, be able to limit the likelihood of liability further with contractual exclusions of liability.

The Effect of the Exclusion Clause in the User Agreement

An online reputation system provider may be able to reduce its exposure to liability using a contractual exclusion clause. Before continuing to consider eBay, it is important to note that some online reputation system models do not involve a contract with potential plaintiffs. For example, sites such as Epinions.com and Ratemyprofessors.com contain statements about parties who may not have agreed by contract to submit to public comment, including possibly defamatory or trade libelous comment. In such cases, the provider of the online reputation system would be unable to point to contractual restrictions of liability in defence.

Even if an online reputation system provider requires users of its system to agree to contractual terms, such as eBay's User Agreement, this is not the end of the inquiry into potential liability. Courts may find the exclusion of liability clause to be inapplicable or unenforceable.

Exclusion clauses can be problematic when they are included in standard form consumer contracts, which are often carefully drafted in favour of a party who has superior bargaining power and experience (see, e.g., Waddams, 2005, para. 471). The concern is that suppliers might use standard form contracts to excuse themselves for liability for serious deficiencies in the quality of goods or services provided (Waddams, 2005, para. 471). This problem has been addressed by statute as well as by certain common law doctrines devised by judges.

An example of a statutory response to this problem is found in the Ontario *Consumer Protection Act, 2002,* S.O. 2002, c.30, Schedule A, which provides that suppliers of services in the context of consumer agreements are deemed to warrant that the services are of "a reasonably acceptable quality" (s.9(1)). Furthermore, any term purporting to negate this deemed warranty is void (s.9(3)).

Judges have devised various techniques to avoid injustice where an exclusion clause appears to be unfair. One such technique is that courts will often interpret any ambiguity in an exclusion clause against the interests of the party who drafted it (the "contra proferentum" rule). Courts demand clarity in exclusion clauses. Unless the exclusion clause expressly, or by necessary implication, covers the act that is said to give rise to liability, the exclusion clause may not offer much protection against liability arising from that act (Fridman, 2002, p. 616). Section 11 of the Ontario *Consumer Protection Act, 2002* codifies a version of the "contra proferentum" rule for consumer agreements, providing that "any ambiguity that allows for more than one reasonable interpretation of a consumer agreement provided by the supplier to the consumer...shall be interpreted to the benefit of the consumer."

Courts sometimes resist applying an exclusion of liability clause where to do so would be unfair or unreasonable (Waddams, 2005, para. 481-482). An example of this is found in *Robet v. Versus Brokerage Services Inc.* (2001), which concerned an online brokerage service. A negligent data entry error at the defendant brokerage (Versus) resulted in the duplication of orders. The plaintiff discovered and tried to fix the problem by selling the excess shares. Without informing its customers of the error and without verifying whether the customers had self-corrected by selling the shares themselves, Versus rectified these errors, leaving the plaintiff in a "short" position. The plaintiff had to cover the "short" position at a large loss. Versus argued that it was not liable due to the exclusion clause in the service agreement, which excluded liability arising from erroneous transmissions of information. The court rejected this argument. It found that a certain reasonable degree of accuracy in processing and reporting of transactions is an essential element of online brokerage services, and customers would be unlikely to purchase services from a provider that disclaimed all responsibility to provide services of reasonable quality. In this case, the gross negligence of the defendant was beyond the type of conduct that the parties could reasonably have agreed would be covered by the exclusion clause.

The eBay User Agreement that is concluded with Canadian users contains clauses that exclude and limit liability (eBay, 2005j). A potential user must accept the User Agreement before being permitted to transact on eBay.

Clause 3.1 of the eBay User Agreement warns users that eBay is not an auctioneer and that it is not involved in the transactions between buyers and sellers. It further states that it has no control over "the quality, safety or legality of the items advertised, the truth or accuracy of the listings, the ability of sellers to sell items or the ability of buyers to pay for items," and it "cannot ensure that a buyer or seller will actually complete a transaction."

In clause 3.3, eBay states the following:

We use many techniques to verify the accuracy of the information our users provide us when they register on the Site. However, because user authentication on the Internet is difficult, eBay cannot and does not confirm each user's purported identity. Thus, we have established a user-initiated feedback system to help you evaluate with whom you are dealing. We also encourage you to communicate directly with potential trading partners through the tools available on the Site. You may also wish to consider using a third party escrow service or services that provide additional user verification. See our Buying and Selling Tools page.

According to clause 3.4, the user releases eBay from "claims, demands and damages (actual and consequential) of every kind and nature, known and unknown, suspected and unsuspected, disclosed and undisclosed, arising out of or in any way connected with [a dispute with one or more users]."

In clause 3.5, eBay warns users that it does not control the information provided by other users, some of which may be inaccurate or deceptive. It asks users to "[p]lease use caution, common sense, and practice safe trading when using the Site." Clause 3.5. further provides that users agree to accept the risks that others may act under false pretenses, and that eBay is not responsible for the acts or omissions of the users.

Clause 11 of the User Agreement indicates that the eBay services are provided "as is" without any representation, warranty, or condition. Clause 12 provides that should eBay be liable for damages related to its site or its services, the damages are capped at the greater of $150 or the fees paid to eBay in the preceding 12 months by the user concerned.

These clauses seem to exclude potential claims related to defamation. In particular, clause 3.4 provides that users release eBay from any claims related to disputes with other users. Since a defamation claim against eBay would be based on eBay's role in publishing or republishing a defamatory statement by another user, section 3.4 arguably addresses this situation.

The analysis of whether the User Agreement's exclusion clause would be effective against a claim that the Feedback Forum is misleading is more complicated. It is true that eBay has disclaimed all liability arising out of disputes between users. It has also emphasized its lack of control over, knowledge about, and responsibility for the honesty of other users. Users must, in fact, agree to assume the risks that others may be dishonest (clause 3.5). It would seem then that a plaintiff could not complain of being exposed to these risks.

Nevertheless, an argument exists that weakens the effect of the exclusion clause. There is an ambiguity in the provisions of the User Agreement that is arguably compounded by the various statements made on the Web site about the trustworthiness and utility of the feedback. Several clauses warn that eBay cannot ensure the trustworthiness of other users, and eBay disclaims responsibility for the acts and omissions of other users. Clause 3.5 urges users to practice "safe trading." Against this background, clause 3.3 might be interpreted as offering the means to practice "safe trading," including using feedback to evaluate other users. As a result, the entire User Agreement might be interpreted as further endorsing the feedback system rather than limiting liability for potential misrepresentation about the feedback system's efficacy. Given that ambiguity in exclusion clauses is to be resolved against the drafting party, this appears to be a weakness in eBay's attempt to limit its liability.

It would be advisable for providers of online reputation systems, such as eBay's, to be careful to avoid overstating the utility of their systems, and to ensure that they more clearly and specifically disclaim responsibility for losses resulting from reliance on their systems.

Conclusion and Future Trends

Online reputation systems offer interesting potential economic, social, and political benefits and challenges. They support collective decision making in a manner that may reduce the gate-keeping power of intermediaries. As their use becomes more widespread, potential frictions will emerge and aggrieved parties will increasingly turn to the law for solutions.

Most of the online reputation systems of today were developed based on ad hoc principles and ideas. As these complex and powerful systems are introduced and become widely used, it is important to ensure that they conform to the social and legal conventions that govern the societies in which they are used. Therefore, adjustments are often necessary to make the systems conform to these conventions. On the other hand, these new computerized reputation systems raise novel issues that are not always clearly addressed by existing legal principles. Some uncertainty regarding the appropriate and likely legal response will necessarily exist as the law follows its slow path of evolution.

There are many different types of online reputation systems today, and the relevant legal issues are likely to vary according to the type under consideration. This chapter has chosen the example of eBay's Feedback Forum for analysis because of the accumulated body of empirical studies of the system, as well as because the Feedback Forum has already been the subject of lawsuits in the United States. Clearly, the legal analysis might vary somewhat for other online reputation systems. It is also important to note that laws and regulations vary by jurisdiction, creating a challenge for online businesses (including providers of online reputation systems) that operate across borders. The nature of the rules applicable in other jurisdictions should be considered where potential users are located in those other jurisdictions. Despite this legal variability, the same types of problems can be expected to arise in the common law countries, which share numerous legal values and assumptions.

As discussed in this chapter, some of the potential liabilities under the Canadian common law that face online reputation system providers such as eBay are claims in defamation arising from statements made in the Feedback Forum as well as claims in negligent misrepresentation arising from eBay's apparent overstatement of the reliability of the feedback. Although these are novel and challenging claims to make, there are circumstances under which plaintiffs might arguably succeed. Contractual exclusions of liability may assist an online reputation system provider in limiting exposure to liability, but providers should be aware that these clauses must be carefully drafted as any ambiguity is generally resolved by a court against the drafting party.

Turning to the future, the evolution of online reputation systems will also introduce another important variable into the legal issues raised by this technology. One question of interest with respect to the regulation of online reputation systems is whether reputation data can be shared by different organizations for different applications. An example of shared reputation data is the credit rating database used by banks and many other organizations. The online reputation systems discussed in this chapter are generally owned by one organization, for instance the eBay reputation system. Would it not be useful if a user with a good reputation in the eBay marketplace could use his or her reputation in the Amazon marketplace? Businesses often develop "proprietary reputation systems for their community, with the side effect of locking users into that service if they wish to maintain their reputation" (Bonawitz, Chandrasekhar, & Viana, 2004). The development of shared online reputation systems requires further technical study on the type of trust information that could be shared among a given class of applications. Besides the credit rating, there may be many other types of trust information useful for different types of human activities. Further work is also required on the design and implementation of shared reputation systems and the legal issues that would be raised by such systems.

Acknowledgments

The authors gratefully acknowledge the support of the Ontario Research Network for Electronic Commerce (ORNEC), the University of Ottawa and its Faculty of Law in the preparation of this chapter. We also benefitted from the helpful research assistance of Christine Higgs, Maxine Ethier, Derek van Dusen, and Talitha Nabbali. The authors are affiliated with the Faculty of Law (Chandler), the School of Information Technology and Engineering (el-Khatib, von Bochmann, and Adams), and the School of Management (Benyoucef) at the University of Ottawa.

References

Bailey, B. P., Gurak, L. J., & Konstan, J. A. (2003). *Trust in cyberspace*. Retrieved October 22, 2005, from http://orchid.cs.uiuc.edu/publications/bailey-lea-trust.pdf

Bajari, P., & Hortacsu, A. (2004). Economic insights from Internet auctions: A survey. *Journal of Economic Literature, 42*(2), 457-486.

Barrick Gold v. Lopehandia. (2004). 71 O.R. (3rd) 416 (Ont. C.A.).

Blaze, M., Feigenbaum, J., Ioannidis, J., & Keromytis, A. D. (1999). The role of trust management in distributed systems security. In J. Vitek & C. D. Jensen (Eds.), *Secure Internet programming: Security issues for mobile and distributed objects* (pp. 185-210). New York: Springer.

Block-Lieb, S. (2002). E-reputation: Building trust in electronic commerce. *Louisiana Law Review, 62*, 1199.

Bonawitz, K., Chandrasekhar, C., & Viana, R. (2004). *Portable reputations with EgoSphere*, MIT Internal Report.

Botiuk v. Toronto Free Press Publications Ltd. (1995). 126 D.L.R. (4th) 609 (S.C.C.).

Brown, R. E. (1994). *The law of defamation in Canada* (2nd ed.). Toronto: Carswell.

Cabral, L., & Hortacsu, A. (2005). *The dynamics of seller reputation: Evidence from eBay.* Working Paper. Retrieved December 5, 2005, from http://pages.stern.nyu.edu/~lcabral/workingpapers/CabralHortacsu_June05.pdf

Calkins, M. M. (2001). My reputation always had more fun than me: The failure of eBay's feedback model to effectively prevent online auction fraud. *Richmond Journal of Law & Technology, 7*, 33.

Cameron, D. D., & Galloway A., (2005). Consumer motivations and concerns in online auctions: An exploratory study. *International Journal of Consumer Studies, 29*(3), 181-192.

Carter v. B.C. Federation of Foster Parent Associations. (2005). 257 D.L.R. (4th) 133 (B.C.C.A.); [2004] B.C.J. No. 192 (B.C.S.C.).

Competition Act, R.S.C. (1985). c. C-34.

Consumer Protection Act 2002. (2002). S.O. 2002, c.30, Sched.A.

Dellarocas, C. (2001). Building trust on-line: The design of reliable reputation reporting. *Sloan Working Paper* 4180-01. Retrieved 5 December 2005, from http://papers.ssrn.com/abstract=289967

Dellarocas, C., & Resnick, P. (2003, April 26-27). Online reputation mechanisms: A roadmap for future research—a summary report. In *First Interdisciplinary Symposium on Online Reputation Mechanisms*, Cambridge, MA. Retrieved December 12, 2005, from http://ccs.mit.edu/dell/papers/symposiumreport03.pdf

eBay. (2005a). *eBay Inc. announces third quarter 2005 financial results*. Retrieved December 5, 2005, from http://investor.ebay.com/releases.cfm

eBay. (2005b). *Creating a seller's account*. Retrieved December 5, 2005, from http://pages.ebay.com/help/sell/seller_account.html

eBay. (2005c). *Evaluating a member's reputation*. Retrieved December 5, 2005, from http://pages.ebay.com/help/feedback/evaluating-feedback.html

eBay. (2005d). *Feedback policies: Overview*. Retrieved December 5, 2005, from http://pages.ebay.com/help/policies/feedback-ov.html

eBay. (2005e). *Making your feedback public or private*. Retrieved December 5, 2005, from http://pages.ebay.com/help/policies/feedback-public.html

eBay. (2005f). *Marketplace safety tips, feedback*. Retrieved December 5, 2005, from http://pages.ebay.com/securitycenter/mrkt_safety.html

eBay. (2005g). *Buying and paying*. Retrieved December 5, 2005, from http://pages.ebay.com/securitycenter/buying_paying.html

eBay. (2005h). *Feedback abuse, withdrawal and removal.* Retrieved December 5, 2005, from http://pages.ebay.com/help/policies/feedback-abuse-withdrawal.html

eBay. (2005i). *eBay policy tutorial: Feedback.* Retrieved December 5, 2005, from http://pages.ebay.com/help/tutorial/feedbacktutorial/intro4.html

eBay. (2005j). *User agreement.* Retrieved December 12, 2005, from http://pages.ebay.ca/help/policies/user-agreement.html

eBay. (2006a). *Process for eBay standard purchase protection program.* Retrieved March 11, 2006, from http://pages.ebay.ca/help/tp/esppp-process.html

eBay. (2006b). *The PayPal buyer protection.* Retrieved March 11, 2006, from http://pages.ebay.ca/paypal/pbp.html

Epinions. (2005). *FAQs the web of trust.* Retrieved December 5, 2005, from http://www.epinions.com/help/faq/?show=faq_wot

Federal Trade Commission. (2002). Commercial alert complaint requesting investigation of various Internet search engine companies for paid placement and paid inclusion programs. *Letter to search engines.* Washington, D.C., USA. Retrieved November 27, 2005, from http://www.ftc.gov/os/closings/staff/commercialalertattatch.htm

Fridman, G. H. L. (2002). *The Law of Torts in Canada* (2ⁿᵈ ed.). Toronto: Carswell, 2002.

Gentry v. eBay, Inc. (2002). 99 Cal. App. 4ᵗʰ 816 (Calif. C.A.).

Gilbert, A. (2003, April 30). FTC, states, take on on-line auction fraud. *CNET News.com* Retrieved December 5, 2005, from http://news.com.com/FTC,+states+take+on+online-auction+fraud/2100-1017_3-999009.html

Gillette, C. P. (2002). Reputation and intermediaries in electronic commerce. *Louisiana Law Review, 62,* 1165.

Grace v. eBay Inc. (2004). 120 Cal. App. 4ᵗʰ 984 (Cal. Ct. Appeal).

Hercules Management Ltd. v. Ernst & Young, [1997] 2 S.C.R. 65 (S.C.C.).

Hitlin, P., & Rainie, L. (2004). Pew Internet project data memo: Online rating systems. *Pew Internet & American Life Project.* Retrieved November 27, 2005, from http://www.pewinternet.org/pdfs/PIP_Datamemo_Reputation.pdf

HSBC Bank Canada v. Dillon Holdings Ltd. (2005). O.J. No. 2331 (Ont. S.C.J.).

Jøsang, A., Ismail, R., & Boyd C. (2005). A survey of trust and reputation systems for on-line service provision. In *Decision support systems* (forthcoming). Preprint retrieved December 12, 2005, from http://security.dstc.edu.au/papers/JIB2005-DSS.pdf

Kagal, L., Finin, T., & Joshi, A. (2001). Moving from security to distributed trust in ubiquitous computing environments. *IEEE Computer, 34*(12), 154-157.

Klar, L. (2003). *Tort Law* (3ʳᵈ ed.). Toronto: Thomson Canada Ltd.

Konrad, R. (2002, June 5). eBay touts anti-fraud software's might. *CNET News.com.* Retrieved December 5, 2005, from http://news.com.com/eBay+touts+anti-fraud+softwares+might/2100-1017_3-932874.html

Kollock, P. (1999). The production of trust in online markets. In E. J. Lawler et al. (Eds.), *Advances in group processes* (Vol. 16). Greenwich, CT: JAI Press. Online version retrieved November 27, 2005, from http://www.sscnet.ucla.edu/soc/faculty/kollock/papers/online_trust.htm

Linden, A. M. (2001). *Canadian Tort Law* (7th ed.). Markham: Butterworths Canada Ltd.

Mann, R. J. & Belzley, S. R. (2005). The promise of Internet intermediary liability. *William and Mary Law Review, 47*, 239-307.

MCW, Inc. v. Badbusinessbureau.com. (2004). U.S. Dist. LEXIS 6678.

Nagy v. Manitoba Free Press. (1907). 39 S.C.R. 340 (S.C.C.).

National White Collar Crime Center and Federal Bureau of Investigation. (2004). *IC3 2004 Internet fraud—crime report.* Retrieved December 5, 2005, from http://www.nw3c.org/downloads/data_trends_report2004.pdf.

Nissenbaum, H. (2001). Securing trust online: Wisdom or oxymoron? *Boston University Law Review, 81*, 635-664.

Queen v. Cognos Inc. (1993). 1 S.C.R. 87 (S.C.C.).

Rapscallion22. (2005, November 8). Abuse of feedback system. *eBay Forum Discussion.* Retrieved December 5, 2005, from http://forums.ebay.com/db1/thread.jspa?threadID=1000128294&start=0

Resnick, P., & Zeckhauser R. (2001, February 6). Trust among strangers in Internet transactions: Empirical analysis of eBay's reputation system. Working paper version. Retrieved December 12, 2005, from http://www.si.umich.edu/presnick/papers/ebayNBER/index.html. Revised version published (2002) in M. R. Baye (Ed.), *The economics of the Internet and e-commerce*, volume 11 of *Advances in Applied Microeconomics.* Elsevier Science.

Resnick, P., Zeckhauser R., Friedman, E., & Kuwabara, K. (2000). Reputation systems. *Communications of the ACM, 43*(12), 45-48.

Resnick, P., Zeckhauser, R., Swanson, J., & Lockwood, K. (2004). The value of reputation on eBay: A controlled experiment. *Working Paper prepared for June 2002 ESA Conference*, Boston. Initial draft 2002, revised draft March 12, 2004. Retrieved December 5, 2005, from http://www.si.umich.edu/~presnick/papers/postcards/

Robet v. Versus Brokerage Services Inc. (2001). O.J. No. 1341 (Ont. S.C.J.).

Rustad, M., & Koenig, T. (2005). Rebooting cybertort law. *Washington Law Review,80*, 335-416.

Schneider v. Amazon.com. (2001). 108 Wn. App. 454 (Wash. Ct. App. 2001).

Shi, J., von Bochmann, G., & Adams, C. (2004). A trust model with statistical foundation. In T. Dimitrakos & F. Martinelli (Eds.), *Proceedings IFIP Workshop on Formal Aspects in Security and Trust* (pp. 145-158). Toulouse: Springer.

Shi, J., von Bochmann, G., & Adams, C. (2005, July 25). Dealing with recommendations in a statistical trust model. In *Proceedings of the AAMAS Workshop on Trust in Agent Societies,* Utrecht, The Netherlands.

Slack v. Ad-Rite Associates Ltd. (1998). O.J. No. 5446 (Ont. Gen. Div.).

Sookman, B. (2002). *Computer, Internet and electronic commerce law*. Toronto: Thomson Carswell.

Suzuki Motor Corp. v. Consumers Union. (2003). 330 F. 3d 1110 (9th Circuit).

Thompson, N. (2003, June 23). More companies pay heed to their word of mouse. *The New York Times*, Late Edition, p. 4.

Tran, H., Hitchens, M., Varadharajan, V., & Watters, P. (2005). *A trust based access control framework for P2P file-sharing systems.* Presented at the Hawaii International Conference on System Sciences (HICSS-38), Honolulu, HI.

United States, Federal Trade Commission. (2005). *Online auctions: A guide for buyers and sellers.* Retrieved December 5, 2005, from http://www.ftc.gov/bcp/conline/pubs/online/auctions.htm

Vizetelly v. Mudie's Select Library Ltd. (1900). 2 Q.B. 170 (Eng. C.A.).

Waddams, S. (2005). *The law of contracts.* Aurora, Ontario: Canada Law Book.

Wang, Y., & Vassileva, J. (2004). Trust-based community formation in peer-to-peer file sharing networks. In *Web intelligence* (pp. 341-348). IEEE Computer Society.

Wearden, G. (2004, December 7). Judge raps eBay over fraud. *CNET News.com.* Retrieved December 5, 2005, from http://news.com.com/Judge+raps+eBay+over+fraud/2100-1038_3-5481601.html

Wolverton, T. (2002, March 25). Hackers find a new way to bilk eBay users. *CNET News.com.* Retrieved December 5, 2005, from http://news.com.com/2100-1017-868278.html

Wolverton, T. (2002b, June 28). Fraud lingers despite eBay efforts. *CNET News.com.* Retrieved December 5, 2005, from http://news.com.com/Fraud+lingers+despite+eBay+efforts/2100-1017_3-940427.html

Section II

Trust Technologies in E-Services

Chapter V

Holistic Trust Design of E-Services

Stéphane Lo Presti, Royal Holloway, University of London, UK

Michael Butler, University of Southampton, UK

Michael Leuschel, Heinrich-Heine Universität Düsseldorf, Germany

Chris Booth, QinetiQ, UK

Abstract

As a central issue of modern e-services, trust has to be tackled early during the development phases. We present and compare, in this chapter, various works and methodologies that contribute to this aspect. A holistic trust design methodology that combines useful aspects encountered in the existing works is then described in detail. It is based on a systematic analysis of scenarios that describe the typical use of the e-service by using a trust analysis grid. The trust analysis grid is composed of 11 trust issue categories, which cover the various aspects of the concept of trust, and is used to guide the design of the computing system by analyzing and refining the scenarios, and providing hints at the suitability of technologies for the scenario. We illustrate this methodology in several examples.

Introduction

Trust has recently been recognized as a crucial and central property of modern systems that provide e-services in a variety of contexts. Because failing to address this issue correctly may have a profound and costly impact on the e-service development, the issue of trust must be tackled early during the development, so as to identify and mitigate it as early as possible. This chapter covers methodologies that help to do so.

Trust is a human notion that goes beyond technical aspects of the system. It is important that it is not confused with other concepts, for example, security, so that users understand and thus have confidence in the system. This aspect is reinforced by the rapid growth of e-services developed in, for example, pervasive computing (Huandg, Ling, & Ponnekanti, 1999) or multiagent systems (Hanssens, Kulkarni, Tuchinda, & Horton, 2002).

Trust defies traditional analysis in that it encompasses a wide range of other issues at a high level of abstraction, for example, security, risk, social engineering, or the law, in an ever-increasing complex arrangement. The recent literature on trust (see Jøsang, Ismail, & Boyd; Rindeback & Gustavsson, 2004; or Staab, Bhargava, Lilien, Rosenthal, Winslett, & Sloman, 2004, for example) shows a number of ways with which trust can be dealt. But the literature lacks a holistic point of view that can help understand which techniques or technologies are best in various contexts and circumstances.

The design phase of the system development is the most appropriate time for analysis of trust in the system. This is the approach used to tackle more traditional issues like risk (Storey, 1996) and security (Anderson, 2001), and it has proven successful in improving the quality of systems. It can be seen as a process whose output is a set of requirements that must be addressed in the subsequent phases of the development.

Based on those two ideas of holistic design, trust is considered, in this chapter, as an evolving, contextual, and composite belief that one principal (trustor) has that another principal (trustee) will perform certain actions with certain expected results, when not all information about those actions is available. The various elements of this definition will be detailed in the remainder of this chapter.

The first section presents current works on methodologies to help design trustworthy e-services. Then we present a methodology that builds upon the current understanding of trust and improves on the existing trust design methodologies. It provides a holistic analysis framework to help design trustworthy e-services where the user is the focus of attention. This framework is applied to several realistic systems under development, including e-health and e-learning, in the next section.

Existing Methodological Work
Tackling the Trust Issue

There is a huge corpus of work on the issue of trust, but few concentrate on this issue during the design of a system development, and fewer propose methodologies to help the design process. We present here representative contributions to this topic, and discuss their advantages and disadvantages as holistic trust design methodologies.

Typologies of Trust

There are many general works that analyze and decompose the notion of trust so as to provide general guidelines and understanding into this notion. Some of them suggest, in particular, the holistic nature of the concept of trust, by combining together the various aspects of trust presented in other works.

Though these works provide a necessary and fundamental insight into the notion of trust that any holistic trust design methodology should provide, and in particular a basic decomposition into its more elemental properties, they are not sufficient by themselves for devising an e-service design methodology as they provide no concrete help to the e-service designer.

TRUST-EC E-Commerce Requirements

The TRUST-EC project (Jones & Morris, 1999) lists the common applications in e-commerce and analyzes how they consider trust, taken as a kind of reliance of system stakeholders that is more general than dependability. The list of nonfunctional requirements for trust for the e-commerce business derived from this analysis is comprised of confidentiality, integrity, availability, identification, prevention, traceability, quality, risk management, and authentication. This work concludes on the possible necessity of *"a requirements process for e-business, based on the framework, which will assist developers in structuring both the process of eliciting trust requirements (by providing a checklist of issues to be discussed with different stakeholders), and the way in which such requirements are documented"*(Jones & Morris, 1999).

McKnight and Chervany's Conceptual Framework

McKnight and Chervany (1996) analyze research papers on trust, taken from a wide range of domains: management, sociology, economics, politics, science, psychology. They summarize the various views on trust in a conceptual framework based on six constructs, which themselves are decomposed into more elements. The basic concepts of the generic definition of trust of McKnight and Chervany are trusting intention, trusting behavior, trusting beliefs, system trust, dispositional trust, and situational decision. These general concepts are refined into notions like feelings of security, vulnerability, honesty, situational normality, belief-in-person, or trust stance. This work is probably the one that provides the best view on the holistic nature of trust, in that it gathers information from domains whose problems are quite orthogonal, and it shows the intrinsically diverse and interwoven structure of trust. On the other hand, it covers such a wide scope of trust issues that it is difficult to use it concretely.

Jøsang, Ismail, and Boyd's Analysis of Trust-Related Applications and Models

Jøsang, Ismail, and Boyd (2005) give a more technical overview of the research on trust, in particular by focusing on modern reputation systems. They describe five trust classes (borrowed from Grandison and Sloman's [2000] classification) that describe the various layers of the concept of trust, namely provision trust, access trust, delegation trust, identity trust, and context trust. These classes are defined in the context of a trust purpose that enables to instantiate the classes in a given situation. The semantics of trust considered in a given application are then described against two dimensions: the levels of subjectivity and specificity. Many examples of modern systems using reputation are presented, for example eBay (2006), or Slashdot (2006).

General Methodologies

This section presents methodologies to help in various aspects of the design of systems and e-services where trust is central. The following methodologies are based on ad-hoc concepts and methods, but will show the possible approaches currently taken to design trustworthy systems.

Security Requirements Specification Method

Tan, Titkov, and Poslad (2002) devise an abstract security model that they apply to the case of an e-banking service implemented as a multiagent system. This model is based on the concepts of assets, safeguard to protect the asset, threat to the asset, and profile to specify policies and relationships between the previous concepts. A graphical notation is used to illustrate the model, where security domains are shown as groupings of concepts and profiles. The various assets are then described more precisely in the case of the e-banking scenario, where the various services needed are modeled as assets.

This analysis enables to discuss the various service design issues in the e-banking scenario. But first the methodology is aimed at multiagent systems, though it could still be used more generally at a conceptual level, and secondly, the analyzed issues are related to the more technical side of trust, namely security, and they require expert knowledge (authentication, security policies). The ideas underlying this approach are good, but not developed enough to make it a holistic trust design methodology.

Matrix Model

Tan's trust matrix model (Tan, 2003) is a means to analyze trust-building services between trading partners in e-commerce. It proposes to represent an e-service in the form of a grid. The grid rows correspond to properties of the service grouped into three layers. The grid columns correspond to a theoretical decomposition of the notion of trust into four reasons, namely, social signs, personal experience, understanding, and communality. Each reason is divided into two sources, depending on whether they correspond to trust created by a party of the transaction or a control mechanism.

The trust analysis in this framework is suited to the examination of a particular service offered by a system. It is also quite precise in that it considers a lot of trust issues, but those issues are specific to the kind of services examined in this work, namely business-to-business first trade situation. This approach is very rich in terms of the holistic view it provides into trust, but weak in terms of design features, as it is not aimed at this task.

Decompositional Model of Trust Used in System Design

Yan and Cofta (2003) define trust domains as areas of mobile communication where the definition of trust, which is a set of statements and goals, is common between the various elements. Gaps between these trust domains, implied by the subjectivity of the trust definitions, are bridged with particular components that are responsible for ensuring trust at a level above the one of the domains. The methodology is based on a graphical representation of entities, domains, and their interconnections, enabling a view of the system at a higher level of abstraction.

This methodology brings intuitiveness to system design and enables one to treat the trust issue at a variable level of granularity, but it lacks accurateness to express more specific properties and localized problems, and it does not provide clear guidelines to help the system designer understand the various trust issues. It is in particular unclear what the application of the methodology would bring to examples other than the one presented.

Holistic Analyses of Trust Relationships

In the context of virtual communities, Ishaya and Mundy (2004) indicate that the potential barriers to trust development and management are fivefold: sociological, psychological, technological, legal, economic. They develop mechanisms to support the provision of trust, summarized by three tables that present relevant questions to ask about the elements of trust, the trust building process, and the security factors.

Similarly, Grimsley and Meehan (Grimsley, Meehan, & Tan, 2004) consider trust from the perspective of Internet-mediated community relations and decompose it into various dimensions that are not necessarily orthogonal. The community trust compact and an experience management matrix described in this work are based on three dimensions, corresponding to the notions of information, control, and influence. These two conceptual tools are represented by tables guiding the design of the project under consideration.

These two works present a holistic view on trust mainly focused on the sociopsychological phenomenon, and where the subjective aspects of trust are captured by many concepts and notions expressed in long questions. These textual approaches at design are not satisfactory as they add a layer of subjectivity and are prone to errors. Furthermore, they are very difficult to apply to technical systems, as they mainly consider abstract properties of human systems.

Framework to Derive Trust Assumptions

Haley, Laney, Moffett, and Nuseibeh (2004) apply principles of requirements engineering to security systems with the goal of deriving trust assumptions during the system-level analysis. A graphical notation is used to define domains. Interfaces, phenomena, and constraints are described in context and problem frame diagrams. Constraints explored in this work are security requirements that help identify threats and vulnerabilities at the system-level. The constraints are completed by trust assumptions that help satisfy the security requirements and that specify the system designer's point of view on trust.

This approach provides powerful features for e-service design, but it considers trust in the technical sense, that is, implicit assumptions in the security model that need to be made explicit. The subjective, and thus holistic, nature of trust is not represented. Though apparently intuitive, the graphical notation can rapidly lead to cluttered diagrams that impede on an effective design.

The i* Graphical Design Framework

The *i** framework (Yu & Cysneiros, 2002; Yu & Liu, 2001) is a framework proposed to model nonfunctional requirements (privacy and security) in multiagent systems. A composite graph is used to represent the relationships between actors of a system. Relationships are of four types: goal, task, resource, and *softgoal* (goals that have no qualitative measure of satisfaction and are attached to graph edges). Trust relationships are expressed as softgoals. The strategic dependency (SD) and strategic rationale (SR) models enable one to view the system at various levels of abstraction. An *i** graph looks like a scenario annotated with interrelated keywords.

The *i** framework is interesting as it focuses on a user-centered scenario describing the e-service under consideration in its context of daily use, and uses intuitive graphical features to represent properties. But as illustrated in (Yu & Cysneiros 2002), *i** graphs can very quickly become unreadable, and thus unusable to the e-service designer.

Methods with a Formal Background

This section covers some methodologies that use formal methods to design and specify the electronic system. Computing science formal methods stem from mathematics and aim to help design, develop, analyze, and validate software so that it is correct, error-free, and robust. The formal dimension of these methodologies provides a basis for automated reasoning and tool support, thus greatly easing the work of the designer and opening the door for systematic analysis.

TROPOS

TROPOS (Giorgini, Massaci, Mylopoulos, & Zannone, 2004, 2005) is a graphical meth-odology for modeling and representing the various system dependencies with the aim of analyzing trust requirements in security properties of electronic systems. TROPOS extends the i^* framework (see previous section) by defining new concepts (actor, resource) and relationships (delegation, negative authorization) with the goal of focusing on trust. The diagrammatical notation is formalized into the logical language Datalog so that the specifi-cation can be checked automatically with software. A CASE tool has been devised to draw TROPOS diagrams and check its correctness.

TROPOS builds upon i^* and extends it with more precise security notions. It removes the disadvantage of needing to manage the complexity of its graph thanks to the formalization. On the other hand, this approach requires some knowledge of formal verification that may not be available in the design project.

CORAS

The CORAS methodology (Braendeland & Stolen, 2004; Vraalsen et al. 2005, pp. 45-60) implements risk assessment techniques using an extension of the UML semiformal method. The expressiveness of UML profile is extended conceptually by introducing normative modalities borrowed from deontic logics so that legal risks can be better specified. It cov-ers the risk dimension of trust, but does not explain any definition of trust. It requires and enables the system designer to use the definition most suited for his system. Various tools are available to use the methodology (Vraalsen et al., 2005, pp. 402-405) and a fully formal view of CORAS is under development.

The CORAS approach is close to software engineering as it uses the UML notation to model the system, and it bases its analysis on a scenario. In these scenarios, a hierarchy of assets describes trust that must be protected from threats, vulnerabilities, and incidents. Evaluating in detail the risks associated with the system under examination enables one to propose the solution to trust issues. The CORAS analysis methodology is partitioned into five subpro-cesses that are establish the context; identify risks; analyze risks; evaluate risks; treat risks. This sequence is completed by a monitoring and review process that runs in parallel and can restart the sequence of subprocesses.

Conclusion

A study of the existing works reveals that a decomposition of trust is central to any trust design methodology. General methodologies focus on a functional subset of properties, more well known and less subjective, except for holistic analyses of trust relationships (Grimsley et al., 2004; Ishaya & Mundy, 2004). But this limitation removes the holistic nature of trust, in that focusing on a subproperty while eluding to others transforms the issue from trust to a different concept (e.g., security, risk).

Most methodologies adopt an ad-hoc approach, without building on traditional design meth-odologies. This makes the tackling of the trust issue in e-service design more difficult and costly, and thus constitutes an impediment to the adoption of such methodologies in e-service development. While methodologies using a graphical representation bring intuitiveness to this task, it is quickly limited because of graph cluttering, though this can be improved as in TROPOS (Giorgini et al., 2004, 2005) and CORAS (Vraalsen et al., 2005, pp. 45-60; Vraalsen et al., 2005, pp. 402-405) via tool-support. This later methodology is based on traditional design methodologies (risk analysis, UML), but mainly focuses on risk. (Haley et al., 2004) is also based on existing requirements engineering methods.

Textual notations are not limited by the graphical notation and can express complex notions in a human-understandable way, but it is only useful to the designer if guided as in the matrix model, as long descriptions are prone to misinterpretations and difficult to use. Furthermore, these notations can easily be incorporated into existing design methodologies, without the need to modify the design process.

A Holistic Trust Design Phase

As seen in the previous section, it is still quite difficult to find an existing methodology able to help in designing e-services so as to make them globally trustworthy. It is particularly difficult in computing systems where the subjectivity induced by plain text English is in conflict with the operational nature of computing systems. This is made even more difficult in the context of emerging and changing technologies, where the level of abstraction is quite low and the focus is centered on the user.

We describe a holistic methodology to analyze trust during the design of a system that focuses on the system user and provides insight into the subjective nature of the system. This meth-odology can be seen as a holistic trust design phase that is added at the start of the system development. Many of the subjective facets of trust are captured by this methodology, as

Figure 1. The holistic trust design

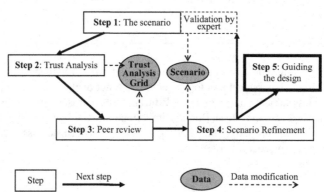

well as objective concepts that are more directly applicable to real-world applications. The holistic trust design phase is composed of five steps that are structured as shown in Figure 1. Each step of the holistic trust design is described in the following sections. We then illustrate the methodology on several examples.

Step 1: The Scenario

Because of the human-centric nature of trust and modern e-services, it is critically important that trust is explored from the user's perspective, rather than in terms of abstract concepts or security features, so as to appreciate the impact of particular trust issues on the users of the system. The holistic trust design phase reflects this imperative by working on *scenarios*. The scenarios form the foundations of the methodology, and their development and analysis provide a valuable holistic view of trust that can guide the design of the electronic system.

A *scenario* is a short, fictional narrative, set in the near future, that describes people's daily lives, concentrating on their use of e-services under examination. The scenarios are user-focused and usually avoid descriptions of how the technology works unless such descriptions clarify the users' interactions with the system.

It is important that the scenarios reflect the way in which people would use the e-services to support them in their daily lives, in order to fit the technology to the task rather than the opposite. It is critical that the scenarios are validated by subject-matter experts so that they plausibly depict people and processes within the application domain. This validation should be done, if possible, by a person external to the trust analysis and the system design, so that his/her opinion is not biased towards the technical environment proposed.

When writing scenarios, there is a trade-off between length and accuracy, but for the purpose of system development, scenarios should focus on a specific set of features provided by the systems. The writing of scenarios is thus eased, but this may limit the scope of the results, as a longer scenario can introduce interactions between elements that would be independent in smaller scenarios. Scenarios are living documents that will evolve during the process of trust analysis to meet the needs of the users and of the system designer. Their iterative development provides insight into the system and enables system designers to explore the various dimensions of their system.

Step 2: The Trust Analysis

The second step and foundation of the holistic trust design phase involves the *trust analysis grid*. A sketch of a trust analysis grid (TAG) is given in Table 1. The rows of the grid correspond to vignettes in the scenario. The columns of the grid correspond to categories of trust issues that will be checked against the vignettes.

These trust issue categories are also grouped into *trust issues group* for the sake of convenience (see next sections). This choice of rows and columns is particularly suited to the study of scenarios, as it enables the reviewer to follow the flow of narration vertically.

Table 1. Trust analysis grid

Vignette in the scenario	Trust Issue Categories										
	Data		System					Subjective			
	Source vs. Interpretation	Accuracy	Audit Trail	Authorization	Identification	Availability	Reliability	Personal Responsibility	Reasoning	Usability	Harm
First vignette	X			XX			Y		YYY		physical

Vignettes

Since scenarios are written in a narrative style, only certain sentences and pieces of sentences are of interest for analyzing the trust issues. A vignette corresponds to one or several pieces of one or several sentences of a scenario, and constitutes a cohesive group with regards to the trust issues. The pieces of sentence of interest to the trust analysis are indicated by formatting them in *italic*, the rest being pieces of the sentence that do not concern the trust analysis, but are displayed to ease the reading of the TAG. The various vignettes are examined in the order where they appear in the scenario.

Trust Issue Categories

A trust issue category corresponds to a specific property that represents one of the different facets of trust. They complement each other and are denoted by column labels in the TAG. These categories have been determined by successive analysis of various scenarios developed and a study of the state of the art on trust. We assume that the generalizations that we derived from the trust analysis are plausible because they have been derived from the user's interaction with the system represented in the plausible scenarios.

Each trust issue category denotes a facet of the notion of trust that is directly observed in a vignette, rather than being the consequence of such an observation. For example, the category *Source vs. Interpretation* generally may follow from the category *Reasoning*, though this latter observation is not directly observable in the scenario at that point. The eleven trust issue categories are:

- **Source vs. Interpretation:** An interpretation is data that has been obtained after the processing of other data (the source). The interpretation is generally less trusted than the source data itself.

- **Accuracy:** The level of detail of information determines how precisely trust can be evaluated in the system. The higher the accuracy, the more confident users will be that they can trust this particular part of the system.

- **Audit trails:** An audit trail lists all the actions performed, who performed them or gave permission to perform them, and the events occurring in the system. This information should not be modifiable, or at least a modification should be detected and recorded along with the previous version.

- **Authorization:** Any agent accessing a piece of information or requesting a service must have the permission from the system to do so, which in turn may require that the user has authorized it (or not denied it).

- **Identification:** Identity is important to differentiate the participants and communicate with one of them. On the other hand, this identity may be limited (e.g., pseudonym) in certain contexts in order to provide privacy.

- **Reliability:** This property indicates that a service operates according to its specification. Similarly, the property can refer to the integrity of the data produced by the service.

- **Availability:** Availability corresponds to the temporal constraints on a service that ensure that the flow of action in the system is not stopped for a period of time longer than expected.

- **Personal Responsibility:** The system cannot check everything, but some things people do will affect the system's trust. A person must remain responsible for the actions he/she performs, since they are not mediated by a trusted system. The property of accountability is important to put a significant level of trust in the system.

- **Reasoning:** Each participant manipulates the data to process it, in order to make decisions or answer a request. This process can weaken the trust another participant has in the system if this reasoning does not appear correct.

- **Usability:** This aspect of trust encompasses various elements, like the intrusiveness of the mechanisms used to interact with the user, or its usefulness. It is a crucial element of trust in computer systems as they can greatly impede the user. If a system is hard to use correctly, it may then be used incorrectly, and this will in turn reduce the trust.

- **Harm:** At the heart of trust is the notion of avoiding harm, since trust is a belief based on uncertain and approximate knowledge. It encompasses situations like loss of privacy (in the sense that personal data has been accessed against the will of its owner), breach of confidentiality, loss of financial assets, physical or emotional damage, and more generally, risk.

Trust Issues Groups

The trust issue categories are grouped together into groups that correspond to properties at a higher level of abstraction. They are only used to organize the trust issue categories according to their abstract similarities. The three trust issue groups are:

- **Subjective Categories**

  Trust issue categories: *Personal Responsibility, Reasoning, Usability, Harm*

  Trust is inherently subjective in that it reflects the point of view of the trustor. The subjective categories involve the agent's internal state and knowledge, and express its beliefs. They also provide part of the context that is used to interpret trust relationships.

- **System Categories**

  Trust issue categories: *Audit Trail, Authorization, Identification, Availability, Reliability*

  These categories relate to the underlying components and services of the computing system used in the scenario. This system may involve a physical device, a computer program, or a more general socioeconomic system.

- **Data Categories**

  Trust issue categories: *Source vs. Interpretation, Accuracy*

  These two categories describe the properties of the data from the point of view of trust.

Grid Cells Values

The TAG is populated with values that can be of various forms, each providing slightly different means to represent the trust issues. The grid cells of the TAG can contain:

- An **X** mark

X indicates that this particular trust issue applies in its general stance in this vignette; the marks **XX** and **XXX** indicate values that are *more*, or respectively *much more*, important as those marked with an **X** on the same row; on the other hand, **X** cell values are not comparable between different rows.

If in a given row, with four filled cells, one needs to relate two of them in terms of importance (for example **X** and **XX**) and also relate the two others, but independently from the first two, then one can use different letters **X** and **Y** for the two pairs of values. The second one could be for example **Y** and **YYY**.

- The name of a more precise issue

It is sometimes necessary to indicate more precisely which aspect of the trust issue category is involved in a given vignette. This is done by putting a word as a cell value. For example, the trust issue category *Harm* can be refined into **physical** or **financial**.

- A signed number

A natural number represents the scale of the trust issue for a given vignette, 1 being the least important (but still present, as 0 is not used and instead the cell is empty) and increasing values indicating more important occurrence of the trust issue. The number is preceded with a negative sign (-) to represent the fact the contribution of this vignette to the trust issue is negative, that is, it is an issue. On the contrary, a positive sign (+) is used to denote the fact that the vignette addresses the particular trust issue. Note that values corresponding to the trust issue category *Harm* are always negative.

Colors are also used to represent our judgment about the trust issues, as they emphasize that these judgments are subjective. Two colors, a light and a dark, are used to represent visually the convention expressed by the number sign. It can be used in conjunction with the number value, or alone to give more visual information.

Step 3: Peer Review

In the third step of the holistic trust design phase, the initial examination of trust issues in step 2 undergoes peer review and cross-checking. Peer review supports the extraction of trust issues from the perspective of another potential user, who may have a different view on trust issues. It may be thus the occasion to discover some missing trust issues by complementing the reviewer's point of view.

In practice, the peer review is a very useful exercise as it forces the reviewers to explain and clarify their trust analysis. The peer review is typically done during a meeting where the reviewers go through their TAGs and compare them. Since trust is a subjective matter, they may argue on whether or not a particular trust issue arises at one point of the scenario. This disagreement may mean that a choice between contradicting requirements must be made by the system designer.

Disagreements occurring during the peer review may also be the consequence of trust analyses made from the point of view of users of the system who have a different roles; for example, an end user and a system administrator. The trust analyses are not generally compatible due to contradictory requirements occurring between the roles, but the peer review ensures that the overall approach to analyzing the e-services is consistent.

Step 4: Scenarios Refinement

In the fourth step, scenarios are refined by adding new text and vignettes, or removing existing ones to address comments that have been made during the peer review. The purpose of the scenarios is to provide a framework that illustrates possible applications of the system, and to extract the most relevant trust issues. It is important that the scenarios reflect the trust concerns of all the stakeholders involved, and it should be updated to represent different priorities. However, these concerns evolve as the trust analysis progresses and makes explicit the various trust issues.

When scenarios are updated, the sequence of steps is then executed again. The updated scenarios are validated by the domain experts who first validated it (Step 1), another trust analysis is made (Step 2), a peer review is organized (Step 3), and the scenarios are possibly refined another time (Step 4). This sequence is iterated until reviewers and system designers believe that the scenarios cover all the functionalities of the system and the trust analyses depict in a satisfying fashion the understanding of the system.

Step 5: Guiding the Design of the System

The four previous steps provided some insight into the trust issues underpinning the systems, and are a means to explore the possible solutions provided by the system. In that sense, it follows the traditional design phase in software development based on use-cases. The last and final step of the holistic trust design phase consists in using the TAG to draw some guidelines in order to make design decisions.

Identifying Significant Areas

A simple visual examination of the TAG can give the system designer an overview of where the areas that are significant regarding trust are in the scenarios. Because of its visual nature and the fact that its vertical dimension corresponds to the sequential flow of a scenario, the TAG can be viewed as a map of the trust issues in the system under examination. The various *areas* of this map can give us some guidance on how to best design the system.

Firstly, we can decompose the TAG into three areas corresponding to the three groups of trust issue categories Subjective, System, and Data. This abstract typology of trust indicates the kind of expertise that is required for designing the system. A Subjective-group system may require a system designer with knowledge of social science and/or the law, and human-computer interface. A System-group system corresponds to a system where the infrastructure plays a central role and where a technical experts in e-services may best practice his/her abilities. A Data-group system may need to be designed by an expert in data management and processing and/or privacy and data usage.

Secondly, we can also examine each column of the TAG individually. The columns that are full indicate that the corresponding trust issue is predominating in the system. This means that the system components proposed to solve this trust issue category in the design are given special attention and that enough resources are devoted to them. Ideally, the trust issue categories that have the most cell values in the TAG should require an additional verification pass following the system design. This verification should be made in reverse order, so that the most full trust issue category is verified last, and should carefully check that these concerns are mitigated.

Thirdly, a row or a sequence of rows where a lot of cell values are present probably indicates a crucial point in the scenario. This corresponds to a part of the system that is critical regarding trust and where additional attention must be paid. Another subscenario may be created to describe, in more precise terms, how the user interacts with the system and the system behavior, and then a new trust analysis can be run. Following the system design, this point in the scenario must be verified thoroughly.

Matching Technologies Against Scenarios

Rather than using the previous guidelines, one can try to analyze the TAG in a more systematic way to draw some more precise conclusions. Though it is not easy because of the subjective nature of the trust issues that are represented, it can still shed an interesting light on the design issues and, in particular, its technical feasibility. As the purpose of our approach is to help in the design of e-services, any means to understand how best to do this is beneficial to the e-service designer.

In order to introduce the technological elements into the holistic trust design, a TAG of the various common technologies and techniques used in modern e-services is used. An example of such a technology TAG is presented in Table 2. We then have two TAGs: one corresponding to the scenario and the other one to the technologies. The suitability of a particular technology at a given point (sequence of vignettes) in the scenario is given in terms of how close its pattern (a row of 11 cell values) matches the area corresponding to this point in the TAG of the scenario.

This pattern-matching technique differs from the previous heuristic method in that it relates the informal analyses of scenarios and the technologies, and provides a point of anchorage for a more formal approach. As a scenario and its TAG are refined through the iterative sequence of steps of the holistic trust design, the technology TAG is completed to match the system's technological needs.

Examples

We describe here three examples of concrete applications of the holistic trust design phase that will help to understand it and demonstrate its usefulness. For the sake of brevity, some stories have been truncated and unnecessary elements were removed. The trust analysis is presented in the form of the trust analysis grid, using various cell value formats for the different scenarios. Step 3 of the holistic trust design phase is not discussed for the sake of conciseness.

E-Healthcare

We present a scenario in the context of e-healthcare. In this futuristic but realistic scenario, various police and health workers collaborate on a crash scene. The scenario actors are performing their work and duties using computer devices and e-services to improve the patient treatment.

Table 2. Technology TAG

| Technology | Trust Issue Categories | | | | | | | | | | |
| | Data | | System | | | | | Subjective | | | |
	Source vs. Interpretation	Accuracy	Audit Trail	Authorization	Identification	Availability	Reliability	Personal Responsibility	Reasoning	Usability	Harm
Wireless Network			X	X	X	X	X	X		X	X
Grid Computing				X	X	X	X		X	X	X
Peer-to-Peer Network			X	X	X	X		X			X
Sensors	X	X		X		X		X		X	
Data Records	X		X		X	X		X	X		X
Network Traffic	X	X					X			X	
Audio and Video Data	X	X		X			X	X		X	
Speech Data	X	X					X		X	X	
Pads				X				X	X	X	
Location and Context		X							X		
HUDs										X	X
Personal Agents	X	X	X			X		X	X	X	
Service Agents		X	X		X	X	X		X		
Encryption						X					
Digital Signatures				X				X			
Authorization Mechanism			X		X	X	X	X			
Authentication		X		X	X		X			X	
Time Limited Leases			X	X	X	X	X	X		X	
Domain-based Security				X	X					X	

The Scenario

Neil is driving to work when suddenly, brake lights flare and Neil is jolted alert. There seems to be a wall of slowing cars and smoke is pouring from the wheels of the car in front. Neil's car was too close to avoid a collision. As the motorway grinds to a halt, it appears that three cars have crashed. Other motorists have managed to avoid the initial accident on both sides, but some have had minor collisions.

The emergency services already know much of the situation. As soon as the cars' airbags were triggered by the crash, the cars transmitted a distress call, including their location (given by the navigation systems) and the number of occupants (detected by simple pressure sensors in the seats). The first car's phone was too badly damaged to transmit its call, but for 999 calls it was able to piggyback on the phone of the second car using short-range networking.

The emergency control room dispatches a small number of police, fire, and ambulance vehicles immediately. The incoming calls from other motorists, and images from a traffic camera on a nearby bridge, seem to confirm the seriousness of the accident, and further vehicles are dispatched. The controller also sends an incident support vehicle to assist with clearup. The information known so far is shared between all of the vehicles en route. Information on traffic flow and speed is also shared between the vehicles to enable them to avoid blocked or slow routes. The dispatch and arrival of the vehicles is logged automatically to provide statistics on response times.

The traffic police are first on scene, and begin making the area safe as best they can. The video feed from their speed camera is available to the control room, but at low bandwidth. A still image is shared with the vehicles en route though. The police confirm the number of vehicles involved, and the number of casualties. They quickly take a few evidential photos of the scene, and begin basic first responder treatment. These photos are shared with the en route vehicles and the hospitals.

Neil is awake now. One of the policemen is trying to hand him over to the first paramedic on scene, but the policeman is told to keep holding Neil's head still while the paramedic triages the other casualties. He informs the ambulances and the control room of his findings by radio. The control room enters this information into the log for the incident, which is shared with the receiving hospitals.

The ambulances are arriving on scene and, after checking with the firefighters that the scene is secure, the paramedics continue treatment. They record their assessment and treatment onto normal paper report forms, but these are backed by smart clipboards that record and recognize the handwriting and ticked boxes, and can forward that information, if required. Each patient is given an RFID tag, normally on a wristband, to enable the incident records to follow them around the system.

Neil seems to be relatively unhurt, but is immobilized with a cervical collar and board until spinal injury can be ruled out. The spinal board, sadly, doesn't have any sensors yet, but it does have an embedded RFID tag to identify which ambulance organization it belongs to. The firefighters are busy cutting up the car in front, and one of them is taking a few quick photos with his helmet camera for the incident support crew, to give them some idea of the scene.

Trust Analysis

We present in Table 3 the TAG for the scenario described previously. Due to the high number of actors and situations described, the TAG is quite big, but it could be split into smaller TAGs if necessary.

An interesting vignette in this scenario with regards to the technologies envisaged in pervasive systems is the *piggybacking* of the first car's phone. In this situation, the *piggybacking* implies that the phone call does not originate from the *source* and that some sort of *authorization* system enabled the first car's phone to use the resources of an unknown car around it. The *availability* of this technology is here paramount, but on the other hand could

Table 3. TAG of the e-healthcare scenario

Vignette in the scenario	Data		System					Subjective			
	Source vs. Interpretation	Accuracy	Audit Trail	Authorization	Identification	Availability	Reliability	Personal Responsibility	Reasoning	Usability	Harm
three cars have *crashed*		X									X
motorists have *managed to avoid* the ... accident	X		X					X			
minor collisions		X									
emergency services already know *much of* the situation		X						X			X
the cars *transmitted* a distress call			X			X	X				
piggyback on the phone of the second car	X			X		X					X
emergency control room *dispatches...* vehicles			X						X		
the *seriousness* of the accident		X									
The information known so far is *shared*				X		X		X			
The dispatch and arrival of the vehicles is *logged*			X			X					
traffic police are *first* on scene			X					X			
making the area *safe*											X
The *video feed...* at *low bandwidth*	X	X	X			X					X
the *number* of vehicles involved, and the *number* of casualties		X	X				X				
evidential photos of the scene	X		X				X	X			
begin *basic first responder treatment*				X				X			
These photos are *shared*	X			X		X	X				
the paramedic *triages* the other casualties							X		X		
enters this information into the *log*			X			X					X
shared with the receiving hospitals	X			X		X	X				
the scene is *secure*											X
normal paper report forms	X									X	
smart clipboards that *record* and *recognize* the handwriting and ticked boxes, and can *forward* that information	X		X	X			X		X		

Table 3. continued

RFID tag				X					X	X
the incident records	X		X							
The spinal board, sadly, doesn't have any *sensors* …		X			X	X				
… but it does have an embedded RFID tag				X					X	X

lead to abuses (*harm*) if the call serves other purposes than emergency. All other trust issue categories were not represented here.

Guiding the Design

This long scenario was part of the bunch of scenarios that helped devise the design methodology and improve the trust analysis grid by going through several rounds of analysis. Though realistic and validated by a first aider, the system was not designed and developed further. The scenario is here to illustrate the first steps of the holistic trust design phase, but design and development are not part of the requirements.

The scenario and TAG enable to look at the system and services from two different viewpoints, thus separating functionalities from properties. For example, the scenario made use of technologies not yet fully implemented (pervasive network, RFID), but providing the right functionalities and the TAG lead to hard requirements on these technologies (availability, harm).

Theme Park

This scenario is set in the context of a pervasive theme park, named Vaughn Park, that is fully equipped with pervasive computers that provide e-services to the customers. Park tickets are embedded with location technology (e.g., wi-fi, RFID that enable to provide context-dependent services. The focus of this scenario is a virtual queuing system where users can queue for a ride and play a treasure hunt game that will guide them to the ride.

This scenario contains a hypothetical part (between brackets) that illustrates the expressive power of the holistic trust design, where various design branches can be explored by adding optional features and situations.

The Scenario

Janet and John are having a great time at Vaughn Park, but now that they have been on all the rides they wanted to, except for Hubris, which has a long queue, they are beginning to get a little bored. They and their parents have joined Hubris' queue, but there is an estimated wait of over an hour until they'll be able to ride. Their parents suggest that they try one of the pervasive games the park offers.

The information kiosk can tell that they're waiting for Hubris, and it also knows that Janet and John have been on many of the rides that are likely to interest them, so it thinks that the Treasure Hunt game is a good candidate for them. Indeed it is, so they choose to play the game.

The first clue is a simple one: "Can you find a big squirrel?" (If they weren't old enough to be reading yet, they could be given picture-only clues, but only if their parents played along with them.) Janet remembers that there is a squirrel on one of the merry-go-rounds in the green area.

When they find the merry-go-round they go up to an information kiosk. The kiosk knows they are playing Treasure Hunt, and that they are looking for a big squirrel. The one on the merry-go-round isn't the one it had in mind, so it displays a message saying "Good try! But this one isn't big enough; can you find a bigger one? It's quite close!"

John notices a topiary cat on the other side of the merry-go-round, and wonders whether there might be some more topiary nearby.

What a surprise! There is the squirrel, sculpted in the hedging. And neither of them had noticed it at all when they were on the merry-go-round! The nearby kiosk congratulates them warmly, and asks them to find a big cleaning implement. They don't really know what to look for, so they don't move. The kiosk gives them a bigger clue: "who might use a cleaning implement, but not necessarily for cleaning?" That's it! Off they go, to the haunted house, which has a witch!

After successfully solving several more clues, the final clue leads them to Hubris, where they find their parents waiting. Their ride is great, and they go home afterwards talking very fast with a lot of excitement about the great day out.

Trust Analysis

Before we give the TAG in Table 4, we detail the analysis of one vignette of the scenario. This vignette is when the children do not understand what they should be looking for, and the kiosk gives them a clue. The piece of sentence of interest here is the *bigger clue*. It is a *usability* feature, as it will make the Treasure Hunt game more usable to the children. It also requires the system to *reason* about the situation, for example, detect that the children are waiting for a clue because they are not standing in front of the kiosk. The input of this process is the activity of the children they are standing in front, which is their *personal responsibility*, while the output is a clue, which should *reliably* help the children. The other categories do not apply to this piece of sentence of interest.

Table 4. TAG of the theme park scenario

Vignette in the scenario	Data		System					Subjective			
	Source vs. Interpretation	Accuracy	Audit Trail	Authorization	Identification	Availability	Reliability	Personal Responsibility	Reasoning	Usability	Harm
estimated wait of over an hour		time									
The information kiosk *can tell…*									X		
… that *they* are waiting					X	X		X			
it also *knows* that Janet and John have been			X						XX		
rides that are *likely* to interest them	XX							X	XX		
So the system *thinks* that			X						XX		
they *choose* to play the game			X						X		
If they were not old enough to be reading yet, they could be given picture-only clues, but only if their parents played along with them								XX	X	XX	X
The kiosk *knows* they are playing Treasure Hunt					X			X	X		
the one it had *in mind …*				X					X		
… so it *displays* a message								X		X	X
The nearby kiosk *congratulates them warmly*					X			X	X	X	
They *don't really know* what to look for								X			X
The kiosk gives them *a bigger clue*							X	X	X	X	
the final clue leads them to Hubris				X				X	X	X	

Guiding the Design

We first notice that the TAG is mostly filled with trust issues from the group *Subjective*. This is explained by the fact that the pervasive theme park is a closed environment and this greatly simplifies the security requirements. Furthermore, the services provided are not data-intensive. This indicates that the application described in the scenario is a quite subtle application, what corresponds to intuition that it is user-friendly, and that the emphasis should be put on the perception of the system by the user during the design.

From the point of view of individual trust issue categories, *Personal Responsibility* and *Reasoning* are the ones that are most filled. The first category corresponds to the fact that the user has the total freedom to walk around the pervasive theme park during the game and he/she is responsible for his/her actions when looking for the clues, while the system is not interacting with him/her. The second category underlines the fact that the game corresponds to a hunt and must be adapted to the way the user performs it. To make the application more trustworthy, the user expects the system to act with him/her in a way consistent with the status of the hunt. The system designer shall include inference and proactive capabilities of good quality.

Finally, no row distinguishes itself from the others, notably due to the overall importance and continuous presence of trust issues from the *Subjective* group. This may be explained by the fact that the application is focused on the user whose mobility avoids concentrating the system capabilities into one particular part of the scenario.

E-Learning

This last example describes uses of an e-learning application named ShowNTalk. This commercial application allows pupils to create and show presentations on PDAs, and is aimed at improving the reading, writing, presentational, and IT skills of primary school pupils. The scenario served as a basis for the implementation of its first prototype, while the TAG helped in identifying the trust issues and improving the application.

The Scenario

Liz, a primary school teacher, has decided to assign her class of pupils an assignment to do on their PDA's. The children will prepare a multimedia presentation on the different types of cloud formations, working individually on their PDA's.

After creating an introductory slide about clouds on his PDA, Sam notices his geography book has a chapter on cloud formations. Sam uses the PDA to take a picture of a page in a book that has a picture of a cumulus cloud and some text describing it. He uses the voice annotation feature to record himself reading aloud the text on the page. He later finds a page in the same book about stratus clouds but there's no picture, so he uses the stylus on the PDA to input the text from the book and adds a voice recording of the text. When looking outside, Sam spots a cirrus cloud in the sky and goes outside to use the camera function to take a picture of the cloud and add some text using the stylus.

Later in the day, the pupils present their work to their teacher using the slideshow option in the software. The software automatically scrolls through the slides, showing the pictures and text whilst playing any audio files present with each. Liz asks each pupil to upload their work to the server.

After her pupils have gone home Liz reviews some of the presentations, starting with Sam's. She checks Sam's previous work on the server and notices a comment saying that his reading needed some work. From his latest presentation, she notices that his reading of the text on many of the slides is much better, so she adds a comment to the presentation stored on the server.

Table 5. TAG of the e-learning scenario

Vignette in the scenario	Trust Issue Categories										
	Data			System				Subjective			
	Source vs. Interpretation	Accuracy	Audit Trail	Authorization	Identification	Availability	Reliability	Personal Responsibility	Reasoning	Usability	Harm
Liz gives assignment to pupils											
Sam takes picture of page in book											
Sam records himself reading text from book											
Sam copies text from book into PDA using stylus											
Sam takes pictures of cirrus cloud											
Sam adds text to slide about cirrus cloud											
Sam uses slideshow options											
Sam uploads work to server											
Liz reviews some presentations											
Liz checks Sam's previous work on server											
Liz notices a comment											
Liz adds a comment											

Trust Analysis

The following TAG in Table 5 uses a light color for issues that need to be addressed and a dark color for those are addressed.

Guiding the Design

The trust analysis reveals various strengths and weaknesses of the system with regard to trust. On the positive side, the trust issue categories *Availability*, *Reliability*, and *Usability* are well addressed. This shows that the application depicted in the scenario is user-friendly, as these trust issue categories are among the ones that are perceived directly by the user.

The TAG shows that the ShowNTalk application has several limitations in the areas of *Identification* and *Authorization*, two security properties. For example, there is no way to record which pupil is using a given PDA, or whether the pupil is entitled to synchronize his work with the school's server. The trust analysis shows clearly that addressing these two trust issue categories should reduce greatly the number of trust issues in the system (at least from the point of view of this scenario, which is representative of the system use). This analysis result led the development team to introduce a login system on the PDA and an access control list on the server. The prototype tests showed that this design improved the trustworthiness of the prototype, and that this was overall a good design decision, as it was focused on a specific part of the system and used standard security components.

The introduction of these security components in the system affects the *Usability* issue, which needs to be addressed in the next version of the application, notably by improving the GUI and considering HCI aspects of the application. This is a more traditional aspect of the design that can now be considered separately from the holistic trust design.

Future Trends

As trust and e-services get more pervasive in computing systems, reliance on them will increase too, and understanding the various aspects composing trust will be as important as mastering how these aspects are composed. As each aspect of trust gets more and more diverse and complex (Jøsang et al., 2005), design will be particularly important in order to ensure the trustworthiness of whole systems. This trend should follow the general trend in the software industry to try to address significant issues as early as possible during the development process.

The subjective side of trust encompasses, at the moment, the facets of trust that are understood the least; for example, usability (see Bottoni, Costabile, Levialdi, Matera, & Mussio, 2000) for a rare example, and the law. These topics will get more attention as trust is better understood by researchers and developers, and this trend will increase as more applications will use trust and users will have to consider this issue more often.

While independent aspects of trust are better understood (dynamics, risk, etc.), the study of their combination will become critical. Standardization efforts will help in introducing some coherence in the field, as well as activities proposing to compare the various propositions like the agent reputation and trust testbed (ART Testbed, 2006).

Security is a growing concern nowadays, as vulnerabilities become more difficult to find and threats cause increasing damages. In many ways, trust is tied to security, though this relationship is not well understood yet. Anderson (2001) highlights the need for security usability, while the 14th International Workshop on Security Protocols (, 2006) proposes to "put the human back in the protocol" because he is "directly aware of the security requirement, or has access to the correct system state at the outer level of abstraction." This later aspect is reminiscent of the holistic nature of trust.

Conclusion

If modern e-services are to be successful, compelling applications will not be enough to make it enter people's daily lives. More efforts are needed to both find a suitable way to implement it and to make it trustworthy. Trust is a key notion in these systems. It supports both a better understanding of the system by the user, and a better representation of the user's needs and concerns, since it is a concept inspired by a human notion.

Many, in recent years, proposed ways to address part of the trust issue, but few tried to tackle the problem from a holistic point of view, where the various parts are put in the perspective of real systems. The holistic nature of trust is difficult to capture, as well as its subjective nature. Firstly, the issue has to be tackled early during the development cycle so as to think about the system as a whole rather than concentrate on its parts. Secondly, scenarios, or use-cases, are intuitive and powerful means to explore the system ideas by putting them in the context of its use. Lastly, guidelines should be provided on the various facets of trust issues, rather than imposing a particular definition of trust. An important point here is that they should guide the system designers at an adequate level of abstraction.

Many methodologies exist, but most do not address these requirements as they tackle specific aspects of trust or are difficult to apply to the design of concrete e-services. They put on the system designer the responsibility of bringing together the various parts that can be gathered from the different methodologies.

On the contrary, the previous requirements are addressed by the holistic trust design presented in this chapter: as it is a process preceding the system design, it centers on scenarios, and the trust analysis grid guides the designer during the analysis of the system. The holistic trust design phase is based on five steps, and revolves around the scenarios and the TAG by iterating the steps until a stable design of the system is achieved from the point of view of trust. By focusing on domain expert-validated scenarios, the design phase stays close to the user concerns that are crucial to achieve trustworthiness. By providing an abstract decomposition of trust that covers a wide range of topics, it helps the system designer to identify the trust issues and to try to mitigate them in subsequent rounds of trust analysis.

References

Anderson, R. (2001). *A guide to building dependable distributed systems*. John Wiley and Sons.

ART Testbed. (2006). Retrieved March 25, 2006, from http://www.lips.utexas.edu/art-testbed

Bottoni, P., Costabile, M. F., Levialdi, S., Matera, M., & Mussio, P. (2000). Trusty interaction in visual environments. In *Proceedings of the 6th ERCIM Workshop USER INTERFACES FOR ALL (UI4ALL)*, Florence, Italy (pp. 263-277).

Braendeland, G., & Stolen, K. (2004). Using risk analysis to assess user trust. In *Proceedings of the Second International iTrust Conference* (LNCS 2995, pp. 146-160). Oxford, UK: Springer.

eBay. (2006). Retrieved March 25, 2006, from http://www.ebay.com

Fourteenth International Workshop on Security Protocols. (2006, March 27-29). Retrieved March 25, 2006, from http://homepages.feis.herts.ac.uk/~strrjh/SP2006

Giorgini, P., Massaci, F., Mylopoulos, J., & Zannone, N. (2004). Requirements engineering meets trust management. In *Proceedings of the Second International iTrust Conference* (LNCS 2995, pp. 176-190). Oxford, UK: Springer.

Giorgini, P., Massaci, F., Mylopoulos, J., & Zannone, N. (2005). Modelling social and individual trust in requirements engineering methodologies. In *Proceedings of the Third International iTrust Conference* (LNCS 3477, pp. 161-176). Paris, France: Springer.

Grandison, T., & Sloman, M. (2000). A survey of trust in Internet applications. *IEEE Communications Surveys and Tutorials, 3*(4), 2-16.

Grimsley, M., Meehan, A., & Tan, A. (2004). Managing Internet-mediated community trust relations. In *Proceedings of the Second International iTrust Conference* (LNCS 2995, pp. 277-290). Oxford, UK: Springer.

Haley, C., Laney, R., Moffett, J., & Nuseibeh, B. (2004). Picking battles: The impact of trust assumptions on the elaboration of security requirements. In *Proceedings of the Second International iTrust Conference* (LNCS 2995, pp. 347-354). Oxford, UK: Springer.

Hanssens, N., Kulkarni, A., Tuchinda, R., & Horton, T. (2002). Building agent-based intelligent workspaces. In *Proceedings of the International Conference on Internet Computing, IC'2002* (Vol. 3, pp. 675-681). Las Vegas, NV: CSREA Press.

Huandg, C., Ling, B. C., & Ponnekanti, S. (1999). Pervasive computing—what is it good for? In *Proceedings of the ACM International Workshop on Data Engineering for Wireless and Mobile Access*, Seattle, WA (pp. 84-91).

Ishaya, T., & Mundy, D. (2004). Trust development and management in virtual communities. In *Proceedings of the Second International iTrust Conference* (LNCS 2995, pp. 266-276). Oxford, UK: Springer.

Jones, S., & Morris, P. (1999, April 8-9). TRUST-EC: Requirements for trust and confidence in commerce: Report of the workshop held in Luxembourg. *European Communities EUR Report, 2*.

Jøsang, A., Ismail, R., & Boyd, C. (2005). A survey of trust and reputation systems for online service provision. *Decision Support Systems, (to appear)*.

McKnight, D. H., & Chervany, N. L. (1996). *The meanings of trust*. (Tech. Rep. No. 96-04, MISRC Working Paper Series): University of Minnesota, Management Information Systems Research Center.

Rindeback, C., & Gustavsson, R. (2004). Why trust is hard—challenges in e-mediated services. In *Proceedings of the 7th International Workshop on Trust in Agent Societies* (LNCS 3577, pp. 180-199). New York: Springer.

Slashdot. (2006). Retrieved March 25, 2006, from http://slashdot.org

Staab, S., Bhargava, B., Lilien, L., Rosenthal, A., Winslett, M., & Sloman, M. (2004). The pudding of trust. *IEEE Intelligent Systems Journal, 19*(5), 74-88.

Storey, N. (1996). *Safety-critical computer systems.* Addison-Wesley.

Tan, J., Titkov, L., & Poslad, S. (2002). Securing agent-based e-banking services. In *Trust, Reputation, and Security: Theories and Practice (AAMAS 2002 International Workshop)* (LNAI 2631, pp. 148-162): Springer.

Tan, Y. H. (2003). A trust matrix model for electronic commerce. In *Proceedings of the First International iTrust Conference* (LNCS 2692, pp. 33-45). Crete, Greece: Springer.

Vraalsen, F., Braber, F., Lund, M., & Stolen, K. (2005). The CORAS tool for security risk analysis. In *Proceedings of the Third International iTrust Conference* (LNCS 3477, pp. 402-405). Paris: Springer.

Vraalsen, F., Lund, M., Mahler, T., Parent, X., & Stolen, K. (2005). Specifying legal risk scenarios using the CORAS threat modelling language. In *Proceedings of the Third International iTrust Conference* (LNCS 3477, pp. 45-60). Paris: Springer.

Yan, Z., & Cofta, P. (2003). Methodology to bridge different domains of trust in mobile communications. In *Proceedings of the First International iTrust Conference* (LNCS 2692, pp. 211-224). Crete, Greece: Springer.

Yu, E., & Cysneiros, L. (2002). Designing for privacy in a multi-agent world. In *Trust, Reputation, and Security: Theories and Practice (AAMAS 2002 International Workshop)* (LNAI 2631, pp. 209-223). Springer.

Yu, E., & Liu, L. (2001). Using the *i** strategic actors framework. In *Trust in Cyber-Societies, Integrating the Human and Artificial Perspectives* (LNAI 2246, pp. 175-194): Springer.

Chapter VI

Two-Layer Models for Managing Distributed Authenticity and Trust

Rolf Haenni, University of Berne & Berne University of Applied Sciences, Switzerland

Jacek Jonczy, University of Berne, Switzerland

Reto Kohlas, University of Berne, Switzerland

Abstract

This chapter describes the difficulty of managing authenticity and trust in large open networks. Participants of such networks are usually unknown to each other. Questioning somebody's authenticity and trustworthiness is thus a natural reflex and an important security prerequisite. The resulting problem of properly managing authenticity and trust is an emerging research topic. The chapter proposes a common conceptual framework and compares it to several existing authenticity and trust models. The goal is to increase the awareness that authenticity and trust are not separable and to promote the corresponding two-layer requirement.

Introduction

The past few years have seen a remarkable growth of computer networks. This development is driven by many new groundbreaking applications such as electronic mail, online auctions, peer-to-peer file sharing, electronic commerce, VoIP phoning, online banking, electronic voting, virtual discussion groups, chat rooms, online dating, and many more. Most of these applications run on *open networks*, most notably on the *Internet* or on corresponding subnetworks thereof. These networks are mostly characterized by a large and dynamic group of geographically widespread participants, who often stay anonymous or use pseudonyms or nicknames. The large size and the anonymity of such networks imply that most participants do not know each other in person. This is a fundamental source of many severe security problems, and it raises the important question of *trust* relative to a potential communication partner. In the context of open networks and with respect to an unknown network participant X, trust has at least two facets:

- **Identity trust:** Is X the person (s)he claims to be?
- **Reliability trust:** Will X be a reliable service provider, business partner, customer, etc.?

Identity trust is particularly important if the transmitted information is confidential, for example in electronic mails. Confidentiality is usually achieved by means of cryptographic techniques such as public-key encryption, but it is only guaranteed as long as authentic public keys are used. The problem of establishing identity trust is thus closely related to the problem of public-key authentication. In this chapter, we will refer to it as the *authenticity problem*. Authentic public keys are also a prerequisite for achieving data integrity by means of digital signatures.

Reliability trust is not primarily related to the transmitted information between two network participants, but rather to the commercial or interpersonal transaction that comes afterwards. The winner of an online auction, for example, is interested in promptly receiving the auctioned item from the seller. His primary concern is the quality of the service offered; the seller's identity is secondary. The seller has a similar view, as the main concern is receiving a prompt payment, independently of the buyer's identity. These views are typical for most electronic commerce relationships between a seller and a buyer. Similar views have the users of peer-to-peer networks, where not revealing the identity (i.e. to stay anonymous) is even a desirable property. In this chapter, reliable network participants will be called *trustworthy*, and the problem of judging somebody's trustworthiness is simply the *trust problem*.

Network participants, who know each other in person or from dealing with each other in the past, may have a direct basis to judge themselves authentic and/or trustworthy. This is what we call *direct authenticity* and *direct trust*, respectively, which is based on their first-hand experience. In general, that is, between unknown network participants without mutual first-hand experience, the only way to establish authenticity and trust is by means of direct statements from third parties. The most prominent examples of such third-party statements are *certificates*, *recommendations*, and *ratings*. A certificate approves the authenticity of somebody's public key. Recommendations and ratings are similar, but they usually refer to somebody's trustworthiness. Certificates, recommendations, and high ratings are *positive* statements, whereas low ratings are *negative* statements. As a general term for any type of such third-party statements, we follow the suggestion of Jonczy and Haenni (2005, 2006), and call them *credentials*.

A collection of credentials forms the *evidence*, from which indirect authenticity and trust is derivable. One can think of a credential as a bit string or a digital file representing the statement made by the issuer. To make credentials resistant against forgeries, it is crucial to *digitally sign* them. This is what we call *digital signature requirement*. It requires the issuer of a statement to possess a public/private key pair. The (secret) private key is necessary to generate the signature, whereas the (nonsecret) public key is distributed to allow the signature to be verified. If a signature is successfully verified with a given public key, it means that the credential was definitely issued by the holder of the corresponding private key. The remaining problem then is to verify the authenticity of the public key, for which further credentials are necessary. Establishing authenticity and trust is therefore a recursive problem of verifying corresponding credentials. This implies that the authenticity and trust problems are interrelated.

The main message of this chapter is that any attempt to separate the authenticity and trust problems is futile. One hand washes the other: authenticity depends on trust, and trust depends on authenticity. A formal model should therefore have (at least) two trust *layers*, one for authenticity (identity trust) and one for trust (reliability trust). This is what we call a *two-layer requirement*. Such models are generally called *multilayer models* (or *two-layer models* if the number of layers is restricted to these two). We will give an overview of existing one-layer and two-layer models. Special attention will be given to *credential networks*, a two-layer model that includes many other (one- and two-layer) models as special cases.

Basic Definitions and Terminology

This section is an attempt to build up a common conceptual framework for the subsequent discussion of various one- and two-layer models. In its essence, the approach is similar to the *abstract trust model* described in Mahoney, Myrvold, and Shoja (2005), but the discussion will be more detailed and formally more precise. The most important concepts are *authenticity* and *trust*. Both of them are related to *entities* and *identities*.

Entities and Identities

Entity is the general term commonly used for persons, agents, systems, groups, organizations, and so forth. If an entity acts in a computer network, it is also called *participant* or *user*. Entities are the principal objects of trust relationships. We will look at situations where a *local* entity tries to derive indirect trust relative to a *remote* entity. The necessary evidence usually stems from *intermediate* entities. Local entities are sometimes called *owner* (of the evidence). Formally, the set of all available and relevant entities will be denoted by **E**. Entities may have some computational power, for example, for the encryption and decryption of messages. In the context of this chapter, we require each entity $E \in \mathbf{E}$ to be linked to a unique *identifier*, that is, an unambiguous name, description, or list of attributes of the entity. The unambiguity of these identifiers allows us to use symbols like E simultaneously as the identifier of an entity and for the real-world entity itself. In other words, a distinction between entities and their unique identifiers is no longer necessary, and this allows us to use these concepts interchangeably.

An *identity* is a label or a description used to refer to an entity (Mahoney et al., 2005). Typical examples of identities are pseudonyms, e-mail addresses, public keys, fingerprints (of public keys), PINs, and so forth, or combinations of them. Note that an entity may have several identities, for example, several e-mail addresses, but a given identity is usually assumed to unambiguously belong to a single entity. This latter requirement often disqualifies simple names as adequate identities. Mathematically, the connection between entities and identities is thus a *one-to-many* relationship. In the context of this chapter, we require the identities to include exactly one public key, whereas other elements such as nicknames or e-mail addresses are optional. The reason for this is the above-mentioned digital signature requirement, which will be discussed more profoundly in one of the following subsections. To keep the formal setting as simple as possible, we will denote both the set of possible public keys and the set of possible identities by $\mathbf{K}$. Accordingly, we will use the concepts of public keys and identities interchangeably.

The main difference between unique identifiers and multiple identities is the idea that entities may create their own identities, while their unique identifiers are supposed to be globally determined and therefore not self-assigned. In the case of a given identity, this poses the problem of authenticity, that is, the question of whether the identity belongs to a certain entity or not. The set of all identities belonging to an entity E will be denoted by $\mathbf{K}_E \subseteq \mathbf{K}$.

Authenticity

Within the conceptual framework of this chapter, *authenticity* is related to the validity of a binding between an identity (or a public key) and an entity. The verification of such a binding is called *authentication*. Our convention to include exactly one public key in each identity allows us to call a binding *authentic*, whenever the entity in the binding is in possession of the matching private key. In such a case, it is sometimes convenient to talk about authentic (or valid) public keys rather than authentic bindings. Formally, the set of all possible entity/identity bindings is given by the Cartesian product $\mathbf{B} = \mathbf{E} \times \mathbf{K}$, and the set of authentic bindings is a subset $\mathrm{A}ut \subseteq \mathbf{B}$.

Authentication means thus to verify whether a given binding $(E, K) \in \mathbf{B}$ is an element of $\mathrm{A}ut$ or not. This is the same as to prove the truth of a proposition $\mathrm{A}ut(E, K)$, which holds whenever entity E is in possession of a matching private key (relative to the public key included in $\mathbf{K}$). This is the formal definition of the *authenticity problem* mentioned in the introduction. Another view is to look at $\mathrm{A}ut$ as an indicator function $\mathrm{A}ut: \mathbf{B} \rightarrow \{0,1\}$. The use of the indicator function underlines that authenticity is always *absolute*, that is, the set $\Omega_A = \{0,1\}$ of so-called *authenticity values* is restricted to 0 (not authentic) and 1 (authentic). We will see next that this restriction is one of the diverging characteristics between authenticity and trust.

Trustworthiness

Trust is a relationship between two entities, whereas *trustworthiness* is a property of a single entity. It is possible to first formalize trust and then derive trustworthiness from it, but our primary focus here is on trustworthiness. Both trust and trustworthiness are *trust scope* or *subject-matter* specific and *time-dependent*, that is, an entity K may be trustworthy with respect to scope S at time t, but not with respect to another scope S' or at another time t'. A trust scope limits thus the application of trust to a specific purpose or domain of action, such as being a reliable seller or buyer in the context of online auctions (Jøsang, Ismail, & Boyd, 2006). In the following, we will focus on trust scopes and not further discuss the aspect of time. Let the set of all possible trust scopes be denoted by **S**. This allows us to express a situation where an entity $E \in \mathbf{E}$ is considered trustworthy with respect to a scope $S \in \mathbf{S}$ by $Trust_S(E)$.

Trust and trustworthiness can be *absolute* or *gradual*. In the absolute case, we may look at $Trust_S(E)$ as a proposition that is either true or false (like the propositions $Aut(E, K)$ in the previous subsection). For each trust scope $S \in \mathbf{S}$, this defines a corresponding subset $Trust_S \subseteq \mathbf{E}$ of trustworthy entities. Generally, there is no connection between the sets $Trust_S$ and $Trust_{S'}$ of different trust scopes S and S'. The determination of these sets is the *trust problem* mentioned in the introduction.

Gradual trust requires some measure or quantification to express various degrees of an entity's reliability in successfully accomplishing a task of a certain scope S. In Mahoney et al. (2005), this measure is called *trust value*. The set of all possible trust values will be denoted by Ω_T. In addition to Boolean sets like $\{0,1\}$ or $\{no, yes\}$, we may consider discrete sets like $\{1,...,10\}$ or $\{none, low, medium, high, full\}$, or continuous sets like the unit interval $[0,1]$ or percentages $[0,100]$. Independently of the actual choice, we assume Ω_T to be *ordered*. The maximal value is then supposed to represent the special case of "fully trustworthy,". whereas the minimal value stands for "fully untrustworthy". The topic of trust values is extensively discussed in Marsh (1994) and Shi, Bochmann, and Adams (2004).

For a given set of trust values Ω_T, one can think of trustworthiness as a function $Trust_S : \mathbf{E} \rightarrow \Omega_T$. Absolute trust corresponds to the Boolean case of $\Omega_T = \{0,1\}$, where the $Trust_S$ function degenerates into the indicator function of the previously-mentioned set of trustworthy entities. This is certainly an important special case, but in general, we need to consider cases like $Trust_S(E) = high$ or $Trust_S(E) = 0.8$.

In some particular situations, all entities of a certain community may agree to (implicitly) attribute the maximal trust value to some specific entities. Such an agreement is called *trust root* (Mahoney et al., 2005). Entities that are the subject of a trust root are called (central) *authorities*, and a model with a formally specified trust root is called *centralized*. Note that any centralized model can be transformed into an equivalent decentralized one, just by explicitly assigning maximal trust values to all authorities.

Statements and Credentials

With respect to an unknown remote entity $E \in \mathbf{E}$ and a given identity $K \in \mathbf{K}$, establishing authenticity or trust requires some sort of third-party *statements* or *declarations* from intermediate entities. We make a general distinction between *authenticity statements* of the form $\text{Aut}(E, K) = x, x \in \Omega_A$, and *trust statements* of the form $Trust_S(E) = x, x \in \Omega_T$. With $\mathbf{D}$ (for declarations) we denote the set of all possible authenticity or trust statements, and *issuer*$(D) \in \mathbf{E}$ refers to the issuing entity of the statement $D \in \mathbf{D}$. A statement is called *positive* (*negative*), if the corresponding authenticity or trust value x is maximal (minimal) within Ω_A or Ω_T, respectively. If x is neither maximal nor minimal in a non-Boolean set Ω_T, the trust statement D is called *mixed*. Furthermore, it is common to call positive authenticity statements *certificates* and positive trust statements *recommendations*. In Jonczy and Haenni (2005, 2006), negative authenticity and trust statements are called *revocations* and *discredits*, respectively, and mixed statements are called *ratings*.

As we will see, it is often useful to consider the case of *weighted* statements. The idea is to allow the issuing intermediate entity to express her/his personal confidence in the statement. Formally, if $D \in \mathbf{D}$ is a statement, then the *weight* (or *confidence weight*) assigned to it is a value *weight*$(D) \in [0,1]$ in the unit interval. The two extreme cases of full and no confidence correspond to *weight*$(D) = 1$ and *weight*$(D) = 0$, respectively. Note that *weight*$(D) = 0$ makes D valueless and corresponds to not issuing D at all. Some authors call a pair (x, ω), where $x \in \Omega_T$ is a trust value (w.r.t. an entity's trustworthiness) and $\omega \in [0,1]$ a confidence weight (w.r.t. an issued statement), an *opinion* (Jøsang, 1999a; Theodorakopoulos, 2004; Theodorakopoulos & Baras, 2004).

To make a weighted statement fraud resistant, it is indispensable that the issuer E adds some sort of *digital signature*. This is what we call *digital signature requirement*. Without a digital signature, it is not possible to verify the origin of the statement, that is, it could have been issued by any entity, including the one to which the statement refers. This would be an open door for malicious entities and frauds. The general term we propose for a digitally signed and weighted statement is *credential*. It consists of the statement with its confidence weight, the identity (public key) used to generate the signature, and the signature itself. Credentials are thus tuples $C = (D, \omega, K, \sigma)$ with $D \in \mathbf{D}$, $\omega = weight(D)$, $K \in \mathbf{K}_E$, and $\sigma = sign(S, \omega, K)$. With *sign* we denote the procedure that generates a digital signature with respect to its parameters. It may be based on cryptographic techniques such as RSA encryption and hash functions, but this is not further specified here. $\mathbf{C}$ denotes the set of all possible credentials.

The verification of a credential $C \in \mathbf{C}$ is a procedure which uses the public key included in K to check whether σ is a valid signature with respect to D, ω, and K. Again, we do not further specify the cryptographic techniques on which the verification procedure is based. A successfully verified credential guarantees that the statement actually stems from the entity behind the identity (i.e., the entity holding the corresponding private key), but it says nothing about the issuing entity E itself and its trustworthiness. For this, it is necessary to verify the authenticity of the binding between K and E. If the verification fails, the credential has probably been compromised and should not be further considered.

Multilayer Models

A particular trust scope is somebody's ability or reliability to issue meaningful credentials. This is actually a very important scope, since accepting credentials as the basic pieces of evidence to solve the authenticity and trust problems always implies some sort of trust with respect to the issuers. Let us call the scope of this particular type *issuer trust scope* and denote it by S_I. To take different credentials into account, some authors such as Maurer (1996) make a distinction between different levels of issuer trust and corresponding scopes. Other authors find it convenient to assume a *generic trust scope, S_G*, that covers all possible types of trust, including issuer trust.

A model with at least two layers, one for authenticity and one for issuer trust or generic trust, is called a *two-layer model*. This is the minimal requirement we impose. It is crucial to have these two layers, because the actual value of a credential depends on both the authenticity and trustworthiness of the issuer. The two basic types of two-layer models are depicted on the left-hand side and in the middle of Figure 1. Some concrete models are restricted to a single trust layer, but we consider them inherently insecure (see next section). Models with further layers for other trust scopes are generally called *multilayer models*. Of particular interest are three-layer models with authenticity on the first layer, issuer trust on the second layer, and the (application-dependent) *principal trust scope S_P* on the third layer, as depicted on the right hand side of Figure 1. Concrete three-layer models have not yet been proposed.

Evidence and Evaluation

A collection of successfully verified credentials $\Gamma \subseteq \mathbf{C}$ is the *trust evidence* on which authenticity and trust is evaluated. The *evaluation* itself is the process of judging an entity's trustworthiness or a public key's authenticity on the basis of the available trust evidence. The evaluation is called *local*, if the trust evidence depends on the entity performing the evaluation, otherwise it is called *global*. In two- or multilayer models, the evidence may contain statements about authenticity and various types of trust, and therefore we expect conclusions about both authenticity and trust from the evaluation. One can thus think of the evaluation as a procedure or mechanism that takes some trust evidence as input and outputs some sort of qualitative or quantitative judgments with respect to the propositions $Aut(E, K)$ and $Trust_S(E)$. Let the set Θ of possible outcomes of an evaluation be called *evaluation set* and its elements *evaluation values*. The result of an evaluation is then a value $eval(Aut(E, K), \Gamma) \in \Theta$ or $eval(Trust_S(E, K), \Gamma) \in \Theta$. In Mahoney et al. (2005), these functions are called *trust metrics*.

Candidates of possible evaluation sets are the ones used for trust values, but we may additionally consider discrete sets {*reject, accept*} or {*reject, accept, undecided*}, or Cartesian products like $[0,1]^2$ or $[0,1]^3$. The evaluation values in the case of such Cartesian products are thus pairs (w, y) or triples (x, y, z) of values in the unit interval, that is, points in the unit square or unit cube, respectively. This type of outcome is typical if the underlying mechanism makes use of some sort of nonadditive probability theory like *Dempster-Shafer theory* (Shafer, 1976), *probabilistic argumentation* (Haenni, 2005a), or *subjective logic* (Jøsang, 1997). We will later see examples of this, especially in the closing section on credential networks.

Figure 1. The basic types of two- and three-layer models

Existing One-Layer Models

Many of the existing trust models do not accomplish the two-level requirement. The primary goal of such *one-layer models* is the evaluation of somebody's trustworthiness with respect to a single principal trust scope, that is, they are not concerned with authenticity and thus cannot impose the digital signature requirement. In some models, like in the eBay trust model or in NICE, this principal trust scope is very much application-oriented. Other one-layer models such as GRTM/HLTT consider several levels of issuer trust. The BBK model makes a distinction between issuer trust and principal trust without considering authenticity. An overview of these basic types and examples of one-layer models are shown in Figure 2. Gray boxes highlight the primary focus of the respective models.

One-layer models are also called *reputation systems*. Since they are not equipped with digital signatures and do not worry about authenticity, they are easily vulnerable against attacks of malicious or dishonest entities. An example of such an attack is an entity's attempt to strengthen its reputation by using different identities to issue several (positive) self-credentials. In the same way, it is easily possible to weaken the reputation of a fully trustworthy entity. Despite their vulnerability, some reputation systems are very successful in practice, especially in the context of online auctions. The rest of this section gives a short overview.

Online Auction Systems: eBay

An important application area of trust and reputation systems is the virtual world of online auctions. By far the most successful system worldwide is *eBay*. It defines an online marketplace with several million registered users and almost one billion listed items. In such a tremendous commercial network, buyers and sellers are usually not known to each other. One can look at it as an "anonymous community of ad-hoc buyers and sellers" (Mahoney et al., 2005), for which trust is an indispensable requirement. The fact that trust plays a central role is expressed by the following quote retrieved from the eBay Web site:

The key to eBay's success is trust. Trust between the buyers and sellers who make up the eBay community. And trust between the user and eBay, the company.

After a successful eBay transaction, the buyer and seller are allowed to rate each other by leaving some *feedback*, consisting of a *rating* (positive, negative, or neutral) and a short com-

Figure 2. Basic types and examples of existing one-layer models

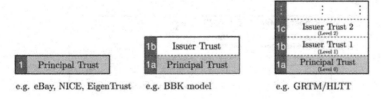

e.g. eBay, NICE, EigenTrust   e.g. BBK model   e.g. GRTM/HLTT

ment. The feedback ratings are the key factors for buyers and sellers to determine whether another registered user is trustworthy. The collection of somebody's feedback ratings forms the so-called *member profile*. Surprisingly, the number of complaints has consistently been a remarkably small percentage of all eBay transactions, and feedback profiles contain very few negative comments. An example of a possible eBay member profile is shown in Figure 3.

Formally, feedback ratings are trust statements with respect to the set $\Omega_T = \{positive, negative, neutral\}$ of possible trust values. No confidence weight is attached. The evaluation essentially consists of counting the number of ratings for each possible value. This leads to the simple profile statistic shown Figure 3. Its main component is the percentage of positive feedback, that is, $\Theta = [0,100]$ is the set of possible evaluation values. eBay's trust evaluation is global, but the decision to accept a seller as sufficiently trustworthy is left to the potential buyers. To some extent, by showing corresponding statistics for different time periods, eBay takes into account that trust is time dependent.

The aspect of authentication is not included in eBay's underlying reputation system, but the company seems to understand its importance. To prevent fraudulent use, they provide a registration service that requires all eBay users to guarantee identification through one's credit card information. This allows eBay to keep track of its users and to minimize the possibility of dual accounts for one person, without compromising the members' anonymity with self-selected user names. Note that eBay is the authority of its own centralized trust model. For further information about eBay's security and trust management, we refer to Boyd (2002). For legal aspects in the context of eBay's reputation system, see Chandler, El-Khatib, Benyoucef, Bochman, and Adams (2006).

NICE

Another one-layer model is proposed by *NICE*, a platform for implementing cooperative applications over the Internet (Lee, Sherwood, & Bhattacharjee, 2003). The name is a recursive acronym for *NICE is the Internet Cooperative Environment*. One important goal of cooperative infrastructures is to enhance the cooperation between users of a (mostly distributed) application. In peer-to-peer applications, for example, cooperation relates to the willingness of users to provide their share of resources to the system, that is, to other users. In the context of NICE, a distributed scheme for trust inference has been developed with the focus on peer-to-peer networks. In this trust management system, users can assign and infer trust values for other users. The inferred trust values represent the degree to which a user considers other users to be cooperative, and these values may be used then to price resources in the system.

Figure 3. The member profile of a registered eBay user

Member Profile: rolf (10779 ☆)				
Feedback Score:	10779	Recent Ratings:		
Positive Feedback:	99.3%		Past Month	Past 6 Months	Past 12 Months
Members who left a positive:	10853	⊕ positive	1109	6734	10759
Members who left a negative:	73	⊘ neutral	3	16	28
All positive feedback received:	16146	⊖ negative	0	13	26
Learn about what these numbers mean.		Bid Retractions (Past 6 months): 0		

The model is based on the assumption that a peer-to-peer system can be decomposed into a set of two-party transactions. A second assumption is that the system contains a set of "good" nodes (or users) that perform nearly all of their transactions correctly and entirely. Based on these assumptions, the system allows good users to identify other good users, leading to so-called *cooperative peer groups*. In these groups, each participant completes a transaction with high probability.

For all transactions in the system, each involved participant produces a so-called *cookie*, which is a signed statement about the quality of the transaction. Even though digital signatures are imposed, there are no statements concerning the validity of the involved public keys. After a successful transaction between a *consumer X* and the *provider Y* of a resource, *X* signs a cookie stating that the transaction with *Y* has been successfully completed. *Y* may then store this cookie and use it later to prove its own trustworthiness to other users, including *X*. With the progress of the system, more and more cookies are stored at different users, which leads then to a trust graph on which the trust evaluation is based.

The quality of a transaction is expressed by the so-called *cookie value*, a real number $x \in [0,1]$. A valued cookie is thus a trust statement of the form $Trust(Y) = x$, that is, the set of possible trust values is the unit interval $\Omega_T = [0,1]$. Weighted statements or authenticity statements are not supported. The lack of authenticity statements (authenticity is implicitly assumed) makes NICE a one-layer model.

The first step of the evaluation process consists in the traversal of the trust graph resulting from all accomplished transactions and the collection of the necessary direct and third-party cookies. This resulting subgraph forms then the evidence on which the (local) evaluation is based. NICE proposes two possible metrics called *strongest path* and *weighted sum of strongest disjoint paths*, both of them resulting in an inferred trust value in the evaluation set $\Theta = [0,1]$. These metrics are efficiently computable, but they are rather more pragmatic than theoretically well founded.

BBK Trust Model

Another popular one-layer model is the one proposed in Beth, Borcherding, and Klein (1994) as an extension of the approach described in Yahalem, Klein, and Beth (1993). It diverges from other one-layer models like eBay and NICE in the sense that it is not bound to a specific application area. We will call it *BBK (trust) model* or BBKM for short.

BBKM makes a distinction between two different trust scopes called *direct trust* and *recommendation trust*. Direct trust refers to the belief in an entity's capabilities with respect to a given task or service, whereas recommendation trust refers to the belief in an entity's capability to decide whether another entity is trustworthy (in the given trust class) or to reliably recommend other entities. This is exactly what we mean with *principal trust* and *issuer trust*, respectively, with the main focus on principal trust. BBKM does not further specify the direct (principal) trust, but it gives some examples of so-called *trust classes*, that is, tasks like the generation of cryptographic keys, identification, keeping secrets, and so on. We consider BBKM a one-layer model, because it does not impose digital signatures with a corresponding authenticity layer.

In BBKM, trust and trustworthiness is regarded as a relationship between two entities rather than a property of a single entity. Corresponding trust statements are essentially of the form $Trust_{S_P}(X,Y)=x$ for direct trust and $Trust_{S_I}(X,Y)=x$ for recommendation trust. The trust value x depends on the number of X's positive experiences with Y (with respect to the total number of experiences) and gives thus an estimation of the probability that Y behaves well when being trusted. The possible trust values are thus real numbers in the unit interval $\Omega_T=[0,1]$. No confidence weights are permitted.

The evaluation process consists then in applying the *BBK trust metrics* to a set of different trust relationships between entities. This metric consists of some *inference rules* that are used to derive indirect trust relationships from the given evidence. In this way, all possible paths between two users are considered in the corresponding trust graph. The results are values in the unit interval, thus $\Theta=[0,1]$ is the set of possible evaluation values. No restrictions are imposed on the locality of the evaluation.

In its present form, BBKM is vulnerable in the presence of malicious entities. Such entities may manipulate the computation of the metrics by creating additional artificial relationships that then would alter the resulting evaluation values. This is the point on which the usefulness of BBKM was questioned in the literature (Reiter & Stubblebine, 1999). However, by requiring all trust statements to be digitally signed, it would be possible to extend BBKM to a proper nonvulnerable two-layer model, just by considering *identification* (identity trust) as the principal trust scope.

Other Existing One-Layer Models

The *EigenTrust* reputation system is another model used in the context of peer-to-peer file-sharing networks (Kamvar, Schlosser, & Garcia-Molina, 2003). Its main contribution is an algorithm that is supposed to decrease the number of downloads of inauthentic files in such networks. For that purpose, each peer has assigned a unique global trust value based on the peer's history of uploads. The main problem addressed is the aggregation of local trust values of all peers without the use of a centralized system. Local trust values are defined like in the eBay model as the sum of ratings of individual transactions between two peers.

The approach chosen is based on the notion of transitive trust: if peer X trusts peer Y with (normalized) value $x \in [0,1]$, and Y trusts Z with (normalized) value $y \in [0,1]$, then X is supposed to trust Z with value $z=x \cdot y \in [0,1]$. In general, this indirect trust value is the sum of such products over all intermediate peers. Such sums are considered as the components of a matrix C_X, and when the (normalized) local trust values are interpreted as probabilities, the so-called *local trust matrix* C_X defines a Markov chain. The stationary distribution $\mathbf{t}_X$ of this Markov chain converges, after many iterations, to the eigenvector of C_X, and is the same for all peers X. The components t_Y of this global trust vector $\mathbf{t}$ represent the global trust values and quantify how much trust the system as a whole assigns peer Y.

In most of the existing trust management systems, it is possible to see the available evidence as a directed graph (often called *trust graph*), where the nodes represent entities, and the edges some sort of trust relationships between the entities. The edges are usually labeled with a trust or confidence value. If these values are interpreted as probabilities, the problem of evaluating an entity's trustworthiness turns out to be a *two-terminal reliability problem* of a corresponding *reliability network* (Colbourn, 1987). This is the motivation behind the so-called *generic reliability trust model* (GRTM) proposed in Mahoney et al, (2005).

GRTM introduces a trust metric called *hop-count limited transitive trust* (HLTT). Different levels of trust are supported, similar to Maurer's MCV model (see next section). A statement on the ground level 0 means that the issuing entity X trusts entity Y with respect to a principal trust scope. A statement on a higher trust level $i > 0$ means that X trusts Y as a recommender on level $i - 1$, and so on. Each trust statement has an attached trust value, $x \in [0,1]$, that is interpreted as the probability of a successful interaction between X and Y. The HLTT metric is then applied to derive indirect trust statements with respect to the principal trust scope on level 0.

The *Reiter-Stubblebine trust metric* also takes a directed graph as input (Reiter & Stubblebine, 1997, 1999), but the nodes of the graph are public keys, without references to any entities. A directed edge from a key K_1 to another key K_2 represents a certificate that has been signed by the owner of K_1 and assigns certain attributes to the public key K_2. Each edge from K_1 to K_2 has an assigned trust value, called *insurance label*, that represents the amount of money for which the owner of K_1 will be liable to the user (who is applying the metric) if the attributes bound to K_2 are incorrect. In order to authenticate a key K_T (the *target key*), user X applies the trust metric to the graph by supplying, as additional input parameters, the key K_T and a trusted key K_S (the *source key*). The evaluation returns then the amount (of money) for which the name-to-key (or name-to-K_T) binding is insured by going through all disjoint paths from K_S to K_T in the graph. These ideas are similar to the ones proposed in Levien and Aiken (1998).

Numerous other trust and reputation systems have been proposed. Some of them use the concept of so-called *trust-management engines*, like *PolicyMaker* (Blaze, Feigenbaum, & Lacy, 1996) and *KeyNote* (Blaze, Feigenbaum, & Keromytis, 1999). The focus of these systems is on authentication and access control. A similar approach is taken by the *REFEREE* system (Chu, Feigenbaum, LaMacchia, Resnick, & Strauss, 1997), which is a general-purpose language with a primary focus on trust management for Web browsing. A survey of these systems is given in Blaze, Feigenbaum, Ioannidis, & Keromytis (1999).

Existing Two- or Multilayer Models

One-layer models are particularly popular in the communities of electronic commerce and peer-to-peer networks. This is a consequence of the fact that these applications are primarily concerned with trust, much more than with authenticity; but authenticity is one of the avowed goals in the areas of cryptography and secure communications, that is, it is not a surprise that these are the roots of most existing two- or multilayer models. The most prominent example is the so-called *web of trust* in PGP, a popular and widely used implementation of public-key cryptography for e-mail security. Its primary goal is authenticity (of public keys), but to accomplish this goal, it includes a superposed trust layer. PGP's web of trust was the motivation for a number of similar approaches. We will have a look at some of them in the rest of this section. In Figure 4 we give an overview, and indicate the corresponding supported layers. Again, gray boxes represent the approaches' primary focus.

PGP's Web of Trust

One of the first and most popular software applications for encryption and authentication based on public-key cryptography is pretty good privacy (PGP). It is mostly used to secure electronic mail. The first version had been developed by Phil Zimmermann in the early 1990s (Zimmermann, 1994). Its popularity is due to the fact that it was open-source from the early beginnings. In the meantime, PGP turned into a commercial product, but nonproprietary successors such as OpenPGP and GnuPG (GNU Privacy Guard) are available today. The PGP protocol defines standard formats for encrypted messages, signatures, and certificates, as well as a simple trust model.

Zimmermann was faced with the problem to develop a system that allowed the users of a global network to exchange their public keys in an authentic way. Establishing a hierarchical organization of central *certification authorities* seemed not to be the right solution, as this would have left too much power in their hands. Moreover, every PGP user should be allowed to decide whom to trust and to which degree. This was Zimmermann's motivation to develop a simple two-layer trust model called *web of trust* (WOT).

The basic idea in WOT is to let all PGP users issue public-key certificates, that is, digitally signed positive authenticity statements. Negative or weighted statements are not permitted. The issuing entity is called *introducer*. In the context of PGP, it is more common to talk about *signing a key* rather than issuing a certificate, and somebody's evidence, that is, a collection of certificates, is a *key ring*. PGP does not support general trust statements between arbitrary users, but the *owner* of a key ring is allowed to assign a respective trust value from the set $\Omega_T=\{no\ trust,\ marginal\ trust,\ full\ trust\}$ to the public key of each introducer. PGP trust values are thus assigned to identities. They represent the owner's belief that the entity behind the identity is a reliable certificate issuer.

PGP is thus a restricted two-layer model with a primary focus on authenticity. The (local) evaluation is a simple mechanism that determines for each public key in the key ring a value in the set $\Theta=\{valid,\ invalid\}$. PGP also defines *marginally valid* public keys, but they are considered as *invalid* by default. A key is considered *valid*, if one of the following three local conditions holds:

1.   The key belongs to the owner.

2.   The key is signed by at least one *fully trusted* introducer with a *valid* key.

3.   The key is signed by at least two *marginally trusted* introducers with *valid* keys.

Figure 4. Examples of existing two- or multilayer models

Requiring at least *one* fully trustworthy (second rule) or *two* marginally trustworthy (third rule) introducers are the default values, but different (higher) values may be chosen by the owner.

The WOT model is simple and efficient, but it has also some deficiencies. One problem is the lack of a continuous set of trust values. Another problem is the fact that trust values are assigned to identities (public keys) instead of entities. Consider a marginally trustworthy entity who uses two different identities to sign the same key. The second rule then makes the entity look fully trustworthy, which is not true. Further problems are caused by the *locality* of the trust value combination. As it has been pointed out in Haenni (2005b), this may lead to counterintuitive conclusions.

Haenni's Key Validation Model

A simple extension of PGP's web of trust is the *key validation model* (KVM) proposed in Haenni (2005b). KVM adopts all the basic elements and restrictions of WOT, except that continuous trust values in the set $\Omega_T=[0,1]$ are allowed. A given trust value $x \in \Omega_T$ is interpreted as the subjective probability $x=p(Rel(X))$ that the entity X is a reliable introducer. In its basic form, KVM requires trust statements to be issued by the owner of the key ring, that is, general trust statements between arbitrary users are not permitted. The last part of Haenni (2005b) mentions the possibility of such *recommendations*, but the discussion is rather cursory. The same holds for the possible inclusion of *revocations*, that is, negative authenticity statements. We will therefore not consider recommendations and revocations to be part of KVM.

For the (local) evaluation, KVM suggests to use a theory of uncertain reasoning called *probabilistic argumentation* (Haenni, 2005a ; Haenni, Kohlas, & Lehmann, 2000). The idea is to describe the evidence included in a key ring by a set Σ of logical sentences. This set of sentences and the given probabilities (trust values) are then used to compute so-called *degrees of support* $dsp(h) \in [0,1]$ and *degrees of possibility* $dps(h) = 1 - dsp(\neg h) \in [0,1]$ of the hypotheses $h=Aut(X, K)$. Intuitively, degrees of support measure the weight of the available evidence that supports a hypothesis h, whereas degrees of possibility refer to the weight of the evidence that supports $\neg h$. Both measures are posterior probabilities of logical provability.

The restriction of KVM to positive authenticity statements, together with the resulting absence of negative evidence, leads to $dps(Aut(X, K)) =1$ for all possible bindings (X, K), that is, degree of support remains as the only relevant measure. The evaluation values in KVM are thus single values $dps(Aut(X, K))$ in the unit interval $\Theta=[0,1]$. KVM suggests to accept a public key as authentic, if the corresponding degree of support surpasses a certain user-defined threshold. The validities of all other keys remain undecided. Note that KVM resolves some of the previously mentioned problems of WOT, but the necessary computations are considerably more expensive. Recently, the basic form of KVM has been realized as a GnuPG extension (Jonczy et al., 2006).

Maurer's Confidence Valuation

A more expressive and flexible extension of PGP's web of trust is Maurer's model of *confidence valuation* (MCV) for public-key authentication in decentralized public-key infrastructures (Maurer, 1996). MCV was the first two-layer model to support both authenticity statements (certificates) and trust statements (recommendations) between arbitrary users. Maurer's model has been readopted in Kohlas and Maurer (2000), and recently extended in Marchesini and Smith (2005) by including time, revocations, and other issues. The model imposes the statements to be weighted and digitally signed. MCV's primary goal is authentication, but by recognizing the need of at least one superposed trust layer, it could as well be used for evaluating trust. Maurer's goal is to define a method that has precise semantics and is as expressive as possible. MCV consists of two parts, first a *deterministic* (unweighted) model, and second a probabilistic (weighted) model based on *probabilistic logic* (Nilsson, 1986). Both cases are restricted to Boolean sets $\Omega_A = \Omega_T = \{0,1\}$ and positive statements.

In the deterministic model, the set $View_X$ consists of the collection of evidence and assumptions of an entity X. The pieces of evidence and their possible conclusions are called *statements*. Based on the initial set of statements, entity X may derive further statements by applying different logical *inference rules*. There are two types of such rules, one for authenticity and one for trust. Each of them describes the necessary preconditions for concluding that a public key is authentic or that an entity is trustworthy, respectively. By consecutively applying these inference rules, it may be possible to (logically) prove the authenticity of a given public key. Maurer's deterministic model proposes thus a local evaluation of positive authenticity and trust statements into the Boolean set $\Theta = \{0,1\}$.

The probabilistic model works with the same set of rules $View_X$, but it accounts for the possibility that an entity may not be entirely sure about the truth of an issued statement $S \in \mathbf{D}$. This is what Maurer calls *confidence*, and various degrees of confidence are expressed by corresponding *confidence parameters* $con(S) \in [0,1]$. Clearly, confidence parameters correspond to *weights*, and a statement with an attached confidence parameter is a *weighted statement*. Maurer suggests interpreting confidence parameters as subjective probabilities, reflecting an issuer's belief in the truth of the statement. The (local) evaluation is then a problem of computing indirect confidence values, that is, probabilities that the authenticity of a public key is derivable from the given evidence. The evaluation set in the probabilistic model is thus the unit interval $\Theta = [0,1]$.

A particularity of MCV is the distinction between infinitely many issuer trust scopes called *trust levels*. The idea is that a recommendation on the ith level refers to somebody's trustworthiness on level i-1. Authenticity is regarded as the ground trust level $i=0$. Despite this generality and MCV's soundness and preciseness, it has not yet been integrated in any operational system. One point that was criticized in the literature is the use of probabilities as confidence parameters. In Reiter and Stubblebine (1999), it is argued that probabilities should not be used as confidence parameters, as they *seem to bear no relationship to random experiments*. This is certainly true, but Maurer's original intention was probably a Bayesian (nonfrequentist) interpretation of probabilities as an entity's subjective belief.

Jøsang's Certification Algebra

Another existing two-layer model is Jøsang's *certification algebra* (JCA). Like WOT, KVM, and MCV, it takes into account that authentication cannot be based on public-key certificates alone, but also needs to include the trust relationships between users (Jøsang, 1999a). Mathematically, JCA is based on a theory of uncertain reasoning called *theory of subjective logic* (Jøsang, 1997). Its principal formal concept is the one of an *opinion* $\omega=(b, d, i)$. It consists of three additive real numbers, a degree of *belief* $b \in [0,1]$, a degree of *disbelief* $d \in [0,1]$, and a degree of *ignorance* $i \in [0,1]$, with the restriction of $b+d+i=1$. Opinions can be regarded as points in a two-dimensional barycentric triangle called *opinion triangle* (similar to the one shown in Figure. 10).

With respect to entity X's authenticity and trustworthiness, JCA allows the users to express their believe in statements by opinions ω_{Aut}^{X} or $\omega_{Trust_S}^{X}$, where S refers to the related trust scope. If $\Omega=\{(b,d, i) \in [0,1]^3 : b+d+i=1\}$ denotes the set of all possible opinions (the entire opinion triangle), then $\Omega_A = \Omega_T = \Omega$ are the sets of possible authenticity and trust values. This is a very general view that includes the possibility of positive, negative, and weighted statements.

The evaluation in JCA is based on three operators called *conjunction, recommendation*, and *consensus*. The first two are special cases of *Dempster's rule of combination* (Shafer, 1976). The evaluation computes the combination of all available and relevant opinion statements, from which "overall opinions" ω_{Aut}^{X} or $\omega_{Trust_S}^{X}$ arise. These are again arbitrary elements of Ω, that is, JCA's evaluation set is $\Theta = \Omega$, the set of all possible opinions. Unfortunately, the discussion in Jøsang (1999a) says little about the decision of accepting or rejecting an entity's trustworthiness or a public key's authenticity.

JCA has two major drawbacks. The first one is a problem of dependent certification paths in complex networks, which makes the proposed evaluation procedure inapplicable (Jøsang, 1999b). The second problem is the noncompatibility of the consensus operator with Dempster's rule of combination.

Credential Networks

In this section, we will give a short introduction to a general model that follows the spirit of the previously discussed two-layer models. The evidence providing authenticity and trustworthiness comes in the form of *credentials*, which constitute the central formal concept of this approach. In a decentralized setting, all network participants are allowed to issue credentials. The resulting collection defines a *credential network* (Jonczy & Haenni, 2005, 2006). These networks form the basis for the derivation of indirect trust or authenticity. The main conceptual and computational problem is thus to evaluate a given credential network.

The model proposed here deals with the particular view of a participant or *user* X_0 of a distributed network. U denotes the set of other network users in which X_0 is interested in, and $U_0 = \{X_0\} \cup U$ is the set of all users including X_0. In the context of a given credential network, X_0 is called the *owner* of the network. The problem from the perspective of X_0 is to judge the *authenticity* and/or *trustworthiness* concerning other network users $Y \in U$. To formally describe this, we will use two propositions Aut_Y and $Trust_Y$ as respective abbreviations for $Aut(Y, K)$ and $Trust_{S_G}(Y)$ suggested at the beginning of this chapter. We adopt the simplifying assumption that $Trust_Y$ stands for a generic trust scope S_G.

The goal of the owner is thus to authenticate Y (authenticity problem) or to derive Y's trustworthiness (trust problem), or both. In other words, X_0 wants to prove the truth of Aut_Y and/or $Trust_Y$. It is assumed that Aut_{X_0} and $Trust_{X_0}$ are implicitly true. This means that the owner is absolutely certain about the authenticity of his own public key and his own trustworthiness.

Credentials: Overview and Classification

If we assume that $Y \in \mathbf{U}$ is unknown to X_0, then there is no direct or explicit way for X_0 of proving the truth or falsity of Aut_Y or $Trust_Y$. The judgment of X_0 must therefore rely upon statements about Y's authenticity and trustworthiness issued by third parties, that is, by other users $X \in \mathbf{U} \backslash \{Y\}$ of the network. Such statements are called *credentials* and are required to be *digitally signed*, as suggested in the first part of this chapter.

A credential is always issued by a user $X \in \mathbf{U}_0$, the *issuer*, and concerns another user $Y \in \mathbf{U}_0$, the *recipient*. Furthermore, there is a general distinction between two *classes* T and A of credentials, depending on whether it is a statement about the trustworthiness or the authenticity of the recipient. This reflects the two-layer character of this approach. The convention is to denote A-credentials issued by X for Y by A_{XY} and T-credentials by T_{XY}. In the latter case, the issuer of a credential acts as *trustor*, whereas the recipient plays the role of the *trustee*. Note that the owner X_0 may as well issue and receive credentials, and issuing self-credentials A_{XX} or T_{XX} is not prohibited.

In addition to the two classes A and T, there is another distinction between three different *signs* +, −, and ± for *positive*, *negative*, and *mixed* credentials, respectively. The intuitive idea here is that the issuer of a credential may either want to make a positive or a negative statement about the authenticity or trustworthiness of another network user. A mixed statement can be seen as a *rating*. The combination of classes and signs yields six different credential types, as shown in Figure 5. Further details on these types are discussed in the following subsections.

Another feature of the model allows the issuer of a credential, by assigning a value $\pi \in [0,1]$, to specify the *weight* of the credential. The values $\pi = 0$ and $\pi = 1$ are the two extreme cases of minimal and maximal weight, respectively. In the case of a positive or negative credential, we assume the assigned value π to represent the confidence weight of an absolute (positive or negative) statement. In the case of a mixed credential, we suppose the weight to be understood as a trust value $\pi \in \Omega_T$ or authenticity value $\pi \in \Omega_A$. Formally, a credential is a 5-tuple $C = (class, sign, issuer, recipient, weight)$ with $class \in \{T, A\}$, $issuer \in \mathbf{U}_0$, $recipient \in \mathbf{U}_0$, $sign \in \{+, -, \pm\}$, and $weight \in [0,1]$. To distinguish between the two classes, and to make the formal notation more compact, the convention adapted from Jonczy and Haenni (2005, 2006) is to denote A-credentials by:

$$A_{issuer,\ recipient}^{sign,\ weight} = (A,\ sign,\ issuer,\ recipient,\ weight),$$

Figure 5. The six credential types with the corresponding graphical representation. A-credentials constitute the first layer (authenticity), whereas T-credentials form the second layer (generic trust).

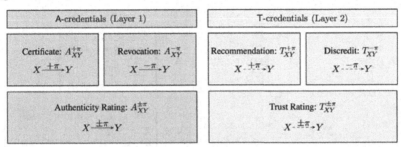

and T-credentials by:

$$T^{sign,weight}_{issuer,recipient} = (\mathsf{T}, sign, issuer, recipient, weight).$$

An example of a positive A-credential of weight 0.8 is $A^{+0.8}_{XY} = (A, +, X, Y, 0.8)$, whereas $T^{\pm0.7}_{XY} = (T, \pm, X, Y, 0.7)$ is a mixed T-credential of weight 0.7. Both of them are issued by X and concern the same recipient Y. Graphically, an A-credential issued by user X for user Y is represented as a solid arrow pointing from X to Y, labeled with its sign and weight. Similarly, a T-credential is represented as a dashed arrow. Figure 5 shows all possible credentials with their respective graphical representations.

The foregoing discussion allows us now to define a credential network $\mathbf{N}$ owned by user X_0 as a quadruple $\mathbf{N}=(\mathbf{U}_0, X_0, \mathbf{A}, \mathbf{T})$, where $\mathbf{A}$ and $\mathbf{T}$ denote sets of A- and T-credentials, respectively. For a pair of users $X, Y, \in \mathbf{U}_0$, each set $\mathbf{A}$ and $\mathbf{T}$ is restricted to include at most one credential $A_{XY} \in \mathbf{A}$ and $T_{XY} \in \mathbf{T}$, respectively. Note that this does not exclude cases in which both sets $\mathbf{A}$ and $\mathbf{T}$ include a credential between the same issuer X and recipient Y. In other words, X may issue at most one A-credential for Y, and at the same time, X may also issue (at most) one T-credential for Y.

An example of a credential network is depicted in Figure 6 as a weighted, directed multigraph. The nodes represent the users, the owner being emphasized by a double circle. The network consists of six users, nine A-credentials (six positive, two negative, one mixed), and eight T-credentials (five positive, two negative, one mixed).

Certificates and Recommendations

Positive A-credentials are called *certificates*. If X issues a certificate $A^{+\pi}_{XY}$ of weight π for recipient Y, it means that X acts as a guarantor for the authenticity of Y's public key. The numerical parameter π expresses X's personal confidence in issuing a certificate for Y. A certificate A^{+1}_{XY} of maximal weight $\pi=1$ is called *absolute*. Note that issuing a certificate A^{+0}_{XY} of minimal weight $\pi=0$ is like issuing no certificate at all.

Figure 6. Example of a credential network

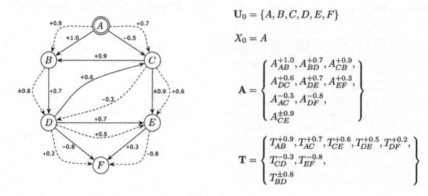

$$U_0 = \{A, B, C, D, E, F\}$$

$$X_0 = A$$

$$A = \left\{ \begin{array}{l} A_{AB}^{+1.0}, A_{BD}^{+0.7}, A_{CB}^{+0.9}, \\ A_{DC}^{+0.6}, A_{DE}^{+0.7}, A_{EF}^{+0.3}, \\ A_{AC}^{-0.5}, A_{DF}^{-0.8}, \\ A_{CE}^{\pm0.9} \end{array} \right\}$$

$$T = \left\{ \begin{array}{l} T_{AB}^{+0.9}, T_{AC}^{+0.7}, T_{CE}^{+0.6}, T_{DE}^{+0.5}, T_{DF}^{+0.2}, \\ T_{CD}^{-0.3}, T_{EF}^{-0.8}, \\ T_{BD}^{\pm0.8} \end{array} \right\}$$

The logic behind a certificate issued by X for Y is analogue to Maurer's (MCV) model and works as follows: in order to prove the authenticity of Y, X must be authentic and trustworthy at the same time, which is expressed by the propositions Aut_X and $Trust_X$. Because X may only be partially confident in the statement expressed by the certificate, $A_{XY}^{+\pi}$ only holds with a certain probability that corresponds to the weight π. In other words, to prove authenticity, it is necessary to have at least one reliable certificate from an authentic and trustworthy issuer. This principle is illustrated in Figure 7(a).

In a similar way, positive T-credentials are called *recommendations*. A recommendation $T_{XY}^{+\pi}$ represents thus X's opinion that Y is trustworthy. Again, $\pi=1$ means that the recommendation is absolute, whereas $\pi=0$ implies that X has no opinion at all, which is equivalent to not issuing a recommendation. In general, π expresses X's confidence in the statement about Y. The logic behind recommendations is similar to the logic behind certificates, that is, to prove the trustworthiness of the recipient Y, it is necessary to have at least one recommendation $T_{XY}^{+\pi}$ whose issuer X is authentic and trustworthy. Figure 7(b) visualizes this principle.

Revocations and Discredits

With respect to trustworthiness and authenticity, the evidence provided by certificates and recommendations is always positive. We will now consider the case of *negative* evidence

Figure 7. (a) A certificate issued by X for Y proves the authenticity of Y. (b) A recommendation issued by X for Y proves the trustworthiness of Y.

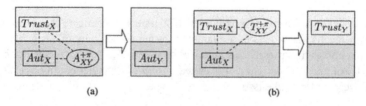

(a)   (b)

Figure 8. (a) A revocation issued by X for Y disproves the authenticity of Y. (b) A discredit issued by X for Y disproves the trustworthiness of Y.

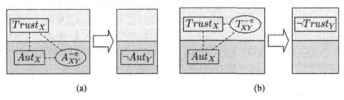

(a)   (b)

in the form of *revocations* and *discredits*. Intuitively, a revocation is a signed statement that somebody's public key is *not* authentic, whereas a discredit is a signed statement that somebody is *not* trustworthy.

Formally, a revocation issued by X for Y is a negative A-credential $A_{XY}^{-\pi}$. A revocation can thus be regarded as a negative certificate, which leads to "negative" authenticity, expressed by the negative literal $\neg Aut_Y$. Similarly, a discredit is a negative T-credential $T_{XY}^{-\pi}$, which may serve as a proof for $\neg Trust_Y$. As before, the weight π indicates the issuer's confidence in the respective statement. The logic behind revocations and discredits is analogue to certificates and revocations, except that they are possible proofs for the negative literals $\neg Aut_Y$ and $\neg Trust_Y$, respectively, as shown in Figure. 8.

In the literature, it is usually supposed that revocations are either issued by a central authority or by the owner of a key, for example, in the case of a lost or compromised private key in order to revoke the appertaining public key (key revocation) or to revoke corresponding digital certificates (Sadighi Firozabadi, & Sergot, 2003). Here we allow all network users to be potential issuers of revocations, and those will always refer directly to the authenticity of a public key.

Ratings

Mixed statements are called *ratings*. Again, depending on what it is related to, we need to distinguish between *authenticity ratings* and *trust ratings*, respectively. The idea is that the issuer of a trust rating, for example, may want to rate somebody's trustworthiness on a continuous scale with *fully trustworthy* and *completely untrustworthy* at the two extreme ends. Here, the weight specified by the issuer will therefore play the role of a trust value (of the recipient) rather than a confidence value (of the issuer).

A trust rating issued by X for recipient Y is thus a mixed T-credential $T_{XY}^{\pm\pi}$ with an attached trust value $\pi \in \Omega_T = [0,1]$. The issuer X of such a rating expresses his knowledge about the recipient's trustworthiness, that is, $T_{XY}^{\pm\pi}$ means that Y's trustworthiness is rated with value π. For example, a trust rating of weight $\pi = 0.8$ confirms that the recipient is reliable in 80% of all cases, and in the remaining 20% of cases he is not reliable.

In an analogue way, authenticity ratings are mixed A-credentials $T_{XY}^{\pm\pi}$ with an attached authenticity value $\pi \in \Omega_A = [0,1]$. For the sake of generality, we allow here arbitrary authenticity values in the full range from 0 to 1. This is in conflict with the prerequisite that authenticity values are always absolute, and general authenticity ratings may thus not be very useful in practice. But to underline the general character of the model, they are not explicitly excluded.

The logic behind trust and authenticity ratings is as follows. Under the condition that X is both authentic and trustworthy, $T_{XY}^{\pm\pi}$ implies $Trust_Y$ and $T_{XY}^{\pm\pi}$ implies $A_{XY}^{\pm\pi}$ with probability π, but at the same time they imply $\neg Trust_Y$ and $\neg Aut_Y$ with probability $1-\pi$, as shown in Figure. 9. Note that this is like combining a recommendation with a discredit or a certificate with a revocation, respectively. This is why ratings are called *mixed* credentials.

Evaluation

For a given credential network, the question that arises now is how to evaluate it. On the basis of the evidence encoded in the network, and with respect to a particular user $X \in \mathbf{U}$, the primary goal is to quantitatively judge the authenticity (of a given public key) and trustworthiness of X. The judgment will return a pair of evaluation values on a continuous scale between 0 and 1, that is, elements of the evaluation set $\Theta=[0,1]^2$. The owner of the credential network may then use this information to decide whether a public key or a service is acceptable or not.

The approach proposed in Jonczy and Haenni (2005) is to initially translate the credential network into a *probabilistic argumentation system* (Haenni, 2005a; Haenni et al., 2000). The main part of a probabilistic argumentation system is a set Σ of propositional sentences describing the available knowledge. The idea thus is to express a given credential network by logical sentences, like in MCV (Maurer, 1996). This translation is mainly a question of expressing the boxes and arrows of the above figures with appropriate propositions and logical operators.

The problem then is to derive from the given knowledge base possible proofs for some hypotheses of interest Aut_X and $Trust_X$. The evaluation process consists of two parts. In the first *qualitative* part, the problem consists in finding sets of so-called (minimal) *arguments* and *counter-arguments* (Jonczy & Haenni, 2005). The second *quantitative* part of the evaluation consists in computing the probabilistic weights of these arguments and counter-arguments. This leads to a pair of evaluation values called *degree of support* (dsp) and *degree of possibility* (dps). These values are interpreted as follows: $dsp(Aut_X)$ and $dsp(Trust_X)$ are the probabilities that Aut_X respectively $Trust_X$ are supported by arguments, while $dsp(Aut_X)$ and $dsp(Trust_X)$ are the probabilities that $\neg Aut_X$ respectively $\neg Trust_X$ are not supported by arguments, and thus remain possible.

Figure 9. (a) An authenticity rating issued by X for Y confirms Y's (partial) authenticity. (b) A trust rating issued by X for Y confirms Y's (partial) trustworthiness.

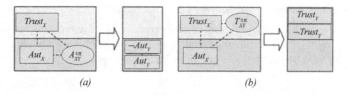

Consider the example from one of the previous subsections. The evaluation of the credential network from Figure 6 leads then to the results shown in Table 1.

The owner A receives of course maximal support for both, authenticity and trust. B also has maximal support for authenticity due to the absolute certificate from A. The presence of negative evidence decreases the degrees of support as well as possibility for any user, except for A. The possibility of B's authenticity is also maximal since there is no negative evidence that could lower the authenticity of B.

For a given pair of values $dsp(h)$ and $dps(h)$, there are three possible decisions with respect to h: (1) accept h, (2) reject h, or (3) leave h open. To decide whether to accept or reject the hypotheses $Trust_X$ and Aut_X for a user X, the owner may define an *acceptation threshold* $\lambda \in [0,1]$ and accept Aut_X whenever $dsp(Aut_X) \geq \lambda$ and accept $Trust_X$ whenever $dsp(Trust_X) \geq \lambda$. Note that not accepting a hypothesis is not necessarily a reason to reject it. For this, it may be necessary to define a *rejection threshold* $\eta \in [0,1]$, that is, Aut_X is rejected for $dps(Aut_X) \leq \eta$ and $Trust_X$ is rejected for $dps(Trust_X) \leq \eta$. Note that $\eta < \lambda$ is a necessary condition to exclude the case of simultaneously accepting and rejecting a hypothesis. If a hypothesis is neither accepted nor rejected, it means that the available information is insufficient to make a decision, that is, more credentials are needed.

From the owner's point of view, there are many possible strategies concerning the decision about a hypothesis. To make this point clearer, suppose the owner defines the following two decision strategies:

- **Strict acceptation policy (SAP):** The owner chooses a high acceptation threshold λ (e.g. 0.9) and also a high rejection threshold η (e.g. 0.8). In this case, only a few hypotheses will be accepted (if any) and some will be rejected.

- **Loose acceptation policy (LAP):** The owner chooses a rather low acceptation threshold λ (e.g. 0.6) and a medium rejection threshold η (e.g. 0.5). Compared to an SAP, more hypotheses may be accepted and only few will be rejected (if any).

In this example, let us now see how the owner will decide in the case of a SAP with $\lambda=0.9$ and $\eta = 0.8$. In this case, only three hypotheses are accepted, namely Aut_B and of course Aut_A and $Trust_A$. The owner may thus consider user B as being authentic. There are also three hypotheses rejected: Aut_C, Aut_F, and $Trust_D$. The owner thus considers C and F as unauthentic and D as untrustworthy. All other hypotheses are left open because they are neither accepted nor rejected.

Table 1. Degrees of support and possibility obtained from the credential network in Figure 6

	User X					
	A	B	C	D	E	F
$dsp(Aut_X)$	1.000	1.000	0.117	0.513	0.248	0.009
$dps(Aut_X)$	1.000	1.000	0.491	0.866	0.980	0.729
$dsp(Trust_X)$	1.000	0.869	0.683	0.631	0.168	0.052
$dps(Trust_X)$	1.000	0.965	0.976	0.764	0.953	0.911

Following a LAP with $\lambda=0.6$ and $\eta=0.5$, the owner's decisions turn out differently. Beside the three hypotheses accepted in the example, further ones are accepted, namely $Trust_B$, $Trust_C$, and $Trust_D$. The owner thus additionally considers the users B, C, and D as being trustworthy. But here, Aut_C is the only rejected hypothesis, that is, C is considered as being unauthentic. The remaining hypotheses are left open.

In Figure. 10, pairs of degree of support and degree of possibility are shown as points in the *opinion triangle* (Jøsang, 1999a) for both decision scenarios. The bottom right corner stands for $dsp=1$, the bottom left corner stands for $dps=0$, and the top corner means $dps-dsp=1$. The two thresholds λ and η are shown as values on the unit interval between the left and the right bottom corner.

Special Cases

From the perspective of credential networks, let us now discuss the relation to existing two- and one-layer models. We will use $\mathbf{A}^+$, $\mathbf{A}^-$, and $\mathbf{A}^{\pm}$ to denote sets of positive, negative, and mixed A-credentials, respectively, and $\mathbf{T}^+$, $\mathbf{T}^-$, and $\mathbf{T}^{\pm}$ for sets of T-credentials. If $\mathbf{C}$ is an arbitrary set of credentials, then this notational convention allows us to write:

$$\mathbf{C} = \mathbf{A} \cup \mathbf{T} = \mathbf{A}^+ \cup \mathbf{A}^- \cup \mathbf{A}^{\pm} \cup \mathbf{T}^+ \cup \mathbf{T}^- \cup \mathbf{T}^{\pm}$$

for the decomposition of $\mathbf{C}$ into corresponding subsets.

Maurer's model allows positive evidence in the form of certificates and recommendations with corresponding confidence values, but no negative or mixed statements (Maurer, 1996). If we neglect Maurer's distinction between different levels of issuer trust, we get credential networks of the following form:

$$\mathbf{N}_{Maurer} = (\mathbf{U}_0, X_0, \mathbf{A}^+, \mathbf{T}^+).$$

Figure 10. Hypotheses lying within the left subtriangle are rejected, those lying within the right subtriangle are accepted, and the remaining hypotheses are left open. (a) SAP with $\lambda=0.9$ and $h=0.8$, (b) LAP with $\lambda=0.6$ and $\eta=0.5$.

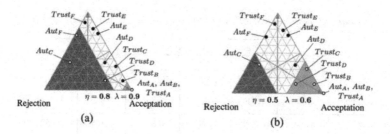

In Haenni's model (2005b), all certificates are absolute. Furthermore, the owner X_0 is required to specify explicit trust values for all users in the network. This is like requiring the owner to issue trust ratings with corresponding weights for all users. Let $\mathbf{T}^{\pm}_{X_0 \mathbf{U}}$ denote such a set of trust ratings issued by X_0, that is, one for each user $X \in \mathbf{U}$. Furthermore, we consider (absolute) revocations to be part of Haenni's model, but not recommendations. If we denote the sets of absolute certificates and revocations by $\mathbf{A}^+$ and $\mathbf{A}^-$, respectively, Haenni's model corresponds to:

$$\mathbf{N}_{\text{Haenni}} = (\mathbf{U}_0, X_0, \mathbf{A}^+ \cup \mathbf{A}^-, \mathbf{T}^{\pm}_{X_0 \mathbf{U}}).$$

The situation in a PGP web of trust is similar to Haenni's model. All certificates are absolute, and the owner of the web of trust is required to specify trust values for all users. However, because the possible trust values are restricted to *fully trustworthy*, *marginally trustworthy*, and *untrustworthy*, it's like restricting the possible weights of the trust ratings to the set $\Omega = \{0, 0.5, 1\}$. A set of such trust ratings for all users is denoted by $\mathbf{T}^{\pm\{0,0.5,1\}}_{X_0 \mathbf{U}}$. If we do not consider revocations to be part of the PGP model (PGP allows only revocations affecting the issuer's own public key), then we get the following particular kind of credential network:

$$\mathbf{N}_{\text{PGP}} = (\mathbf{U}_0, X_0, \mathbf{A}^+, \mathbf{T}^{\pm\{0,0.5,1\}}_{X_0 \mathbf{U}}).$$

In a centralized public-key infrastructure, it is assumed that (at least) one entity X_{CA} is a fully trustworthy *certificate authority*. All certificates are absolute, and with one exception they are all issued by X_{CA}. The one that is not issued by X_{CA} is a certificate issued by X_0 for X_{CA}. Let $\mathbf{U}_{CA} = \mathbf{U}_0 \cup \{X_{CA}\}$ be the extended set of users that includes a certificate authority X_{CA}. If $\mathbf{A}^{+1}_{X_{CA}}$ denotes a set of absolute certificates all issued by X_{CA}, then a centralized public-key infrastructure (PKI) is a credential network with the following characteristics:

$$\mathbf{N}_{\text{CA}} = (\mathbf{U}_{CA}, X_0, \mathbf{A}^{+1}_{X_{CA}} \cup \{A^{+1}_{X_0 X_{CA}}\}, \{T^{+1}_{X_0 X_{CA}}\}).$$

In many reputation networks, all the statements are ratings, but they are usually not required to be digitally signed. Furthermore, the focus is on trust only. In the terminology of credential networks, this is like assuming all public keys to be authentic, which corresponds to a situation in which X_0 issues absolute certificates for all users $X \in \mathbf{U}$. If $\mathbf{A}^{+1}_{X_0 \mathbf{U}}$ denotes such a set of absolute certificates issued by X_0, then:

$$\mathbf{N}_{\text{Reputation-Network}} = (\mathbf{U}_0, X_0, \mathbf{A}^{+1}_{X_0 \mathbf{U}_0}, \mathbf{T}^{\pm})$$

forms a reputation network in the above sense.

Future Trends and Conclusion

The introduction of information technologies into most business and social activities is resulting in complex networks of electronic relationships. Trust and authenticity play a crucial role in the functioning of these networks, especially to ensure the security of transactions and contracts between network entities. Managing trust and authenticity in the context of such networks and virtual communities is thus a strongly emerging area, but the development of satisfactory and general solutions is a very difficult task. Previous work in this area has explored many different directions, and it consists of mathematical models, pragmatic ad-hoc solutions, and analytical or empirical studies. The research is often focused on certain domains like peer-to-peer networks, reputation systems, or public-key infrastructures. As a first conclusion, it seems that the appropriateness of a solution depends on the specific application.

Another observation is that today's models and solutions come from two different worlds, namely from *theory* and from *practice*. Theoretical models are mostly developed and discussed by academics, while the design and realization of most practical solutions is the work of application-oriented companies or practitioners. Some of the theoretical approaches have led to very general and mathematically sound models, but most of them are difficult to implement and inefficient when it comes to computing exact solutions. On the other side, existing solutions from the practice are often quite pragmatic and designed to be efficient, but most of them lack of a generality and some are mathematically not properly founded. The focus lies thus on efficiency and ease-of-use rather than generality and mathematical soundness.

These motivations and goals make perfect sense in their respective worlds, but they are often conflicting and thus difficult to combine. This problem is similar to the more general tradeoff problem of usability vs. security: which level of technical complexity are users willing to accept in order to avoid frauds, loss of privacy, or loss of sensitive data? As there is no general answer to this, future research should focus on finding the optimal consensus or compromise between computational efficiency, ease-of-use, mathematical correctness, and generality of the model.

Within the academic community, there is a growing research interest on trust-based networks in different disciplines. Several ongoing research projects deal with trust in networks from the point of view of security, which is mainly a computer science perspective. Unfortunately, this view is still quite disconnected from other related contributions, for example, from sociology, experimental economics, or physics. For the further development towards more realistic theoretical models and real-world oriented implementations, it would certainly be fruitful to explore the possible integration of the research from all affected areas. Related to the topic of network-based trust, this integration will be one of the major challenges in the near future.

The analysis presented in this chapter is a security-oriented view of computer scientists. The discussion aims at clarifying key notions like entities, identities, authenticity, and trust-worthiness. The result is a classification of existing systems in terms of so-called *layered* models. This view is the consequence of the *digital signature requirement*, which seems to be crucial to avoid frauds from malicious or dishonest entities. Consequently, the chapter proposes and defends the *two-layer requirement*, which imposes a model to include at least two layers, one for trust and one for authenticity. Stressing out this mutual dependency between trust and authenticity is one of the primary goals of this chapter.

Another goal of this chapter is to give an overview of existing approaches. Some of them satisfy the previously mentioned requirements, some of them do not. The discussion includes an attempt to define the basic notions like trust and authenticity with maximal generality and preciseness. It turns out, that most existing models are easily transferable into this general terminology, which may be useful to better understand and compare their properties and characteristics. Particular attention is given to the *credential network* model, currently one of the most general existing models.

Acknowledgments

This research is supported by the Swiss National Science Foundation, project no. PP002--102652, and the Hasler Foundation, project no. 2042. Special thanks also to Michael Wachter for careful proofreading and helpful comments.

References

Beth, T., Borcherding, M., & Klein, B. (1994). Valuation of trust in open networks. In *ES-ORICS'94, 3rd European Symposium on Research in Computer Security* (pp. 3-18). Springer.

Blaze, M., Feigenbaum, J., Ioannidis, J., & Keromytis, A. D. (1999). The role of trust management in distributed systems security. In *Secure Internet programming: Security issues for mobile and distributed objects* (pp. 185-210). London: Springer.

Blaze, M., Feigenbaum, J., & Keromytis, A. D. (1999). KeyNote: Trust management for public-key infrastructures (position paper). In *6th International Workshop on Security Protocols*, Cambridge, UK (pp. 59-63).

Blaze, M., Feigenbaum, J., & Lacy, J. (1996). Decentralized trust management. In *SP'96: IEEE Symposium on Security and Privacy* (pp. 164-173).

Boyd, J. (2002). In community we trust: Online security communication at eBay. *Journal of Computer-Mediated Communication, 7*(3). Retrieved from http://jcmc.indiana.edu/vol17/issue3/boyd.html

Chandler, J., El-Khatib, K., Benyoucef, M., Bochmann, G., & Adams, C. (2006). Legal challenges of online reputation systems. In *Trust in e-services: Technologies, practices and challenges* (to appear).

Chu, Y. H., Feigenbaum, J., LaMacchia, B., Resnick, P., & Strauss, M. (1997). REFEREE: Trust management for Web applications. *Computer Networks and ISDN Systems, 29*(8-13), 953-964.

Colbourn, C. J. (1987). *The combinatorics of network reliability*. New York: Oxford University Press.

Haenni, R. (2005a). Towards a unifying theory of logical and probabilistic reasoning. In F. B. Cozman, R. Nau, & T. Seidenfeld (Eds.), *ISIPTA'05, 4ᵗʰ International Symposium on Imprecise Probabilities and Their Applications*, Pittsburgh, PA (pp. 193-202).

Haenni, R. (2005b). Using probabilistic argumentation for key validation in public-key cryptography. *International Journal of Approximate Reasoning, 38*(3), 355-376.

Haenni, R., Kohlas, J., & Lehmann, N. (2000). Probabilistic argumentation systems. In D. M. Gabbay & P. Smets (Eds.), *Handbook of defeasible reasoning and uncertainty management systems* (Vol. 5: Algorithms for Uncertainty and Defeasible Reasoning, pp. 221-288). Dordrecht, Netherlands: Kluwer Academic Publishers.

Jonczy, J., & Haenni, R. (2005). Credential networks: A general model for distributed trust and authenticity management. In A. Ghorbani & S. Marsh (Eds.), *PST'05: 3ʳᵈ Annual Conference on Privacy, Security and Trust*, St. Andrews, Canada (pp. 101-112).

Jonczy, J., & Haenni, R. (2006). Implementing credential networks (accepted). In *iTrust'06, 4ᵗʰ International Conference on Trust Management*, Pisa, Italy (pp. 164-178).

Jonczy, J., Wythrich, M., & Haenni, R., (2006). A probabilistic trust model for GnuPG. In *23c3* (accepted), *Chaos communication Congress 2006*, Berlin, Germany.

Jøsang, A. (1997). Artificial reasoning with subjective logic. In A. C. Nayak & M. Pagnucco (Eds.), *2ⁿᵈ Australian Workshop on Commonsense Reasoning*, Perth, Australia.

Jøsang, A. (1999a). An algebra for assessing trust in certification chains. In *NDSS'99: 6ᵗʰ Annual Symposium on Network and Distributed System Security*, San Diego, CA.

Jøsang, A. (1999b). Trust-based decision making for electronic transactions. In L. Yngström & T. Svensson (Eds.), *NORDSEC'99: Fourth Nordic Workshop on Secure IT Systems*, Stockholm, Sweden.

Jøsang, A., Ismail, R., & Boyd, C. (2006). A survey of trust and reputation systems for online service provision. In *Decision support systems* (to appear).

Kamvar, S. D., Schlosser, M. T., & Garcia-Molina, H. (2003). The EigenTrust algorithm for reputation management in P2P networks. In *WWW2003, 12ᵗʰ International World Wide Web conference*, Budapest, Hungary (pp. 640-651).

Kohlas, R., & Maurer, U. (2000). Confidence valuation in a public-key infrastructure based on uncertain evidence. In H. Imai & Y. Zheng (Eds.), *PKC'2000, Third International Workshop on Practice and Theory in Public Key Cryptography* (pp. 93-112). Melbourne, Australia: Springer.

Lee, S., Sherwood, R., & Bhattacharjee, S. (2003). Cooperative peer groups in NICE. In *IEEE- INFOCOM'03, 22ⁿᵈ Annual Joint Conference of the IEEE Computer and Communications Societies*, San Francisco (pp. 1272-1282).

Levien, R., & Aiken, A. (1998). Attack-resistant trust metrics for public key certification. In *Security'98, 7ᵗʰ USENIX Security Symposium*, San Antonio, TX (pp. 229-242).

Mahoney, G., Myrvold, W., & Shoja, G. C. (2005). Generic reliability trust model. In A. Ghorbani & S. Marsh (Eds.), *PST'05: 3ʳᵈ Annual Conference on Privacy, Security and Trust*, St. Andrews, Canada (pp. 113-120).

Marchesini, J., & Smith, S. W. (2005). Modeling public key infrastructures in the real world. In D. Chadwick & G. Zhao (Eds.), *EuroPKI'04, 2nd European PKI Workshop: Research and Applications* (pp. 118-134). Canterbury, UK: Springer.

Marsh, S. P. (1994). *Formalising trust as a computational concept.* Unpublished doctoral dissertation, University of Stirling, Scotland, UK.

Maurer, U. (1996). Modelling a public-key infrastructure. In E. Bertino, H. Kurth, G. Martella, & E. Montolivo (Eds.), *ESORICS, European Symposium on Research in Computer Security* (pp. 324-350). Springer.

Nilsson, N. J. (1986). Probabilistic logic. *Artificial Intelligence, 28*(1), 71-87.

Reiter, M. K., & Stubblebine, S. G. (1997). Toward acceptable metrics of authentication. In *SP'97: 18th IEEE Symposium on Security and Privacy*, Oakland, CA (pp. 10-20).

Reiter, M. K., & Stubblebine, S. G. (1999). Authentication metric analysis and design. *ACM Transactions on Information and System Security, 2*(2), 138-158.

Sadighi Firozabadi, B., & Sergot, M. (2003). Revocation in the privilege calculus. In *FAST'03: 1st International Workshop on Formal Aspects in Security and Trust* (pp. 39-51).

Shafer, G. (1976). *The mathematical theory of evidence.* Princeton, NJ: Princeton University Press.

Shi, J., Bochmann, G., & Adams, C. (2004). A trust model with statistical foundation. In *FAST'04, 2nd International Workshop on Formal Aspects in Security and Trust*, Toulouse, France (pp. 145-158).

Theodorakopoulos, G. (2004). *Distributed trust evaluation in ad-hoc networks.* Unpublished master's thesis, University of Maryland, College Park, MD.

Theodorakopoulos, G., & Baras, J. S. (2004). Trust evaluation in ad-hoc networks. In M. Jakobsson & A. Perrig (Eds.), *WiSe'04, ACM Workshop on Wireless Security* (pp. 1-10). Philadelphia: ACM Press.

Yahalem, R., Klein, B., & Beth, T. (1993). Trust relationships in secure system—a distributed authentication perspective. In *IEEE Symposium on Research in Security and Privacy* (pp. 150-164).

Zimmermann, P. R. (1994). *The official PGP user's guide.* MIT Press.

Chapter VII

Information Valuation Policies for Explainable Trustworthiness Assessment in E-Services

Karen K. Fullam, University of Texas at Austin, USA

K. Suzanne Barber, University of Texas at Austin, USA

Abstract

Information e-services are useful for exchanging information among many users, whether human or automated agent; however, e-service users are susceptible to risk of inaccurate information, since users have no traditional face-to-face interaction or past relational history with information providers. To encourage use of information e-services, individuals must have technology to assess information accuracy and information source trustworthiness. This research permits automated e-service users—here called agents—acting on behalf of humans, to employ policies, or heuristics, for predicting information accuracy when numerous pieces of information are received from multiple sources. These intuitive policies draw from human strategies for evaluating the trustworthiness of information to not only identify accurate information, but also distinguish untrustworthy information providers. These policies allow the agent to build a user's confidence in the trust assessment technology by creating justifications for trust assessment decisions and identifying particular policies integral to a given assessment decision.

Introduction

Increasingly, e-services are becoming a common method of exchanging information among a wide range of users. Information e-services include Web sites like eBay (eBay, 2006), which utilizes a centralized reputation exchange mechanism to assess the trustworthiness of buyers and sellers, and Epinions (Epinions, 2006), which provides a forum for information exchange about the quality of goods and services. Online information exchange, however, leaves users susceptible to risk of inaccurate information, since users have no traditional face-to-face interaction or no past relational history with information providers. Thus, information sources find it easier to lie about the information they provide, since retribution may be difficult.

To avoid the influence of untrustworthy information sources, system designers have historically emphasized "hard security" measures, including such technologies as user authentication and encrypted transmission. Even with infrastructure protections in place to verify users and ensure transmission integrity, critical security questions remain unanswered—about user authenticity, intent, and competence (Falcone, Pezzulo, & Castelfranchi, 2002), and self-confidence (Barber & Kim, 2002a)—that suggest potential vulnerabilities. These questions can only be answered by considering the content of provided information. Specifically, the trustworthiness of incoming information and information providers must be examined to identify accurate information, especially when hard security measures fail.

If the public is to be encouraged to utilize such information e-services, individuals must be provided with technology to assess information accuracy and the trustworthiness of information sources. Information trustworthiness assessment accomplishes three purposes: (1) e-service users receive more accurate information, (2) untrustworthy information providers are identified and isolated, and (3) the user's confidence in the trust assessment technology leads to increased utilization of the e-service. However, since the accuracy of information can depend on numerous factors, such as the trustworthiness of the provider and the age of the information, this information trustworthiness assessment problem is no simple task.

This information trust assessment research permits automated e-service users—here called agents—acting on behalf of humans, to employ a set of policies (Fullam & Barber, 2004), or heuristics, for predicting the accuracy of information when numerous pieces of information are received from multiple sources. These intuitive policies draw from human strategies for evaluating the trustworthiness of information. The information valuation policies, to be discussed, not only identify accurate information, but also distinguish untrustworthy information providers. An agent's use of these information valuation policies builds the human user's confidence in the trust assessment technology by creating justifications for trust assessment decisions that point out the particular policies integral to a given assessment decision.

The information selection algorithm presented here values incoming information—according to expected accuracy—based on a set of intuitive information valuation policies that justify the derived estimate. Information valuation policies are defined based on estimated source trustworthiness, corroboration by other sources, and certainty expressed by the source. The algorithm values incoming information against these policies, evaluating tradeoffs in cases of policy conflicts, and information with highest estimated quality is given priority when information is merged to form estimates. The direct mapping from policies to algorithm implementation provides intuitive justification for an estimate's derived alternatives and their certainties.

The objective of this research is to develop an information selection algorithm, based on the notion of information valuation, that provides estimate justification while maintaining estimates that are accurate and expressive of possible alternatives. The proposed algorithm is designed for deriving accurate estimates from source information. The estimates generated through this algorithm convey information about the certainty of the derived belief. The algorithm is based on a set of intuitive policies for prioritizing source information based on quality; these policies provide the human e-service user with justification for the resulting estimates. By examining intuitive bases for building certainty about source information, we design an algorithm that not only gives an accurate certainty assessment, but also provides justification for the human user. Information valuation is necessary to provide certainties for all possible alternatives, so a method for gauging the reliability, or accuracy, of incoming information is necessary. While the policies for deciding this accuracy depend on many factors, an obvious element is information source trustworthiness, which is difficult to predict. Since the trustworthiness of the information source is a vital component to assessing the value of information, a representation for predicted source trustworthiness is developed and presented here.

This research makes a major contribution in terms of generating decision-making information for human e-service users. An information selection algorithm based on intuitive policies challenges trust-modeling research to examine information quality assessment in terms of a number of factors, not only information source reliability. Basing information prioritization on these policies promotes traceability in algorithm construction. In addition, justification for derived information subject estimates is provided, a useful feature for any domain in which humans are the ultimate decision-making authority. The explanation of estimate calculation promotes confident human-agent interaction by providing the human with an understanding of how estimates are generated.

Background

Any e-service user, whether human or automated agent, relies on correct information to make online decisions. This information may be related to address locations on a map-providing service, such as Maporama (Maporama International, 2006) or Google Maps (Google, Inc., 2006a); stock quotes from a ticker service like MarketBrowser (Leading Market Technologies, 2006) or MSN Money (Microsoft, 2006); prices of goods for purchase at comparison shopping sites like Shopzilla (Shopzilla, Inc., 2006) or Pricegrabber (Pricegrabber.com, LLC., 2006); the reputations of e-service providers on referral networks such as Epinions (Epinions, 2006) or Amazon (Amazon.com, Inc., 2006); or the trustworthiness of potential acquaintances in online social networks such as MySpace (MySpace.com, 2006) or orkut (Google, Inc., 2006b). Users of these e-services must obtain accurate information, know the certainty of that information, and have justification for why the information is correct.

The e-service user must estimate the true values of many types of information, here called information subjects. Users need more than just single-value answers for these information subject estimates; alternative answers and certainties for each possible answer must often be considered. Importantly, when automated e-service agents represent human users, they must additionally satisfy any doubts of the human superior by supplying justification for provided answers. For example, an online purchasing agent must estimate the trustworthiness of sellers before selecting a potential transaction partner. The purchasing agent might be on alert for conflicting reports about a seller's reputation. Further, the agent may wait to select a seller until reputations can be confirmed to a specific degree of certainty. Also, the agent might have to explain the surety of its reputation assessment to a human before gaining the human's confidence and permission to purchase.

Unfortunately, an e-service agent can never know the absolute truth about its information estimates because the data it collects is uncertain. Information received through online communications with other agents or humans may be compromised if the communication channel is not secure. Information sources may be incompetent or dishonest. The agent must make its information estimates by merging uncertain information from all sources—including humans and other agents—to calculate information subject estimates it asserts to be true with a given degree of certainty. The agent needs its set of estimates to answer the following questions:

What is the agent's *best* estimate of an information subject?

From the information an agent receives from sources, including communication from humans and other agents, the agent's information selection algorithm must generate an accurate estimate of an information subject. Estimate correctness improves when the value, or accuracy, of incoming information is examined, and priority is given to more valuable information during estimate calculation. The field of trust evaluation attempts to model the reliability, or accuracy, of information sources to identify trustworthy providers of information (Jurca & Faltings, 2002), but little attention has been devoted to assessing the trustworthiness of information itself. Additionally, most trust assessment techniques represent information subjects as logical statements whose answers are estimated as either true or false (Barber & Kim, 2002b). Related work in belief maintenance (Flouris & Plexousakis, 2001; Gardenfors, 1988) also assumes logical representations for belief estimates, though recent work in continuous and hybrid belief maintenance (Lerner, 2002) has examined representing beliefs about continuous variables. An agent must have the flexibility to generate estimates for logical statements as well as variables, whose answers might be in the set of real numbers, for example. This research presents an estimate representation accommodating both types of information subjects, as well as an information selection algorithm application to continuous-variable-type information subjects.

How certain is the agent of this estimate?

The agent must not only generate an accurate estimate, but also assess the quality, or accuracy of that estimate. Certainty allows the agent to enumerate all estimate possibilities then distinguish the most accurate among them. The agent's level of certainty about an information subject estimate may determine whether or not an action is taken. Many, including Halpern (1989) and Barber and Kim (2002a), have investigated quantifying an agent's confidence in a calculated estimate. However, these certainty calculations, based on Bayesian probability computations, are nonintuitive and difficult to explain to a human attempting to understand the agent's calculation process. In addition, certainty is represented as a value between zero and one (zero means no certainty and one means complete certainty); arbitrary meaning is given to values between the upper and lower bounds. The information selection algorithm presented here makes certainty calculation a straightforward process, explained through the characteristics of the source information, such as source trustworthiness, corroboration of the information, and certainty of the source in its communicated information. Further, a representation of certainty is presented such that each certainty value is tied to a unique probability that an estimate is true.

What are the justifications for each of the agent's estimates and certainties?

In situations where the ultimate e-service user is a human, justification (based on intuitive principles) of all possible information subject estimates and their certainties may be required to satisfy the user's doubts about how the estimates were derived. The formation of an estimate should be traceable to provide a user with justification for each calculated alternative and its proposed likelihood. Research examining trust in information sources (Dragoni & Giorgini, 2003) can provide justification based on a source's estimated reliability, or trustworthiness. However, other factors such as number of sources reporting, certainty conveyed by those sources, amount of corroboration between sources, and timeliness of their information should also play a straightforward role in the calculation of estimates and certainty on those estimates.

While significant research has been conducted in addressing portions of the problems presented, this research focuses on the need for an information selection algorithm addressing all three of these requirements held by an e-service agent.

Policies for Information Valuation

This research seeks to allow a set of intuitive policies to guide algorithm construction. These policies not only provide guidelines for building an accurate information selection algorithm, but yield necessary justification for the human e-service user concerning confidence in resulting answers. To form these policies, general principles are identified for quality-based information valuation, many of which can be based on observations about how humans tend to value information.

Several factors affect an agent's information subject estimate calculation process, including (1) values of source-reported information, (2) number of sources reporting, (3) agreement among source information (4) certainty conveyed by the reporting source, (5) perceived source trustworthiness as modeled by the agent, and (6) age of source information at time of estimate calculation. The agent might also be influenced by prior estimates about the same information subject; these prior estimates might be effectively classified as information of which the provider is the agent itself (with a corresponding perceived trustworthiness). The estimate's consistency with other estimates the agent maintains might also be a factor. However, for this research, we assume the agent maintains only an estimate about a single fact (e.g., the trustworthiness of a seller), as well as trustworthiness information about reporting sources; the agent makes no inferences about the relationship between different facts.

Since an agent may not know the true value of an information subject, it has no basis to judge the quality of source information based on a source's communicated values alone. However, the agent can follow general policies for identifying information most valuable to the estimate derivation process. These policies (Fullam & Barber, 2004), identified next, have been selected because they (1) are based on arguments for information valuation in the trust community and (2) represent intuitive information valuation heuristics employed by humans, making the resulting information selection easily explainable. However, the policies are naïve heuristics when implemented in isolation; hence, each policy includes a discussion of the policy's limitations and necessary assumptions, as well as harmful ways information sources might influence the agent's resulting estimate. However, later explanation will show that an algorithm employing a compromise of all policies can identify robustly the most valuable information for estimate calculation. This research attempts to design an optimally accurate algorithm in light of these policy differences and combined utility.

1.   **Priority of maximum information:** An agent should incorporate information from as many sources as possible. Information from each source has some intrinsic value, in the sense that more information increases the agent's likelihood of achieving greater accuracy. Simple statistics show that given information from a greater number of independent sources, the variance of the true mean decreases; thus, the derived estimate should be closer to the information subject's true value. This concept works best with many reporting sources and assumes that sources are statistically independent in their reporting; in other words, there can be no collusion or common inaccuracy among information sources.

This policy is limited, because in many cases, the agent's derived answer will be more accurate if the agent can exclude information it deems inaccurate by other means. Given this policy, an information source can influence the agent's estimate only based on whether or not it chooses to communicate information to the agent.

2.   **Priority to corroborated information:** An agent should give priority to information that can be corroborated (Fallis, 2004). High value should be assigned to information that is similar to other information, while low value should be assigned to information that is significantly different from other information. An information source can influence the agent's estimate if it is able to communicate information that is consistent with the information conveyed by the group of information sources as a whole.

This policy is limited in that an agent will highly value poor information if the majority of sources inadvertently are providing inaccurate, yet consistent input. In addition, this policy assumes no collusion occurs between information sources to mislead the agent by providing uniform, incorrect information.

3.   **Priority for source certainty:** An agent should give priority to information from sources conveying high certainty on that information (Barber & Kim, 2002a). Likewise, if a source conveys a low certainty on its information, the agent should place

a low value on that information. If the information source is proficient at conveying a quality certainty assessment, that certainty assessment will be an indication of the accuracy of the information.

This policy is limited in situations where a reliable source claims low certainty on its information, while an unreliable source claims high certainty. In these cases, the imprecision of the reliable source might be more valuable than the known mistakenness of an unreliable source. The policy also assumes that information sources are honest and competent in conveying their confidence in the information they provide. In addition, this policy might be dangerous, since it allows a source to influence the agent simply through the certainty the source communicates, regardless of source reliability or actual data quality.

4.   **Priority to reliable sources:** An agent should give priority to information from sources it estimates to be most reliable (Abdul-Rahman & Hailes, 1999; Roorda, van der Hoek, & Meyer, 2002). If a reporting source is estimated by the agent to be a provider of quality information (in other words, the source has a high reputation), based on past experience or recommendations from other entities, then the agent should place a high value on the information provided by that source. Conversely, if the agent estimates that the source reports poor quality information (the source has a low reputation), the agent should assign a low value to the provided information.

A high-quality source should convey a low certainty along with unreliable information. An information source can influence the agent's estimates, and the agent's trust model of the source, via this policy based on the quality of information it communicates to the agent. This policy also requires the agent to model source trustworthiness, which can be a complicated task; the agent's model of source trustworthiness is assumed to be accurate, and the source's true accuracy, modeled as its error probability distribution, are assumed to be static. This policy fails to consider that trustworthy sources can occasionally provide inaccurate information; although this research may assume that a source's trustworthiness characteristics are static over time, the accuracy of individual reports generated from those characteristics may vary widely from report to report. Much attention will be given to the topic of building models of information source trustworthiness, in terms of accuracy of both values and certainties, in the future sections.

5.   **Priority to recent information:** An agent should give priority to information it estimates to be most recent (Fullam & Barber, 2005). Conversely, if the information is old, then it should be considered less valuable. Since the true value of an information subject is more likely to have changed as more time passes, older information is less likely to be accurate.

Through this policy, a source can influence the agent's estimates by ensuring that it consistently supplies information to the agent, so the agent always has recent information. The policy is limited by the possibility that older information from a more-trustworthy source might be more accurate than more recent information from an inaccurate source. Additionally, in order to assign relative value to information of different ages, the agent must know the rate at which truth about an information subject changes; the faster the information subject changes, the more quickly information loses value. The complexity of this problem is beyond the scope of this research.

An Information Selection Algorithm Based on Information Valuation Policies

To explain how estimates are computed using information valuation policies, an estimate representation much first be discussed. Estimates are based on an information subject v, where v is any variable or statement that evaluates to some continuous or discrete set of values X^v (X^v is the universal set of possible values for v). Let X_a^v be called the set of all possible values for v believed by a to exist; hence, $X_a^v \subseteq X^v$. Then, an estimate B_v about v is uniquely defined by the tuple $< v, X_a^v, \phi_a^v, a, t>$, where ϕ_a^v is a set of probabilities asserted by a over X_a^v and t is the time at which the estimate is calculated. As an example, if X_a^v represents a continuous set such as the set of real numbers (where v is a continuous variable), ϕ_a^v might consist of a continuous distribution function. There is a tradeoff between the representational complexity of the distribution function shape chosen to represent the estimate and the function's precision; for example, a multimodal distribution may be more difficult to represent, yet a better description of v than a normal distribution. A communicated report C_{s_i} is a message from information source s_i that minimally includes the information v, $X_{s_i}^v$, and s_i, but may also include $\phi_{s_i}^v$ and t, where $X_{s_i}^v$ and $\phi_{s_i}^v$ represent, respectively, the set of possible values and the probability distribution over those values that s_i communicates to a. For now, we shall define estimate calculation simply as some process by which an agent a utilizes a set of information source reports C_a to derive an estimate B_v about v.

In the estimate definition we propose, certainty is implicitly maintained by the set of probabilities ϕ_a^v. In cases where X_a^v is a continuous set, certainty can be defined as the asserted probability that the true value, x_T, of the information subject is within a specified small radius δ of a given value. Formally, for a given $x' \in X_a^v$, certainty that x_T is in the range x' - δ to x' + δ is given by:

$$\text{certainty}(x', \delta) = \int_{x'-\delta}^{x'+\delta} \phi_a^v(x)dx$$

for a selected interval radius δ. This definition of certainty allows increased expressiveness; certainty that x_T is in the range x' - δ to x' + δ can be calculated for any $x' \in X_a^v$, not only for some asserted single-value result.

The algorithm designed in this section attempts to accomplish several objectives. First, it must be able to generate alternatives and certainties for each information subject by calculating the agent a's estimate distribution, ϕ_a^v, from several information source distributions. Second, it should provide justification for the resulting estimate distribution by enumerating reasons for value assessments of information contributing to the calculated estimate.

The following sections explain how each policy can be incorporated into the information selection algorithm. In particular, a prominent policy for valuing information is based on the perceived trustworthiness of the information source; source trustworthiness can be difficult to predict, and so significant effort is devoted to constructing information source trust models. Finally, in merging policies into a single algorithm, tradeoffs between policies will become evident, and so conflicts must be resolved.

Several assumptions are made in the construction of this algorithm. To simplify the algorithm's illustration, the types of estimates that are computed are limited to only estimates about continuous variables, particularly useful in domains such as reputation calculation in online social networks. For simplicity, probability distributions for these estimates are represented as normal distributions. Also, this information selection algorithm forms estimates only from new source information received in the current timestep. Hence, old estimates maintain no residual influence over current estimates (although in future work, previous estimates could be modeled as information of which the agent itself is the source). Finally, the computation of an estimate about a single information subject v is considered independent from any information the agent might maintain about other information subjects. Thus, the existence of possible inference rules linking estimates about different information subjects is ignored. The single exception to this assumption pertains to reputations, which are estimates about information source trustworthiness; the agent builds reputation estimates from data it maintains about past source information quality.

One additional assumption is made concerning information source trustworthiness characteristics. A source's true accuracy is defined in terms of the source's probability distribution of error between the mean of the reported distribution and the true value of the information subject, as well as the accuracy of the source's certainty assignment (denoted by the standard deviation of the reported distribution). This research assumes that a source's accuracy parameters are static over time. However, since each report is generated based on error probability distributions, the accuracy of a single report can vary widely from timestep to timestep.

As shown in Figure 1, each information source s_i first sends an information report C_{s_i} to the agent. All reports about a single information subject v are collected in the set C_a. Next, the agent evaluates the worth of each report according to one or more policies (which may include the modeling of information source trustworthiness). The valuation process performs a binary inclusion decision, assigning weights of either zero or one to each piece of information. The estimate distribution ϕ_B is then derived from included information sources; if the estimate distribution is described by a normalized Gaussian, then the estimate distribution mean, μ_B, and standard deviation, σ_B, are computed. A "naïve" information selection algorithm would include all information sources (assigning a weight of one to each piece of information) and calculate the estimate distribution mean and standard deviation as:

$$\mu_B = \frac{\sum_{i=1}^{n} \mu_{s_i}}{n}$$

$$\sigma_B = \sqrt{\frac{\sum_{i=1}^{n}(\sigma_{s_i}^2 + (\mu_{s_i} - \mu_B)^2)}{n}}.$$

Figure 1. Estimate calculation process with trust-modeling information valuation

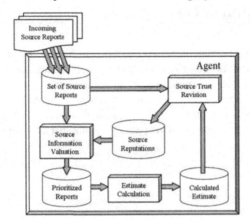

Calculation of estimate certainty, however, should assume greater accuracy with larger numbers of contributing sources. If source data are independent, then we can assert that the mean, μ_{s_i}, of each source distribution is taken from a distribution whose mean is the true value, x_T, of the belief subject and whose standard deviation is some σ. If the average of the source distribution means μ_{s_i}, for $i = 1$ to n, is denoted by $\bar{\mu}$, then the collection of $\bar{\mu}$ values (over all samples) forms a distribution whose mean is x_T, and whose standard deviation is $\frac{\sigma}{\sqrt{n}}$. Thus n sources, instead of 1 source, narrow the confidence interval for $\bar{\mu}$ by a factor of $\frac{1}{\sqrt{n}}$. In other words, averaging one source distribution may yield $\bar{\mu}$ such that $P(|\bar{\mu} - x_T| \leq d)$. Averaging n source distributions will yield a value for $\bar{\mu}$ such that $P\left(|\bar{\mu} - x_T| \leq \frac{d}{\sqrt{n}}\right) = p$. Since the proportion $\frac{1}{\sqrt{n}}$ determines the impact of the number of information sources on the closeness of $\bar{\mu}$ to x_T, the belief certainty calculation can be modified to account for better accuracy with more information sources by dividing the naïve belief certainty by $\sqrt{n}$. Thus σ_B, when accounting for number of information sources becomes:

$$\sigma_B = \frac{\sqrt{\dfrac{\sum\limits_{i=1}^{n}(\sigma_{s_i}^2 + (\mu_{s_i} - \mu_B)^2)}{n}}}{\sqrt{n}}.$$

Simplifying,

$$\sigma_B = \sqrt{\frac{\sum\limits_{i=1}^{n}(\sigma_{s_i}^2 + (\mu_{s_i} - \mu_B)^2)}{n}}.$$

Selecting Information Based on Information Characteristics: Certainty Maximization Algorithm

Maximizing the agent's estimate certainty can assist in finding the tradeoffs between obtaining maximum information, maximizing source certainty, and maximizing source agreement. If the estimate standard deviation σ_B is an accurate measure of the closeness of the estimate distribution mean μ_B to the information subject's true value x_T, then minimizing σ_B should yield a distribution most closely aggregated around x_T. Recall that the estimate distribution standard deviation, when accounting for number of information sources, can be calculated as:

$$\sigma_B = \sqrt{\frac{\sum_{i=1}^{n}(\sigma_{s_i}^2 + (\mu_{s_i} - \mu_B)^2)}{n}}.$$

The agent must find the combination of information sources that minimizes σ_B. Starting from a single most promising source, each additional source increases σ_B by both the $\sigma_{s_i}^2$ term (the source standard deviation) and the $(\mu_{s_i} - \mu_B)^2$ term (the distance of the distribution mean from the aggregate distribution mean), and decreases σ_B by increasing the number of sources, n, by one. Unfortunately, ranking information sources in order of best contribution (small $\sigma_{s_i}^2$ and $(\mu_{s_i} - \mu_B)^2$ terms) involves infeasibly complex computation since the value of the $(\mu_{s_i} - \mu_B)^2$ term changes depending on which source is added (μ_B changes depending on the means of included source distributions), and since some sources may have larger $\sigma_{s_i}^2$ terms and smaller $(\mu_{s_i} - \mu_B)^2$ terms, or vice versa. As a guide, μ_B can be calculated when including all sources except outliers, and sources can be prioritized in order of minimal value of $\sigma_{s_i}^2$ and $(\mu_{s_i} - \mu_B)^2$ summed terms. Then σ_B can be calculated for the group of included sources each time the next highest-ranking source is added to the group (this time using the μ_B as computed only from the included group). The group that results in the smallest calculated value for σ_B denotes the sources that should be allowed to contribute to the estimate calculation. The belief distribution mean and standard deviation can then be calculated from only the selected group of sources.

Table 1 demonstrates example calculations required to determine which source information will be included in the estimate calculation. First, the distribution reported by Source 8 is determined to be an outlier based on a standard outlier test (see Fullam, 2003 for more details about outlier testing). A preliminary estimate mean is calculated from the remaining information from Sources 1 through 7. Sources are then sorted in order of increasing magnitude of contribution to estimate standard deviation. Then for groups of size 1 to 8, the predicted estimate standard deviation is calculated. For the example shown, only Sources 1 through 6 should be included in the estimate calculation process (the addition of Sources 7 and 8 yield higher values for the estimate standard deviation).

Since the strategy of ordering sources assumes that the preliminary μ_B is calculated from a group of sources that may not be the final contributing group, some sources may be unfairly excluded from the contributing group. To avoid unfair exclusion of sources, it is reasonable to err on the side of maximum information, and adopt the group of agents for whom σ_B is

Table 1. Calculation of belief certainty maximization

Source n	Source Mean (μ_{s_i})	Source Standard Deviation (σ_{s_i})	Source Standard Deviation Term $(\sigma_{s_i}^2)$	Difference of Means Term $(\mu_{s_i} - \mu_B)^2$	Contribution to Estimate Standard Deviation $\sigma_{s_i}^2 + (\mu_{s_i} - \mu_B)^2$	Predicted Estimate Standard Deviation When Including Sources 1 Through n
1	222.34	0.190	0.036	0.000	0.036	0.191
2	222.21	0.300	0.090	0.022	0.112	0.193
3	222.65	0.220	0.048	0.084	0.133	0.177
4	222.56	0.320	0.102	0.040	0.142	0.163
5	222.03	0.230	0.053	0.109	0.162	0.153
6	221.98	0.170	0.029	0.144	0.173	0.145
7	222.75	0.440	0.194	0.152	0.346	0.150
8*	218.95	0.430	0.185	11.628	11.813	0.449

*Note: Preliminary outer mean $(\mu_B) = 222.36$; *outlier, not included in calculation of μ_B*

within some small interval from the minimal calculated σ_B. This certainty maximization algorithm allows a small estimate standard deviation allowance of 10% larger than the minimum hypothesized standard deviation. By this allowance, information from Source 7 would be included in the estimate calculation process.

The equation used in this research for calculating estimate standard deviation (and subsequently, estimate certainty) is accurate; hence, selecting information by maximizing estimate certainty effectively identifies the most accurate information based on characteristics of the information itself. The certainty maximization algorithm weighs tradeoffs between three information valuation policies based on (1) maximum information, (2) information corroboration, and (3) source certainty.

Selecting Information Based on Information Source Trustworthiness: Error Minimization Algorithm

Evaluating source information based on a source trustworthiness policy is more difficult than using other policies. Policies regarding maximum information, source certainty, and source agreement are based at most on the content of the communicated source report. However, policies regarding source trustworthiness require that a model of source trustworthiness be built up as a result of the agent's interactions with the information source. Consequently, the following sections identify policies for building reputations and discuss how reputations can affect information valuation. Throughout this research, we define an agent's trust in an information source as the agent's confidence that the information source will (1) provide accurate information, and (2) convey an accurate certainty assessment of the information provided. Further, we use a simplified definition of reputation as an agent's estimate of its own trust in an information source (see Barber & Fullam, 2003 for a detailed discussion of trust and reputation concepts beyond the scope of this chapter).

Policies for Evaluating Information Source Trustworthiness

In determining how to build reputation models of information source trustworthiness, we can identify useful policies for assessing information source trustworthiness. A source's trust model is built up by the agent over time, and a trustworthiness assessment for a given timestep depends on (1) content of source-reported information, (2) content of the derived estimate, (3) certainty conveyed by the reporting source, (4) certainty associated with the derived estimate, and (5) the relative ages of source-reported information and the derived estimate.

1. **Reward for accurate information:** An agent must decide the value of information received from sources, ideally, by comparing source information against the true value of the information subject. Because an agent does not have knowledge of the information subject's true value, it must substitute its final, calculated estimate (as derived from *all* source information) as the standard against which source information must be evaluated. Therefore, an information source's reputation benefit should be proportional to the similarity between the source's information and the agent's calculated estimate. Conversely, an information source's reputation loss should be proportional to the disagreement between the source's information and the agent's calculated estimate (Jonker & Treur, 1999). Information sources are thus motivated to convey information as accurately as possible. This policy assumes the agent's derived estimate is an accurate model of the information subject's true value.

2. **Penalty or reward of conveyed certainty:** When a source communicates a high level of certainty on its information, the source accepts a prospect of greater risk/reward to its reputation, which should be credited (or discredited) greatly if the information is found to be similar (or dissimilar) to the agent's derived estimate (Barber & Kim, 2002a). Alternatively, when a source communicates a low level of certainty on its information, its reputation should be credited (or discredited) only slightly if the information is found to be similar (or dissimilar) to the agent's derived estimate, because the source is effectively declaring "I don't know." This motivates the information source to convey certainty assessments that are as accurate as possible, since the source will lose credibility for assigning high certainty to inaccurate information and, likewise, forgo an opportunity cost (reputation credit) for assigning low certainty to accurate information.

3. **Strength of belief certainty:** When an agent has high certainty on a calculated estimate, it assumes a good model of the information subject's true value and can more confidently credit or discredit source reputations; however, when an agent is less certain of its calculated estimate, it should take caution in revising source reputations, acknowledging that its estimate may be inaccurate. Therefore, if an agent has a high certainty on a calculated estimate, it should greatly credit (discredit) a source's reputation if the source's information is found to be similar (dissimilar) to the agent's estimate. Alternatively, if an agent has a low certainty on a calculated estimate, it should only slightly credit (discredit) a source's reputation if the source's information is found to be similar (dissimilar) to the agent's estimate (Barber & Kim, 2002a). This policy assumes the agent's calculated certainty on the estimate is accurate.

4.   **Age of information:** Because the true value of an information subject can change over time, a source should not be held accountable for differences between its information and the true value due to a time difference between when the report is received by the agent and when the estimate is calculated. Instead, sources reporting data claimed to be more recent should be held to higher accountability. As a result, if a source's information is old, relative to the age of the calculated estimate, the source's reputation should be credited (discredited) only slightly, whereas if the source's information is recent, the source's reputation should be greatly credited (discredited) (Fullam & Barber, 2005). This policy motivates an information source to communicate, promptly, data that is recent (to its best knowledge), or else convey a low certainty on the information. Unfortunately, since temporal issues are not considered in this research, integration of source promptness in modeling the source's reputation will be left for future work.

Algorithm Based on Source Trustworthiness

Each source's trustworthiness is modeled as a distribution of source distribution mean raw error (compared to the estimate distribution mean). To build a normal distribution ρ_{s_i} reflecting the accuracy of the source s_i's distribution mean, after each timestep t in which a new estimate is calculated, the error, α, between the source distribution mean and estimate distribution mean, is calculated as:

$$\alpha(t) = \mu_{s_i}(t) - \mu_B(t).$$

The distribution ρ_{s_i} after N timesteps, can be described by its mean, μ_{ρ,s_i}, and standard deviation, σ_{ρ,s_i}, where:

$$\mu_{\rho,s_i} = \frac{\sum_{t=1}^{N}\left(\frac{1}{\sigma_B(t)\sigma_{s_i}(t)}\alpha(t)\right)}{\sum_{t=1}^{N}\left(\frac{1}{\sigma_B(t)\sigma_{s_i}(t)}\right)}, \text{ and}$$

$$\sigma_{\rho,s_i} = \sqrt{\frac{\sum_{t=1}^{N}\left(\frac{1}{\sigma_B(t)\sigma_{s_i}(t)}(\mu_{\rho,s_i} - \alpha(t))^2\right)}{\sum_{t=1}^{N}\left(\frac{1}{\sigma_B(t)\sigma_{s_i}(t)}\right)}}.$$

By examining the raw error distributions of all sources, predictions can be made to minimize the absolute value estimate error from the information subject's true value given different combinations of n sources. Given each source's raw error distribution ρ_{s_i}, averaging values taken from each source's distribution yields a predicted estimate error ρ_B described by a normal distribution with mean and standard deviation given as:

$$\mu_{\rho,B} = \frac{\sum_{i=1}^{n} \mu_{\rho,s_i}}{n}$$

$$\sigma_{\rho,B} = \frac{\sqrt{\sum_{i=1}^{n} (\sigma_{\rho,s_i}^2)}}{n}.$$

The predicted estimate error distribution can then be converted to a predicted mean absolute error. Representing error as a distribution is necessary, since source error precision, or consistency, as measured by source error standard deviation, is a factor in calculating mean absolute value error. A tradeoff emerges between sources that are accurate, on average, yet inconsistent (high error standard deviations), and sources that may be consistent, yet inaccurate, on average. When evaluating sources based on their mean absolute value error, both source accuracy and precision are weighed. The distribution, ρ_B, modeling the predicted raw error of the estimate distribution mean from the information subject's true value, is directly correlated to the absolute value error of the estimate distribution mean from the information subject's true value. Minimizing this absolute value error can determine which sources should be included in the estimate calculation. The following discussion explains how mean absolute value error can be calculated from the estimate's predicted raw error distribution.

If an estimate's raw error distribution is ρ_B, then the predicted estimate mean absolute value error can be calculated as:

$$\text{Mean absolute value error} = \int_{-\infty}^{+\infty} |x| \rho_B(x) dx.$$

If ρ_B is a normal distribution described by $(\mu_{\rho,B}, \sigma_{\rho,B})$, then the previous equation is expanded to

$$\text{Mean absolute value error} = \int_{-\infty}^{+\infty} |x| \frac{1}{\sigma_{\rho,B}\sqrt{2\pi}} e^{-\frac{(x-\mu_{\rho,B})^2}{2\sigma_{\rho,B}^2}} dx.$$

Though this integral seems complex, it is simple to assess for some cases. Figure 2 illustrates three cases:

1. $|\mu_{\rho,B}| = 0$
2. $0 < |\mu_{\rho,B}| < 4\sigma_{\rho,B}$
3. $|\mu_{\rho,B}| > 4\sigma_{\rho,B}$

Figure 2. Error distributions with different mean conditions

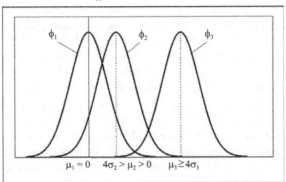

When ρ_B has a mean of zero, the mean absolute value error can be expressed as:

$$\text{Mean absolute value error} = \sigma_{\rho,B} \sqrt{\frac{2}{\pi}}.$$

Thus, although a source's error may average to zero, the standard deviation of the error distribution gives insight into the source's error precision. Low error standard deviations identify more favorable sources that are consistently accurate (low absolute value error), while high standard deviations correlate to sources that are inconsistent (high absolute value error).

In cases where nearly the entire error distribution is either positive or negative, as given by the rule $|\mu_{\rho,B}| > 4\sigma_{\rho,B}$, the mean absolute value error can be approximated as:

$$\text{Mean absolute value error} \approx \mu_{\rho,B}.$$

For these error distributions, the magnitude of error signified by the distance of $\mu_{\rho,B}$ makes examining error consistency insignificant. In cases where $0 < |\mu_{\rho,B}| < 4\sigma_{\rho,B}$, integration must be performed to get a value for the mean absolute value error. In other words, both the magnitude of average error $\mu_{\rho,B}$ and error precision, signified by $\sigma_{\rho,B}$, are factors in determining mean absolute value error.

The combination of information sources yielding the lowest mean absolute value error is the optimally accurate combination, and sources that are too inaccurate are excluded from the estimate calculation process. Information from included sources can be used to derive the estimate distribution mean and standard deviation. Finally, reputations of all sources (not just those contributing to the estimate calculation), can be revised by adding the error information from the newest timestep to the source error distribution, ρ_{s_i}.

The prospect of trying all possible combinations of sources might seem complex. However, information sources can be ordered so that testing only a few combinations is necessary. If sources have error means near zero, then sources can be ordered from least standard deviation to greatest. Then only the estimate error standard deviation must be calculated for groups starting with only the lowest standard deviation source then iteratively adding the next lowest. If source error distribution means are significantly larger than four times the error distribution standard deviations, sources can simply be ordered by increasing error distribution means. Ordering sources is slightly more difficult when sources have error distribution means between zero and four times the error distribution standard deviations. In this case, sources can be sorted by individual source absolute value error.

This error minimization algorithm is susceptible to instability, since important decisions about what information to include can be made, in the first few timesteps, based on no or incomplete source error distributions. As a result, this algorithm is modified to first build source error distributions during the first 20 timesteps, while using a naïve belief revision algorithm, before switching to the filtering of sources based on reputations.

Merging Selection Methods: All-Policy Algorithm

The final algorithm must merge the two selection methods that attempt to maximize estimate certainty and minimize predicted estimate error. Figure 3 demonstrates the process of merging policies. Selection to maximize estimate certainty is based on heuristics about clues in the communicated source information. Selection to minimize predicted estimate error is a stronger technique, because it is based on past source performance. However, predicting estimate error requires reputation models of information source trustworthiness that must be built up through interactions between the agent and information sources over many timesteps. A comprehensive algorithm must weigh a source's long-term trustworthiness record against the characteristics of a single piece of information.

The all-policy algorithm builds reputations during the initial timesteps while using the certainty maximization algorithm. Once reputations have stabilized, the algorithm attempts to select sources based on source trustworthiness characteristics. If sources can be eliminated, the estimate distribution is calculated according to error minimization. If no sources can

Figure 3. Process of merging policies

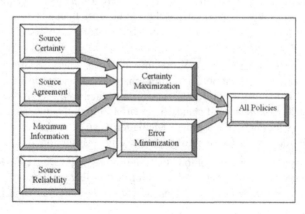

be identified as sufficiently untrustworthy, the all-policy algorithm then attempts to select source data based on characteristics of the information itself. Then the estimate distribution is calculated, with only the selected information, according to certainty maximization.

Providing Justification Through Algorithm Policies

Basing the all-policy algorithm on policies for information valuation provides justification to the human e-service user for the value and certainty of the calculated estimate. Upon completion of the estimate distribution calculation, the estimate can be presented to the human, in terms of the distribution mean μ_B (also known as the most likely value, x^*), along with distribution standard deviation, σ_B, which is inversely related to the certainty of the estimate. To justify the estimate probability distribution, the number of reporting sources can be listed, as well as details about the contributing sources and rejected sources. For included sources, the distributions of error of means, ρ_{s_i}, should demonstrate sufficient source trustworthiness. In addition, if no distinction between source reputations can be made, results should show how characteristics about the source information itself cause source data to

Figure 4. Estimate justification when reputations are insufficient

be rejected. An included source's contribution to estimate distribution standard deviation, shown by the impact of its $\sigma_{s_i}^2$ and $(\mu_{s_i}-\mu_B)^2$ terms, should be sufficiently small. For each rejected information source, a reason for exclusion should be given, either based on the source's reputation for inaccuracy or nonconformity of its information from the rest of the provided source information.

Figure 4 displays example output that might accompany an estimate calculation. In this example, nine sources report information. Since this estimate calculation occurs at Timestep 2, reputations for accurate and inaccurate sources appear similar, and the algorithm does not have sufficient source trust models to distinguish between accurate and inaccurate sources. As a result, the algorithm performs a second step in which it chooses sources based on characteristics of the provided information itself. From the data shown, each additional source, after the source with the lowest standard deviation contribution (Source 7), increases the predicted estimate standard deviation. Looking at the source distributions, this may be because each source's distribution is considered "distant" from every other distribution (distributions to not overlap significantly). Therefore, all sources other than Source 7 are excluded from the estimate calculation process. Because of its low contribution to estimate standard deviation, Source 7 happens to be the source closest to the distribution mean as calculated by all sources except outliers.

Figure 5 shows a second example of estimate calculation output. In this case, reputations are sufficiently developed to show a distinction between accurate sources, and one inaccurate source (Source 0). Further, the type of Source 0's untrustworthiness is shown; although Source 0 has a mean error near zero, the standard deviation of its error is much larger than that of the other sources. As a result, Source 0 is excluded from the estimate calculation process, and the estimate is determined from distributions provided by the other eight sources.

Figure 5. Estimate justification when reputations are sufficient

```
[java] time = 1986
[java] Performing Estimate Calculation
[java]
[java] Will evaluate based on source characteristics.
[java]
[java] Source 0 reputation mean: -0.011994542235696034
[java] Source 0 reputation standard deviation: 1.8678809614673941
[java]
[java] Source 1 reputation mean: -0.026884241127515293
[java] Source 1 reputation standard deviation: 0.45547649972640086
[java]
[java] Source 2 reputation mean: 0.04290372051125848
[java] Source 2 reputation standard deviation: 0.4719911391863596
[java]
[java] Source 3 reputation mean: 0.0014684282320005916
[java] Source 3 reputation standard deviation: 0.4801553057674544
[java]
[java] Source 4 reputation mean: 0.03697692480332428
[java] Source 4 reputation standard deviation: 0.46031282596506884
[java]
[java] Source 5 reputation mean: 0.009219522177546414
[java] Source 5 reputation standard deviation: 0.4953939541591729
[java]
[java] Source 6 reputation mean: -0.048098107273136
[java] Source 6 reputation standard deviation: 0.4428978195825331
[java]
[java] Source 7 reputation mean: -0.0012935740965261521
[java] Source 7 reputation standard deviation: 0.4884312246610267
[java]
[java] Source 8 reputation mean: -0.0032240366182671354
[java] Source 8 reputation standard deviation: 0.3888613214324404
[java]
[java] Source 0.0 is excluded because of poor reputation.
[java]
[java] Calculated estimate mean: 250.29323751881844
[java] Calculated estimate standard deviation: 0.16133149700620628
```

Experiments

The following experiments in this section compare the algorithms listed; a number of scenarios are specified to delineate cases in which each algorithm performs best according to a truth interval probability metric.

Domain Description

Because the information selection algorithm described in this research is domain-independent, it can be applied to numerous domains with similar results. In a single experiment run, an e-service agent is employed, for example, to determine the trustworthiness of an online seller. The agent obtains information (for example, the seller's percentage of satisfactory transactions) from several sources; each source s_i reports approximated information as a normal probability distribution ϕ_{S_i} by specifying distribution mean, μ_{S_i}, and standard deviation, σ_{S_i}.

In constructing experiments, each source is designed with accuracy characteristics of either "reliable" or "unreliable." Reliability is defined by (1) the source's accuracy in communicating information (for example, seller's satisfactory transaction rate), and (2) the source's accuracy in assessing the certainty of the communicated information. Source i's accuracy is described by a mean and standard deviation (μ_{rel,S_i}, σ_{rel,S_i}) describing a probability distribution of the source's error between its reported distribution mean (μ_{S_x} or μ_{S_y}) and the seller's true satisfactory transaction rate. Given this definition, the mean of the error probability distribution corresponds to accuracy of source values to true values, and the standard deviation of the error probability distribution corresponds to the source's consistency, or precision of the source values. Thus, a source classified as "reliable" has a mean error and/or a distribution standard deviation less than that of a source classified as "unreliable." Source certainty accuracy is described by whether the source reports the optimal probability distribution standard deviation (σ_{S_x} or σ_{S_y}) as $|x_T - \mu_B|$, or a default, inaccurate, small standard deviation of 0.01. A small default standard deviation is chosen, since sources are likely to inflate their reported certainty in order to influence the believing agent. A source classified as "reliable" should assign more accurate certainties to its reports than certainties reported by a source defined as "unreliable."

Experiment Parameters

Four types of experiments are conducted to compare the following algorithms:

1. The **naïve, noninformation-valuating algorithm,**
2. The **certainty maximization algorithm**, which combines the maximum information, source certainty, and source agreement policies by including those sources that maximize calculated estimate certainty,

3.   The **error minimization algorithm**, which combines the maximum information and source reliability policies by including those sources that minimize the expected error between the estimate mean and the true value of the information subject, and

4.   The **all-policy algorithm**, which combines certainty maximization and error minimization strategies.

Each algorithm version is assessed given varying states of source trustworthiness as described in Table 2. Each experiment requires the specification of (1) number of information sources, n, (2) number of information sources, n_r, designated as "reliable," (3) number of sources, n_u, designated as "unreliable," (4) "reliable" source error specification, as given by a mean and standard deviation of the probability distribution of the source's error from true seller satisfactory transaction rate (μ_r, σ_r), and (5) "unreliable" source error specification, also given by mean and standard deviation of the source's error probability distribution (μ_u, σ_u). Experiment 1 maintains a constant ratio of unreliable to total sources of 1/3 and varies the total number of sources between 3 and 30. In Experiment 2, the ratio of unreliable sources to total number of sources is varied from 1/9 to 9/9 with a constant total number of 9 sources. Experiments 3 and 4 vary the degree of error in unreliable sources; Experiment 3 varies unreliable source mean error between 0 and 20 with a constant error standard deviation of 2.0, and Experiment 4 varies unreliable source error standard deviation between 1 and 23 with a constant mean error of 0.0.

Experiments are conducted for each of the algorithm versions for each of three certainty reporting scenarios (Table 3). In Scenario 1, all reliable and unreliable sources report accurate

Table 2. Experiment variable specifications

Experiment No.	1	2	3	4
Number of Sources (n)	{3, 6, 9, 12, 15, 18, 21, 24, 27, 30}	9	9	9
Number of Reliable Sources (n_r)	{2, 4, 6, 8, 10, 12, 14, 16, 18, 20}	{9, 8, 7, 6, 5, 4, 3, 2, 1}	6	6
Number of Unreliable Sources (n_u)	{1, 2, 3, 4, 5, 6, 7, 8, 9, 10}	{1, 2, 3, 4, 5, 6, 7, 8, 9}	3	3
Mean Error (μ_r)	0	0	0	0
Reliable Source Error Standard Deviation (σ_r)	0.5	0.5	0.5	0.5
Unreliable Source Mean Error (μ_u)	0	0	{0, 2, 4, 6, 8, 10, 12, 14, 16, 18, 20}	0
Unreliable Source Error Standard Deviation (σ_u)	2	2	2	{1, 3, 5, 7, 9, 11, 13, 15, 17, 19, 21, 23}

Table 3. Experiment scenario specifications

Scenario	Reliable Source Reported Standard Deviation	Unreliable Source Reported Standard Deviation
1	$x_T - \mu_B$	$x_T - \mu_B$
2	$x_T - \mu_B$	0.01
3	0.01	0.01

location probability distribution standard deviations $\sigma_{S_{\rho_x}}$, defined as $|x_T - \mu_B|$. In Scenario 2, only reliable sources report accurate probability distribution standard deviations, while unreliable sources report a default, inaccurate, small standard deviation of 0.01. In Scenario 3, reliable and unreliable sources report default standard deviations of 0.01. Scenario 1 is considered unlikely, since it is improbable that unreliable sources would be good at approximating accurate probability distribution standard deviations. Scenario 2 is considered more probable; reliable sources are more likely to be good at correctly approximating their certainty on the information they report, while unreliable sources are less likely. However, experimental results will focus on Scenario 3, in which it is assumed that all sources may be poor at estimating their certainty. Scenario 3 is emphasized because, in most cases, no assumptions can be made concerning the quality of source certainty evaluations. Nonetheless, Scenarios 1 and 2 will also be discussed briefly as well.

Experiment Metric

Algorithms are evaluated according to a single metric that incorporates both accuracy of estimate distribution mean and accuracy of estimate certainty assessment. This metric computes the fraction of the probability distribution ϕ_B assigned to an interval surrounding the information subject's true value x_T. Hence, the tradeoff between accurate estimates with inappropriately low certainty assessments and inaccurate estimates with appropriate certainty assessments is acknowledged. This metric maximizes the probability assigned to a truth interval within the estimate distribution ϕ_B:

Metric: Pick the algorithm for which the truth interval probability, averaged over N timesteps, is maximized, where average truth interval probability for a selected (small) interval radius δ is defined as:

$$\text{Truth interval probability} = \frac{\sum_{i=1}^{N}\left(\int_{x_T - \delta}^{x_T + \delta}\phi(x)dx\right)}{N}.$$

In evaluating these experiments, $\delta = 0.01$.

Figure 6. Truth interval probability by number of total sources

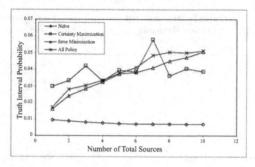

Figure 7. Truth interval probability by number of unreliable sources

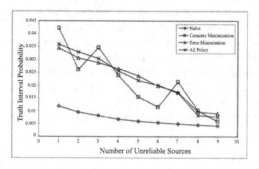

Figure 8. Truth interval probability by unreliable source mean error

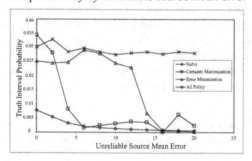

Experimental Results

First, results will be presented for Scenario 3, in which all sources report default standard deviations of 0.01. In Experiment Number 1, as the total number of sources increases (Figure 6), truth interval probability for all algorithms, except the naïve algorithm, increases. Both

Figure 9. Truth interval probability by unreliable source error standard deviation

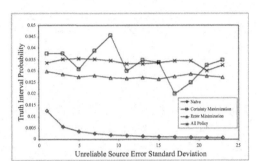

Figure 10. Truth interval probability by number of total sources, Scenario 1

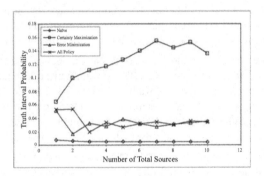

selection algorithms, the certainty maximization and error minimization algorithms, maintain relatively large truth interval probabilities. However, the certainty maximization algorithm is highly volatile. The all-policy algorithm not only outperforms the error minimization algorithm, but provides more stability than the certainty maximization algorithm, since it relies on both certainty maximization and error minimization components.

As the number of unreliable sources increases (Experiment Number 2), the truth interval probability decreases. For the variations shown in Figure 7, the all-policy and error minimization algorithms maintain similar truth interval probabilities. These two algorithms exhibit more stability than the certainty maximization algorithm, although certainty maximization achieves higher truth interval probabilities for some numbers of unreliable sources.

Figure 8 shows truth interval probability as unreliable source error mean increases (Experiment Number 3). For most algorithms, truth interval probability quickly drops as unreliable source error mean increases. The error minimization algorithm accommodates higher levels of unreliable source error, but also drops in performance (in correlation with its performance according to estimate distribution mean and standard deviation errors). Importantly, the all-policy algorithm maintains consistently high truth interval probabilities and is not affected by

Figure 11. Truth interval probability by number of total sources, Scenario 2

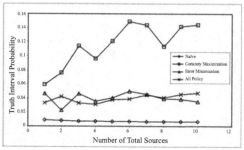

increasing source unreliability. The all-policy algorithm maintains consistently low error of belief distribution mean and error of belief distribution standard deviation. It is best able to identify and exclude unreliable sources, but also select information based on characteristics of the information itself in cases when trust models are not sufficiently helpful.

In Experiment Number 4, as unreliable source error standard deviation increases (Figure 9), again, the two intermediate selection methods (the error minimization and certainty maximization algorithms) maintain high levels of truth interval probability. However, the certainty maximization algorithm is highly volatile as unreliability increases. The all-policy algorithm not only consistently maintains higher truth interval probabilities than the error minimization algorithm, but provides more stability than the certainty maximization algorithm.

We now present a brief discussion of results for Scenario 1 (in which all sources report accurate certainty assessments) and Scenario 2 (in which only reliable sources report accurate certainty assessments). Though discussion of results focuses on the broader case of Scenario 3, in which no sources report accurate certainty assessments, interesting algorithm behavior can be observed when additional information is known about the tendencies of sources to report accurate certainty assessments. Figure 10 shows truth interval probability as the total number of sources increases (Experiment Number 1), according to Scenario 1. The certainty maximization algorithm maintains the highest truth interval probabilities, showing that reputation modeling is not helpful under Scenario 1. Figure 11 shows truth interval probability under Scenario 2 as the total number of sources increases. Again, the certainty maximization algorithm maintains the highest truth interval probabilities, rendering reputation modeling unnecessary in cases where reliable sources report exact certainty assessments.

The results presented here show that given Scenario 3, in which all sources report a default, inaccurate standard deviation, both intermediate selection algorithms (error minimization and certainty maximization) perform better than the naïve algorithm by maintaining higher truth interval probabilities. However, the certainty maximization algorithm demonstrates significant instability. The all-policy algorithm combines the benefits of both intermediate algorithms by achieving high truth interval probabilities and improved stability over the certainty maximization algorithm. Results related to Scenario 1 and Scenario 2, in which all or reliable sources report accurate certainty assessments, show that the certainty maximization algorithm maintains the highest truth interval probabilities. These results show that reputation modeling is not useful in cases where sources provide adequate certainty assessments.

From Theory to Application: Information Valuation in E-Services

Information valuation can be applied to e-services such as map providing, stock tickers, comparison shopping, referral networks, and online social networks. The following example applications—map-providing services and online social networking services—demonstrate how a human user can benefit from employing an information valuation agent to perform calculations on his behalf.

Map-providing services are used to calculate travel times to destinations. However, a map-providing service may use out-of-date maps, may position destinations in incorrect locations, or may use inconsistent travel speeds, yielding different travel times to destinations. An agent employing information valuation techniques can request the same time-to-destination information from multiple map-providing services then use information valuation to select the best subset of travel time answers. In the process, the agent can discard outlier information (travel times that do not agree with the majority of reported times) and keep track of providers' reputations (based on past travel time accuracy). Next, the agent can calculate the travel time based on the best subset of answers, providing the human user with both a certainty about the calculated travel time (based on number of answers received, reputations of the service providers, etc.) and a justification for the calculated travel time, including the reasons for excluding any unsatisfactory providers.

In online social networks, human users form connections to other humans based on mutual interests. However, users are in danger of networking with unsafe individuals and being exposed to harm, should they reveal personal information or agree to meet the unsafe individual in person (The Associated Press, 2006). Therefore, human users find it important to judge the reputation of another user before establishing an acquaintance, or "friendship" relationship with that user. To form a reputation opinion about an individual, a user can query his existing friends to ask them about the individual. An agent employing information valuation techniques can request that its friends provide a numeric rating representing the trustworthiness of the questionable individual. The agent can then compute a combined trustworthiness rating, taking into account the number of friends providing ratings, friends' certainties about their own trustworthiness assessments, agreement among the friends' ratings, and the agent's estimates of each friend's ability (trustworthiness) to make such assessments. The resulting trustworthiness rating of the questionable individual can then be provided to the human user, along with the agent's confidence in the estimate. Most importantly, the human user is provided with traceable justification for the trustworthiness rating; this justification is useful because (1) it may prevent human users from irrationally accepting questionable friends in online social networks and (2) in extreme cases, it provides authorities with evidence for identifying harmful online predators.

Future Trends

Several assumptions are made in this chapter; each of these assumptions helps pave the path for future research. While the algorithm presented in this chapter assumes source accuracy characteristics to be static, to the contrary, many real-world e-service domains are populated with information sources—both humans and agents—whose abilities and intentions change over time. Reputation models, which account for temporal dynamics, must be employed to evaluate how a source's reputation evolves over time.

Further, the experiments conducted in this research assume no information sources enter or leave the online system (start or stop communicating with the believing agent) once the experiment has begun. A more sophisticated algorithm would be required to assign new reputations to information sources entering the system if dynamic entry of information sources is permitted. The problem of bootstrapping reputation models of new agents is certainly a pressing problem online, where new e-service Web sites are created daily, and in e-services such as eBay, where users may change their identities at will (Barber, Fullam, & Kim, 2003; Fullam, Klos, Muller, Sabater, Schlosser, Topol et al., 2005).

Conclusion

This research presents an information selection algorithm based on intuitive policies for information valuation. Justification for the derived estimate, in terms of a valuation of the information used to create the estimate, is provided as explanation for the calculated estimate. Policies for valuation of information, based on characteristics of the information and the sources providing it, are delineated as guidelines for algorithm construction. In addition, each policy is traceably incorporated into the estimate calculation process to provide justification for estimate certainties. Finally, since modeling of information source trustworthiness can be complicated, significant effort is devoted to constructing these reputation models.

This research identifies five policies for valuing source information based on giving priority to (1) maximizing the number of contributing sources, (2) information from most certain sources, (3) information most in agreement with other source reports, (4) information from the most accurate sources, and (5) information that is most recent. Each of these policies (except for the recent information policy, which is reserved for future work) is incorporated into an information-valuating all-policy algorithm. The traceability of this merging of policies is seen through intermediate algorithms, each based on a subset of policies, as well as the all-policy algorithm:

1.   The certainty maximization algorithm, which combines the maximum information, source certainty, and source agreement policies by including those sources that maximize calculated estimate certainty.

2.   The error minimization algorithm, which combines the maximum information and source reliability policies by including those sources that minimize the expected error between the estimate mean and the true value of the information subject.

3.   The all-policy algorithm, which combines certainty maximization and error minimization strategies.

Tradeoffs emerge between evaluating information based on the predicted trustworthiness of information sources vs. evaluating information based on the characteristics of the information itself. Experimentation shows the superiority of an algorithm incorporating all information valuation policies to algorithms based on a subset of policies. In addition, an algorithm based on policies for information valuation provides justification for calculated estimates by producing reasons why more valuable information is given priority over less valuable information.

This research makes a major contribution toward assisting e-service users in obtaining accurate information from online sources. An information selection algorithm based on intuitive policies challenges trust modeling research to examine information quality assessment in terms of a number of factors, not only information source trustworthiness. The all-policy algorithm, presented in this research, experimentally assesses tradeoffs between source trustworthiness, source agreement, source-reported certainty, and number of reporting sources to optimally value information used in the estimate calculation process. Most importantly, the algorithm weighs a source's long term reputation against the estimated quality of a single report from that source, based on the report's characteristics, as compared against information from other sources. This is important in situations where sources considered "unreliable" might occasionally provide accurate information, or in cases where source trust models are not yet sufficiently built up to be useful. Experimental results show that application of information valuation policies to estimate calculation yields significant improvement in estimate accuracy and precision over naïve, no-policy estimate calculation. In addition, basing information valuation on intuitive policies promotes traceability. Justification for derived estimates is provided, a useful feature for any e-service domain in which human users are the ultimate decision-making authority.

References

Abdul-Rahman, A., & Hailes, S. (1999). *Relying on trust to find reliable information*. Paper presented at the International Symposium on Database, Web and Cooperative Systems (DWACOS'99), Baden-Baden, Germany.

Amazon.com, Inc. (2006). *Amazon*. Retrieved March 10, 2006, from http://www.amazon.com

The Associated Press. (2006) *Boys' MySpace.com prank results in arrest*. Retrieved March 13, 2006, from http://www.cnn.com

Barber, K. S., & Fullam, K. (2003). Applying reputation models to continuous belief revision. In *The Workshop on Deception, Fraud, and Trust in Agent Societies at Autonomous Agents (AAMAS-2003)*, Melbourne, Australia (pp. 6-15).

Barber, K. S., Fullam, K., & Kim, J. (2003). Challenges for trust, fraud, and deception research in multi-agent systems. In R. Falcone, K. S. Barber, L. Korba, and M. Singh (Eds.), *Trust, reputation, and security: Theories and practice* (pp. 8-14). Berlin: Springer.

Barber, K. S., & Kim, J. (2002a). Belief revision process based on trust: Agent evaluating reputation of information sources. In R. Falcone, M. Singh, and Y.-H. Tan, (Ed.) *Trust in cyber-societies: Integrating the human and artificial perspectives* (LNCS 2246, pp. 73-82). Berlin: Springer.

Barber, K. S., & Kim, J. (2002b). Soft security: Isolating unreliable agents. In *The Workshop on Deception, Fraud, and Trust in Agent Societies at Autonomous Agents (AAMAS-2002)*, Bologna, Italy (pp. 8-17).

Dragoni, A. F., & Giorgini, P. (2003). Distributed belief revision. *Autonomous Agents and Multi-Agent Systems, 6*(2), 115-143. Berlin: Springer.

eBay. (2006). *eBay*. Retrieved March 10, 2006, from http://www.eBay.com

Epinions. (2006). *Epinions*. Retrieved March 10, 2006, http://www.epinions.com

Falcone, R., Pezzulo, G., & Castelfranchi, C. (2002). Quantifying belief credibility for trust-based decision. In *Proceedings of the Workshop on Deception, Fraud, and Trust in Agent Societies at Autonomous Agents (AAMAS-2002)*, Bologna, Italy (pp. 41-48).

Fallis, D. (2004). On verifying the accuracy of information: Philosophical perspectives. *Library Trends, 52*(3), 463-487.

Flouris, G., & Plexousakis, D. (2001). *Belief revision in propositional knowledge bases.* Paper presented at the 8th Panhellenic Conference on Informatics, Nicosia, Cyprus.

Fullam, K., & Barber, K. S. (2004). Using policies for information valuation to justify beliefs. In *Proceedings of the Third International Joint Conference on Autonomous Agents and Multiagent Systems (AAMAS-2004)* (pp. 404-411). Washington DC: IEEE Computer Society.

Fullam, K., & Barber, K. S. (2005). A temporal policy for trusting information. In R. Falcone, K. S. Barber, J. Sabater, and M. Singh (Eds.), *Trusting agents for trusting electronic societies* (pp. 75-94). Berlin: Springer.

Fullam, K., Klos, T., Muller, G., Sabater, J., Schlosser, A., Topol, Z., Barber, K. S., Rosen-schein, J., Vercouter, L., & Voss, M. (2005). A specification of the agent reputation and trust (ART) testbed: Experimentation and competition for trust in agent societies. In *Proceedings of the Fourth International Joint Conference on Autonomous Agents and Multiagent Systems (AAMAS-2005)* (pp. 512-518). New York: Association for Computing Machinery.

Gardenfors, P. (1988). *Knowledge in flux: Modeling the dynamics of epistemic states.* Cambridge, MA: MIT Press.

Google, Inc. (2006a). *Google maps*. Retrieved March 10, 2006, from http://maps.google.com

Google, Inc. (2006b). *orkut*. Retrieved March 10, 2006, from http://www.orkut.com

Halpern, J. Y. (1989). The relationship between knowledge, belief, and certainty: Preliminary report. In *Proceedings of the Fifth Workshop on Uncertainty in Artificial Intelligence*, Windsor, Ontario, Canada (pp. 143-151).

Jonker, C. M., & Treur, J. (1999). Formal analysis of models for the dynamics of trust based on experiences. In *The 9th European Workshop on Modeling Autonomous Agents in a Multi-Agent World: Multi-Agent System Engineering (MAAMAW-99)*, Valencia, Spain (pp. 221-231).

Jurca, R., & Faltings, B. (2002). Towards incentive-compatible reputation management. In *The Workshop on Deception, Fraud, and Trust in Agent Societies at Autonomous Agents (AAMAS-2002)*, Bologna, Italy (pp. 92-100).

Leading Market Technologies. (2006). *MarketBrowser*. Retrieved March 10, 2006, from http://www.marketbrowser.com

Lerner, U. N. (2002). *Hybrid Bayesian networks for reasoning about complex systems*. Doctoral Dissertation, Stanford University.

Maporama International. (2006). *Maporama*. Retrieved March 10, 2006, from http://www.maporama.com

Microsoft. (2006). *Market report: Stock ticker*. Retrieved March 10, 2006, from http://news.moneycentral.msn.com/briefing/StockTicker.asp

MySpace.com. (2006). *MySpace*. Retrieved March 10, 2006, from http://www.myspace.com

Pricegrabber.com, LLC. (2006). *PriceGrabber*. Retrieved March 10, 2006, from http://www.pricegrabber.com

Roorda, J., van der Hoek, W., & Meyer, J. (2002). Iterated belief change in multi-agent systems. In *The First International Joint Conference on Autonomous Agents and Multi-Agent Systems (AAMAS-2002)* (pp. 889-896). New York: Association for Computing Machinery.

Shopzilla, Inc. (2006). *Shopzilla*. Retrieved March 10, 2006, from http://www.shopzilla.com

Chapter VIII

Trust Management Tools

Tyrone Grandison, IBM Almaden Research Center, USA

Abstract

After entering the realm of computing over a decade ago, the term trust management has evolved to encompass many concepts and mechanisms that bring it closer to its intuitive interpretation. This chapter will outline the evolution and present the catalyst(s) for each phase in its metamorphosis. In each stage, trust management tools were constructed to showcase the current understanding in the field. These tools will be discussed and their strengths, domains of application, and scope for improvement presented. The foundation of trust management technology can be found in security notions, for example credentials, in mathematical computation and in formal (and informal) reputation models. Each of these categories and their hybrids will be highlighted. This chapter should leave the reader with (1) a holistic view of the trust management problem, (2) a clear differentiation of trust management from other fields (and terms) in the computer security arena, and (3) knowledge of the appropriate domain of usage for each system.

Introduction

Trust management entered the computer science academic discourse through the work of Blaze, et al. (Blaze, Feigenbaum, & Lacy, 1996) and has directly spawned the creation of several trust management systems, namely Policymaker (Blaze, Feigent, & Strauss 1998), KeyNote (Blaze, Feigenbaum, Ioannidis, & Keromytis, 1999) and REFEREE (Chu, Feigenbaum, LaMacchia, Resnick, & Strauss, 1997). However, upon closer inspection (Grandison & Sloman, 2000) it becomes apparent that the *trust management* referred to by Policymaker-based systems is directed at addressing the complexity of the two-step authentication and authorization process (Blaze, Ioannidis, & Keromytis, 2003) and not tackling the trust management problem in its entirety.

In recent years, the research community (Carbo, Molina, & Davila, 2003; Riegelsberger, Sasse, & McCarthy, 2005; Ruohomaa & Kutvonen, 2005; Suryanarayana & Taylor, 2004) has recognized that trust management involves not only security controls, but also privacy controls (Seigneur & Jensen, 2004), reputation management (Carbo et al., 2003; Krukow, 2004; Shmatikov & Talcott, 2005; Zacharia & Maes, 2000), risk management (Grandison, 2003), experience management (Azzedin & Maheswaran, 2002), trusted behavior modeling (Agudo, Lopez, & Montenegro, 2005; Carbone, Nielsen, & Sassone, 2004; Jøsang, 1996), and adaptive credential negotiation (Biskup & Karabulut, 2003; Winsborough, Seamons, & Jones, 1999). This led to the development of new classes of trust management systems, which will be presented later.

The objectives of this chapter are to discuss what trust management is and is not, to present the current set of trust management solutions, and to highlight how each can be used in the e-services environment. It is outside the purview of this chapter to focus on technologies that engender trust, such as privacy management or risk management technology; rather, the emphasis will be on technology deemed as addressing the trust management problem.

After perusing this chapter it is hoped that (1) an e-services practitioner will have a basic understanding of the trust management tools that could be a part of the systems building arsenal, and (2) a manager will have a rudimentary comprehension of trust management issues. The starting point for our conversation is a clear understanding of trust management.

Defining Trust Management

Currently, the term *trust management* has a similar level of implied comprehension and intuitive interpretation as the term *trust* (see Chapter I). Blaze et al. (1996) provided the earliest definition of trust management for computer systems, which is that trust management is:

A unified approach to specifying and interpreting security policies, credentials, relationships which allow direct authorisation of security-critical actions.

This was the dominant view of trust management until the turn of the 21st century. As previously stated, this perspective was narrow in scope. The reason for this is embedded in the dilemma faced by the security community at the time. The dilemma is defined in the following context. The Internet was not designed with security in mind. Cryptography was used as a solution to the network's security problems, but the problem with cryptography was that it required complex key management. The solution to this problem was to create public key infrastructures (PKIs). The trust in the certificate authority and the keys in a PKI led to a trust problem, which is the trust management problem that Blaze refers to. Thus, Blaze et al. (1996) do not focus on the problem of managing trust, but on the problem of managing public key authorisation. Blaze's problem can be succinctly stated as that of allowing public keys to be authorised and linked directly to their allowable actions.

Eventually, e-commerce and distributed systems researchers and practitioners saw the need to address trust management in order to hasten the acceptance of their systems. However, Blaze's definition was not sufficient. Jøsang and Tran (2000) defined trust management in e-commerce as:

The activity of collecting, codifying, analysing and presenting security relevant evidence with the purpose of making assessments and decisions regarding E-commerce transactions.

This definition offered a broader, more abstract, and more intuitive interpretation of the trust management problem than presented in Blaze et al. (1996). Jøsang and Tran stressed the need for trust assessment to be based on evidence that can be practically collected and then used for decision-making. This emphasis was made because systematic and reliable ways of obtaining evidence in the e-commerce environment were nonexistent at the time. However, Jøsang and Tran neglected to expound on the issues surrounding the encoding, analysis, and presentation of this evidence.

Grandison and Sloman (2003) extended Jøsang and Tran's (2000) definition to make it directly applicable to a distributed systems environment. They stated that trust management is:

The activity of collecting, encoding, analysing and presenting evidence relating to competence, honesty, security or dependability with the purpose of making assessments and decisions regarding trust relationships for Internet applications.

Evidence could include credentials such as certificates for proof of identity or qualifications, risk assessments, usage experience, or recommendations. Analysis includes identification of possible conflicts with other trust requirements. Thus, trust management is concerned with collecting the information required to make a trust relationship decision, evaluating the criteria related to the trust relationship, and monitoring and reevaluating existing trust relationships. As trust in e-services requires these facets to be addressed, this definition is the most appropriate.

In the course of developing trust management tools, the term trust management has been incorrectly used as a synonym for similar terms that are closely related, but not the same thing.

What Trust Management is Not?

Trust management literature (Biskup & Karabulut, 2003; Blaze, Feigent, & Strauss, 1998; Carbo et al., 2003; Chu, 1997; Foley, 2002; Freudenthal & Karamcheti, 2003; Khare & Rifkin, 1998; Kolluru & Meredith, 2001) has used the terms trust, access control, authorization, and authentication interchangeably. This is a mistake (Blaze et al., 2003; Grandison, 2001; Grandison, 2003; Grandison & Sloman, 2001). The four terms are distinct.

The difference between *trust* and *access control* can be shown through a simple example. When Jane trusts Semantix to provide network security testing services, it does not necessarily imply that Jane will allow Semantix unfettered access to her network to perform tests. The principle is trust does not necessarily imply access control rights and vice versa. For some situations, it may be true that trust may lead to access rights being granted, but being trusted does not automatically mean that access will be given. *Authorisation* can be viewed as a policy decision assigning access control rights for a subject to perform specific actions on a specific target with defined constraints. Thus, authorisation is the outcome of the refinement of a more abstract trust relationship. For example, if I develop a trust relationship with a particular service provider, then I may authorise that service to install monitoring software on my computer and hence set up the necessary access control rights to permit access. Thus, a trust relationship may lead to a positive authorisation decision, but it is not a guarantee. *Authentication* is the verification of an identity of an entity, which may be performed by means of a password, a trusted authentication service, or using more complex tokens, such as certificates. Thus, *trust* and *authentication* should not be used interchangeably.

Not surprisingly, the terms *trust management, access control management, authorisation management,* and *authentication management* have also been used interchangeably. This is a practice that leads to confusion and contention, and hampers the development of technology for trust management, which includes all these concepts.

With this in mind, it makes sense that trust management tools have been built that address one or more of the topics previously mentioned.

Trust Management Tools

On a conceptual level, trust management involves evidence preparation and collection, trust specification, trust establishment, trust analysis, and trust monitoring (Grandison, 2003). Most current trust management tools address at most three of these phases. Thus, trust management tools are still maturing.

Initial systems were credential-based. The next set was based on computational theory around the evaluation of trust levels. The third set is built on the notion of reputation, and the final set is a combination of all others. Each of these categories of trust management tools will be discussed further.

Credential-Based Tools

The notion of security is relatively well-understood and easiest to address when tackling a topic as complex as trust management. Thus, the majority of trust management tools have been security-focused, that is, credential based. The current set of credential-based trust management solutions is public key certificates (Network Associates, 1990), PICS (Evans, Feather, Hopmann, Presler-Marshall, & Resnick, 1997; Krauskopf, Miller, Resnick, & Treesee, 1996; Miller, Resnick, & Singer), PolicyMaker (Blaze et al., 1996; Blaze, Feigent, & Strauss, 1998), KeyNote (Blaze, Feigent, & Strauss, 1998), REFEREE (Chu et al., 1997), RT (Li & Mitchell, 2003), IBM Trust Establishment (IBM, n.d.; IBM, 2000), SD3 (Jim, 2001), Fidelis (Yao, Moody, & Bacon, 2003), TCG (Compaq et al., 2005) and Trustbuilder (Winsborough et al., 1999), There are also a few other nameless trust management systems in this category. A representative example will be presented.

A thorough description of the operation, benefits, and concerns of these tools was presented in Grandison and Sloman (2000). Thus, only the core of each technology will be presented in this section. A study of the differences between the credential-based models was presented in Weeks (2001) and Ruohomaa and Kutvonen (2005).

Our discussion will start with two basic systems (i.e., public key certificates and PICS) and walk through a timeline of other systems that build upon these technologies.

Public Key Certificates

Public key certificates are used for authentication, which is a part of the trust establishment process. Certificates are issued by a certification authority (CA), and only verify that a particular public key is owned by a particular entity. The CA does not vouch for the trustworthiness of the key owner, but simply authenticates the owner's identity. A PKI is the repository that is used to hold certificates. Simple PKI (SPKI) is an instance of a PKI that has received a lot of attention in the trust management world (Biskup & Karabulut, 2003; Weeks, 2001).

The trust model surrounding the popular public key certificate systems tend to be either hierarchical, for example, X.509 (Sun, 2001), or ad-hoc, for example, PGP (Network Associates, 1990). Both types of systems have problems. PGP lacks official mechanisms for creating, acquiring, and distributing certificates. Thus, it may not be suited for e-services, unless additional technology is brought to bear. X.509's rigid hierarchical structure may lead to unnatural business alliances between competing companies that violate the expected flow of trust. If this is used in e-services, then there should be other trust mechanisms in place that reduce or eliminate this exposure. Generally, public key certificates are useable where a trust relationship needs to be established based on the identity of the parties involved.

PICS

Platform for Internet content selection (PICS) was developed by the World Wide Web Consortium (W3C) to solve the issue of protecting children from pornography on the Internet.

The core idea behind PICS (Evans et al., 1997; Krauskopf et al., 1996; Miller et al.) is that it provides a filter between the potential viewer and Web documents. PICS is essentially a way to establish trust between the viewer and content provider.

PICS defines standards for the format and distribution of labels, which are metadocuments describing Web documents. It does not specify a vocabulary that a label must use, nor does it state which labels are important for a particular circumstance.

PICS could be used in e-service scenarios where the provider is allowing access to online documents. Thus, a consumer is trying to create a trust relationship with delivered content based on the ratings of the content and personal choices.

PICSRules is a powerful tag-based language that allows access to online resources. The PICS standard and PICSRules language allow for both trust specification and trust establishment to be performed. The usefulness of the PICS framework is limited by the quality of rating services used in the solution configuration and by the correct specification of the rules (which can be complex and nonintuitive). Also, though the lack of a standard vocabulary offers flexibility in specification, it also means reduced interoperability and the need for translation services.

PolicyMaker

PolicyMaker (Blaze et al., 1996; Blaze et al., 1998) is a trust management system built at AT&T Research Laboratories that states what a public key is authorised to do. Traditional certificate systems did not bind access rights to the owner of the public key within the certificate framework. These systems required a two-step process to take place: (1) the binding of a public key to its owner, which occurs within the certificate framework, and (2) the binding of access rights to the identified key owner, which occurs outside the certificate framework. PolicyMaker enables both steps to be merged into a single step that binds access rights to a public key.

The Policymaker system is built on a query engine and is geared towards authorization mapping. In a typical scenario, an application gives the PolicyMaker engine, a (set of) requested action(s), a set of credentials, and a policy; the engine tries to prove that the credentials contain a proof that the requested action(s) complies with the policy. For e-services, PolicyMaker may be used to establish the relationship between a public key (and the entity it represents) and its allowable trusted rights.

PolicyMaker does not address the problem of how to discover that credentials are missing and does not have support for negative assertions.

KeyNote

KeyNote (Blaze et al., 1998) is the successor to PolicyMaker and was developed to improve on the weaknesses of PolicyMaker. It has the same design principles of assertions and queries but includes two additional design goals: standardisation and ease of integration.

In KeyNote, the query engine is tasked with more responsibility than that of PolicyMaker's. PolicyMaker assumed that the calling application would perform a lot of the critical functionality, such as signature verification. The conceptual operation of KeyNote is exactly the same as PolicyMaker; and is focused on trust establishment. KeyNote suffers from the same issues mentioned for Policymaker. In Blaze et al. (2003), they present information on the future direction of the KeyNote tool.

REFEREE

REFEREE (Rule-controlled environment for evaluation of rules and everything else) (Chu et al., 1997) is a trust management system based on PolicyMaker and developed by Yang-Hua Chu, for making access decisions relating to Web documents. It considers a PICS label as the stereotypical Web credential and uses the same theoretical framework as PolicyMaker to interpret trust policies and administer trust protocols, which are represented as software modules.

Like PolicyMaker and KeyNote, REFEREE is a recommendation-based, query engine so it needs to be integrated into a host application. In this context, recommendation refers to evidence or advice given to a user to help in the decision-making process. REFEREE suffers from the same issues as PICS and, with the exception of negative assertions, the same issues as PolicyMaker. For e-Services, REFEREE is also essentially a tool for trust establishment based on document ratings.

RT

Role-based trust management framework (RT) (Li & Mitchell, 2003; Li, Mitchell, & Winsborough, 2002) is based on role-based access control (RBAC), credential management, and delegation logic. An RT principal has an associated (set of) role(s). A user can specify the granting or revoking of access rights by modifying the set of associated roles. Like KeyNote, RT has a deduction engine that is conceptually similar in functionality.

However, RT has defined semantics for its policy language, addresses the issue of credential chain discovery, uses a unified vocabulary, and has facilities for delegation. However, at its core, it performs the same function as KeyNote using the same kind of tokens, that is, public keys.

IBM Trust Establishment

IBM states that the underlying trust implications for an e-business transaction may be addressed using certificates. Certificates can be issued by various bodies, vouching for an entity in a particular role; for example, vouching for someone's status as a buyer, seller, trade, and so forth. IBM developed a role-based access control model that uses certificates, a Java-based trust establishment module and a trust policy language (TPL). The system is similar to PolicyMaker, but permits negative rules preventing access. The default certificate scheme used is X.509 v3, though other certificate formats are supported.

The trust establishment module validates the client's certificate and then maps the certificate owner to a role. The certificate need not bind to a user's identity, but could just state that the user has a particular attribute or a public key can be used to map onto an anonymous role (IBM; IBM, 2000).

This technology suffers from the same issues discussed in the section of public key certificates, as well as the discovery of missing credentials concern. For trust enablement in e-services, IBM trust establishment can be used in a similar manner as public key certificates and PolicyMaker.

SD3

Secure dynamically distributed datalog (SD3) (Jim, 2001) is a trust management system that uses logic to represent security policies. It consists of a high-level policy language, a local policy evaluator, and a certificate retrieval system. The policy language is an extension of datalog, which is a database programming language. SD3 is an extension of work done by Gunter and Jim on QCM (Gunter & Jim, 2000), which is a system for automatic certificate management. Like PolicyMaker, KeyNote, and REFEREE, SD3 is a recommendation-based query system. Unlike these other systems, SD3 uses a logic-based language as its default notation.

After the scenario is coded into a program, evaluation is started by passing this program, a query, and the input certificates to the SD3 optimiser. An optimised set of rules is then passed to the SD3 core evaluator. The evaluator produces an answer to the query and a proof that the answer follows from the security policy (specified in the program). Before the answer is returned, the proof is checked and incorrect proofs are reported as errors. Thus, SD3 is conceptually very similar to KeyNote. The difference between the two systems lies in the nature of their specification languages and their verification mechanism. In both cases, SD3 tends to be more explicitly logic-based. SD3 suffers from the same problems as KeyNote does. SD3 can be utilized in the same manner as the other public key-based recommendation systems.

Fidelis

Fidelis (Yao et al., 2003) is a policy-driven trust management framework that originates from the work on open architecture for secure, Internetworking services (OASIS) (Hayton et al., 1998), which is a role-based architecture for distributed authorization management. Yao et al. (2003) state that the Fidelis policy framework is an abstract, conceptual foundation that is used as a starting reference point for the implementation of a policy language. Conceptually, the Fidelis framework assumes the same view of trust management as PolicyMaker-based systems. However, Fidelis defines policies and credentials differently from PolicyMaker-based systems, and includes the notions of a trust network and trust conveyance.

The syntax and semantics of FPL has a strong association with first-order predicate logic. The primary issues with Fidelis are that (1) there seems to be no differentiation between the various degrees of trust that may be possible, (2) though a policy is checked against the trust network, there seems to be no means of arbitrarily analysing the policy with respect to the trust network, (3) it is not clear how the Fidelis system would handle policy specifications from principals using different local languages in order to perform policy evaluation, and

(4) the assumption of the abstract nature of the framework is weakened by the key-centric perspective taken in defining its basic elements.

For e-services, Fidelis is best utilized when establishing a trust relationship, where the base credentials are keys.

TCG

Trusted Computing Group (TCG), which was formally Trusted Computing Platform Alliance (TCPA), is a consortium of companies to make the computer platform trustworthy. It was formed by Compaq, HP, IBM, Intel, and Microsoft. The motivation behind the decision to create an alliance was the realization by these companies that customers viewed their products as not worthy of their trust. In their own words:

.... came to an important conclusion: the level, or amount, of trust they were able to deliver to their customers, and upon which a great deal of the information revolution depended, needed to be increased and security solutions for PC's needed to be easy to deploy, use and manage.

In the TCG main specification document and the TCG PC specific implementation document, data structures and processes are defined that allow a computer system to verify all its components as trusted starting from *boot time*. TCG is heavily rooted in using cryptography to verify each and every component being used on a system; from BIOS, to operating system (OS) components to software running on top of the OS. More information on the integrity checking process can be found in Grandison (2003).

The TCG repository suffers from the same problems faced by PKIs. The framework may also lead to more dangerous scenarios, where end user privacy may inadvertently infringe or consortium members may be given an unfair business advantage (the ability to effectively shut out any rival software by labeling them from an untrustworthy source). Some other problems with the TCG framework are outlined in Anderson (2002). A detailed description of the TCG initiative can be found in their "Design Philosophies and Concepts" paper (Compaq et al., 2005).

Trustbuilder

Trustbuilder (Barlow, Hess, & Seamons, 2001; Seamons, Winslett, & Yu, 2001; Winsborough et al., 1999; Winsborough et al., 1999) is a trust negotiation framework that extends the work on IBM Trust Establishment Framework. Trustbuilder seeks to address the problem of establishing trust between strangers through credential exchange. In this context, a credential is defined as a digitally signed assertion by a credential issuer about a credential owner. Assertions are essentially a set of attribute-value pairs. A sensitive credential is one that contains private information. Parties engage in a protocol of credential exchange to reach a successful negotiation decision. However, not all negotiations are successful. The information required by each party may be set at a value that prohibits a successful negotiation.

The TrustBuilder framework is focused on trust establishment, but does not include facilities for handling credentials regarding negative assertions, and assumes nothing about the consistency of the credential expressions.

The Nameless

Kagal, Undercoffer, Perich, Joshi, and Finin (2002) describe a trust management framework that uses a system of rights and delegations, as well as digital certificates, to facilitate trust management. Their architecture assumes that each group of agents is protected by security agents that are responsible for authorizing access to services/resources within the group. The idea is that a client can request access to a resource or service by providing its identity information, along with any delegations it may have to the security agent for the domain. The security agent uses its policies to verify the identity and delegations of the client, granting access only if everything is valid. This system uses a specification language that seems to be derived from work done by Jajodia and Subrahmanian (1997) and combines it with work done by Blaze et al. (1996).

The common thread between credential-based systems is the use of a piece of evidence and some defined policy to determine if a trust relationship should be established. There is no explicit representation of trust level computation.

Computation-Based Tools

Computation-based trust management tools focus on using contextual cues, which vary from system to system, to evaluate the level of trust that should be placed on a trustee requesting the establishment of a trust relationship. In this section, Poblano (Chen & Yeager, 2000), SECURE (English et al., 2002), and a system developed by Shrobe and Doyle (2000) will be discussed.

Poblano

Poblano (Chen & Yeager, 2000) is an attempt to build a decentralized trust model based on the JXTA platform. The JXTA project is concerned with designing and implementing free software that would enable the easy creation, use, and maintenance of peer-to-peer networks. Poblano is based on the assumption that each individual has his or her opinion on the trustworthiness of another. It is believed that these opinions can be collected, exchanged, and evaluated. The initial application areas for this distributed trust model were (1) a reputation guided searching system, and (2) a recommendation system for security purposes.

The broader objective of this project was to allow the model to be adapted to work in any scenario where distributed trust relationships are used. The model describes trust relationships between peers and also between peers and codat (code and data), a protocol that allows the dissemination of trust and algorithms for the updating of trust. Each peer has information available to it on either the group or its confidence in the codat and peer, and about the risk involved. Using this information, the model describes the formulas and mechanisms used to calculate trust values and propagate trust information. The first concern with the Poblano trust model is that the equations for calculating/updating trust are simple and arbitrary. Thus, the accuracy and general applicability of this formula is questionable. The second issue with the model is that it seems specifically designed for solving the problem of searching distributed networks and the validation of the search results and sources. The third problem is that it may suffer from the same key problems faced by public key certificates. Finally, the Poblano framework appears to have no facilities for the specification of constraints. This may limit its usability in e-service environments.

SECURE

The SECURE project is a collaborative research effort involving the Trinity College Dublin and the Universities of Aarhus, Cambridge, Geneva, and Strathcylde. The purpose of this effort is to provide entities in a decentralized environment with the ability to reason about trust in the context of partial information, where risk is a significant consideration.

The project is founded on a computational model of trust that is used for reasoning about trust and for the deployment of verifiable security policies. The system utilizes recommendation and trust values, that is, pairs of belief and disbelief measures, to calculate the scenario-specific risk value for particular transactions. Assuming that each entity has a threshold risk value, and based on the computed risk value on the transaction, a positive or negative trust decision is made. The SECURE system can be used for e-services trust establishment. However, the issue of the consistent and appropriate assignment of default values is not addressed in this system.

The Nameless

In Shrobe and Doyle (2000), an active trust management system for autonomous adaptive survivable systems is proposed. Survivable systems tend to assume absolute trust. This assumption is not feasible given the nonexistence of an impenetrable and incorruptible trusted computing base (TCB). Shrobe and Doyle (2000) propose the development of a survivable system that could function in an imperfect environment. The system should constantly collect and analyse security-related data from a broad variety of sources, including the application systems, intrusion detection systems, system logs, network traffic analysers, and so forth. The nature and scope of the collected data are determined by the user of this system and their particular needs. The result of these analyses forms their trust model, which is a probabilistic representation of the trustworthiness of each computational resource in the system. The applications use this trust model to help decide which resources should be used to perform each major computational step by maximizing the ratio of expected utility of performing a task to the associated risk.

Reputation-Based Tools

Reputation-based systems (Carbo et al., 2003; Shmatikov & Talcott, 2005; Zacharia & Maes, 2000) assume that the basis for trust is an entity's reputation and not necessarily the credentials presented. These systems are event driven and use some identity token as the starting point to uncover the reputation of the presenting agent. Formal reputation-based trust management systems are still new to the research community. I am trying to refer to conceptual descriptions of the systems rather than go through them all, because the conceptual function is the same; the change lies in the reputation calculation and dissemination.

An example of an emerging system is that proposed by Shmatikov and Talcott (2005). They describe a formal model for reputation-based trust management, where restrictions on an agent's behavior are encapsulated in licenses; and good and bad behavior interpreted as license fulfillment and license violation. Reputation is modeled as a set of licenses; some completed, some *in process*, some violated, some misused. A trust decision is based on the current set of licenses for the requesting agent.

Hybrid Tools

Hybrid tools incorporate reputation, computation, and credential mechanisms. The two instances that will be presented here are SULTAN (Grandison, 2003) and QTM (Freudenthal & Karamcheti, 2003).

SULTAN

The SULTAN trust management system (Grandison, 2001; Grandison, 2003; Grandison & Sloman, 2002; Grandison & Sloman, 2003) was developed by the Distributed Software engineering group at Imperial College - London to take a step towards more holistic trust management systems. It is constructed on notions of statements of trust, distrust, negative recommendations, and positive recommendations and includes functionality to include risk and experience information in a trust decision.

The system is centred on tooling, that is, the specification editor, the analysis engine, the risk service, the trust monitor, and the trust consultant, which provides decision support to the end user. SULTAN makes no assumption on the nature of the mechanism used in trust establishment, that is, use of security credentials, reputation information, risk profiles, and so forth.

The problem with the SULTAN TMF is that it is not lightweight, with respect to memory and analysis execution time. Though geared for analysis, establishment, and monitoring, SULTAN should only be used in e-services scenarios that go beyond the strictly credential-only scenarios.

QTM

Quantified trust management (QTM) (Freudenthal & Karamcheti, 2003) extends role-based access control and public key-based trust management with features that allow the direct expression of partial trust in delegations. QTM allows the specification of a reliability measure (a probability in the range [0..1]) for agents in their particular roles. The set of rules pertinent to a particular trust decision are collected and *composite* trust value.

QTM may be viewed as an augmented access control engine with the ability to handle notions of partial trust in entities. Thus, like PolicyMaker-based systems, it is can be used for trust establishment. However, the nontreatment of the consistent and reliable assignment of the reliability measures is a problem faced by QTM. As of 2003, QTM is still work in progress.

Summary

Figure 1 illustrates the timeline of trust management tools, which is based on the earliest publication date of documents on these solutions.

From the discussion, it can be gleamed credential-based systems should be used in e-services environments where only trust establishment is pertinent. This is true of computation-based and reputation-based systems. These systems need to be utilized in conjunction with tools that address trust monitoring and update, experience management, and other important aspects of trust management, such as the hybrid tools. Hybrid and reputation-based systems (also some computational ones) seem to be a natural fit for e-services because the notions modeled seem more intuitive to the domain.

For each trust management system, with the exception of public key certificates, there is a specification notation that allows trust policy expression. Thus, commonality exists the ability to express trust specifications.

Figure 1. A timeline of trust management tools

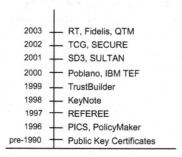

2003	RT, Fidelis, QTM
2002	TCG, SECURE
2001	SD3, SULTAN
2000	Poblano, IBM TEF
1999	TrustBuilder
1998	KeyNote
1997	REFEREE
1996	PICS, PolicyMaker
pre-1990	Public Key Certificates

Explicit comparison of all these tools is difficult given that most systems are an evolution of core technology, and each iteration provides improvement on the previous incarnation while leaving the core problems in tact.

Future Trends

The presentation of the story of trust management and the solutions developed to address this problem highlights three major concerns that drive the development of future trust management systems.

The first concern is that there is an overreliance of public key technology. This translates to an overemphasis on security controls; when successful e-service deployments will emphasize reputation, privacy, experience, and risk. The implication is that there needs to be a creation of trust management tools that more closely match the e-services trust problem domain. Thus, more systems with foundations in the privacy, risk, and reputation arena should be expected.

The second concern is the lack of focus on evolution of the trust relationship. The majority of trust management systems in use neglect to model the fact that trust relationships evolve and need to be monitored. These systems will evolve beyond the assumption that only trust relationship establishment matters and start to incorporate functionality for trust monitoring, update and propagation.

The final concern is the implied assumption that trust and security concepts are interchangeable. As trust management systems are deployed and feedback is gathered from the end-users, there will be an appreciation of the difference and a demand for systems that address a broader spectrum of the trust management problem.

In essence, the three concerns lead to the same outcome, trust management tools that are more holistic and that go beyond the current paradigm.

Conclusion

An exposition of the origin of the phrase trust management was given and an explanation about why it was flawed was presented. An evolving list of trust management definitions was provided and the rationale for the choice of a definition of trust management for e-services was highlighted.

Trust management for e-services is defined as:

The activity of collecting, encoding, analysing and presenting evidence relating to competence, honesty, security or dependability with the purpose of making assessments and decisions regarding trust relationships for e-services.

A clear differentiation between trust management, access control management, authorisation management, and authentication management was given, because the terms are often mistakenly used interchangeably.

Then an overview of the various credential-based, computation-based, reputation-based, and hybrid tools with highlights on how they can be used in e-services. It was realized that for e-services, either a hybrid or reputation-based system is a more natural fit. For other systems, they must be combined with other technology to address a wider section of the trust management problem.

References

Agudo, I., Lopez, J., & Montenegro, J. A. (2005). A representation model of trust relationships with delegation extensions. In P. Herrmann, V. Issarny, & S. Shiu (Eds.), *Third International Conference on Trust Management (iTrust 2005)*, Paris (LNCS 3477, pp. 116-130).

Anderson, R. J. (2002). *TCPA / Palladium frequently asked questions, Version 1.0*. Retrieved January 23, 2006, from http://www.cl.cam.ac.uk/~rja14/tcpa-faq.html

Azzedin, F., & Maheswaran, M. (2002). Integrating trust into grid resource management systems. In *International Conference on Parallel Processing 2002 (ICPP 2002)* (pp. 47-54).

Barlow, T., Hess, A., & Seamons, K. E. (2001). Trust negotiation in electronic markets. In *Eighth Research Symposium in Emerging Electronic Markets*, Maastricht, Netherlands. Retrieved January 24, 2006, from http://isrl.cs.byu.edu/pubs/rseem2001.pdf

Biskup, J., & Karabulut, Y. (2003). Mediating between strangers: A trust management based approach. In *2nd Annual Public Key Infrastructure (PKI) Research Workshop*, Gaithersburg, MD: NIST. Retrieved January 20, 2006, from http://middleware.internet2.edu/pki03/presentations/07.pdf

Blaze, M., Feigenbaum, J., Ioannidis, J., & Keromytis, A. (1999). *The KeyNote Trust Management System, Version 2* (RCF 2704). Retrieved February 8, 2006, from http://www.crypto/papers/rfc2704.txt

Blaze, M., Feigenbaum, J., & Keromytis, A. D. (1998). KeyNote: Trust management for public-key infrastructures. In *Security Protocols International Workshop*, Cambridge, UK. Retrived January 20, 2006, from http://www1.cs.columbia.edu/~angelos/Papers/keynote-position.pdf

Blaze, M., Feigenbaum, J., & Lacy, J. (1996). Decentralized trust management. In *IEEE Conference on Security and Privacy*. Oakland, CA: IEEE Computer Society Press.

Blaze, M., Feigenbaum, J., & Strauss, M. (1998). Compliance checking in the PolicyMaker trust management system. In (Ed.), *Financial Cryptography: Second International Conference* (pp. 251-265). Anguilla, British West Indies: Springer-Verlag.

Blaze, M., Ioannidis, J., & Keromytis, A. D. (2003). Experience with the KeyNote trust management system: Applications and future directions. In P. Nixon, & S. Terzis (Eds.), *First International Conference on Trust Management (iTrust 2003)*, Heraklion, Crete, Greece (LNCS 2692, pp. 284-300).

Carbo, J., Molina, J. M., & Davila, J. (2003). Trust management through fuzzy reputation. *International Journal of Cooperative Information Systems 12*(1), 135-155.

Carbone, M., Nielsen, M., & Sassone, V. (2004). A calculus for trust management. In K. Lodaya, & M. Mahajan (Eds.), *24th International Conference on Foundations of Software Technology and Theoretical Computer Science*, Chennai, India (LNCS 3328, pp. 161-172).

Chen, R., & Yeager, W. (2000). *Poblano: A distributed trust model for peer-to-peer networks.* Sun Microsystems. Retrieved January 14, 2006, from http://www.jxta.org/docs/trust. pdf

Chu, Y.-H. (1997). *Trust management for the World Wide Web.* Massachusetts institute of Technology. Unpublished masters thesis. Retrieved January 16, 2006, from http://www. w3.org/1997/Theses/YanghuaChu/

Chu, Y.-H., Feigenbaum, J., LaMacchia, B., Resnick, P., & Strauss, M. (1997). *REFEREE: Trust management for Web applications.* Retrieved January 17, 2006, from http://www. farcaster.com/papers/www6-referee/

Compaq et al. (2005). *TPM main: Part 1 Design principles, Version 1.* Retrieved March 8, 2006, from https://www.trustedcomputinggroup.org/specs/TPM/tpmwg-main-rev62_Part1_Design_Principles.pdf

English C., Nixon, P., Terzis, S., McGettrick, A., & Howe, H. (2002). Dynamic trust models for ubiquitous computing environments. In *Workshop on Security in Unbiquitous Computing (UBICOMP) 2002.* Retrieved March 3, 2006, from http://www.teco. edu/~philip/ubicom2002ws/organize/paddy.pdf

Evans, C., Feather, C. D. W., Hopmann, A., Presler-Marshall, M., & Resnick, P. (1997). *PICSRules 1.1.* Retrieved March 8, 2006, from http://www.w3.org/TR/REC-PICS-Rules

Foley, S. N. (2002). Trust management and whether to delegate. In B. Christianson, B. Crispo, J. A. Malcolm, & M. Roe, M. (Eds.), *9th International Workshop on Security Protocols* (LNCS 2467, pp. 151-157). Cambridge, UK: Springer-Verlag.

Freudenthal, E., & Karamcheti, V. (2003). *QTM: Trust management with quantified stochastic attributes* (Tech. Rep. No. TR2003-848). New York: Courant Institute of Mathematical Sciences, New York University. Retrieved January 20, 2006, from http://csdocs. cs.nyu.edu/Dienst/Repository/2.0/Body/ncstrl.nyu_cs%2fTR2003-848/pdf

Grandison, T. (2001). Trust specification and analysis for Internet applications. In *2nd IFIP Conference on E-Commerce, E-Business, E-Government (I3e 2002)*, Lisbon, Portugal. Retrieved January 16, 2006, from http://www.eyetap.org/~maali/trust-papers/I3e2002. pdf

Grandison, T. (2003). *Trust management for Internet applications.* Unpublished doctoral dissertation, Imperial College - University of London, UK.

Grandison, T., & Sloman, M. (2000). A survey of trust in Internet applications. *IEEE Communications Surveys and Tutorials, 4*(4), 2-16.

Grandison, T., & Sloman, M. (2003). Trust management tools for Internet applications. In P. Nixon, & S. Terzis, S. (Eds.), *First International Conference on Trust Management (iTrust 2003)*, Heraklion, Crete, Greece (LNCS 2692, pp. 91-107).

Gunter, C.A. & Jim, T. (2000). Policy-directed certificate retrieval. *Software: Practice & Experience, 2000, 30*(15) 1609-1640.

Hayton, R., Bacon, J., & Moody, K. (1998, May). OASIS: Access control in an open, distributed environment. In *IEEE Symposium on Security and Privacy* (pp. 3-14). Oakland CA: IEEE Computer Society Press.

IBM. (n.d.). *IBM trust establishment policy language*. Retrieved March 3, 2006, from http://www.haifa.il.ibm.com/projects/software/e-Business/TrustManager/PolicyLanguage.html

IBM. (2000). *Access control meets public key infrastructure, or: Assigning roles to strangers*. Retrieved January 6, 2006, from http://www.haifa.ibm.com/projects/software/e-Business/papers/Paper_Trust.pdf

Jajodia, S. S. P., & Subrahmanian, V. (1997). A logical language for expressing authorizations. In *IEEE Symposium on Security and Privacy* (pp. 31- 42). Oakland, CA: IEEE Press.

Jim, T. (2001). SD3: A trust management system with certified evaluation. In (Ed.), *IEEE Symposium on Security and Privacy* (pp. 106-115). Oakland, CA: IEEE Computer Society.

Jøsang, A. (1996). The right type of trust for distributed systems. In *ACM New Security Paradigms Workshop* (pp. 119-131). Lake Arrowhead, CA.

Jøsang, A., & Tran, N. (2000). *Trust management for e-commerce*. Retrieved January 17, 2006, from http://citeseer.nj.nec.com/375908.html

Kagal, L., Undercoffer, J., Perich, F., Joshi, A., & Finin, T. (2002). *A security architecture based on trust management for pervasive computing systems*. Retrieved January 14, 2006, from http://ebiquity.umbc.edu/_file_directory_/papers/15.pdf

Khare, R., & Rifkin, A. (1998). Trust management on the World Wide Web. *Peer-reviewed Journal on the Internet 3*(6). Retrieved Janury 15, 2006, from http://www.firstmonday.org/issues/issue3_6/khare/index.html

Kolluru, R., & Meredith, P. H. (2001). Security and trust management in supply chains. *Information Management and Computer Security, 9*(5), 233-236.

Krauskopf, T., Miller, J., Resnick, P., & Treesee, W. (1996). *PICS label distribution label syntax and communication protocols, Version 1.1*. Retrieved February 8, 2006, from http://www.w3.org/TR/REC-PICS-labels

Krukow, K. (2004). *On foundations for dynamic trust management*. Technical report, University of Aarhus, Denmark. Retrieved January 16, 2006, from http://www.brics.dk/~krukow/research/publications/online_papers/Progress.pdf

Li, N., & Mitchell, J. C. (2003). RT: A role-based trust-management framework. In *DARPA Information Survivability Conference and Exposition (DISCEX)*, Washington, DC. Retrieved January 16, 2006, from http://theory.stanford.edu/people/jcm/papers/rt_discex03.pdf

Li, N., & Mitchell, J. C. (2003). Datalog with constraints: A foundation for trust management languages. In V. Dahl, & P. Wadler (Eds.), *Fifth International Symposium on Practical Aspects of Declarative Languages* (LNCS 2562, pp. 58-73).

Li, N., Mitchell, J. C., & Winsborough, W. H. (2002). Design of a role-based trust management framework. In (Ed.), *2002 IEEE Symposium on Security and Privacy* (pp. 114-130). IEEE Computer Society. Retrieved January 15, 2006, from http://www.cs.purdue.edu/homes/ninghui/papers/rt_oakland02.pdf

Miller, J., Resnick, P., & Singer, D. *PICS rating services and rating systems (and their machine readable descriptions), Version 1.1*. Retrieved January 8, 2006, from http://www.w3.org/TR/REC-PICS-services

Network Associates. (1990). An introduction to cryptography. In *PGP 6.5.1 user's guide* (pp. 11-36). Network Associates Inc.

Riegelsberger, J., Sasse, A. M., & McCarthy, J. D. (2005). The mechanics of trust: A framework for research and design. *International Journal of Human-Computer Studies, 62*(3), 381-422.

Ruohomaa, S., & Kutvonen, L. (2005). Trust management survey. In P. Herrmann, V. Issarny, & S. Shiu (Eds.), *Third International Conference on Trust Management (iTrust 2005)*, Paris (LNCS 3477, pp. 77-92).

Seamons, K. E., Winslett, M., & Yu, T. (2001). Limiting the disclosure of access control policies during automated trust negotiation. In *Network and Distributed System Security Symposium*, San Diego, CA. Retrieved January 13, 2006, from http://dais.cs.uiuc.edu/pubs/winslett/ndss2001.pdf

Seigneur, J. M., & Jensen, C. D. (2004). Trading privacy for trust. In C. Jensen, S. Poslad, & T. Dimitrakos (Eds.), *Second International Conference on Trust Management (iTrust 2004)*, Oxford, UK (LNCS 2995, pp. 93-107).

Shmatikov, V., & Talcott, C. (2005). Reputation-based trust management. *Journal of Computer Security, 13*(1), 167-190.

Shrobe, H., & Doyle, J. (2000). Active trust management for autonomous adaptive survivable systems (ATMs for AAsss). In P. Robertson, H. Shrobe, & R. Laddaga, (Eds.), *1st International Workshop on Self-Adaptive Software (IWSAS 2000)* (pp. 40-49). Springer-Verlag.

Sun. (2001). *X.509 certificates and certificate revocation lists (CRLs)*. Retrieved October 12, 2005, from http://java.sun.com/products/jdk/1.2/docs/guide/security/cert3.html

Suryanarayana, G., & Taylor, R. N. (2004). *A survey of trust management and resource discovery technologies in peer-to-peer applications* (Tech. Rep. No. UCI-ISR-04-6). Irvine, CA: University of California, Irvine.

Weeks, S. (2001). Understanding trust management systems. In (Ed.), *IEEE Symposium on Security and Privacy* (pp. 94-105). Oakland, CA: IEEE Computer Society.

Winsborough, W. H., Seamons, K. E., & Jones, V. E. (1999). *Automated trust negotiation: Managing disclosure of sensitive credentials*. IBM Transarc White Paper.

Winsborough, W. H., Seamons, K. E., & Jones, V. E. (1999). Negotiating disclosure of sensitive credentials. In *Second Conference on Security in Communication Networks*, Amalfi, Italy. Retrieved January 24, 2006, from http://isrl.cs.byu.edu/pubs/scn99.pdf

Yao, W. T., Moody, K., & Bacon, J. (2003). Fidelis: A policy-driven trust management framework. In P. Nixon, & S. Terzis (Ed.), *First International Conference on Trust Management (iTrust 2003)*, Heraklion, Crete, Greece (LNCS 2692, pp 301-317).

Zacharia, G., & Maes, P. (2000). Trust management through reputation mechanisms. *Applied Artificial Intelligence, 14*(9), 881-907.

Section III

Trust Practices in E-Services

Chapter IX

Building Consumer Trust for Internet E-Commerce[1]

George Yee, National Research Council Canada, Canada

Abstract

The growth of the Internet is increasing the deployment of e-commerce B2C services within such areas as e-retailing, e-learning, and e-health. However, a major impediment to the growth of e-commerce on the Internet is the lack of consumer trust in the provider of the e-service (Van Slyke, Belanger, Comunale, 2004). This chapter presents a literature survey of recent contributions to building trust in e-commerce, followed by a description of seven ways for the B2C Internet service provider to build trust in the use of its services among consumers.

Introduction

Accompanying the growth of the Internet has been the availability of a diverse number of e-services. Most consumers are familiar with online banking or online retailing via the Internet. Other Internet-based services such as e-learning (online courses), e-government (online government services such as tax information), and e-health (online medical advice and others) are becoming more commonplace as well. Yet, the pace of such growth can be many times the current rate if consumers found these services trustworthy. According to Van Slyke et al. (2004), worldwide Internet commerce was expected to reach $8.5 trillion in 2005, of which online retail sales is the most evident, with U.S. consumers spending $51.3 billion online in 2001, $72.1 billion in 2002, and a projected $217.8 billion in 2007. However, Van Slyke et al. (2004) also report that not all forecasts are as rosy: while total online spending is increasing, per person online spending is quickly declining. These authors indicate that concerns over privacy and trust are among the most important factors that turn an online buyer into a nonbuyer. Kim and Prabhakar (2004) examine the role of trust in consumers' first adoption of Internet banking. They report that consumers' initial trust in the e-banking service is necessary for making use of the service and that this initial trust is based on trust for the "e-channel," the electronic channel through which service transactions are conducted (i.e., the Internet). Kim and Prabhakar (2004) state that trust of the e-banking service calls for trust in the provider of the service (the bank) and trust in the e-channel.

This chapter has two main objectives. The first objective is to present a literature survey of recent contributions to building trust for e-commerce. The second objective is to provide a description of seven methods that can be taken by the B2C Internet service provider to increase consumer trust in its services. These methods are (1) branding, (2) seal of approval (including privacy seals), (3) trustable user interface, (4) trusted subproviders, (5) reputation, (6) insurance, and (7) economic incentives. Thus, the reader will gain from this work: (a) an awareness of what research has been done in the area of building trust for e-commerce, and (b) knowledge of seven practical approaches that can be used to make B2C services trustworthy to consumers (and thereby increase sales and profits).

It is useful in a chapter on "trust" to define the meaning of trust. Gefen (2002) defines trust as "a willingness to be vulnerable to the actions of another person or people" or "the expectation that commitments undertaken by another person or organization will be fulfilled." Gefen (2002) also states that "overall trust is the product of a set of trustworthiness beliefs" that are primarily about the ability, integrity, and benevolence of the trusted party. "Integrity is the belief that the trusted party adheres to accepted rules of conduct, such as honesty and keeping promises. Ability is beliefs about the skills and competence of the trusted party. Benevolence is the belief that the trusted party, aside from wanting to make a legitimate profit, wants to do good to the customer." Of course, trust is important for many social and business relationships, setting the stage for interactions and expectations. Trust is even more important for e-commerce than ordinary commerce, since the business environment of the Web is less verifiable and less controllable. When consumers supply private information needed by a Web service, they expose themselves to possible unethical use and disclosure of their data.

The remainder of this chapter is organized as follows. The "Literature Survey" section summarizes the content and findings of recent works on building trust for e-commerce. The section "Seven Ways to Build Consumer Trust for Internet E-Commerce" describes the seven methods mentioned above for building trust. The section "Future Trends" discusses the likely evolution of trust and e-commerce in the coming years. Finally, the section "Conclusion" concludes the chapter.

Literature Survey

Many papers describing trust and e-commerce have appeared in recent years in response to the growth of the Internet and e-commerce. We present a nonexhaustive review of some of the more recent papers here (Table 1), categorizing them according to the following focus areas: "overall trust factors," "trust models and frameworks," "aspects of trust or methods for trust," "trust in specific sectors or geographic areas," "privacy and security," and "user interface issues." It is recommended that the reader peruse this table to find entries of interest and then read the corresponding original papers, as the summaries and key findings in the table may not do the original papers justice. In addition to the review here, we will refer to these papers in the remaining sections of this work as appropriate.

Table 1. Survey of recent papers on trust in e-commerce

Focus Area / Paper	Summary of Content	Key Findings
Overall Trust Factors		
Araujo & Araujo (2003). Developing trust in Internet commerce.	Describes factors that can influence a consumer's trust; also presents key elements for improving such trust.	A weighted checklist or automated tool can be developed to improve the trustworthiness of Web sites.
Gefen (2002). Reflections on the dimensions of trust and trustworthiness among online consumers.	Based on the premise that trust is multi-dimensional, proposes a three dimensional scale of trustworthiness dealing with integrity, benevolence, and ability; shows the importance of examining each dimension individually.	May be better to regard online consumer trustworthiness beliefs as a set of interrelated beliefs about the vendor rather than as one overall assessment; need to realize that trust may be multi-dimensional as well as uni-dimensional.
Kim & Tadisina (2005). Factors impacting customers' initial trust in e-businesses: An empirical study.	Uses previous studies and logical reasoning to define initial trust and examines its predictors. Empirical results explaining the factors impacting customers' initial trust in e-businesses are also presented.	The results provided evidence that Web site quality has the largest effect on customers' beliefs that an e-business had competence and goodwill. Other predictors like company profile and supporting organization, had lesser effects. Authors caution that these results should be used with caution since they were based on old data gathered under limited conditions.

Table 1. continued

Van Slyke et al (2004). Factors influencing the adoption of Web-based shopping: the impact of trust.	Using the literature on trust and diffusion of information, discusses the role of trust on consumers' intention to use B2C e-commerce; presents the results of a consumer survey to determine the influence of trust on decisions to make purchases.	Perceptions of trust are related to intentions to shop on the Web. Further, perceived ideas of relative advantage, complexity, compatibility, and image are also related to such intentions. While trust is important, the influence of trust seems to be less than some other factors.
Trust Models and Frameworks		
Bhattacharya & Saha (2004). Trust dimensions in e-retailing: A strategic exploration.	Focuses on development of trust through understanding and risk analysis as perceived by the consumer; provides a conceptual model and framework for future studies on why people are apprehensive to buying on the Internet.	Tips to help providers gain the trust of their customers; building trust is a long-term proposition; propensity of customers to trust an online shopping process can only be supported, not controlled, since trust needs to be earned.
Chen & Park (2004). Trust and privacy in electronic commerce.	Proposes a research model with trust and privacy as two endogenous variables along with other exogenous variables such as independent self-construal, interdependent self-construal, technological knowledge, and Web site quality, that are expected to affect the trust level and privacy concerns of Internet consumers.	Identified several major factors that affect trust and privacy in e-commerce; proposed eight hypotheses regarding trust, privacy, and self-construals. An example of a hypothesis is (Hypothesis 3) *Internet consumers with interdependent self-construals will have lower level of privacy concerns when shopping online.*
Chen, Gillenson, & Sherrell (2004). Consumer acceptance of virtual stores: A theoretical model and critical success factors for virtual stores.	Proposes a theoretical model, the Model of Consumer Acceptance of Virtual Store, for predicting consumer acceptance of virtual stores. Results of testing this model are also presented.	The proposed model can explain and predict consumer acceptance of virtual stores substantially well. The authors give advice to modify model input and parameters for additional research studies.
Kong & Hung (2006). Modeling initial and repeat online trust in B2C e-commerce.	Proposes an integrated model of online trust, and identifies the fundamental drivers of the online trust attitude formation process by adopting the dual cognitive processing notions of the Elaboration Likelihood Model of persuasion. Attempts to identify the fundamental drivers of information processes that lead to customers' trust decisions.	Identified two fundamental drivers that aid customers in their trust decision-making processes: motivation and ability to process relevant information. Authors believe that their model provides a basis to understand the relationships between initial and repeat customer online trust.
McKnight, Kacmar, & Choudhury (2003). Whoops... did I use the wrong concept to predict e-commerce trust? Modeling the risk-related effects of trust vs. distrust concepts.	Makes the point that mistrust is better suited at addressing issues of high risk (e.g., perceptions that the Web is risky), and proposes a model making use of both trust and mistrust to better predict high risk Web constructs.	E-commerce risk needs to be addressed by both trust and distrust concepts. Disposition to trust tends to affect low- or medium-risk constructs; disposi-tion to distrust tends to affect high risk constructs (e.g., willing-ness to depend on the Web site).

Table 1. continued

Nefti, Meziane, & Kasiran (2005). A fuzzy trust model for e-commerce.	Presents a trust model based on fuzzy logic. The authors argue that fuzzy logic is suitable for trust evaluation because it takes into account the uncertainties within e-commerce data. The trust model is validated using two case studies.	The fuzzy trust model addresses many issues that other trust models do not, such as taking into account the fuzzy nature of trust and the use of a substantial number of variables. Future trust systems should allow customers to rank trust variables according to their own perception and experience.
Salam, Iyer, Palvia, & Singh (2005). Trust in e-commerce.	Provides a comprehensive framework, based on four main research themes, for understand-ing trust in the context of Internet-enabled exchange re-lationships between consumers and Web-based vendors.	Trust is complex, containing technological, behavioral, social, psychological, and organizational interaction elements. Technical approaches to establishing trust are necessary but not sufficient. A comprehensive view of how consumer trust evolves related to specific actions is needed.
Serva, Benamati, & Fuller (2005). Trustworthiness in B2C e-commerce: An examination of alternative models.	Presents a study to clarify and advance the theoretical conceptualization of trustworthi-ness within a B2C context by synthesizing previous research and testing three alternative conceptualizations.	Viewing trustworthiness as a one-dimensional construct may be limited, in that it may not fully represent the underlying data. Instead, trustworthiness is better represented as a multidimensional construct, and both first and second-order conceptualizations are useful in e-commerce trust research, depending on purpose.
Tsygankov (2004). Evaluation of Web site trustworthiness from customer perspective, a framework.	Proposes a trust evaluative framework with 20 evaluation positions for use in reviewing commercial Web site trustworthiness from the customer perspective.	It would be useful to have a set of rules and recommendations for establishing trusted e-commerce environments. The presented framework may be used for evaluation of commercial Web site trustworthiness rate.
Yang, Hu, & Chen (2005). A Web trust-inducing model for e-commerce and empirical research.	Presents a Web trust-inducing model consisting of four dimensions, namely graphic design, structure design, content design, and social-cue design, along with four hypotheses. Presents the results of an online survey carried out to test the model and hypotheses. Identifies 12 trust-inducing features that can be applied to foster optimal levels of trust in customers.	Results of this study support the majority of the original model features. Some relationships did not receive significant support from the data, but the original model seems to hold fairly well after some moderate revision. The revised model is a reasonable starting point for developing a friendly interface for inducing trust in e-commerce.
Zhang, Kang, & He (2005). Towards a trust model with uncertainty for e-commerce systems.	Presents a trust model to account for the uncertain nature of trust using the cloud model. The traditional cloud model is extended to reason and describe the uncertainty of trust relationships scientifically and effectively.	Compared the proposed trust model with three other trust models in simulation experiments; results show that the proposed model performs better than the other three models. The proposed model has been applied in real e-commerce systems.

Table 1. continued

Aspects of Trust or Methods for Trust		
Atif (2002). Building trust in e-commerce.	Proposes a trust Web model based on a distributed search algorithm and a network of trusted intermediaries that can establish a trusted channel through which end parties deal virtually directly and risk free with each other.	Future e-commerce systems must support trust services to gain loyalty from both consumers and providers. The proposal here builds trust by negotiating a customers' request to complete a transaction using a sequence of trustworthy intermediaries.
Kim & Prabhakar (2004). Initial trust and the adoption of B2C e-commerce: The case of Internet banking.	Presents a conceptual model proposing that initial trust in the electronic channel as a banking medium and trust in the bank are major determinants of consumer acceptance.	A significant relationship exists between initial trust in the electronic channel and the adoption of Internet banking. However, trust could be neces-sary but not sufficient for the adoption of Internet banking.
Kim, Steinfield, & Lai (2004). Revisiting the role of Web assurance seals in consumer trust.	Examines consumers' awareness of Web assurance seal services and consumers' perceived importance of assurance seals found on B2C Web sites.	Consumer education increases the perceived importance of the seals, but consumers still are not likely to use these seals as indicators of site trustworthiness.
Kim & Kim (2005). A study of online transaction self-efficacy, consumer trust, and uncertainty reduction in electronic commerce transaction.	Explores self-efficacy as a factor that influences trust during an online transaction. Self-efficacy is an important factor in explaining motives and motivations of individual behaviors and choices.	Self-efficacy plays an important role in online transactions by negatively influencing perceived risk and positively influencing consumer trust. Online trans-action self-efficacy is a stronger predictor of risk perception than disposition to trust.
Lee, Ahn, & Han (2006). Analysis of trust in the e-commerce adoption.	Studies the trust of virtual communities to better understand and manage e-commerce. Proposes a theoretical model to clarify the factors as they are related to a Technology Acceptance Model. In particular, the relationship between trust and intentions is hypothesized.	When the users of a virtual community consider information exchange between one another, they are more sensitive to the trust between members than the trust in service providers. However, when they are interested in online purchasing, trust in service providers has a stronger impact on intention to purchase than trust between members.
Moores (2005). Do consumers understand the role of privacy seals in e-commerce?	Describes a study aimed at answering the basic question of whether online consumers understand or care about privacy seals and whether such measures have any impact on their online shopping.	While respondents to the study understand that privacy seals have something to do with promoting trust online, they are generally unaware of what a site must do to acquire a seal, or even what a genuine seal actually looks like. Furthermore, while almost all of the respondents had bought online, less than one-third would only trust a site with a seal. Serious questions need to be asked of the role of privacy seals in developing online trust.

Table 1. continued

Moores & Dhillon (2003). Do privacy seals in e-commerce really work?	Examines whether privacy seals in e-commerce really work.	Good news: the three main seals (TRUSTe, WebTrust, BBB-Online) have sensible data privacy principles and strive to ensure compliance by recipient Web sites. Bad news: Serious abuses by recipient sites continue. Perhaps legislation is required.
Salam, Rao, & Pegels (2003). Consumer-perceived risk in e-commerce transactions.	Examines consumer-perceived risks of transactions over the Internet focusing on the financial dimension. A framework is developed to identify critical aspects that need to be present or developed to reduce perceived risk.	One way to reduce consumer-perceived risk is to develop institutional trust using financial and social institutions as guarantors of e-commerce activity. Another way is for vendors to offer economic incen-tives (e.g., competitive pricing).
Tang, Thom, Wang, Tan, Show, & Tang (2003). Using insurance to create trust on the Internet.	Examines the use of insurance as a proxy in order to create trust for e-commerce activities over the Internet.	People surveyed were enthu-siastic about using insurance to effect trust, but expressed reservations about paying for it. The insurance value proposition needs further study but arguments can be made for its viability.
Trust in Specific Sectors or Geographic Areas		
Barnard & Wesson (2004). A trust model for e-commerce in South Africa.	Proposes a trust model for e-commerce in South Africa based on guidelines identified as significant for e-commerce in South Africa.	Guidelines identified can be applied to the design and eval-uation of e-commerce sites. The guidelines and the trust model together can improve the usability and level of consumer trust in South African e-commerce.
Kim, Ferrin, & Rao (2003). A study of the effect of consumer trust on consumer expectations and satisfaction: the Korean experience.	Proposes an e-commerce framework for the relationship between consumer trust, satisfaction, and expectation. The proposed models are tested using Internet consumer behavior data from two major Korean universities.	Both consumers' trust and expectation have positive influ-ences on consumers' satisfaction. The more consumers trust the seller, the higher the expectation they have, and the more likely to be satisfied. Consumer satis-faction may also affect the future trust and expectation of the consumer.
Luo & Najdawi (2004). Trust-building measures: A review of consumer health portals.	Analyzes trust building measures used by 12 major health portals and identifies the potential effects of these measures on consumer trust.	Each trust building measure affects the trustworthiness of the portal in different ways. Such measures are widely deployed, but the number and type used vary considerably among the portals.
Siau & Shen (2003). Building customer trust in mobile commerce.	Explores various facets of gaining consumer trust for mobile commerce.	Customer trust is crucial for the success of mobile commerce. Building this trust is complex, involving technology and business practices.
Sillence, Briggs, Fishwick, & Harris (2004). Trust and mistrust of online health sites.	Examines the question of how trust develops for online health information Web sites.	There is evidence for a staged model of trust in which visual appeal determines early decisions to mistrust sites, while credibility and personalization of informa-tion content influences the decision to select or trust them.

Table 1. continued

Sillence, Briggs, Fishwick, & Harris (2005). Guidelines for developing trust in health Web sites.	Similar to Sillence et al. (2004). Explores the question of how people decide which health Web sites to trust and which to reject.	Design guidelines for health Web sites. Staged model of trust as in Sillence et al. (2004). Within a health domain, it appears that personalization, site impetus, and social identity are especially important for site acceptance.
Privacy and Security		
Korba, Yee, Xu, Song, Patrick, & El-Khatib (2005). Privacy and trust in agent-supported distributed learning.	Explores the challenges, issues, and solutions for satisfying requirements for privacy and trust in agent-supported distributed learning.	Described many aspects of building privacy into agent-supported distributed learning. Not all described technologies would be required for every e-learning environment; need to use them where required, including in other types of e-business.
Levy & Gutwin (2005). Security through the eyes of users: Improving understand-ing of Web site privacy policies with fine-grained policy anchors.	Tackles the problem of understanding Web site privacy policies that make it difficult for the consumer to determine the cause and origin of conformance conflicts.	Integrated Privacy View that uses fine-grained policy anchors to present visual conformance information in the context of specific input fields. Users prefer this approach and could better determine the existence and source of privacy conflicts.
Nilsson, Adams, & Herd (2005). Building security and trust in online banking.	Examines the question of what influences users' perceptions of online banking security and trust.	One challenge for online banking is to maintain the balance between perceived trust, security, and usability for users. Authentication mechanisms can have a significant impact upon perceived trust in online banking.
Roussos & Moussouri (2004). Consumer perceptions of privacy, security, and trust in ubiquitous commerce.	Discusses the market forces that make the deployment of ubiquitous commerce infra-structures a priority for grocery retailing. Report on a study on consumer perceptions of security and privacy for MyGrocer, a recently developed ubiquitous commerce system.	Rather than focusing solely on the trustworthiness of a system, design should also address the affective aspects of interaction between ubiquitous commerce services and the consumer. It is unlikely that without allowing some degree of control over the system, consumers will be persuaded to use it. Indeed, controlling the flow of personal data is core in developing a trusting relationship between consumer and retailer.
Spiekermann, Grossklags, & Berendt (2001). E-privacy in 2nd generation e-commerce: Privacy preferences vs. actual behavior.	Examines the relationship between study participants' self-reported privacy preferences and their actual private data disclosing behavior during an online shopping episode.	In the study, participants disclosed private information contrary to their stated preferences. Therefore, current approaches to protect online privacy such as EU data protection regulation or P3P may not be effective since they assume that consumers will act according to their preferences.

Table 1. continued

User Interface Issues		
Barnard & Wesson (2003). Usability issues for e-commerce in South Africa: An empirical investigation.	Discusses an empirical study conducted in South Africa to determine if there were any usability problems on three well-known South African e-commerce sites and one international site.	A comparison of the strengths and weaknesses of each site. The five best and five worst features of the sites. Example best feature: home page gives clear indication of what site sells. Example worst feature: supply enough detail to enable product comparison.
Fang & Salvendy (2003). Customer-centered rules for design of e-commerce Web sites.	Describes a study in which real customers were interviewed to obtain information on what they liked and what difficulties they had in each stage of e-commerce Web site operation.	Nineteen most important design rules addressing customer concerns on home page, navigation, categorization, product information, shopping cart, checkout, and registration, and customer service.
Hussin, Keeling, Macaulay, & McGoldrick (2005). A trust agent for e-commerce: looking for clues.	Reviews the concept of trust in e-commerce and investigates 90 e-commerce Web sites to identify the presence of "clues" in the Web sites that signal the presence of several types of trust attributes; tests the presence of "clues" and trust attributes on Web sites against consumer perceptions of trustworthiness.	The results show that the clues correspond to the consumer search strategy for trust attributes. The clues are used as a basis for developing a personal trust agent (PTA) to assist consumers in assessing the trustworthiness of e-commerce Web sites.
Korba et al. (2005). Privacy and trust in agent supported distributed learning.	For this category of User Interface Issues, contains a section discussing the building of trustworthy user interfaces for distributed learning systems.	Interface design techniques, if properly used, can increase users' feelings of trust and reduce their perceptions of risk. Giving due consideration to users' privacy needs in terms of comprehension, consciousness, control, and consent, and making sure that the service satisfies these needs will be an important step for a usable and trusted environment.
Lanford & Hübscher (2004). Trustworthiness in e-commerce.	Examines the multifaceted notions of trust and trustworthiness and how they can be applied to e-commerce stores. Argues that high usability does not imply that the store is also trustworthy; formulates design guidelines for designing for trust.	Design guidelines for making a site more trustworthy, for example, fulfill the customer's expectations, show technical competence, let the user feel in control. Many e-commerce sites need major improvements to be successful. Improved usability is definitely key, but so is trustworthiness.
Pu & Chen (2006). Trust building with explanation interfaces.	Explores the potential of building users' trust with explanation interfaces. Presents major results from a survey that identified the most promising areas for investigating design issues for trust-inducing interfaces. Describes a set of general principles for constructing explanation interfaces that mostly contribute to trust formation.	Explanation interfaces have the greatest potential for competence-inspired trust with its users. A recommender agent's competence is positively correlated with users' intention to return, but not necessarily with their intention to purchase. An organization-based explanation interface should be more effective than the simple "why" interface, since it would be easier to compare different products and make a quicker decision.

Table 1. continued

Riegelsberger (2003). Interpersonal cues and consumer trust in e-commerce.	Investigates the effect of visual interpersonal cues (e.g., photo-graphs) on consumers' trust in e-commerce. Human trust decisions are also based on affective reactions, which can be triggered by interpersonal cues.	First results: visual interpersonal cues such as photographs have an effect on consumers' decision making. However, this effect strongly depends on context variables as well as individual differences.

The above survey indicates that much work has been done in terms of trust models and frameworks for understanding the role of trust in e-commerce. All studies point to the same conclusion, that trust plays a key role in consumers' decisions to adopt e-commerce. Some of the more interesting conclusions arrived at by these authors include (i) consumers' private information disclosure behavior may not follow their stated privacy preferences (Spieker-mann, Grosssklags, & Berendt, 2001), (ii) the type of authentication mechanism used affects the level of user trust in online banking (Nilsson et al., 2005), (iii) technical approaches (i.e., security technology) for creating trust are necessary but not sufficient (Salam et al., 2005), (iv) trust could be necessary but not sufficient for consumers to adopt Internet banking (Kim & Prabhakar, 2004), (v) consumers may not use seals of approval (aka Web assurance seals) as indicators of Web site trustworthiness (Kim et al., 2004), and (vi) privacy seals do not appear to work as expected and their roles need to be seriously questioned (Moores, 2005; Moores & Dhillon, 2003).

These authors represent excellent references for our presentation of the seven methods to build trust in e-commerce (next section).

Seven Ways to Build Consumer Trust for Internet E-Commerce

The following seven methods for building trust in Internet e-commerce are known approaches in one form or another. As most of these ideas (except for trusted subproviders and reputation) are already well described by other authors, we will keep our descriptions to a minimum and refer the interested reader to these other authors. In addition, these methods are presented here for information purposes only and not to be construed as recommendations. Finally, the methods differ in effectiveness and at least one is controversial.

Branding

Branding refers to the association of an unknown product or a service to a name that is well known and trustworthy among consumers. The intention (and hope) is that the trustworthi-ness of the name will be transferred to the product or service in the eyes of the consumer, that is, the consumer will also believe that the product or service is trustworthy. Branding is well described in terms of a company, a product, and a third party in Araujo and Araujo (2003).

An example of branding in e-commerce can be found in Amazon.com, where the consumer can directly purchase goods (usually used goods) from third-party sellers using the Amazon.com Web site. In this way, the third-party sellers hope to enjoy the trustworthiness and reputation that consumers associate with Amazon.com.

Seal of Approval (including privacy seals)

A seal of approval is an attestation by a recognized and trusted party that the receiver of the seal has lived up to or complied with a set of standards of good conduct, reliability, or trustworthiness. This is an old idea (e.g., Good Housekeeping Seal of Approval on household products) applied to modern e-commerce where the e-commerce Web site displays one or more seal(s) of approval to show that it is trustworthy, as attested to by the recognized and trusted parties. Seals of approval can be specialized to approve different aspects of a consumer's Web site experience (e.g., Verisign Secure Site seal, BBBOnline Privacy seal). There is some controversy as to whether consumers are aware of these seals (Kim et al., 2004) and whether they really work as expected (Moores, 2005; Moores & Dhillon, 2003). Since, the main problem in this controversy appears to be lack of consumer awareness and recognition of the seals, perhaps the answer lies in educating consumers on the seals. However, Kim et al., (2004) state that although consumer education increases the perceived importance of the seals, consumers are still not likely to use them as indicators of Web site trustworthiness. Additional research is needed.

Trustable User Interface

When consumers purchase goods on an e-commerce Web site, they must make decisions about the trustability of the vendor as well as the technology they are using. A number of factors come into play in influencing those trust decisions. One of the most important contributors to trust is a well-designed visual interface. We quote from Korba et al. (2005): "A visual appearance that is clean, uses pleasing colors and graphics, is symmetrical, and is professional looking is usually rated as more trustable. Other design factors that can build trust are the amount of information provided to the user, such as the information on how a system operates and the status of any processing....Predictable performance can also be an important factor, with systems that respond rapidly and consistently, instilling higher levels of trust." Other ideas for building trustable visual interfaces include the use of 19 design rules derived from interviews with real consumers (Fang & Salvendy, 2003), allowing consumers some degree of control over the flow of personal data (Araujo & Araujo, 2003; Lanford & Hübscher, 2004;Roussos & Moussouri, 2004;), fulfilling customer expectations and showing technical competence (Lanford & Hübscher, 2004), and the use of visual interpersonal cues such as photographs (Riegelsberger, 2003).

Trusted Subproviders

A subprovider is a secondary provider that a primary provider uses to supply one or more components of its service. Components of a service could range from a functional component such as data mining to a logistical component such as payment for the service. By using trusted subproviders, the primary provider hopes that the trustworthiness of the trusted subproviders will be transferred to itself in the eyes of the consumer, that is, the consumer will see the primary provider as trustworthy because it uses subproviders that the consumer trusts. The trust effect is similar to branding. The most famous example of a trusted subprovider is Paypal.com for payment services.

In the literature, the closest reference to trusted subproviders is the work by Atif (2002), where the author recommends the use of third-party trusted intermediaries to guarantee payment and delivery. Atif (2002) proposes a "trust Web model based on a distributed search algorithm and a network of trusted intermediaries that can establish a trusted channel through which terminal transacting parties deal virtually directly and risk-free with each other." This approach differs slightly from our use of trusted subproviders in that the intermediaries do not provide components of the service itself but instead act like brokers, forming a trust path between consumer and vendor through which to forward the payment or the goods. Another related work is Salam et al. (2003), who recommend reducing consumer-perceived risk by developing institutional trust using financial and social institutions as guarantors of e-commerce activity. This is similar to the use of trusted intermediaries as guarantors in Atif (2002).

Reputation

The reputation of an e-commerce service provider directly determines whether a consumer will trust the provider's service. The higher the reputation of the provider, the higher the level of trust the consumer will have for the service. Thus, in order to use reputation to build consumer trust in a provider's service, (1) the provider has to be reputable, and (2) there needs to be some way to easily calculate and display the provider's reputation for all consumers to see or access.

The most famous e-commerce reputation system in actual use is the buyer/seller rating system in eBay.com. In this reputation system, buyers rate sellers on how well they carried out their part of the transaction, for example, *goods delivered in a timely manner?*, *goods arrived in condition advertised?*. Sellers rate buyers on how well the buyers fulfilled their end of the bargain, for example, *accurate payment?*, *prompt payment?*. The resultant scores are administered by eBay itself and are posted for all to see. Moreover, the actual text of the buyer or seller rating (e.g., "very fast delivery") is posted as well for all to see. A buyer thinking of making a purchase can check the seller's rating and perhaps peruse the text of all the seller's ratings to make sure the seller has a good reputation before committing to the purchase. By so doing, the buyer can ascribe some trust to the seller if the seller has a good reputation.

A reputation system similar to the one at eBay.com can be set up for general e-commerce providers and consumers. Consumers can rate providers, and vice versa, using the Web site of a trusted authority that would administer the ratings and make sure that ratings are secure and fair. The authority would investigate outlandish ratings to ensure that one party is not "badmouthing" another party. Consumers or providers could then access the authority's Web site to ascertain the reputation of the transacting partner before committing to the transaction. The trusted authority could be a role played by a government agency as a public service and for the good of the economy so that there would be no charges for use of its services. Actually, in traditional commerce, the existing network of Better Business Bureau (BBB) offices, where consumers can lodge complaints against providers, is somewhat like what we are proposing. However, with BBB, consumers do not rate every transaction and consumers themselves are not rated. Nevertheless, traditional commerce consumers can, in many cases, check the BBB for the reputation of a provider.

We did not find any references in the literature to the direct use of reputation to build consumer trust in e-commerce as we describe here. However, other methods such as branding, seal of approval, and trusted subproviders are of course based on the reputation of the name brand, the giver of the seal of approval, and the trusted subprovider, respectively.

Insurance

In today's world, insurance can be found for many areas, as long as the insurance companies find it profitable. It is no surprise then that insurance be proposed as a means of building trust in e-commerce. Tang et al. (2003) is the definitive reference for this method of building trust. In their paper, trust for e-commerce is divided into three types of trust: market space trust (trust that both buyers and sellers must have in the market space where the transaction will occur), buyer's trust (the trust of the buyer that the goods will be delivered as agreed), and seller's trust (the trust of the seller that s/he will be paid for the delivered goods). Tang et al. (2003) then propose specific insurance policies to cover each of the areas in which these types of trust must arise. The different types of trust will then arise as a result of the insurance policies being in place. The authors also conducted interviews with insurance and technology organizations to determine the feasibility of their insurance approach. They report that: "most of the people surveyed and interviewed were enthusiastic about using insurance as a proxy for effecting trust on the Internet. However, there were reservations about paying for such a product." To counter these reservations, the authors cite the example of bottled water, which is a popular purchase item now, but there may have been reservations about paying for bottled water when it was first proposed. Tang et al. (2003) conclude that building e-commerce trust with insurance would provide too many benefits to be ignored. We refer the interested reader to Tang et al. (2003) for the details.

Economic Incentives

The use of economic incentives to build trust in e-commerce refers to incentives to purchase such as reduced pricing, more product for the same price, or free delivery offered by a seller to a potential buyer. The principal behind economic incentives is the observation by researchers (Salam et al., 2003) that some consumers will make purchases if there is sufficient economic incentive, even if their trust level for the vendor is low. In this sense, it may not really be building up the consumer's trust but rather reducing the consumer's perceived risk of the service, that is, the consumer believes that s/he is getting such a good deal that it is "worth the risk." Nevertheless, if the consumer makes the purchase the end result is the same.

Future Trends

Consumer trust for e-commerce is a key enabler of e-commerce success. We have seen how various researchers have tackled the problems of both understanding trust and how it can be built up. This research will of course continue and will involve a melding of diverse disciplines from engineering, computer science, and the social sciences such as psychology and sociology. A rapidly developing area of trust is how to build trust through trustable interfaces, that is, human-machine interfaces that inspire trust in the machine. Another growing area of research that is related to trustable interfaces is the role of usability in building consumer trust. The more usable the device, the more likely it should be trusted. However, the question is: How can usability be improved so that the result inspires trust? Trustable interfaces and usability have important applications in the new field of biometrics, where trust is needed to sooth the consumer's concerns over the use of biometric devices that can be awkward to use. Still, a further area of research will be towards expanding the number of ways of building consumer trust, as described previously.

One goal of improving consumer trust in e-commerce may be stated simply as *arriving at some future state where consumers trust e-commerce to the same extent as they trust brick and mortar commerce*. Achieving this goal will require a thorough understanding of the nature of trust and how to achieve it. It will no doubt require the application of some of the ways of building trust given previously, as well as new methods of building trust that are yet to be discovered. We are still far from achieving this goal, but we have made a reasonable start.

Conclusion

We began by surveying the recent literature on contributions to building consumer trust in e-commerce and found that there are many works in this area, especially on trust frameworks and models. However, all such studies conclude that trust is an important and key factor for e-commerce success. A number of authors had remarkable or counterintuitive findings such as (1) consumers' private information disclosure behavior may not follow their stated privacy preferences (Spiekermann et al., 2001), (2) the type of authentication mechanism used affects the level of user trust in online banking (Nilsson et al., 2005), and (3) technical approaches (i.e., security technology) for creating trust are necessary but not sufficient (Salam et al., 2005). We then proceeded to describe seven practical ways for e-commerce service providers to build consumer trust in their services. Most of these methods are already known and described in the literature but we contributed two, hopefully new ones or variations over existing ones, that as far as we can tell are not in the literature, namely the use of trusted subproviders and the use of reputation. We hope that this work has provided the reader with some useful insights and tools for building trust in e-commerce.

References

Araujo, I., & Araujo, I. (2003, October). Developing trust in Internet commerce. In *Proceedings of the 2003 Conference of the Centre for Advanced Studies on Collaborative Research* (pp. 1-15).

Atif, Y. (2002). Building trust in e-commerce. *IEEE Internet Computing, 6*(1), 18-24.

Barnard, L., & Wesson, J. L. (2003, September). Usability issues for e-commerce in South Africa: An empirical investigation. In *Proceedings of the 2003 Annual Research Conference of the South African Institute of Computer Scientists and Information Technologists on Enablement Through Technology (SAICSIT '03)* (pp. 258-267).

Barnard, L., & Wesson, J. (2004, October). A trust model for e-commerce in South Africa. In *Proceedings of the 2003 Annual Research Conference of the South African Institute of Computer Scientists and Information Technologists on Enablement Through Technology (SAICSIT '04)* (pp. 23-32).

Bhattacharya, K. K., & Saha, S. (2004, October). Trust dimensions in e-retailing: A strategic exploration. In *Proceedings, 2004 IEEE International Engineering Management Conference* (Vol. 2, pp. 825-828).

Chen, J.-C. V., & Park, Y. I. (2004, March 28-31). Trust and privacy in electronic commerce. In *Proceedings of the 2004 IEEE International Conference on E-Technology, E-Commerce, and E-Service (EEE'04)* (pp. 117-120).

Chen, L., Gillenson, M. L., & Sherrell, D. L. (2004). Consumer acceptance of virtual stores: A theoretical model and critical success factors for virtual stores. *ACM SIGMIS Database, 35*(2), 8-31.

Fang, X., & Salvendy, G. (2003). Customer-centered rules for design of e-commerce Web sites. *Communications of the ACM, 46*(12), 332-336.

Gefen, D. (2002). Reflections on the dimensions of trust and trustworthiness among online consumers. *ACM SIGMIS Database, 33*(3), 38-53.

Hussin, A. R. C., Keeling, K., Macaulay, L., & McGoldrick, P. (2005, March 29-April 1). A trust agent for e-commerce: Looking for clues. In *Proceedings of the 2005 IEEE International Conference on E-Technology, E-Commerce, and E-Service (EEE '05)* (pp. 286-289).

Kim, D. J., Ferrin, D. L., & Rao, H. R. (2003, September). A study of the effect of consumer trust on consumer expectations and satisfaction: The Korean experience. In *Proceedings of the 5ᵗʰ International Conference on Electronic commerce (ICEC '03)* (pp. 310-315).

Kim, D. J., Steinfield, C., & Lai, Y. (2004, March). Revisiting the role of Web assurance seals in consumer trust. In *Proceedings of the 6ᵗʰ International Conference on Electronic Commerce (ICEC 2004)* (pp. 280-287).

Kim, E., & Tadisina, S. (2005, January 3-6). Factors impacting customers' initial trust in e-businesses: An empirical study. In *Proceedings of the 38ᵗʰ Annual Hawaii International Conference on System Sciences (HICSS '05)* (pp. 170b-170b).

Kim, K. K., & Prabhakar, B. (2004). Initial trust and the adoption of B2C e-commerce: The case of Internet banking. *ACM SIGMIS Database, 35*(2), 50-64.

Kim, Y. H., & Kim, D. J. (2005, January). A study of online transaction self-efficacy, consumer trust, and uncertainty reduction in electronic commerce transaction. In *Proceedings of the 38th Annual Hawaii International Conference on System Sciences (HICSS '05)* (pp. 170c-170c).

Kong, W.-C., & Hung, Y.-T. (2006, January 4-7). Modeling initial and repeat online trust in B2C e-commerce. In *Proceedings of the 39th Annual Hawaii International Conference on System Sciences (HICSS '06)* (Vol. 6, pp. 120b-12b).

Korba, L., Yee, G., Xu, Y., Song, R., Patrick, A. S., & El-Khatib, K. (2005). Privacy and trust in agent-supported distributed learning. In F. Oscar Lin (Ed.), *Designing distributed learning environments with intelligent software agents* (pp. 67-114). Information Science Publishing.

Lanford, P., & Hübscher, R. (2004, April). Trustworthiness in e-commerce. In *Proceedings of the 42nd Annual Southeast Regional Conference* (pp. 315-319).

Lee, H., Ahn, H., & Han, I. (2006, January 4-7). Analysis of trust in the e-commerce adoption. In *Proceedings of the 39th Annual Hawaii International Conference on System Sciences (HICSS '06)* (Vol. 6, pp. 113c-113c).

Levy, S. E., & Gutwin, C. (2005, May). Security through the eyes of users: Improving understanding of Web site privacy policies with fine-grained policy anchors. In *Proceedings of the 14th International Conference on World Wide Web* (pp. 480-488).

Luo, W., & Najdawi, M. (2004). Trust-building measures: A review of consumer health portals. *Communications of the ACM, 47*(1), 108-113.

McKnight, H., Kacmar, C., & Choudhury, V. (2003, January). Whoops... did I use the wrong concept to predict e-commerce trust? Modeling the risk-related effects of trust vs. distrust concepts. In *Proceedings of the 36th Annual Hawaii International Conference on System Sciences* (10 pp.).

Moores, T. (2005). Do consumers understand the role of privacy seals in e-commerce? *Communications of the ACM, 48*(3), 86-91.

Moores, T. T., & Dhillon, G. (2003). Do privacy seals in e-commerce really work? *Communications of the ACM, 46*(12), 265-271.

Nefti, S., Meziane, F., & Kasiran, K. (2005, July 19-22). A fuzzy trust model for e-commerce. In *Proceedings, Seventh IEEE International Conference on E-Commerce Technology* (pp. 401-404).

Nilsson, M., Adams, A., & Herd, S. (2005, April). Building security and trust in online banking. In *CHI '05 extended abstracts on human factors in computing systems* (pp. 1701-1704).

Pu, P., & Chen, L. (2006, January). Trust building with explanation interfaces. In *Proceedings of the 11th International Conference on Intelligent User Interfaces (IUI '06)* (pp. 93-100).

Riegelsberger, J. (2003, April). Interpersonal cues and consumer trust in e-commerce. In *CHI '03 extended abstracts on human factors in computing systems* (pp. 674-675).

Roussos, G., & Moussouri, T. (2004). Consumer perceptions of privacy, security and trust in ubiquitous commerce. *Personal and Ubiquitous Computing, 8*(6), 416-429.

Salam, A. F., Iyer, L., Palvia, P., & Singh, R. (2005). Trust in e-commerce. *Communications of the ACM, 48*(2), 72-77.

Salam, A. F., Rao, H. R., & Pegels, C. C. (2003). Consumer-perceived risk in e-commerce transactions. *Communications of the ACM, 46*(12), 325-331.

Serva, M. A., Benamati, J., & Fuller, M. A. (2005). Trustworthiness in B2C e-commerce: An examination of alternative models. *The DATABASE for Advances in Information Systems, 36*(3), 89-108.

Siau, K., & Shen, Z. (2003). Building customer trust in mobile commerce. *Communications of the ACM, 46*(4), 91-94.

Sillence, E., Briggs, P., Fishwick, L., & Harris, P. (2004, April). Trust and mistrust of online health sites. In *Proceedings of the SIGCHI Conference on Human Factors in Computing Systems* (pp. 663-670).

Sillence, E., Briggs, P., Fishwick, L., & Harris, P. (2005, May). Guidelines for developing trust in health Web sites. *Special Interest Tracks and Posters of the 14th International Conference on World Wide Web* (pp. 1026-1027).

Spiekermann, S., Grossklags, J., & Berendt, B. (2001, October). E-privacy in 2nd generation e-commerce: Privacy preferences vs. actual behavior. In *Proceedings of the 3rd ACM conference on Electronic Commerce* (pp. 38-47).

Tang, F., Thom, M. G., Wang, L. T., Tan, J. C., Chow, W. Y., & Tang, X. (2003). Using insurance to create trust on the Internet. *Communications of the ACM, 46*(12), 337-344.

Tsygankov, V. A. (2004, March). Evaluation of Web site trustworthiness from customer perspective, a framework. In *Proceedings of the 6th International Conference on Electronic Commerce (ICEC 2004)* (pp. 265-271).

Van Slyke, C., Belanger, F., & Comunale, C. L. (2004). Factors influencing the adoption of Web-based shopping: The impact of trust. *ACM SIGMIS Database, 35*(2), 32-49.

Yang, Y., Hu, Y., & Chen, J. (2005, August). A Web trust-inducing model for e-commerce and empirical research. In *Proceedings of the 7th International Conference on Electronic Commerce (ICEC '05)* (pp. 188-194).

Zhang, G., Kang, J., & He, R. (2005, October 12-18). Towards a trust model with uncertainty for e-commerce systems. In *Proceedings, IEEE International Conference on E-Business Engineering (ICEBE 2005)* (pp. 200-207).

Endnote

[1]   NRC Paper Number: NRC 48509

Chapter X

Developing Trust Practices for E-Health

Elizabeth Sillence, Northumbria University, UK

Pamela Briggs, Northumbria University, UK

Peter Harris, Sheffield University, UK

Lesley Fishwick, Northumbria University, UK

Abstract

The number of people turning to the Internet to meet their various health needs is rising. As the prevalence of this form of e-health increases, so the issue of trust becomes ever more important. This chapter presents a brief overview of e-health and describes how and why people are using the Internet for health advice and information. In order to understand the trust processes behind this engagement, a staged model of trust is proposed. This model is explored through a series of in-depth qualitative studies and forms the basis for a set of design guidelines for developing trust practices in e-health.

Introduction

E-health is a term widely used by many academic institutions, professional bodies, and funding organizations. Rarely used before 1999, it has rapidly become a buzzword used to characterize almost everything related to computers and medicine. As its scope has increased, so have the trust issues associated with the term. A systematic review of published definitions identified a wide range of themes but no clear consensus about the meaning of the term e-health, other than the presence of two universal themes (health and technology) (Oh, Rizo, Enkin, & Jadad, 2005). Eysenbach's (2001) commonly cited definition allows a conceptualization that goes beyond simply "Internet medicine."

E-health is an emerging field in the intersection of medical informatics, public health and business, referring to health services and information delivered or enhanced through the Internet and related technologies.

Despite an absence of any single definition of the concept, the key themes of health and technology allow a wider exploration of the domain from multiple standpoints. E-health can encompass a wide range of technologies (Internet, interactive television, personal, digital assistants, CD-ROMS), a range of health services and information types (family practitioner's surgeries, public settings, consultations, decision making), and a range of different stakeholders (medical professionals, patients and careers, business).

Sixty two percent of Internet users have gone online in search of health information, and it has been estimated that over 21 million people have been influenced by the information provided therein (Pew, 2000). Given the prevalence and use of Web sites concerned with health, the focus of this chapter is specifically on the use of the Internet for health advice and information. There has been a rapid increase in the use of technology, specifically the Internet, in health information and advice. Worldwide, about 4.5% of all Internet searches are for health related information (Morahan-Martin, 2004). Sieving (1999) lists a number of different push and pull factors that have led to this increase, at least from an American perspective. These include an increasingly elderly population and a change in emphasis from healthcare providers treating illness to patients having primary responsibility for maintaining and improving their own health. Meanwhile, a range of content providers have recognized the educational and financial benefits of providing online health information.

Given the range of health advice and information available and the possible delivery modes available, patients are faced with decisions about which information, providers, and technologies to trust. How do people make decisions about trust in this context and how can guidelines for trust practices help in this respect? This chapter aims to explore the issue of trust within the context of e-health. The rest of this chapter is organized as follows. In the next section, we discuss the role of technology in the context of health information and advice. In section "Trust and Mistrust in E-Health," we examine the context of trust in relation to e-health, and in particular online or Web-based health advice and information, and present a staged model of trust that helps reconcile differences in the literature. "Validating the Model" presents a validation of the staged model through in-depth qualitative work.

"Guidelines for Developing Trust in E-Health" draws together the literature and the results of the qualitative work to present a set of guidelines addressing how trust practices can be promoted in e-health and especially Web-based e-health.

The Role of Technology in the Context of Health Information and Advice

Technology has traditionally played an important role within health care. Through physician focused systems such as telemedicine and more recently the development of an electronic patient record system within the UK to an increase in patient-focused information and advice channels, accessing information about health can now be achieved via the telephone, the Internet, or even via the television (BBC Online, 2004). The UK's National Health Service is one service provider exploring new ways of disseminating health information to the general public. The NHS Direct service allows patients to access information online, speak to a nurse on the telephone, or retrieve information via a public access kiosk (Dobson, 2003).

Increasingly, the Internet has been seen as a major source of advice and information on health. More and more patients prefer not to let physicians dictate medical care and as such, have turned to alternative sources of advice. An estimated 80% of adult Internet users in the US (Pew Research, 2003) and over two thirds of Internet users in Europe have turned to the Internet for health information and advice (Taylor & Leitman, 2002). People search online for health information and advice for a number of reasons. Some people want to be better informed, better prepared when meeting the doctor, or are searching for support, alternative answers, or reassurance (Rozmovits & Ziebland, 2004). Over 40% of Europeans said they would like to discuss information found on the Internet with their doctor, and one in five European consumers has asked their doctor about a symptom or diagnosis after having read information online (WHA, 2002). Many people searching online for health advice believe that it will enable them to better deal with their health and will convey health benefits (Mead, Varnam, Rogers, & Roland, 2003).

Time constraints in the consulting room have also led to an increase in online searching. The average length of a doctor's appointment in the UK is currently about 8 minutes. In this short period of time, both the doctor and the patient often find it difficult to explain and discuss all their issues. Patients often find it difficult to recall the specifics of their discussions with the doctor after the consultation (Kalet, Roberts, & Fletcher, 1994). Young people, in particular, are turning to the Internet rather than to a family doctor or a parent to get health information and advice (Kanuga & Rosenfeld, 2004), and the appeal of the Internet is particularly strong for those people who wish advice on important but sensitive matters (Klein & Wilson, 2003). The Internet allows people to communicate and interact with a far greater variety of people across all walks of life. It provides up-to-date information as well as increased social support (Eysenbach, Powell, Englesakis, Rizo, & Stern, 2004). It allows information to be shared in the form of text and images and can put people in touch with the most up-to-date information from some of most eminent sources in the medical profession. The Internet can offer people second and even third opinions and, in short, can provide people with information and advice that they simply cannot find anywhere else.

The advice that health consumers are seeking online ranges from information and advice about treatment decisions, interpreting diagnoses, and understanding any long-term medical implications through to finding support groups, seeking alternative therapies, and understanding drug requirements and drug interactions (Bernhardt & Felter, 2004; Gray, Klein, Noyce, Sesselberg, & Cantrill, 2004; Peterson, Aslani, & Williams, 2003; Reeves, 2001; Ziebland, Chapple, Dumelow, Evans, Prinjha, & Rozmovits, 2004).

But does the Internet leave patients better informed, and does reading online information and following advice lead to better outcomes? Coulson (personal communication), for example, found that people using Internet resources for health topics such as HIV and Aids often took on medical advice that was incorrect. Another key issue is the extent to which users recognize quality advice and information. Despite there being at least 70,000 health related sites available on the Internet (Pagliari & Gregor, 2004) less than half of the medical information available online has been reviewed by the medical profession (Pew Research, 2000), and few sites provide sufficient information to support patient decision making, with many also being heavily jargon laden and difficult to read (Smart & Burling, 2001).

One of the benefits (and the disadvantages) of the Internet is the range of material available regarding health and lifestyle advice. Sites can vary in the type of advice and information they present (see Table 1) and in terms of their scope, health topic, ownership, country of origin, and levels of interactivity. To indicate the range of different sites available, Table 2

Table 1. The range of health Web sites available to consumers

Type of site	Description of site
Web providers and portal sites	Information and advice supplied by Web provider rather than a physical organization. Portals act as catalogues of information providing a gateway to many other sites providing information and advice.
Support groups	Often run by individuals or on behalf of support groups. May be local, national, or global in scale. Often contains forums where consumers can read comments and contribute to discussions.
Charity sites	Registered charity sites provide information and advice on specific health issues and provide a focal point for fund raising activities.
Government Web sites	Provide patient information in the form of news, features, and fact sheets.
Pharmaceutical sites	Sponsored by pharmaceutical companies these sites are often biased in favour of their own drug remedies and regimes.
Sales sites	Sales sites promote and sell certain drugs, medical devices, or health plans, often in addition to some information.
Personal sites	Contains personal experiences of illness and health issues.
Medical databases	Provide access to research papers on health and illness issues.
Media sites	Extensions of print or television media sites that provide the latest news and commentary on health features.
Clinician sites	Information on specific health issues or specialist clinics run by medical professionals.

Table 2. Health Web sites and range of features/services

	Web site		
	Netdoctor http://www.netdoctor.co.uk	**Dipex** http://www.dipex.org	**NHS direct** http://www.nhsdirect.nhs.uk
Domain	General health	High blood pressure	General health
Owner	Web provider	Charity	Government
Type of advice	Patient fact sheets Ask the doctor service News Discussion boards	Personal accounts Medical information Frequently Asked Questions	Health encyclopaedia Self-help guide Clinical evidence-based research reports
Commercial aspects	Health related advertising	Donations requested	None
Notable features	SMS alert service (e.g., contraceptive pill reminder Discussion boards)	Video clips Links to support groups	Locate nearest NHS services facility

provides an overview of three different UK-based sites highlighting their main features and the range of services available on each site.

Given the huge variety of sites available, how are consumers searching for and evaluating the trustworthiness and quality of health Web sites? There is a large body of research assessing the quality of information available on the Internet (Jadad & Gagliardi, 1998; Smart & Burling, 2001; Wyatt, 1997), embracing diverse topics such as Viagra, rheumatoid arthritis, and diabetes. A systematic meta-analysis of health Web site evaluations noted that the most frequently used quality criteria included accuracy, completeness, and readability and design (Eysenbach, Powell, Kuss, & Sa, 2002). Seventy percent of the studies they reviewed concluded that quality is a problem on the Internet.

Almost all of these quality assessments have been conducted from a medical perspective. Relatively few studies have tried to understand the patient experience. Despite forming a cornerstone of NHS IT policy (NHS, 1998) and numerous studies reporting the widespread consumer use of the Internet for health information, relatively few have attempted to understand how different stakeholders access and evaluate the information and the way in which Internet sources affect the patients' experience or health outcomes. Notable exceptions are studies of the way in which patients with HIV or AIDS (Reeves, 2001), cancer (Ziebland et al., 2004), paediatric health information needs (Bernhardt & Felter, 2004), or medicine requirements (Peterson et al., 2003) use online information to help them make treatment decisions, interpret information, find support groups, and seek alternative therapies. Other studies have suggested that whilst the Internet can increase patients' knowledge about their health conditions, they can be left feeling too overwhelmed by the information available online to be able to make an informed decision about their own health care (Hart, Henwood, & Wyatt, 2004). Reviews of quantitative Web-based intervention studies have generally indicated beneficial effects of the Internet on health outcomes, although issues concerning the methodological quality of such studies remain (Bessell, McDonald, Silagy, Anderson, Hiller, & Sansom, 2002). A more recent meta-analysis by Wantland et al. (Wantland, Portillo, Holzemer, Slaughter, &

McGhee, 2004) concluded that in the majority of studies, knowledge and or behavioural outcomes improved for participants using Web-based health interventions.

The paucity of research from the patient perspective is a problem, because we know that ordinary health consumers are likely to adopt different quality criteria to experts, being more readily influenced by the attractiveness of the design, for example (Stanford, Tauber, Fogg, & Marable, 2002). In an empirical study of over 2,500 people who had sought advice online, for example, most began their search via a general information portal—gaining access to information of variable quality indiscriminately (Briggs, Burford, DeAngeli, & Lynch, 2002). Eysenbach and Köhler (2002) noted that consumers (as opposed to experts) failed to check the authorship or owners of the Web site or read disclosure statements, despite suggesting these as important quality markers beforehand. Their study made use of an artificial search task, however, and the authors themselves suggested that people in a "real setting" with a greater stake in the outcome may well pay more attention to the content of the Web sites, in terms of markers of quality. This failure to engage with real Internet consumers in a realistic setting is a common problem in studies of online trust. Thus, there is a real need for systematic explorations of the ways in which people evaluate the trustworthiness of health information and advice online.

Trust and Mistrust in E-Health

The literature suggests that trust is multifaceted, multidimensional, and not easy to tie down in a single space (Marsh & Dibben, 2003). A key point to note is that trust is intimately associated with risk; indeed, it is possible to argue that in the absence of risk, trust is meaningless (Brien, 1998). Even within seemingly simple acts of trust, complex sets of judgements are invoked and a risk assessment is involved. Indeed, some of the trust models that have been developed in recent years have explicitly included risk (Corritore, Kracher, & Wiedenbeck, 2003). In online advice, there is no doubt that people are more willing to trust a site if perceived risk is low. This came out very clearly in a study of over two and a half thousand people who said they had sought advice online (Briggs et al., 2002). Those that sought advice in relatively high risk domains (e.g., finance) were less likely to trust, and subsequently act on, the advice than those who sought advice in low risk domains (e.g., entertainment).

The literature regarding trust in an e-commerce setting provides a useful starting point for exploring the ways in which people evaluate the trustworthiness of health information and advice online (see Grabner-Krauter & Kaluscha, 2003 for a recent review.) Based on this literature, we can assume that various factors are likely to govern the extent to which individuals feel they can trust health advice online. Firstly, they may be influenced by the look and feel of the site; trusting, for example, those sites rated high in visual appeal and mistrusting those sites with poor visual design or with unprofessional errors. Secondly, they may be influenced by the branding of the site or by presence of familiar images or trusted logos. Thirdly, they may be influenced by the quality of information available on the site, trusting those sites with greater perceived expertise, and fourthly, they may be influenced by the extent to which the advice is personalized to the individual, that is, the extent to which the advice appears to come from and be directed to similar individuals (i.e., those with a shared social identity).

Whilst these different factors appear to be important, researchers disagree over their relative importance in fostering trust. For example, some researchers argue that consumer trust (or a related construct, credibility) is primarily driven by an attractive and professional design (Fogg, Kameda, Boyd, Marchall, Sethi, Sockol, & Trowbridge, 2002; Kim & Moon, 1998; Stanford et al., 2002) or is influenced by the presence or absence of visual anchors or prominent features such as a photograph or trust seal (Riegelsberger, Sasse, & McCarthy, 2003). Others argue that trust reflects the perceived competence, integrity predictability, and/or benevolence of the site (Bhattacherjee, 2002; McKnight & Chervany, 2001). A few authors also highlight the importance of personalisation in the formation of trust judgments (Briggs, De Angeli, & Simpson, 2004) or the notion of good relationship management (Egger, 2000).

One way of reconciling these different findings is to consider a developmental model of trust or the way in which trust develops over time. For example, it is worth distinguishing between the kinds of trust that support transient interactions and those that support longer-term relationships (Meyerson, Weick, & Kramer, 1996). Riegelsberger, Sasse and McCarthy (2005), in their model of trust, describe different stages of trust that develop over time: early, medium, and mature forms of trust. A number of authors (Egger 2000, 2001; Sillence, Briggs, Fishwick, & Harris, 2004a) have suggested that three phases are important: a phase of initial trust followed by a more involved exchange that then may or may not lead to a longer-term trusting relationship. If one considers trust in this developmental context, then some of the findings in the literature make more sense. In particular, consideration of a developmental context helps to reconcile the tension between those models of trust, which suggests that it is a concept grounded in careful judgment of institution and process factors such as vendor expertise and experience, process predictability, degree of personalization and communication integrity, and those models that suggest trust decisions depend much more heavily on the attractiveness and professional feel of a site.

A staged model of trust (see Figure 1) makes it possible to distinguish between relatively "hasty" and more "considered" processing strategies for the evaluation of trust in high- and low-risk environments. Chaiken (1980) identified two processing strategies by which an evaluation of trustworthiness may be made: firstly, a heuristic strategy that follows a "cognitive miser" principle, where people base decisions on only the most obvious or apparent information; and secondly, a systematic strategy that involves the detailed processing of message content. A number of other studies in the persuasion literature support the two-process model, namely that people use cognitively intense analytical processing when the task is an important or particularly engaging one, whereas they use affect or other simple heuristics to guide their decisions when they lack the motivation or capacity to think properly about the issues involved. Such different processing strategies also reflect the distinction between the preliminary stage of (1) *intention to trust* and the later stage of (2) *trusting activity* (McKnight & Chervany, 2001).

The process does not stop there, however, and a more realistic assessment of the development of trust should include a third stage in which a trusting relationship develops between the consumer and the Web site. This final stage has been rather overlooked in the trust literature, although it was originally proposed in the Cheskin/Sapient report (1999), and also appears in MoTEC (a Model of Trust for E-Commerce) (Egger, 2000, 2001), where the authors

Figure 1. Staged model of trust

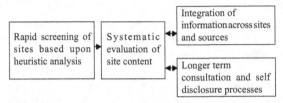

described a stage of trust maintenance. There is, however, little empirical evidence for a staged model of trust in e-commerce. Only two of the studies reviewed by Grabner-Krauter and Kaluscha (2003) investigated real transactions and these were limited to short-term interactions. Most published studies of trust do not investigate the act of trusting, but rather investigate the intention to trust (Briggs et al., 2004).

Stage 1: First Impressions and Heuristic Analysis

Some studies have asked participants to briefly visit a site or sites and then offer some evaluation of trustworthiness. According to Chaiken (1980), such participants would have very low involvement in this process, and we would expect that their trust judgements would be based on first impressions and as such, highly influenced by the attractiveness and ease of use of the site. A number of studies support this.

In their studies on credibility (a concept closely related to trust), Fogg et al. (2002) asked consumers to compare two sites drawn from 1 of 10 different domains, and to make a judgement about which of the sites was more credible. They were asked to supplement this judgement with comments, and notably 46.1% of those comments reflected design qualities, as indicated by the following sample of comments drawn from four participants.

More pleasing graphics, higher quality look and feel.

Not very professional looking. Don't like the cheesy graphics. Looks childish and like it was put together in 5 minutes.

Such comments are remarkably similar to those elicited by Briggs et al. (2002) in a qualitative investigation of trust in sites offering advice and information to potential house buyers (Study 1). In that study, participants had to search for relevant information and then discuss which sites they would return to and which they would reject. Once again, a positive first impression was linked to good design and an absence of amateur mistakes as well as to indications of expertise, while a negative first impression was more explicitly tied to poor design.

Similar results have been noted within the health domain. Peterson et al. (2003) explored consumer experiences in searching for and evaluating information on medicines online. They found that participants reported quickly, rejecting sites that were slow to load, that contained too many graphics, and that had pop-up advertisements. Social cues are also important in the design of trustworthy Web sites. Appropriate graphics and photographs can add to a sense of social presence and inclusion, whilst inappropriate mission statements or alienating language can have the opposite effect (Wang & Emurian, 2005).

Faced with a vast array of information, it is likely that people, and in particular unmotivated students or people under time pressures, will fall back on heuristic processes. Sillence et al. (Sillence, Briggs, Fishwick, & Harris, 2004c) have shown that this rapid screening is very effective in the initial stages of contact with a health Web site. Within a 30-second window, participants were able to efficiently sift information, recognizing and rejecting general portals and sales sites quickly. This may be because such sites have distinctive design features associated with them, but some content processing is also underway.

Good design and credible information do not always go "hand in hand." Sillence et al. (2004c) noted that credible health sites such as those run by BUPA and the NHS were often rejected because they failed to convey through their design the right cues to their content. Well-designed sites with large financial backing, such as those owned by pharmaceutical companies or large sales companies, may well contain credible yet very biased information and advice. Fraudulent Web sites designed to be used in phishing scams are often very well-designed sites containing false information. Experts in the health domain warn against consumers' over reliance on the design of health Web sites as an indicator of credibility (Stanford et al., 2002).

Stage 2: FurtherInvolvement with the Site and Careful Evaluation of Site Content

Those investigations that involved real consumers or that required some protracted engagement with a site or that have asked customers about the general principles underpinning e-commerce transactions have generated a family of trust models with reasonable agreement. In general, the models suggest that trust, which supports online engagement, is influenced by perceived integrity and expertise, predictability, or familiarity of content and reputation (e.g., Bhattacherjee, 2002; Briggs et al., 2002, study 2; McKnight & Chervany, 2001). A number of studies also highlighted the importance of interface factors (ease of use and functionality) that help to reduce the transaction costs of an exchange (e.g. Egger, 2000, 2001; Lee, Kim, & Moon, 2000).

For example, Bhattacherjee (2002) developed a psychometric scale for trust in online transactions that was tested in two field trials and modified accordingly. The resultant seven item scale tapped into three trust elements:

1. **Ability:** both in terms of expertise and information access.

   Example: "Amazon has the skills and expertise to perform transactions in an expected manner."

2. **Integrity:** encompassing issues of fairness of conduct in transactions, customer service, and data usage.

   Example: Amazon is fair in its use of private user data collected during a transaction."

3.   **Benevolence:** in terms of keeping the customers interests in mind in terms of showing empathy and responsiveness to customer concerns.

Example: "Amazon is open and receptive to customer needs."

In a large scale study of credibility conducted at the Stanford persuasion laboratory, over 1,400 participants completed a questionnaire concerned with those factors they felt made Web sites more or less credible (Fogg, Marshall, Laraki, Osipovich, Varma, Fang, et al., 2001). The authors found that "commercial implications" of a Web site negatively affected its perceived credibility. Users penalized sites that had an aggressive commercial flavour. This included sites that required a paid subscription to gain access or sites that had a commercial purpose as opposed to an academic purpose. Bernhardt and Felter (2004) also noted that parents mistrusted commercial sales sites when searching online for health advice for their children. Conversely, sites that convey expertise through the inclusion of authors' credentials and references were viewed in a positive light. External links to outside materials and sources were also seen favourably as evidence of the site's honest and unbiased intention. (Fogg et al., 2001). Within a health context, however, research suggests that perceptions of credibility in relation to commercialism may be more flexible and are highly dependent on topic and content. Walther, Wang, and Loh (2004) found that the presence of advertising on health Web sites only had a deleterious effect on the credibility of sites with .org domains. It actually had a positive effect on .com and educational domains (.edu).

In the health domain, Peterson et al. (2003) found that consumers' opinions on credible sources of information on medicines varied, with some participants viewing pharmaceutical companies as the "official" information on a medicine and others preferring what they considered to be more impartial sources, such as Government organizations and educational establishments. Perceptions of impartiality vary according to the health domain (see our work on the Measles, Mumps, Rubella (MMR) vaccination (Sillence, Brigs, Fishwick, & Harris, 2004b), but remain a key factor in predicting trust. Bernhardt and Felter (2004) found that parents thought that ulterior motives of a site undercut the reliability of the health information they provided.

Stage 3: Subsequent Relationship Development and Integration

As previously mentioned, few studies within the e-commerce trust literature have looked at longer-term relationships between consumer and Web site. This is surprising given that early psychological models of trust between individuals focused explicitly on the build up of a relationship over time.

Trust is a consequence as well as an expectation of action, which means that initial trust judgements will be modified by experience. This interpretation of trust was evident in Rotter's (1967) original view of interpersonal trust, where trust in a generalized other could develop from successful and consistent exchanges with parents and siblings. Gambetta (1988) emphasized the developmental nature of trust by arguing that the point where we shift from saying, "I don't trust X" to "I trust X," is a threshold on this continuum that will vary with individual tendencies (e.g., a disposition to trust) and experience: "trust is not a resource that is depleted through use; on the contrary, the more there is the more there is likely to be" (Gambetta, 1988, p. 234).

Those online studies taking a longer-term perspective on trust emphasize the importance of shared values between customer and vendor. In these studies, trust in a longer term e-commerce relationship is a function not only of competence and predictability, but is highly influenced by the extent to which e-vendors are good communicators and show sensitivity to the personal values and circumstances of the consumer. In this way, good personalization practices are shown to be important for the development of a trusting relationship

In Florian Egger's (2000, 2001) studies of online customers, good personalized communication between customer and vendor was shown to be vital to the development of trust. Egger developed a model of trust for electronic commerce (MoTEC), where trust is initially determined by three factors: (a) the users knowledge of the domain and reputation of the vendor, (b) the impression made by the interface, and (c) the quality of the informational context as assessed by the consumer, but where a fourth factor, relationship management, becomes influential over time:

Relationship management reflects the facilitating effect of timely, relevant and personalized vendor-buyer interactions on trust development (pre-purchase) and maintenance (post-purchase). (Egger, 2001)

Fogg et al. (2001) also noted the influential role of good personalized transactions in their large-scale study of credibility. One of the scales in the questionnaire measured "tailoring" of content and included the following four items:

- The site sends e-mails confirming the transactions you make.
- The site selects news stories according to your preferences.
- The site recognizes that you have been there before.
- The site requires you to register or log in.

Tailoring was found to increase credibility, although the effect was more profound for the older users. In other words, older respondents reported higher credibility evaluations for sites that used some type of tailoring. The role of personalization in online trust was also apparent in a study in which people were asked about advice on the Internet (Briggs et al., 2002). This was an online questionnaire-based study in which a total of 2,893 respondents said they had actually sought advice online. These individuals were asked to give information about the site they had used in terms of issues related to trust as identified in an extensive review of trust literature. In a regression analysis, a clear three-factor model of trust emerged. Personalization was one of these factors and included items such as:

- Did the respondent feel involved in the process?
- Was the site interactive?
- Was the information tailored to the participant?
- Were different courses of action suggested?
- Was a peer commentary available?

Personalization then seems to be an important enabling factor for trust in online advice and indeed in other studies of trust in e-commerce that have explored full engagement with Web sites.

The online community literature also suggests that long-term relationships online are based upon a sense of trust that develops through the exchange of often personal information. The ability to personalize content and to build personalized content is important. The ability to share empathy is also key, especially in health-based communities (Preece & Ghozahti, 2001), but the community context allows individuals some control over disclosure (Gray et al., 2005). Studies within the health domain have examined people's motivations for continued use of the Internet. Rozmovits and Ziebland (2004) noted that in cancer patients, long-term support was the key factor. The Internet was often used to share experience and advice, and to contact support groups and chat rooms. In other health domains, for example, hypertension, personal experiences are also important (Sillence, Briggs, & Herxheimer, 2004).

There is some debate as to the impact of the Internet on health decision making and outcomes, for example, in terms of choosing one form of medication over another or choosing to make a lifestyle choice such as giving up smoking. Coulson (personal communication), for example, found that people using Internet resources for health topics such as HIV and Aids often took on medical advice that was incorrect. However, recent studies indicate that there is some interplay between an individual's use of the Internet and other personal health information sources. Gray et al. (2005) noted that adolescents using the Internet for health advice would check the information that they had received from personal sources on the Internet for consistency. Bernhardt and Felter (2004) also noted that information convergence is a strategy used by parents looking online for health advice about their children, to assess whether or not the information is trustworthy. Parents thought that information that they had read across a number of sites and across a range of different sources (off-line and online) was more trustworthy.

Validating the Model

The staged model of trust proposed by Briggs et al. (2004), and illustrated in Figure 1, reconciles the different findings with regard to the literature concerning online trust. It also allows for the development of guidelines that relate to the stage of engagement with a Web site. As discussed previously, the majority of online trust studies have suffered from using unrealistic settings, unmotivated participants, and from focusing purely upon initial impressions of trust. In keeping with the staged model of trust, we report on a longitudinal in-depth qualitative study that investigates first impressions of a Web site and early analysis of content, as well as longer-term engagement with health Web sites.

The qualitative study is a 4-week investigation of real consumers' attitudes towards online health advice. Four groups of consumers, all with an interest in a specific health issue, searched the Internet for advice over a 4-week period. A variety of data collection methods were used including data logging, log books, verbal protocols, and group discussion. The aim was to elicit the key themes surrounding initial trust and mistrust of health Web sites.

Qualitative Investigations of Trust in Online Health Advice

A novel methodology was developed in order to examine how genuine health consumers search for and appraise online health information and advice. The methodology allows for the examination of people's decision-making processes, in particular with respect to trust, to be observed through the first few seconds of interaction with a Web site to 1 year of engagement.

Four longitudinal studies examining groups of people faced with risky health decisions were undertaken. The health topics were menopause and HRT, hypertension, and healthy living. In addition, a small-scale study examining MMR was also carried out. The methodology is described in more detail in Sillence et al. (2004a). In total, 40 participants (30 females and 10 males) took part in four separate studies focusing on four different health topics. Despite including one solely female health topic, it was anticipated that the final sample would have been more balanced. We can only assume that the gender bias in our sample reflects the higher female interest in health advice within an online setting that has been noted in other studies (Briggs et al, 2002; Pew, 2000) and thus were more willing and committed to take part in the longitudinal study.

The methodology used was the same in each study. Participants were invited to attend a total of four 2-hour sessions at Northumbria University, UK. During all four sessions, participants used the Internet to search for information and advice on the health topic in question, followed by a group discussion with a facilitator. Participants were told to freely surf the Web during Sessions 1 and 4, and were directed to specific Web sites during Sessions 2 and 3. These specific sites were chosen for their trust design elements, and to reflect the range of sites actually used by consumers. All the Web sites visited by the participants were logged and the amount of time spent on each site was recorded. In addition, the participants were asked to record their perceptions of each site visited in a logbook and use this information during the discussion sessions. All the discussions were transcribed and subject to content analysis. At the end of the fourth week, the participants were given diaries in order to record their ongoing information and advice searches over a 6-month follow-up period.

Rejecting or Selecting Health Sites

The first study indicated that during the first 10 seconds of scanning Web sites, participants are keen to find something that is immediately relevant to them and to find content that they can "latch onto." Many of the rejected sites at this stage were portal sites. Portal sites often require participants to carry out a deeper search or to input additional search terms. At 30 seconds, the largest category of sites rejected at this point were sales based. Participants were clearly able to detect and reject signs of commercial activity and a sales orientation very rapidly. At 2 minutes, many sites rejected at this stage were either sales based or were classified as "other related." Some sales sites do not reveal their commercial element until the user has explored the site in some detail. Participants may search through the site and then make a decision to reject the site after discovering its commercial motivation. Figure 2 illustrates the time to reject sites and the type of content the site provided in the case of the HRT and menopause study.

Figure 2. Rejection time and content of sites

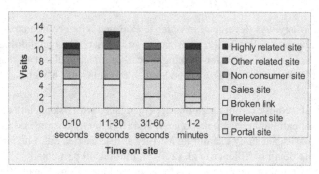

The transcripts from the group discussions and the verbal protocols were examined in terms of the selection (trust) or rejection (mistrust) of Web sites. A number of themes relating to the first impressions of the Web site and characteristics of trustworthy sites emerged. In terms of rejection, the overwhelming majority of comments related to the design of the Web site. The look and feel of the Web site was clearly important to the participants. Visual appeal, plus design issues relevant to site navigation, appeared to exert a strong influence on people's first impressions of the site. Poor interface design was particularly associated with rapid rejection and mistrust of a Web site. In cases where the participants did not like some aspect of the design, the site was often not explored further than the homepage, and was not considered suitable for revisiting at a later date. Negative comments included an inappropriate name for the Web site; complex, busy layout; lack of navigational aids; and pop-up adverts (see P10 in box 1).

The participants mentioned a number of factors in terms of the sites they had selected to explore in more depth. The participants liked sites that contained a great deal of information that was presented in such a manner that an individual could quickly pinpoint their own specific areas of interest. Participants trusted the selected sites because they demonstrated an in-depth knowledge of a wide variety of relevant topics, and put forward unbiased clear information. Participants were more likely to trust the information if they could verify it and cross-check it with other Web sites. Most individuals preferred sites that were run by reputable organizations or had a medical or expert feel about them. They trusted the information on such Web sites, especially when the credentials of the site and its authors were made explicit. Most participants showed some distrust of the advice and information on Web sites sponsored by pharmaceutical companies or those explicitly selling products. This is interesting given that medical expert reviews of HRT and menopause Web sites recommend pharmaceutical sites as providing a comprehensive and credible source of information (Reed & Anderson, 2002). Participants were looking for sites that were written by people similar to themselves, who shared similar interests. In this way, advice feels personalized for them.

Box 1. Examples of features associated with early rejection

Inappropriate sounding names

Well I didn't like it, I think it was possibly the name but I didn't hold out any confidence in something called Netdoctor at all, it sounds more like an IT company to me. (HRT study, P11, 59 years old)

Commercial

It's a very visual thing but then I am a very visual person it has to appeal and the flip side of that is that anything that's covered in ads and pop ups and stuff like that, it's the principle I'm just not interested. (HRT study, P10, 48 years old)

It just looked a bit cheaply made and the donations sign just put me off straight away. (MMR study, P2, Female, 35)

Nothing to latch onto

There was one in particular I was just I went into it and then after a couple of minutes I just thought its too complicated its just too much I can't be bothered with it. (Hypertension study, P13, Female, 52)

Over the Longer Term

We asked the participants in our longitudinal studies to keep diaries over a 6-month period in order to assess how they followed up the information and advice they had read online. The participants were asked to record any sites that they visited during that time and to make a note of what prompted them to go online. We also asked them to note any "off-line" interactions concerning this particular health topic, for example, interactions with health professionals and friends and family. They were asked to make a note of any other resources they had used, for example, television, radio, or newspapers. We were interested to find out when and where the Internet becomes involved in the decision-making process and to assess whether or not information integration had occurred.

Integration

We noted that the Internet was affecting decision making concerning treatments and lifestyle issues differentially across health topics and across individuals. For some participants, online information and advice was affecting their thinking on a week–by-week basis. For others, the affect on their decision-making processes was ongoing over the course of the following year. Here is an example that illustrates how one participant used the information online, how it was integrated with other sources, and overall, how it affected outcomes in terms of decision making.

DT took part in the hypertension study. He was taking medication for his high blood pressure and was unhappy with what he saw as the debilitating side effects. Discussions prior to the

Box 2. Examples of positive features associated with trusted sites

---

Clear and informative content

I found an absolutely marvellous site I was really, really taken with it, it went into so such clear explanations and with a breakdown of the different, oestrogen, progesterone, testosterone and what they actually do and how they link together all along the way it kind of encouraged you at the beginning to work through the site progressively if you wanted to get like a whole raft of background knowledge and then it would help you make decisions, it was great. (HRT, P1, 52 years old)

Impartial information

I suppose it was interesting in the sense that it was so biased against the MMR its useful to read it I mean but basically it was just a self help group website and so again it was like totally propaganda asking for donations and this kind of thing that I found it a bit disturbing actually I didn't like it, it was just so one sided I didn't like it. (MMR study, P1, Female, 33)

A Web site for someone like me

You can go on and find medical information, but what I want to find out is, you know, people giving reports of, right I've got high blood pressure and I've done this and I've done that and it brought my blood pressure down. (Hypertension study, P6, Female, 45)

Familiar language

I like sites that use familiar language, language I am comfortable with not lots of American terms that don't mean anything to me or probably mean different things like drug names for example. (Healthy living study, P2, Male, 35).

It was a British site I guess because it called hot flushes hot flushes not hot flashes like American sites do—that really annoys me that. (HRT study P4, 45 years old)

---

study had left him frustrated since his doctor had advised him that side effects were very unusual for this medication. DT was convinced his symptoms were not normal. During the sessions, he came across one site in particular thta detailed other people's experiences of side effects whilst taking this particular medication. During the group discussions, he told everyone of his findings and his intention to show these results to his doctor. The diaries indicated that he returned to the Web site several times before he visited his doctor. In consultation with his doctor, he had agreed on a change in his medication.

During the follow-up interviews, all the participants expressed the opinion that they were now more careful evaluators of online and off-line content. They also reported a new found confidence with respect to doctors and medical information.

Registration and Self-Disclosure

KK took part in the healthy living study. She was interested in planning a new exercise regime. She looked at ivillage (http://www.ivillage.co.uk) during one of the free search sessions and liked the interactive features of the Web site, such as the calculators, the alert functions, and the large message boards facility. Her diary indicates that she engaged with the site over the longer term. She registered her details with the site in order to be able to post messages and receive e-mail alerts and reminders concerning her personalized exercise plan.

Overall, the participants expressed their desire for personalized advice, but thought that currently it was difficult to obtain online. Often the information on the Web site was felt to be limited and lacking in personal detail. The participants did suggest they would be prepared to disclose more personal information in return for more personalized advice. However, the nature of the personal information was important in this respect. Whilst sites such as BBC's Big Challenge <http://www.bbc.co.uk/bigchallenge> and ivillage <http://www.ivillage.co.uk> offer something more akin to human rather than automated personalized advice, very few of the participants wanted to subscribe to sites such as these or to register their contact details in return for more tailored advice (see Sillence, Briggs, Fishwick, & Harris, 2005c for more detail).

Summary

Initial design appeal is important to users. The speed with which consumers will reject information should provide a salutary lesson regarding the importance of providing the right cues to site content in a highly visible manner. Social identity emerged as a major factor for building trust in online advice. General sites with few identity cues (NHS, Bupa) were seldom selected as trusted sources. Sites with home pages containing relevant information and that offered the opportunity to browse stories from like-minded individuals were viewed very positively. These results add to and extend previous work on trust by Briggs et al. (2002). Once again, personalization and credibility appear to be important factors in predicting whether or not a respondent will act upon the online health advice offered. Additionally, ease of access to useful information also has an important role to play in this respect. This extends the role of usability within online advice and online trust. Good designs combined with the stories that resonate with individual experience are very important factors in building initial trust. There is support for the staged model of trust in which heuristic evaluation and rapid screening is followed up by careful content evaluation and then longer-term engagement with a site. The important trust factors emerging from the studies provide a useful starting point for the development of guidelines for developing trust in e-health.

Guidelines for Developing Trust in E-Health

A composite picture of trust guidelines (taken from the literature and from the studies reported previously) is offered next. The guidelines are split into three sections to reflect the staged model of trust and to suggest the point at which they are most influential in terms of interaction.

Stage 1: Heuristic evaluation

1. Use a professional and attractive design

2. Ensure good ease of use

3. Provide good cues to content on the homepage

4. Maximize the familiarity or predictability of the layout and interaction

5. Do not mix advertising and content—avoid sales pitches and banner adverts

Stage 2: Content evaluation

1. Include background information on the knowledge and expertise of the authors

2. Make clear the motivations of the authors—provide good links to independent Web sites in the same domain to provide reassurances on bias

3. Ensure that the Web site reflects the social identity of the user

4. Offer a personalized service that takes accounts of each user's health needs and preferences

5. Include peer contributions and the ability to contribute to the site

Stage 3: Longer term engagement

1. Ensure content is regularly updated

2. Provide interactive features on the site as well as alternative ways of engaging users, for example, e-mail or text message alerts

3. Enable users to register in order to obtain personalized advice—make clear the purpose of registration and the privacy and security implications

4. Facilitate integration with other Web sites—include good links to other Web sites within the same domain. Provide local off-line addresses and contact details

5. Provide clearly stated privacy policies

Future Trends

We began this chapter with a discussion of some of the reasons why considerations of trust are important in the expanding field of e-health. Let us end the chapter with some explicit considerations of the trust issues raised by future visions of e-health. The changing nature of e-health and its supporting technologies means that the issue of trust becomes ever more important. Health information and advice will no longer solely be accessed from a PC in the home but from public access kiosks in a variety of locations. Health alert systems on mobile phones will mean people receive personal information in public settings. The development of networked health information and the electronic patient record system in the UK means that increasing numbers of people will have access to sensitive health information shared across large networks.

The demand for increasingly personalized e-health services also raises issues of trust and self-disclosure. The qualitative studies reported in this chapter indicate that people desire personalized health services but are reluctant to register their details with Web sites. Work by Sillence and Briggs (in press) also indicated that users found it more difficult to get personalized health advice online compared, for example, to financial advice. The increase in personalization coupled with increasing "public technologies" raises a number of important points regarding privacy and security. Burgoon (1982) described two kinds of privacy, informational privacy and physical privacy, both of which will have to be addressed in future work on e-health.

As increasingly sophisticated Web-based services are being developed, health consumers' trust in the information, and increasingly in the technology that facilitates the transfer of the information, will become of particular importance. Users must be prepared to place their trust not only in the people, but also in the technology that underpins an interaction. Understanding the context for trust, therefore, involves understanding issues of encryption and data security as well as understanding the development of a psychological bond. Bollier (1986), for example, argued that it is vital to distinguish between issues of "hard trust,"—involving authenticity, encryption, and security in transactions, and issues of "soft trust,"—involving human psychology, brand loyalty, and user-friendliness.

We are involved in several related research projects that address these issues, and some things have become clear. Firstly, we need to develop research methods that invite proper participation and involvement. The trust literature is peppered with investigations of users' intention to trust rather than explorations of their trusting behaviour. It is not simply enough to ask people about trust and related issues such as self-disclosure and privacy in the abstract – because, quite simply, what people say and what they do are two different things. Paradigms that allow researchers to investigate the whole cycle of trust from initial trusting dispositions through intention to trust and trusting behaviour have been developed over the past couple of years. These methodologies are currently being refined to include further ways of determining important trust factors in e-health, for example, incorporating measures of individual differences and personalization. The use of eye-tracking, for example, provides another tool in our kit to study the attitudes and behaviours of genuine health consumers engaged in different levels of risky decision making. We also need to know a great deal more about what happens following loss of trust and how the integration process with other sources, for example, healthcare providers, affects decision making. Such questions will be crucial for the development of e-health systems that people can genuinely use.

Conclusion

This chapter has proposed a staged model of trust to help explain the trust processes that are involved with consumers' use of online health advice and information. The studies presented in this chapter have documented some of the factors that can influence people's perceptions of the trustworthiness of online health advice and directly infleunce behaviour. The studies provide support for the staged model of trust and have assisted with the development of guidelines for trust practices in e-health. These guidelines relate to both the design and content features of health Web sites, and will assist in predicting the uptake of health advice. Future work will focus upon the importance of individual differences and personalization in e-health, and will explore the consequences of a loss of trust.

References

BBC Online. (2004). Health advice through your TV. Retrieved November 1, 2005, from http://news.bbc.co.uk/go/pr/fr/-/1/hi/health/4100717.htm

Bernhardt, J. M., & Felter, E. M. (2004). Online pediatric information seeking among mothers of young children: Results from a qualitative study using focus groups. *Journal Medical Internet Research, 6*(1), e7.

Bessell, T., McDonald, S., Silagy, S., Anderson, J., Hiller, J., & Sansom, L. (2002). Do Internet interventions for consumers cause more harm than good? A systematic review, *Health Expectations, 5*(1), 28-37.

Bhattacherjee, A. (2002). Individual trust in online firms: Scale development and initial test. *Journal of management Information Systems, 19*(1), 211-241.

Bollier, D. (1996). *The future of electronic commerce.* A report of the Fourth Annual Aspen Institute Roundtable on Information Technology. Aspen, CO: The Aspen Institute.

Brien, A. (1998). Professional ethics and the culture of trust. *Journal of Business Ethics, 17*(4), 391-409.

Briggs, P., Burford, B., De Angeli, A., & Lynch, P. (2002). Trust in online advice. *Social Science Computer review, 20*(3), 321-332.

Briggs, P., de Angeli, A., & Simpson, B. (2004). Personalisation and trust: A reciprocal relationship? In M.C. Karat, J. Blom, and J. Karat (Eds), *Designing personalized user experiences for eCommerce.* Kluwer.

Burgoon, J. K. (1982). Privacy and communication. *Communication yearbook, 6,* 206-249.

Chaiken, S. (1980). Heuristic versus systematic information processing and the use of source versus message cues in persuasion. *Journal of Personality and Social Psychology, 39,* 752-766.

Cheskin Research and Studio Archetype/Sapient. (1999). *eCommerce trust study.* Retrieved July 16, 2003, from http://www.cheskin.com/p/ar.asp?mlid=7&arid=40&art=0&isu=1

Corritore, C. C. L L., Kracher, B., & Wiedenbeck. S. (2003). On-line trust: Concepts, evolving themes, a model. *International Journal of Human-Computer Studies, 58,* 737-758.

Dobson, R. (2003). News extra: Study reports on use of "touch screen" health kiosks. *British Medical Journal, 326,* 184.

Egger, F. N. (2000). Trust me, I'm an online vendor: Towards a model of trust for e-commerce system design. In *Proceedings of CHI 2000.* ACM Press.

Egger, F. N. (2001). Affective design of e-commerce user interfaces: How to maximise perceived trustworthiness. In *Proceedings of CAHD: Conference on Affective Human Factors Design* (pp. 317-324).

Eysenbach, G. (2001) What is e-health? *Journal Medical Internet Research, 3*(2), e20.

Eysenbach, G., & Köhler, C. (2002). How do consumers search for and appraise health information on the World Wide Web? Qualitative study using focus groups, usability tests and in-depth interviews. *BMJ, 324*, 573-577.

Eysenbach, G., Powell, J., Englesakis, M., Rizo, C., & Stern, A. (2004, May 15). Health related virtual communities and electronic support groups: Systematic review of the effects of online peer to peer interactions. *British Medical Journal, 328*,1166, doi:10.1136/bmj.328.7449.1166.

Eysenbach, G., Powell, J., Kuss, O., & Sa, E-R. (2002). Empirical studies assessing the quality of health information for consumers on the World Wide Web, a systematic review. *Journal of the American Medical Association, 287*(20), 2691-2700.

Fogg, B. J., Kameda, T., Boyd, J., Marchall, J., Sethi,R., Sockol, M., & Trowbridge, T. (2002). *Stanford-Makovsky Web credibiltiy study 2002: Investigating what makes Web sites credible today.* A research report by the Stanford Persuasive Technology Lab and Makovsky & Company, Stanford University. Retrieved from http://www.webcredibility.org

Fogg, B. J., Marshall, J., Laraki, O., Osipovich, A., Varma, C., Fang, N., Paul, J., Rangnekar, A., Shon, J., Swani, P., & Treinen, M. (2001). What makes Web sites credible? A report on a large quantitative study. In *Proceedings of CHI 2001* (pp. 61-66). Seattle, WA: ACM Press.

Gambetta, D. (1988). Can we trust trust? In I. D. Gambetta (Ed.), *Trust: Making and breaking cooperative relations* (pp. 213-237). Oxford: Basil Blackwell.

Grabner-Krauter, S., & Kaluscha, E.A. (2003). Empirical research in online-trust: A review and critical assessment. *International Journal of Human-Computer Studies, 58,* 783-812.

Gray, N. J., Klein, J. D., Noyce, P. R., Sesselberg, T. S., & Cantrill, J. A. (2005). Health information-seeking behaviour in adolescence: The place of the Internet. *Social Science and Medicine, 60,* 1467-1478.

Hart, A., Henwood , F., & Wyatt, S. (2004). The role of the Internet in patient practitioner relationships: Findings from a qualitative research study. *Journal Medical Internet Research, 6*(3), e36.

Jadad, A. R., & Gagliardi A. (1998). Rating health information on the Internet: Navigating to knowledge or to Babel? *Journal of the American Medical Association, 25* 279(8), 611-4.

Kalet, A., Roberts, J. C., & Fletcher, R. (1994). How do physicians talk with their patients about risks? *Journal of General Internal Medicine, 9,* 402-404.

Kanuga, M., & Rosenfeld, W. D. (2004). Adolescent sexuality and the Internet: The good the bad and the URL. *Journal of pediatric and adolescent gynecology, 17*(2), 117-124.

Kim, J., & Moon, J. (1998). Designing towards emotional usability in customer interfaces: Trustworthiness of cyber-banking system interfaces. *Interacting with Computers, 10*, 1-29.

Klein, J. D., & Wilson, K. M. (2003). Delivering quality care: Adolescents' discussion of health risks with their providers. *Journal of Adolescent Health, 30*(3), 190-195.

Lee, J., Kim, J., & Moon, J. Y. (2000). What makes Internet users visit cyber stores again? Key design factors for customer loyalty. In *Proceedings of CHI 2000*, The Hague, Amsterdam (pp. 305-312).

Marsh, S., & Dibben, M. (2003). The role of trust in information science and technology. In B. Cronin (Ed.), *Annual Review of Information Science and Technology, 37* (pp.465-498). Medford, NJ: Learned Information.

McKnight, D. H., & Chervany, N. L. (2001). Trust and distrust definitions: One bite at a time. In R. Falcone, M. Singh, & Y.-H. Tan (Eds.), *Trust in cybersocieties*. Berlin: Springer-Verlag.

Mead, N., Varnam, R., Rogers, A., & Roland, M. (2003). What predicts patients' interest in the Internet as a health resource in primary care in England? *Journal of Health Services Research and Policy, 8*(1), 33-39.

Meyerson, D., Weick, K. E., & Kramer, R. M. (1996). Swift trust and temporary groups. In R. M. Kramer. & T. R. Tyler. (Eds.), *Trust in organizations: Frontiers of theory and research* (pp. 166-195). Thousand Oaks, CA: Sage Publications.

Morahan-Martin, J. M. (2004). How Internet users find, evaluate and use online health information: A cross-cultural review. *CyberPsychology and Behaviour, 7*(5), 497-510.

NHS Exec. (1998, September). *Information for health: An information strategy for the modern* (NHS 199802005).

Oh, H., Rizo, C., Enkin, M., & Jadad, A. (2005). What is eHealth (3): A systematic review of published definitions. *Journal Medical Internet Research, 7*(1), e1.

Pagliari, C., & Gregor, P. (2004). *Literature review of traditional research databases*. Retrieved from http://www.sdo.lshtm.ac.uk/ehealth.html

Peterson, G., Aslani, P., & Williams, K. A. (2003). How do consumers search for and appraise information on medicines on the Internet? A qualitative study using focus groups. *Journal of Medical Internet Research, 5*(4), e33.

Pew Research Center. (2000). *The online health care revolution: How the Web helps Americans take better care of themselves*.Retrieved from http://www.pewinternet.org

Pew Research Center. (2003). *Health searches and email have become more common place, but there is room for improvement in searches and overall Internet access*. Retrieved from http://www.pewinternet.org/

Preece, J., & Ghozati, K. (2001). Observations and explorations of empathy online. In R.R. Rice & J. E Katz (Eds.). *The Internet and health communications: Experience and expectations* (pp. 237-260).Thousand Oaks, CA: Sage publications Inc.

Reed, M., & Anderson, C. (2002). Evaluation of patient information Internet Web sites about menopause and hormone replacement therapy. *Maturitas, 4*, 135-154.

Reeves, P. M. (2001). How individuals coping with HIV/AIDS use the Internet. *Health Education Research,16*(6), 709-719.

Riegelsberger, J., Sasse, M. A., & McCarthy, J. (2003). Shiny happy people building trust? Photos on e-commerce Web sites and consumer trust. In *Proceedings of CHI 2003*. ACM Press.

Riegelsberger, J., Sasse, M. A., & McCarthy, J. D. (2005). The mechanics of trust: A framework for research and design. *International Journal of Human-Computer Studies, 62*(3), 381-422.

Rotter, J. B. (1967). A new scale for the measurement of interpersonal trust. *Journal of Personality, 35*, 651-665.

Rozmovits, L., & Ziebland, S. (2004). What do patients with prostate or breast cancer want from an Internet site? A qualitative study of information needs. *Patient Education and Counselling, 53*, 57-64.

Sieving, P. (1999). Factors driving the increase in medical information on the Web—one American perspective. *Journal Medical Internet Research, 1*(1), e3.

Sillence, E., & Briggs, P. (in press). Please advise: Using the Internet for health and financial advice. *Computers and Human Behavior*.

Sillence, E., Briggs, P., Fishwick, L., & Harris, P. (2004a, April 24-29). Trust and mistrust of online health sites. In *Proceedings of CHI'2004*, Vienna, Austria (pp. 663-670). ACM Press.

Sillence, E., Briggs, P., Fishwick, L., & Harris, P. (2004b, June 5-6). What parents make of MMR and the Internet. *He@lth Information on the Internet, 39*.

Sillence, E., Briggs, P., Fishwick, L., & Harris, P. (2004c, September 6-10). Timeline analysis: A tool for understanding the selection and rejection of health Web sites. In A. Dearden & L. Watts (Eds.), *Proceedings of the Conference HCI 2004: Design for Life*, Leeds, UK (Vol. 2, pp.113-116).

Sillence, E., Briggs, P., Fishwick, L., & Harris, P. (2005c, December). Do health Web sites offer patients personalized information and advice? *He@lth Information on the Internet, 48*, 9-10.

Sillence, E., Briggs, P., & Herxheimer, A. (2004, December). Personal experiences matter: What patients think about hypertension information online. *He@lth Information on the Internet, 42*, 3-5.

Smart, J. M., & Burling, D. (2001). Radiology and the Internet: A systematic review of patient information resources. *Clinical Radiology, 56*(11), 867-870.

Stanford, J., Tauber, E., Fogg, B. J., & Marable, L. (2002). Experts vs. online consumers: A comparative credibility study of health and finance Web sites. *Consumer Web Watch Research Report*. Retrieved August 2003, from http://www.consumerwebwatch.org/news/report3_credibility research/slicebread_abstract.htm

Taylor, H., & Leitman, R. (2002). The future use of the Internet in four countries in relation to prescriptions, physician communication and health information. *Health Care News 2*(13).Retrieved from http://www.harrisinteractive.com/news/newsletters_healthcare.asp

Walther, J. B.,Wang, Z., & Loh, T. (2004). The effect of top-level domains and advertisments on health Web site credibility. *Journal Medical Internet Research, 6*(3), e24.

Wang, Y. D., & Emurain, H. H (2005). An overview of online trust: Concepts, elements and implications. *Computers in Human Behavior, 21*, 105-125.

Wantland, D., Portillo J., Holzemer W., Slaughter, R., & McGhee E. (2004). The effectiveness of Web-based vs. non-Web based interventions: A meta-analysis of behavioral change outcomes. *Journal Medical Internet Research, 11,* 10, 6(4), e40.

WHA. (2002). Internet transforming the doctor patient relationship. Retrieved from http://www.w-h-a.org/wha2/index.asp

Wyatt, J. C. (1997). Measuring quality and impact of the World Wide Web. *British Medical Journal, 314,* 1879-81.

Ziebland, S., Chapple, A., Dumelow, C., Evans, J., Prinjha, S., & Rozmovits, L. (2004). How the Internet affects patients' experience of cancer: A qualitative study. *British Medical Journal, 328,* 564.

Chapter XI

Trust and Privacy Permissions for an Ambient World

Linda Little, Northumbria University, UK

Stephen Marsh, National Council Canada, Canada

Pam Briggs, Northumbria University, UK

Abstract

Ambient intelligence (AmI) and ubiquitous computing allow us to consider a future where computation is embedded into our daily social lives. This vision raises its own important questions and augments the need to understand how people will trust such systems and at the same time achieve and maintain privacy. As a result, we have recently conducted a wide reaching study of people's attitudes to potential AmI scenarios with a view to eliciting their privacy concerns. This chapter describes recent research related to privacy and trust with regard to ambient technology. The method used in the study is described and findings discussed.

Introduction

Ambient intelligence (AmI) and ubiquitous computing allow us to consider a future where computation is embedded into our daily social lives. This vision raises its own important questions (Bohn, Coroama, Langheinrich, Matern, & Rohs, 2005). Our own interest in trust and privacy predates this impending vision, but nonetheless holds a great deal of relevance there. As a result, we have recently conducted a wide-reaching study of people's attitudes to potential AmI scenarios with a view to eliciting their concerns and ideas. This chapter documents the results of this study, and contextualizes them through:

- Considering the concept of AmI and ambient technology, and the social implications of AmI use.

- Exploring relevant existing work in trust and privacy and discuss this in relation to ambient devices.

- Presenting and discussing general user concerns and highlighting problems of exclusion.

When trying to understand how trust and privacy issues are implicated in an ambient world focusing on purely technical approaches is not sufficient. In the e-commerce literature, trust is well documented, traditionally emphasizing the need to develop systems that appear trustworthy (e.g., Shneiderman, 2000). Bødker (2004) argues "technical approaches seem to relate trust directly to the construction of secure systems, thereby implying that users are purely rational, economical actors." In an ambient world, e-services will be accessible anywhere, anytime. Therefore, this chapter considers the social nature of trust and privacy with regard to ambient technology (see Egger, 2003 for a review of trust in e-commerce).

The chapter is structured as follows. In the next section, we comprehensively discuss the concept of privacy and its meaning in both physical and virtual worlds. Following this, we discuss the phenomenon of trust and how, in the AmI future, trust will remain a cornerstone of social interaction. The results and implications for AmI of our study are presented in Section 3. We conclude with a discussion about what privacy and trust considerations might mean in the light of these results, and a preliminary set of guidelines for the design of AmI devices and technology that take these implications into account.

The Concept of Ambient Intelligence

Ambient intelligence (AmI) refers to the convergence of ubiquitous computing, ubiquitous communication, and interfaces that are both socially aware and capable of adapting to the needs and preferences of the user. AmI evokes, or perhaps presages, a near future in which humans will be surrounded by "always-on," unobtrusive, interconnected intelligent objects, few of which will bear any resemblance to the computing devices of today. Mark Weiser (1991) envisaged a world where computers would be implanted in nearly every artefact imaginable. A person might interact with hundreds of computers at anyone point in time, each device invisibly embedded in the environment and wirelessly communicating with each other. These embedded devices will communicate seamlessly about any number of different topics, for example, your present state of health, when you last ate, and what it was you ate. Interactions with other devices and, at the same time, other people, will become anywhere, anytime.

The majority of current work on AmI is driven by technological considerations, despite claims that it is fundamentally a human-centred development that will essentially set people free from the desktop; hence Punie (2003) has argued the societal and user implications of AmI should be made more explicit. One of the particular challenges of AmI is that the user will be involved in huge numbers of moment-to-moment exchanges of personal data without explicitly sanctioning each transaction. In the present, we already carry around devices (mobile phones, personal digital assistants) that exchange personal information with other devices, but we initiate most exchanges ourselves. Nijholt, Rist, and Tuinenbrejier (2004) argue research tends to focus on the interaction with the device or environment, and not with other people or how the user is willing, able, or wants to communicate with the environment or have the environment communicate with them.

As humans are inherently social beings, and our actions are always directly or indirectly linked to other people, how will AmI technologies impact upon our social world? Questions naturally arise: Will people begin to rely to heavily on AmI technology? Will people be comfortable exchanging all types of information, even when it is of a very personal nature? Will the way we socially interact change, and social norms along with it? Will society become one where people feel more at home interacting with their fridge instead of other people? Will AmI technology blur the boundaries between home and the workplace, making a society where efficiency and productivity take precedence over love and leisure time?

The seamless exchange of information has vast social implications. Two important factors that will influence ambient technology adoption and use are trust and privacy issues. Streitz and Nixon (2005) argue "areas of security, privacy, and trust are critical components for the next stages of research and deployment of ubiquitous systems. Moreover, it was identified that these observations are not merely an amplification of the current concerns of Internet users with desktop computers. New approaches are required that take even more into account regarding both the social and technical aspects of this problem to ultimately determine the acceptance of this technology by the general public" (p.35).

This chapter will focus on the social implications of information exchange in an ambient society and not the technical limitations or constraints of such systems. If we consider that the exchange of information is what makes AmI tick, we need to ask questions about information that will have a direct impact on both trust and privacy, including: Who is receiving it? Who has access? Is the receiver credible, predictable, and sensitive? Where is the information being sent and received? In what context is the device used? Does the user have choice and control? How does the device know whom to communicate with, for example, through-personalized agents?

To answer these questions we need to understand privacy and trust, and related underlying variables.

Privacy

Every major advance in information and communication technologies since the late nineteenth century has increased concern about individual privacy (e.g., Brandies & Warren,1890; Price, Adam, & Nuseibeh, 2005). Privacy remains a hot topic, widely discussed by academics and practitioners alike (Kozlov, 2004). AmI brings new and increased risks, including fraud and identity theft, and therefore, we see privacy control as essential in AmI.

There is no universal definition of privacy; the concept is highly complex and involves different perspectives and dimensions. The need and desire for privacy varies between individuals, cultures, social and physical environmental factors (Kaya & Weber, 2003). The desired level of privacy relates to what an individual wants and the achieved level is what they actually obtain.

Research into privacy tends to take an individualist approach and uses North American or Northern European perspectives (e.g., Boni & Prigmore, 2002; Margulis, 2003). Generally, models emphasize the individual's control and choice, and social relationships as either voluntary or as barriers to independence (Fiske, Kitayama, Markus, & Nisbett, 1998). In the western world, privacy definitions tend to involve management of personal information and space. According to Chan (2000), the ability to manipulate space is the primary way individuals achieve privacy. Several concepts have been linked to privacy, for example, self-disclosure, social comparison, social facilitation, and social influence, attitude formation and change (Margulis, 2003).

In the psychological literature, privacy is classified as a human boundary control process that allows access by others according to one's own needs and situational factors (Westin, 1967). However, this definition is not sufficient when considering information exchange in an AmI world. We need to understand how privacy is achieved and maintained in both physical and virtual worlds.

Privacy in the Virtual World

The majority of the human-computer interaction (HCI) literature on privacy tends to focus on exchange and control of information over the Internet (e.g., Cranor, Reagle, & Ackerman, 1999; Jackson, von Eye, Barbatsis, Biocca, Zhao, & Fitzgerald 2003;). The actual term "privacy" is generally used by computer scientists and security specialists to refer to the security of data against various risks or during transmission (Clarke, 1999). Control of personal information is very important no matter where or what type of device is used. Individuals have a right to control and protect their personal information (Nguyen & Truong, 2003).

Future systems will enable more freedom and reduce the physical constraints of time and place. According to Lester (2001), development in technology is considered to be the main culprit responsible for increasing concern over the protection of privacy. As new forms of technology are introduced, personal information may be accessed using a variety of different systems. Whichever type of system people use to access personal information, the concept of privacy is of crucial concern in both the virtual and physical worlds.

However, not everyone shares the same concern; some designers and researchers appear to ignore the importance of privacy and the net effect it has on system use. Kozlov (2004) describes one such debate:

...privacy design is not yet seen as a necessary requirement of an AmI design process in general, and that designers do not feel 'morally responsible' to deliver 'privacy management tools. (p. 6)

We need to differentiate between the physical and virtual world to understand privacy implications. In the physical world, we rely on various cues and signals that can be either physical, for example, architecture or conceptual, for example, perception of space. Through past experience, we are familiar with most contexts and environments; therefore, as humans, we generally comply and perform behaviours in an accepted way. Physical environments are often designed to afford privacy, that is, we can close a door or find a quiet space to talk to friends. The physical world compared to the virtual world is tangible, that is, we experience the physical world through several dimensions. In the virtual world, conceptual cues are often missing or when present, for example, a brand name on the Internet, the actual site might be fraudulent. When exchanging information in the physical world, we generally know who will have access compared to the virtual world.

In an ambient world, information collection, processing, and sharing are fundamental procedures needed for the systems to be fully aware of the user's needs and desires (Dritas, Gritzalis, & Lambrinoudakis, 2005). AmI technologies will act on the user's behalf without their explicit knowledge and the interaction will be invisible. By its very nature, this puts ambient technology and privacy in conflict. We need to understand this conflict and how privacy impacts upon AmI technology adoption and use.

We already know that perceptions of privacy impact upon current technology use (e.g., Little, Briggs, & Coventry, 2005). For example, it is well documented that Internet users have major concerns regarding threat to their privacy and about who has access to the information they provide (Jackson et al., 2003). Cranor, Reagle, and Ackerman (1999) found 87% of users were concerned about the threat to their privacy when online. Also Cranor et al. (1999) found Internet users were less willing to use sites that asked for personally identifiable information, and very uncomfortable providing sensitive information such as credit card details. This further emphasizes the need to understand privacy in an AmI society.

Moor (1997) developed a restricted access theory to understand intrusion, interference, and in particular, informational privacy. He suggests an individual has privacy in a situation with regard to others "if and only if the individual is protected from intrusion, interference and information access by others." Moor gives a vague description of what a "situation" is or could be. He posits situations can mean activity, relationship, or location. Moor also distinguished between naturally private situations (e.g., privacy is protected by the design of the environment) and normatively private situations (e.g., privacy is protected by laws). This approach helps differentiate between having privacy (natural) and having the right to privacy (normative). Although Moor argued privacy can be lost but not violated or invaded in natural situations because there are no norms (e.g., conventional), this does not explain the dynamic nature of how people achieve and maintain privacy in different situations.

Individuals do not always have absolute control about every piece of information about them and once information is disclosed, privacy is lost. However, individuals will disclose information as long as they perceive the benefit will exceed the risk (Thibaut & Kelly, 1959). Bies (2001) identified privacy as a major concern associated with unwarranted disclosure of information. Even when information disclosure is authorized, individuals are concerned with whom the information is disclosed to and the nature of the information disclosed. For example, Cranor, Reagle, and Ackerman (1999) suggest that if the information is disclosed through cookies or disclosure is made to a specific party (e.g., Social Security number) and was not authorized, concern over privacy is more salient.

Fears related to online privacy stem from the technologies' ability to monitor and record every aspect of the user's behaviour (Metzger, 2004). Many users are aware that their privacy is at risk when using the Internet and their online tour can be tracked. Users are aware that after visiting some sites, cookies can get implanted onto their hard drives and they then become a target for unsolicited mail. Users leave data trails almost everyday, for example, credit card use. An individual's data can be collected from the trail he or she leaves behind, and few legal restrictions exist on how the data can be used (McCandlish, 2002). The value of such information increases as more data is collected. At one time, the collection of an individual's personal information was limited to age, address, credit history (personal identity and life history). Now with technologies such as the Internet and surveillance, other data can be collected about a person's behaviour and life: movement, buying history, association with other people, and unauthorized access to electronic records (Arndt, 2005).

Although several programs exist to stop personal details being collected, individuals may not know how to install or use them. Privacy preference protocols and systems such as Platform for Privacy Preferences Project (P3P) (Cranor, 2002), allow users to set preferences in accordance with their privacy needs. When online users are informed that their preferences do not match the privacy policies of each site visited, they can therefore decide whether or not to continue the interaction. However, we must question whether this concept would truly work in an AmI society. Palen and Dourish (2003) argue that as our lives are not predictable, and privacy management is a dynamic response to both the situation and circumstance, prior configuration and static rules will not work. Therefore, disclosure of information needs to be controlled dynamically. Olsen, Grudin, and Horvitz (2005) take an opposite view and suggest individuals can set preferences for sharing information as people tend to have clusters of similar others and therefore, the task is not as complex or particularly difficult to undertake as it first may seem.

When interacting with technology privacy protection and disclosure of information is a two-way process. From the technological viewpoint, for example, use of the Internet, the Fair Information Practice (FIP) (e.g., Federal Trade Commission of America, 2000) suggests companies should give users notice, choice, access, and security. Notice refers to the right of the individual to know what information is being collected and how it will be used. Choice means individuals have the right to object when personal information is collected for another purpose than the one described or shared with third parties. Access refers to the individual's right to see the information and correct errors. Security means companies will honour and ensure data integrity and that data is secure from unauthorized access during both transmission and storage. Practices such as FIP are needed to mediate privacy, empower the individual, increase the users control, and create assurance. These policies also reduce data gathering, data exchanging and data mining and therefore, are important in an ambient society.

Academics, researchers, and industry acknowledge that AmI technologies introduce a new privacy risk (e.g., Price et al., 2005). Privacy control in an AmI world is essential to decrease risks such as fraud and identity theft. Consider the following question: Will users be able to set their own privacy preferences? The answer seems easy, but is it? Humans live, work, and interact with a variety of people and in different environments. The multifaceted nature of human-human interaction requires each individual to set complex sets of privacy preferences dependent upon their situation and circumstance. These preferences would also have to remain stable across place, space, country, and culture.

If AmI technologies are used globally, systems must be designed so that user privacy settings remain secure and unchanged across international boundaries. For example, Europe has a tighter data protection act compared to the U.S. (Dawson, Minocha, & Petre, 2003). Therefore, someone traveling from Europe to the U.S. might find unknown others have access to his or her personal information when entering the country due to the slacker regulation and control of privacy policies related to AmI systems.

Privacy in the Physical World

In the future, individuals will be able to use systems in a multitude of different social environments and be interacting with a variety of people, such as friends, family, or complete strangers.

Concerns already exist about certain technologies used in public places. One such system found in nearly all cities is the surveillance camera. Clark (1999) termed the phrase "dataveillance" to capture the techniques of surveillance and data recording. People have been "watched" and their behaviour recorded in public places for many years. Many arguments exist for the use of such cameras, for example, crime reduction. However, as advances in surveillance technologies are made, many now argue that privacy no longer exists, or that if it does, it is quickly disappearing as our activities are increasingly made public (Brin, 1998; Gotlieb, 1996).

Another area of growing concern for users of technology in public places that violates their privacy is tracking. Users of mobile telephones are already aware their service provider can track their location. However, design specifications in future technologies may mean it is not only the service provider who knows where you are and what you are doing. The future could see systems developed that track users to specific locations whether their device is switched on or off. Tracking will not only be available to the service provider, but to virtually anyone who wants to know where the user is. Although this may be a good idea, for example, in the case of missing persons, it does raise important ethical issues.

A recent study by Consolvo et al. (2005) found individuals are willing to disclose something about their location most of the time. However, the individual will only disclose information when the information is useful to the person requesting it, the request is timely, is dependent upon the relationship he or she has with the requestor, and why the requestor needs the information. These findings highlight the need for control and choice over disclosure of personal information at any one point in time.

Western Models of Privacy

Perception of privacy in the western world often differs from eastern cultures. For example, space in the west is generally considered a mechanism to achieve and maintain privacy, but not as important in eastern cultures. This research employs western approaches to understand and describe privacy. Two western models that have been very influential in privacy research in the discipline of psychology are those developed by Altman in 1975 and Westin in 1967. Both theories are examples of a limited-access approach to privacy (Margulis, 2003). The theories both describe privacy in terms of needs and desires that are control and regulation of access to oneself, and a continuous dynamic regulation process that changes due to internal/external conditions. Both theories acknowledge regulation can sometimes be unsuccessful, different types of privacy exist, and privacy is culturally specific.

Altman (1975) described privacy as an ideal, desired state, or as an achieved end state. If the desired state matches the achieved state then an optimal level of privacy is obtained. Privacy is obtained by selective control of access to the self. Altman suggested that social interaction is at the heart of understanding privacy and that the environment provides mechanisms for regulation. Altman proposed four mechanisms to achieve privacy: verbal (e.g., what is said, tone of voice), nonverbal behaviour (e.g., eye contact in communicating attitudes or intentions), environmental (e.g., personal space, physical aspects of the environment) and culture (e.g., norms, beliefs).

Westin (1967) suggested individuals use a limited-access approach to protect their privacy. He defined privacy as a dynamic process of regulation that is nonmonotonic, that is, an individual can have too much or too little. Westin proposed four types of privacy: solitude (being free from observation by others), intimacy (small group seclusion), anonymity (freedom from surveillance in public places), and reserve (limited disclosure of information to others). The four types serve various functions: personal autonomy (desire to avoid manipulation), emotional release (ability to release tensions from the social world), self-evaluation (ability to contemplate, reflect), limit (set boundaries), and protect communication (share information with trusted others). Westin's model has been extended several times to include other dimensions (e.g., seclusion, not neighbouring, Marshall, 1970). Previous research that highlights the importance of additional dimensions shows how aspects of privacy can be context-specific.

Pedersen (1979, 1999, 1999) further developed Westin's model and categorized privacy into six main types: solitude (freedom from observation by others), reserve (not revealing personal information about one's self to others), isolation (being geographically removed from and free from others observation), intimacy with family (being alone with family), intimacy with friends (being alone with friends), and anonymity (being seen but not identified or identifiable by others). Pedersen suggests that the six types of privacy "represent the basic approaches people use to satisfy their privacy needs."

Although speculative, Burgoon (1982) suggested four dimensions of privacy: physical, psychological, social, and informational. The physical dimension relates to how physically accessible a person is to others, and can be linked to such aspects as environmental design. The psychological dimension refers to a person's right to decide with whom they share personal information and the control of cognitive/affective inputs/outputs such as nonverbal communication. The social dimension is the ability to control social interactions by controlling distance between people. The informational privacy dimension relates to a person's right to reveal personal information to others, which is not always under a person's control.

Privacy Regulation

The regulation of privacy is complicated due to the range of functions it maintains and protects. Levels of perceived privacy can be increased or decreased dependent upon an individuals experience, expectation, other people in the area, the task at hand, and the physical environment. Regulation is considered as a dynamic process with variable boundaries that are under continuous negotiation and management, continuously refined according to circumstance (Palen & Dourish, 2003). Generally, individuals rely on features of their spatial world and the immediate environment. Regulation and control can also be sort by verbal and nonverbal behaviour.

Levels of privacy change dynamically and are affected by both internal and/or external conditions. To gain the desired level of privacy, a person tries to regulate their interaction by altering or maintaining their behaviour dependent upon the situation they find themselves in.

Problems with Privacy

Problems exist when trying to understand and investigate privacy issues that are related to both physical and virtual worlds. No one theory or approach is sufficient to explore this complex topic.

Findings from privacy research in the human-computer interaction (HCI) and computer science areas tend to focus on security aspects of existing or hypothetical systems. However, recent studies are now acknowledging the complex nature of human-human interaction and the need for users to set multiple privacy preferences in an AmI world (e.g., Price et al., 2005).

Privacy research has suffered from a lack of consensus regarding the different dimensions, functions, and definitions of what "the environment" actually consists of. Therefore, we need to consider all dimensions if we are to understand how people achieve and maintain privacy in an AmI society. The dimensions proposed by Westin and Pedersen have been criticized as too confusing and overlapping (Burgoon, 1982). The dimensions appear to ignore physical privacy, that is, the degree to which an individual is physically inaccessible. All of the proposed dimensions implicate psychological functioning; there is no clear differentiation between other types of privacy such as informational. The types of privacy describe interaction with others that occurs in controlled situations and ignores unwanted input.

Although Burgoon's approach to privacy is speculative, it lacks explanation of control over the various dimensions. For example, information pertaining to the social and physical aspects can be temporal, that is, an individual can choose to reveal a certain amount of information at any one time and control the level of interaction, for instance, they may walk away. In comparison, once an individual reveals any type of information in the informational and psychological dimensions, he or she is no longer in control of it and cannot take it back.

Concerns have also been raised in privacy research due to the actual concept itself, that is, individuals both protect and manage it (Pedersen, 1999). No one theory fully describes the objective, physical environment, or how environmental concepts are associated with the independent psychological descriptions of privacy (Margulis, 2003). Margulis states, a complete explanation of privacy needs is required to understand how social activity is situated in context where objective, physical characteristics often affect behaviour.

Levels of control and actual context of the interaction all have a major affect on use of AmI technology and the user. We need to understand how people will regulate, control, and choose when to interact with such devices and who will have access to their personal information.

We know privacy is a multidimensional construct encompassing physical and social judgments (e.g., Pederson, 1999). There are four main dimensions of privacy relevant to AmI research: physical (in what type of environment is the system being used), informational (what type of information is being exchanged), psychological (is the information shared, and if so with whom), and social (who else is present at that time). Each dimension of privacy, that is, informational, psychological, physical, and social needs to be evaluated if we are to understand fully the concept of privacy when related to AmI use. To fully understand privacy, we need to consider how humans interact with each other, how humans interact with technology, how technologies communicate with other technologies, and know the technical constraints of each system.

Trust

There is today a diffuse agreement about the fact that one of the major problems for the success of computer supported society, smart physical environment, virtual reality, virtual organization, computer mediated interaction, etc. is trust*: people's trust in potential partners, information sources, data, mediating agents, personal assistants; and agents' trust in other agents and processes. Security measures are not enough, interactivity and knowledgeability are not enough, the problem is how to build in users and agents trust and how to maintain it.* (Falcone & Castelfranchi, 2001, pp. 55-56)

Trust and privacy are interrelated constructs: the more we trust, the more information we are prepared to reveal about ourselves (Teltzrow & Kobsa, 2004). Social commentators recognize that trust is essential for society (Bok, 1978; Fukuyama, 1996). An interesting picture is emerging about the ways in which individuals make trust judgments in technology-mediated interactions; however, trust judgments are not always made on a rational basis. As trust is multifaceted, several factors are important when understanding AmI use: personalization, motivation, expertise, familiarity, predictability, sensitivity, and the actual source of the information.

Thinking About Trust

For all the studies on the subject (see, for example, Dibben, 2000; Luhmann, 1979, 2000; Misztal, 1996; Sztompka, 1999), trust remains something of an enigma: it is hard to define, hard to see, and difficult to explain, but everyone (at least in certain cultures) seems to know what it is (for a discussion of this, see Dibben, 2000, especially pp. 6-7). While that is somewhat annoying when you are trying to study it, it presents its own opportunities and, to a certain extent, makes life easier when you ask people to talk about it, as in the sessions documented (but it is hard to know, after the fact, what people really *meant*).

The enigmatic nature of trust is reinforced by the sheer volume, nowadays, of research in the area, and the almost pathological need of each and every article to define the phenomenon in some way. In social science alone, for instance "the [...] research on trust has produced a good deal of conceptual confusion regarding the meaning of trust and its place in social life." (Lewis & Weigert, 1985, p. 975). The situation is hardly made better by the plethora of definitions within information and communication technologies, let alone computer security's somewhat muddled understanding of the term. Although, thankfully, similarities exist in most of the extant definitions, they remain different enough to try what is already an overloaded term. In this section, we will try to pick apart the phenomenon with the aim of showing what the similarities are in the definitions, with the modest aim of arriving at something that makes sense in the context of this chapter (a more wide-reaching understanding will wait for a short while longer).

In the context of AmI, trust is a particularly important phenomenon. In the first instance, people are going to be put into situations where they may have to trust their own devices, and be influenced by these same devices. To a large extent, this situation is not unlike what exists now. There are many studies on trust in HCI, user interfaces, eCommerce, and so forth, and their results widely known. For instance, in a static setting, the design of an interface can have dramatic effects on the perceived trustworthiness of the system (for instance, Cheskin, 1999, 2000; Corritore, Kracher, & Wiedenbeck, 2003; Egger, 2000; Fung & Lee, 1999; Karvonen, 1999; Riegelsberger & Sasse, 2001). Indeed, much is also known about the effect on and development of trust in, for example, conversational interfaces (Bickmore & Cassell, 2001), digital systems in general (Corritore et al., 2003), seeking on-line advice (Sillence, Briggs, Fishwick, & Harris, 2004), and even to a lesser extent mobile technology (Siau & Shen, 2003). We find ourselves, then, in a situation where we are capable of at least beginning to understand how to build interfaces and systems that encourage and elicit trust.

There is more to AmI and trust than the interface, or even the system, however (for an excellent review of many AmI implications see Bohn et al., 2005). For starters, it is not just an interface to a single device we are talking about. AmI is a whole environment, all around us, or invisible devices, all potentially "talking" to each other, "behind our backs." The implications on trust, we conjecture, are extreme and somewhat pressing. For instance, am I placing trust in my device, or the devices it talks to, or the environment as a whole? When we consider that AmI is in fact nothing more than a collection of agents doing things for people, where then is the trust placed? In the agents, or the people, or both? Ultimately, AmI is about sharing information that is useful to the people in the environment so that they can enjoy themselves more, get more stuff, have easier lives, and so on. That being the case, the sharing of information and the potentials for transitivity in trust and privacy are amongst the more daunting challenges facing the vision. We think that proper models of and a deep understanding of trust, applied in all of these situations, can help in the design and implementation of not only secure but also usable and socially responsible ambient intelligence environments.

On a final note justifying the need for trust, consider the vision of AmI more closely. In its most pure form, AmI is a connected society of humans and artificial agents, from simple to complex, interacting as only a society can. This, if nothing else, requires us to *encourage, build, and study* trust in that society, because ultimately, a society without trust cannot exist (Bok, 1978; Good, 2000; Luhmann, 1979).

The Generalities: Exploring Definitions of Trust

- Trust is:

  the expectation that arises, within a community, of regular and honest cooperative behaviour, based on commonly shared norms, on the part of other members of that community. (Fukuyama, 1996, p. 26).

- Trust is:

  a state involving confident positive expectations about another's motives with respect to oneself in situations entailing risk. (Boon & Holmes, 1991, p.194)

- *Regardless of the underlying discipline of the authors [...] confident expectations and a willingness to be vulnerable are critical components of all definitions of trust...* (Rousseau, Sitkin, Burt, & Camerer, 1998, p. 394).

- *Trust (or, symmetrically, distrust) is a particular level of the subjective probability with which an agent assesses that another agent or group of agents will perform a particular action, both before he can monitor such action and in a context in which it affects his own action.* (Gambetta, 2000, p. 218).

- *We define trust in the Internet store as a consumer's willingness to rely on the seller and take action in circumstances where such action makes the consumer vulnerable to the seller.* (Jarvenpaa, Tractinsky, & Saarinen, 1999)

As can be seen, several accepted and acceptable definitions of trust exist–the interested reader is referred to (Abdul-Rahman, 2004 (chapters 2 and 3 especially); Dibben, 2000; Marsh & Dibben, 2003; Viljanen, 2005) for more in depth discussions. However, some salient points are important to note.

- The first is that trust is contextual, or situational, that is, it is based in a specific context and can only be generalized (to a greater or lesser extent) outside of that context.

- Secondly, trust exists in situations of risk: there is some discussion as to whether or not that risk is high or not for trust to exist, but in general it is accepted that without some degree of risk, trust is unnecessary.

- Third, there is some requirement for free will (or similar) on the part of the trustee, that is, that they are able to do something which is intentionally or otherwise detrimental to the trustor, just as they are able to do what they are trusted to do.

- Fourth (perhaps more controversially), the phenomenon of trust requires a consideration of alternatives; without such a consideration, with a blind "jumping into" a given situation, the phenomenon at work is not trust, but confidence (cf. Luhmann, 1990). In fact, it is from "confidence" that the concept of "blind trust" grows, with the subsequent argument (see Marsh, 1994) that blind trust is in fact not trust at all.

Rather than reinvent the trust wheel, we propose a definition that has worked relatively well for us in the past, and contains, in a succinct summary, most of the salient points of trust:

Trust is "a positive expectation regarding the behaviour of somebody or something in a situation that entails risk to the trusting party." (Patrick, Briggs, & Marsh, 2005)

What remains is to find out where this definition fits within AmI, what risks are involved, and what expectations are reasonable.

The Specifics: Trust in AmI, a Discussion

The Concept of Context

It is generally agreed that trust is a contextual phenomenon (some say, situationally dependent, meaning almost the same thing). This means that the trust given or received is dependent of who is the trustor or the trustee, the task at hand, the opportunities for betrayal, the potential for gain or loss, and so on. In our own context, it will also bring to bear what tools are being used, what information may or may not be being considered, and so on. It is critically important to bear in mind that the concept of AmI introduces *artificial* trustees to users. The concept of *familiarity* then becomes something of importance in trusting deliberations. According to Luhmann (1990), "trust has to be achieved within a familiar world, and changes may occur in the familiar features of the world which will have an impact on the possibility of developing trust in human relations." (p. 94). Thus, it is difficult to trust what is unfamiliar. In the context of AmI, for many people, the whole *edifice* is unfamiliar, and so a certain lack of trust may be expected, until familiarity is achieved either through use or, as in this work, through demonstrations of how AmI can, for example, benefit the user in specific, familiar contexts (shopping, banking, and so on).

Of course, if Weiser's (1991) original vision of ubiquitous computing (and by extension AmI) is to be realized, what we will see will in fact be nothing: the computers will become the background in which we all live (Bohn et al., 2005). Therefore, how do we conceptualize and explore familiarity and its associated problems? In this instance, does AmI just become another societal tool? If this is the case, what are the implications for trust?

Can We "Trust" (Artificial) Technology?

The question of whether or not it is possible to trust technology has been raised in the past, with equally convincing arguments on either side. On one side (see, for example, Friedman, Kahn, & Howe, 2000), the argument reads that since trust implies a freedom of action on the part of the trustee, it is impossible to refer to the relationship with technology (software, agents, cars, etc.) as one of trust, since technology does not in fact have free will: "people trust people, not technology." (2000, p. 36) In many cases, this is at least a valid argument, but within AmI, the distinction between traditional technology, as seen by the proponents of this argument, and the "free actor" is blurred almost to nonexistence. To illustrate this argument, consider, information sharing between two agents in a closed network. Generally, it really does not matter *what* they share, because no-one is looking at it, and nothing gets done with it. Now, embed these agents in an ambient environment. Suddenly everything changes, but not because the agents have any more or less free will. The crucial addition to this environment is that of people (who, for our purposes, unquestionably *do* have free will!). If a human is able to query the agent(s) for what they know, and use it (on- or off-line), the concept of trust is not just important, but absolutely imperative. Further, the trustee is becoming something of a blurred concept—is it the person who gets the information, or the agent that gives it to them—in other words, should we not think about trusting the agent as a surrogate, to do the right thing with the information it may have?

Largely, the discussion is philosophical, and somewhat moot. Of course we can argue about whether technology can or cannot be validly trusted, but we inadvertently (or not) find ourselves in a situation where people are talking about trust in the environment in a fashion that sounds very much like trusting the technology behind that environment. Further, and critically, thinking in this way enables the people to more quickly assimilate and understand the environment. From an HCI perspective, this understanding, based on potentially flawed arguments though it might be, is a significant achievement (although we would like to wean people off it somewhat, see the next section and Marsh, 2005). Further, in terms of security and privacy, being able to think in terms of trust allows us to conceive much more powerful solutions to practical problems (for more discussion of which, see Patrick et al., 2005).

The Structure of Trust: Rules for Trust Behaviour in AmI

For all its conceptual fuzziness, it is possible to put forward some rules that trust appears to obey. It is worth noting that these rules are still debated hotly amongst trust researchers, but two things apply here: first, it is worth putting up something for discussion to take place around, and second, there appears, at least to these authors, to be a movement towards accepting that these rules are for the most part correct. The rules allow designers and users to be able to reason about what can happen, should happen, or is happening behind the scenes; how, for example, information gets shared with some agents and not others, or how much information gets shared, and so on. To a large extent, defining these rules for trust in AmI is a step along the road towards a system that can explain itself, much like expert systems can explain their chains of reasoning when queried. The interested reader is referred to Viljanen (2005), and Marsh, (1994, esp. ch. 6) for the roots of these observations and rules.

A different slant on some of the rules (especially regarding transitivity, the real "hot" topic) can be found in Chang, Thomson, Dillon, and Hussain (2004):

- **Trust is not symmetric:** that is, it is unidirectional "John trusts Bert" says little to nothing about Bert trusting John. Consider that we walk across the road every day "trusting" that people we do not even know, and who do not know us, will not run us over. Moreover, it is not necessary for Bert to actually *know* that he is trusted by John for it to be the case.

- **Trust is not distributive:** as Viljanen (2005, p. 176) states: "If 'Alice trusts (Bob and Carol),' it does not follow that '(Alice trusts Bob) and (Alice trusts Carol).'" In fact, this has very far-reaching implications for AmI, especially when one considers groups and organizations.

- **Trust is not associative:** "'(Alice trusts Bob) trusts Carol' is not a valid trust expression. However, 'Alice trusts (Bob trusts Carol)' is a possibility" (2005, p. 176). This has implications for transitivity, in fact.

- **Trust is not (strictly) transitive:** In fact, it makes sense in the context of AmI to think of it in some way as weakly transitive, but it is not necessarily the case. It is not possible in any given circumstance to say, however, that if Bert trusts John and John trusts Scott, then Bert trusts Scott. It is a relatively easy step from some of the other rules (especially unidirectionality) to see that this is the case. However, if Bert trusts John and *knows* that John trusts Scott, there may be a way we can infer (and make rules for) Bert trusting Scott to some extent.

When we are thinking about AmI and trust, a very real consideration is how one can trust that the information held about one is given only to those who I trust with it, only for a specific requirement, for only a finite length of time, and so on. These observations are relevant in this context. Only when the individual agents within an AmI environment can reason with rules derived from these observations can we expect AmI to behave in a socially responsible fashion, or to put it another way, at the very least, in a fashion that people can understand and hopefully accept. We are currently developing a system of measurements and rules, that we call Boing, to address this issue.

We cannot fully understand trust without considering risk. Trust and risk are symbiotic concepts, where one cannot fully exist without the other. As Brien (1998) argues in the absence of risk trust is meaningless. Indeed, some of the trust models that have been developed in recent years have explicitly included risk (Corritore et al., 2003). Sillence et al. (2004) state when people seek online advice they are more willing to trust a site if perceived risk is low. Most models of trust implicate personalisation, source credibility, and predictability as predictive factors (see Sillence et al., 2004).

Social Implications

Innovative technologies have been developed over centuries; their impact on society, social structure, and behaviour is well documented (Kostakos et al., 2005). For example, the Internet has had a huge impact on how we interact socially. Even after more than 30 years, the social implications of Internet use are still not fully understood. When we use the Internet, we disclose information about ourselves on nearly every mouse click. The trail we leave behind makes it possible for anyone with the required skill to follow us. The majority of people believe that they can control and regulate the disclosure of their personal informa-tion. However, will people be able to regulate and control all information pertaining to them when using AmI devices? It is not only the control of information that increases concerns in this future world; we must acknowledge that the social implications of such AmI devices are vast. The presence and use of these technologies will be major factors influencing our lives and how we socially interact.

As systems become more ubiquitous and free the user from time and place, research sug-gests that although anytime, anyplace may be possible, it may not always be acceptable (Perry, O'Hara, Sellen, Brown, & Harper, 2001). People have existing expectations about how technology works, and social norms provide cues on how they should interact in any given situation (Jessup & Robey, 2002).

Discussed earlier was the concept of "tracking." Tracking is a departure from existing social norms in that a person knows information about you that you are unaware of, that is, where you are. Generally, when we socially interact with others (e.g., through face-to-face interac-tion or a telephone conversation), we reveal information about ourselves both verbally and nonverbally. The important point is that "we" have made a decision to disclose information to another person, and generally we know who and where he or she is, and vice versa. Will we need to have "lie nodes" built into devices so our presence in every place or space we visit is not accounted for?

We already carry around a voluntary traceable microchip embedded in our mobile telephone. However, will the growth in tracking devices increase and make our lives so predictable that we lose the inherent social process of adventure and value? The introduction of social positioning maps will let us "see before we go" and let others "see where we are." Ahas and Mark (2005) acknowledge that privacy and security of social positioning devices are important issues, but argue "fears people have will most likely diminish in future as people become accustomed to mobile positioning and begin to enjoy the service." They also sug-gest concern over surveillance will also disappear.

Further questions arise related to AmI: How will people manage and control the amount of information revealed at any point in time? Who will people feel comfortable sharing different types of information with? How will people set and evaluate privacy and trust permissions that will govern what is being shared? The AmI challenge is particularly pressing, since in future there will be no obvious physical markers to tell us when we move from private to public cyberspaces (Beslay & Punie, 2002), and so individuals must be given a clearer vision of how and when to control personal data.

The aim of this research is to investigate how people will control information exchange when using AmI devices. To try to understand adoption and use, we need to consider the concepts of trust and privacy and the related underlying variables.

Method

To understand and investigate the concept of AmI technology and subsequent use, key stakeholders provided specific scenarios illustrating the ways in which privacy, trust, and identity information might be exchanged in the future. The stakeholders included relevant user groups, researchers, developers, businesses, and government departments with an interest in AmI development. Four scenarios were developed, related to health, e-voting, shopping, and finance that included facts about the device, context of use, type of service, or information the system would be used for. These scenarios are briefly described next:

Health scenario: Bob is in his office talking on his personal digital assistant (PDA) to a council planning officer with regard to an important application deadline. Built into his PDA are several personalized agents that pass information seamlessly to respective recipients. A calendar agent records and alerts Bob of deadlines, meetings, lunch appointments, and important dates. As Bob is epileptic, his health agent monitors his health and can alert people if he needs help. An emergency management agent takes control in situations when a host of different information is needed; this agent has the most permissions and can contact anyone in Bob's contact list.

Bob is going to meet his friend Jim for lunch when he trips over a loose paving slab. He falls to the ground and looses consciousness. His health agent senses something is wrong and beeps, if Bob does not respond by pressing the appropriate key on the PDA, the agent immediately informs the emergency services. Within seconds, the emergency services are informed of Bob's current situation and his medical history. An ambulance is on its way. Paramedics arrive, examine Bob, and then inform the hospital of Bob's condition on their emergency device. The hospital staff are now aware of Bob's medical history and his present state; therefore, on arrival, he is taken straight to the x-ray department. A doctor receives the x-rays on her PDA. After examining Bob she confirms that he has a broken ankle, slight concussion, and needs to stay in hospital overnight. After receiving treatment, Bob is taken to a ward. His emergency management agent contacts John (Bob's boss) of his circumstance. The emergency management agent transfers the planning application files to John's PDA so the company does not miss the deadline. The agent also informs his parents: letting them know his current state of health, exactly where he is so they can visit, and that his dog needs to be taken care of. As Bob is also head coach at a local running club, the agent informs the secretary Bob will not be attending training the following week. The secretary only receives minimal information through the permissions Bob has set.

Shopping scenario: Anita arrives at the local supermarket, grabs a trolley, and slips her PDA into the holding device. A message appears on screen and asks her to place her finger in the biometric verification device attached to the supermarket trolley. Anita places her finger in the scanner and a personalized message appears welcoming her to the shop. She has used the system before and knows her personalized shopping list will appear next on the PDA screen. Anita's home is networked and radio frequency identification tags are installed everywhere. Her fridge, waste bin, and cupboards monitor and communicate seamlessly with her PDA creating a shopping list of items needed. The supermarket network is set so that it alerts Anita of special offers and works alongside her calendar agent to remind her of any important dates. As she wanders around the supermarket, the screen shows her which items she needs in that particular aisle and their exact location. The device automatically records the price and ingredients of every item she puts into trolley and deletes the information if any item is removed. When Anita is finished, she presses a button on the PDA and the total cost of her shopping is calculated. Anita pays for the goods by placing her finger on the biometric device and her account is automatically debited, no need to unpack the trolley or wait in a queue. The trolley is then cleared to leave the supermarket. Anita leaves the supermarket, walks to her car, and places her shopping in the boot.

E-voting scenario: Natasha decides she wants to vote in the next election using the new online system. She goes online and requests electronic voting credentials. Shortly before polling day, a polling card and separate security card are delivered to Natasha's home. They arrive as two separate documents to reduce the risk of interception. Natasha picks up two of the letters from the doormat and puts the letters in her pocket as she rushes out of the door to head for work. While traveling on the local underground railway system, Natasha decides to cast her vote on her way to work. The letters have provided her with a unique personal voting and candidate numbers that allow her to register a vote for her chosen candidate. She takes out her mobile phone and types her unique number into it. Her vote is cast by entering this unique number into her phone and sending it to a number indicated on the polling card. Her phone then shows a text message: THANK YOU FOR VOTING. YOU HAVE NOT BEEN CHARGED FOR THIS CALL. When Natasha arrives at work, she logs on to the voting site to see if her vote has been registered. While at her computer with her polling cards on the desk in front of her, a colleague looks over her shoulder; she can see that Natasha is checking her vote but cannot see who she has voted for. Once the result of the election has been announced, Natasha checks that the correct candidate name is published next to her unique response number to ensure that the system has worked properly.

Financial scenario: Dave is at home writing a 'to do' list on his PDA. The PDA is networked and linked to several services that Dave has authorized. While writing his list, he receives a reminder from his bank that he needs to make an appointment with the manager related to his yearly financial health check. He replies and makes an appointment for later that day. When he arrives at the bank, he is greeted by the bank concierge system (an avatar presented on a large interface). The system is installed in the foyer of the bank where most customers use the banks facilities. The avatar tells Dave the manager, Mr. Brown, will be with him soon. The avatar notes that Dave has a photograph to print on his 'to do' list and asks if he would like to print it out at the bank as they offer this service. The avatar also asks Dave to confirm a couple of recent transactions on his account prior to meeting Mr. Brown.

The analysis of the shopping and health scenario will be discussed further in this chapter.

Development of Videotaped Scenarios

The elicited scenarios were scripted and the scenes were videotaped in context to develop videotaped activity scenarios (VASc). The VASc method is an exciting new tool for generating richly detailed and tightly focused group discussion and has been shown to be very effective in the elicitation of social rules (Little et al., 2004). VASc are developed from either in-depth interviews or scenarios, these are then acted out in context and videotaped. The VASc method allows individuals to discuss their own experiences, express their beliefs and expectations. This generates descriptions that are rich in detail and focused on the topic of interest. For this research, a media production company based in the UK was employed to recruit actors and videotape all scenarios. The production was overseen by both the producer and the research team to ensure correct interpretation. British Sign Language (BSL) and subtitles were also added to a master copy of the VASc's for use in groups where participants had various visual or auditory impairments.

Participants

The VASc's were shown to 38 focus groups, the number of participants in each group ranged from 4 to 12 people. The total number of participants was 304. Participants were drawn from all sectors of society in the Newcastle upon Tyne area of the UK, including representative groups from the elderly, the disabled, and from different ethnic sectors. Prior to attending one of the group sessions, participants were informed about the aims and objectives of the study. Demographic characteristics of all participants were recorded related to age, gender, disability (if any), level of educational achievement, ethnicity, and technical stance. A decision was made to allocate participants to groups based on age, gender, level of education, and technical stance, as this was seen as the best way possible for participants to feel at ease and increase discussions. As this study was related to future technology, it was considered important to classify participants as either technical or nontechnical. This was used to investigate any differences that might occur due to existing knowledge of technological systems. Therefore, participants were allocated to groups initially by technical classification, that is, technical/nontechnical, followed by gender, then level of educational achievement (high = university education or above vs. low = college education or below), and finally age (young, middle, old). Overall, this categorization process culminated in 24 main groups. Due to poor attendance at some group sessions, these were run again at a later date. Although several participants with physical disabilities attended the main group sessions, two group sessions for people with visual and auditory impairments were carried out at the Disability Forum in Newcastle. The forum was considered to have easier access and dedicated facilities for people with such disabilities.

Technical Classification

To classify participants into technical or nontechnical, six questions based on a categorization process by Maguire (1998) were used. Participants answer the questions using a yes/no response. Responding yes to questions 1, 3, 5, and 6, no to questions 2 and 4 would give a high technical score of 6. If the opposite occurred, this would give a low technical score of 0. Participants in this study who scored 0-3 were classified as nontechnical, while participants who scored 4-5 as technical. The questions were:

- If your personal devices (e.g., mobile telephone or computer) were taken away from you tomorrow, would it bother you?

- Do you think that we rely too much on technology?

- Do you enjoy exploring the possibilities of new technology?

- Do you think technologies create more problems than they solve?

- Is Internet access important to you?

- Do you like to use innovative technology as opposed to tried and tested technology?

Procedure

On recruitment, all participants received an information sheet that explained the study and the concept of AmI technologies. Participants were invited to attend Northumbria University, UK to take part in a group session. The groups were ran at various times and days over a 3-month period. Participants were told they would be asked to watch four short videotaped scenarios showing people using AmI systems and contribute to informal discussions on privacy and trust permissions for this type of technology. They were told all of the other participants in their particular group would be of approximately the same age and gender, and informed the discussion groups would be recorded for further analysis. Participants were not informed about the technical/nontechnical or the level of educational achievement classification that was used. An informal interview guide was used to help the moderator if the discussion deviated from the proposed topic.

At the beginning of each group session, the moderator gave an explanation and description of AmI technologies. After the initial introduction, the first videotaped scenario was shown. Immediately after this, each group was asked if they thought there were any issues or problems they could envisage if they were using that system. The same procedure was used for the other three videotaped scenarios. The scenarios were viewed by all groups in the same order: e-voting, shopping, health, and finance. Once all the videos had been viewed, an overall discussion took place related to any advantage/disadvantages, issues, or problems participants considered relevant to information exchange in an ambient society. Participant's attitudes in general towards AmI systems were also noted.

The moderator structured the discussions using an adaptation of the four-paned Johari Windows's methodology (Luft, 1969), where the four panes represent (1) information shared by the self and others, (2) information available to the self but closed to others, (3) information known by others but unknown to the self, and (4) information as yet unknown by self and others. Each window contracts or expands dependent upon the amount of information an individual wants to disclose. Briggs (2004) has described a means whereby the windows can be used to represent personal disclosure preferences for different agent technologies, organizations, or individuals.

The duration of the sessions was approximately 90 minutes.

Analysis

All group discussions were transcribed then read; a sentence-by-sentence analysis was employed. The data was then open coded using qualitative techniques and several categories were identified. The data was physically grouped into categories using sentences and phrases from the transcripts. Categories were then grouped into the different concepts, themes, and ideas that emerged during the analysis.

The various themes and concepts that emerged from the analysis provided greater insight into the issues regarding information exchange in an ambient society. Different issues related to the user, device, and stakeholder emerged. Further in-depth analysis revealed several constructs related to risk, privacy, trust, and social issues. These constructs were compared in relation to the user, device, and stakeholder. These constructs are depicted in Table 1 (an x is used to depict whether the construct is associated with the user, device, and/or stakeholder).

Table 1. Privacy, trust, and social issues related to AmI use

	Information		
	Device	User	Stakeholder
Trust:			
personalisation	x	x	x
expertise		x	
predictability		x	x
source		x	x
Risk:			
reliance and responsibility	x	x	x
Privacy:			
physical		x	
informational	x	x	x
psychological		x	x
social		x	x
choice		x	
control		x	
security	x	x	x
Social issues:			
exclusion		x	
social and moral values		x	x

In the following section, each concept related to trust, risk, privacy, and social issues is further explained.

Trust Concepts

a.   **Personalization:** the ability of people to personalize an AmI device, use personalized security mechanisms such as biometric verification systems, for example, fingerprints, and the provision of personalized services from the stakeholder. Also, the system's and stakeholder's sensitivity regarding sending and receiving personalized information in a timely manner.

Participants agreed the benefits to some in society having systems that could exchange personal information when appropriate was advantageous. For example, people with medical problems or various disabilities having their health information being disclosed to the relevant people when needed.

Discussion revealed participants concerns over systems being truly sensitive to circumstances under which personal information could legitimately be exchanged. For example, if someone was injured, should the device have permission to inform their next of kin that he or she had been taken to hospital? The transfer of sensitive personal information was discussed. Leakage of sensitive information in inappropriate circumstances was seen as very problematic:

What if one of your agents gets corrupted and starts sending messages here, there and everywhere?

b.   **Source credibility:** linked to motivation and the credibility of the stakeholder. Participants raised concerns over supermarkets using AmI systems to pressure people into buying goods. Concerns were raised over companies having the capacity to create user profiles and monitor people with regard to their shopping habits. This in turn would create health or lifestyle profiles accessible by third parties that would lead to untold consequences.

Participants queried how they could trust "agent" systems, as they perceived they would be linked in some way to different stakeholders. For example, if an agent was used to find information out about a personal loan, would they only return information from company *A* and *B*? The issue of trust transfer (from a trusted to an unknown third party) may be threatening.

c.   **Expertise:** the ability level of the user. Participants discussed problems associated with the user's level of expertise and the complexity of setting preferences for information exchange. In other words, users with little confidence in their own ability to set privacy preferences may find it difficult to place their trust in agent systems.

d.   **Predictability:** the predictability of interaction. Discussions highlighted the dynamic nature of human interaction and that we are not predictable robotic entities. Participants agreed human behaviour is complex and the amount of information related to our everyday lives was too immense to programme preferences into AmI systems. Participants commented that we act and react in different ways depending upon with whom we are interacting, when,and where. Setting up privacy preferences and permissions may become too time consuming, reducing the utility of such systems. Participants expressed concern about the level of control stakeholders would have, and questioned whether they could trust stakeholders to always act in a predictable way.

The kind of ordered, regular lifestyle that you'd have to live for it. I don't know what I'm going to be doing next week. I really don't.

I mean if you know in your own mind what to program into this agent your average day you still haven't had anything taken into consideration about your non-average day, anything could happen out of the blue and the machine will be all to pot because it doesn't fit with what you've programmed into it.

Risk Concepts

a. **Reliance and responsibility:** the user relying too much on the device to exchange information and the responsibility associated with this.

Participants discussed relying on either the system and/or themselves would be problematic. Concern arose over trust in the information received. For example, in the shopping scenario, the user was informed of allergy content in food, participants discussed who would be liable if this information was wrong, especially if they were buying food for another person.

Now if I'm relying on a gadget like that in the store to say this is safe for somebody on a gluten free diet and it's not, what happens, who is liable then, me or the gadget?

Discussion highlighted human fallibility in keeping the system up to date or losing the device (whilst acknowledging the fact that a truly AmI environment may or may not have this problem, we venture to suggest that the loss of something that gives us our identity bears similarities to this concern). Also, if the machine malfunctioned and the user was unaware of this, what would the consequences be? Participants commented systems could not be truly aware of certain facts or always in control. They agreed AmI systems reduce cognitive load, but questioned whether this was advantageous to humans in the long term.

I want to rely on myself and a network of human beings, not a network of communications and little chips.

One is that there has to be a human input somewhere into the system and the reliability of the human input is dependent on the adaptability of that human being. I think we are all intelligent human beings, we're older, we're wiser than we were some years ago and I think we could all put in intelligent information but we can all make mistakes and that is a failing that we have to recognize.

Privacy Constructs

a.   **Physical:** how physically accessible a person is to others. Participants commented that AmI devices would break down the boundaries of physical privacy—making an individual accessible anywhere, anytime. They discussed issues related to leakage of personal information in public settings and especially during interpersonal interaction. Participants queried whether AmI devices could truly be context aware and deliver the correct information in a timely and appropriate fashion.

... you have no privacy, people know where you are, what you are eating, what you are doing, and that really bothers me.

b.   **Informational:** a person's right to reveal personal information to others.The concept of informational privacy was a major concern for all participants. Participant's highlighted complex patterns of personal information would be required to be able to control who receives what and when. Global companies and networks were seen as very problematic–facilitating the transmission of personal information across boundaries, each with different rules and regulations.

Databases can be offshore thereby there are sort of international waters and they are not under the jurisdiction of anyone or the laws of anyone country, you'd have to have global legislation.

Participants acknowledged companies already hold information about you that you are unaware of and this should be made more transparent. Concerns were raised over the probability that stakeholders would collect personal information in an ad hoc manner without informing the person. Data gathering and data mining by stakeholders would create profiles about a person that would contain false information. Participants believed profiling would lead to untold consequence. For example, a person might be refused health insurance as their profile suggests he or she purchases unhealthy food.

It's (information) where it can lead. That's the key to a lot of personal information about you, it's telling you where you live, they (3rd parties) can get details from there and there's companies buying and selling that information.

The device will say "are you sure you want to eat so much red meat because we are going to elevate your insurance premium because of your unhealthy lifestyle."

c.   **Social:** the ability to control social interactions between social actors. Participants discussed the possibility that AmI would foster social isolation. Although systems would, in fact, increase social privacy as less human-human interaction would take place, this was considered very problematic, with enormous negative consequences. Participants commented, in our social world, we already leak information to others in the form of visual cues, for example, items in your shopping trolley, without any serious implications. In the physical world, strangers knowing certain information about you is not problematic; however, people do not want to share the same information with friends. In the physical world, interactions are considered "open" where people can see exactly what is happening compared to the closed nature of the virtual world. One participant described this with reference to a tin opener.

You know if you are using a tin opener, you think oh, I see, but with a computer you can't do anything like that. I mean with a vacuum cleaner you've got a fair idea of what to look for if the thing goes wrong but with a computer. They put computers on the market and they are supposed to be trouble free because they thought they were such a good idea, but if they had waited to iron out all the troubles, it would be another fifty years. You know look at the progress we have made.

d.   **Psychological:** a person's right to decide with whom they share personal information. Psychological privacy emerged as a key barrier to AmI adoption and use. Participants agreed the type of information shared normally depends on who, what, where, and why, but crucially is informed by the type of relationship they have with the other person. If their relationship is close, for example, family, then the majority of information is shared quite freely. However, sharing even with a close family member depends on situation and context. Participants discussed concern over stakeholders sharing personal information with third parties and suggested AmI systems needed transparency at times.

I don't know who has got what information. If I asked anyone are they going to tell me if they didn't want to and how would I know that they were telling me? So it goes into this kind of vacuum, but they are only going to tell me the information they want me to know and they miss the bit that they really don't want me to know, that they do know or not know, I have no way of finding out.

Complex preferences would have to be set for AmI systems and these would need to change dynamically. Participants commented, in some circumstances, relying on agent systems and the use of preset preferences for sharing information was socially unacceptable. This related to how we, as humans, are not predictable, and interact with others in a dynamic way.

One of the main issues is you have got all of these different types of information and how do people actually set the permissions so only person A gets that information and person B gets that and as humans we are continually changing and interacting with more and more people or less people and so the permissions change.

e.   **Choice:** The right to choose. Participants commented little or even no choice would exist in an AmI society. Comments suggested "forced choice" would become the "norm." Participants expressed concern over the right not to reveal information having vast implications leading to exclusion in some circumstances. A sense of being damned, simply because one might choose not to share certain types of information.

f.   **Control:** The right to control. Participants were concerned about reliance on AmI systems reducing personal control. Discussions revealed AmI systems would create "Big Brother" societies that lacked control and choice. Concern was raised over how information would be controlled by stakeholders, that is, receiving information that is considered appropriate.

What I don't like is where it starts taking control of that information from your hands and having information in an electronic device which fair enough you are supposed to have programmed in the first place but once you have programmed it what's your control over it then and it's transmitting information about you to all these various. I don't trust technology enough yet.

That is (AmI system) structuring your life for you. You think you're in control but you're not.

g.   **Security:** security aspects related to transmission and storage of information. Security of AmI systems emerged as key factor that would limit adoption and use. Hacking, access by third parties, leakage, and storage were all areas discussed. Participants differed on the concept of using biometric systems for verification and authentication purposes. Participants classed as technical were more aware of problems related to biometric devices than those from a nontechnical background. Most agreed biometric systems could alleviate the problems of human error (such as forgetting PINs); however, concerns were raised with regard to exclusion when using biometric systems, for example, the ability of the elderly to enroll in and use such systems.

Social Issues

a.   **Exclusion:** Participants commented that exclusion would be a major problem with adoption and use of AmI systems. People would be excluded by age, ability, disability, and membership of specific populations, for example, business communities.

b.   **Social and moral values:** Participants discussed several social and moral issues related to AmI systems. They suggested technologies are now undermining human responsibility. Participants agreed we now interact less socially with others. AmI systems could further decrease social interaction, reduce our social skills, and take away the concept of interpersonal trust.

We are so anti-social anyway, unless Andrew has his friends to the house and I must admit I mean I communicate with a lot of my friends now by text messages whereas before you would have called to them or you know send an email but I see less of people that I care about because it's more convenient to send them a text or an email and I hate it, I really do hate it and I think that's going to encourage more because then you're not even going to have to make the effort to send the text message, your machine is going to be sending them a text message because you're overdue writing to them.

Although some participants in this study liked the idea of using biometric systems to access information and considered this a secure way, other participants viewed this as "depersonalizing" the task at hand. Discussion highlighted how life in general is becoming more depersonalized through increased interaction with technology and less with other human beings. Participants discussed issues related to the fact that if AmI systems were truly "context aware' this depersonalizes human interaction and thought processes.

If he had of collapsed (referring to hospital scenario) *and it wasn't just a, say it was a brain tumour and he only had a few days to live when they got him into hospital and his family were informed of this via an electronic device I just think that's terrible, it's like totally depersonalizing like the medical way of things and I mean I certainly wouldn't like be told by somebody that one of my relatives was going to die or something over a little piece of metal or plastic or whatever it is so I think it's one of those things in theory it all sounds well and good but in reality it just wouldn't work.*

Concerns were raised over the fact existing technologies are often intrusive. Some participants commented that when we disclose information to others, we often do not reveal the truth for various reasons. They contemplated what the consequence of this would be in an AmI world. For example, if a person told his or her partner they were shopping when in fact that was not true, would his or her partner be able to track the person's exact location?

Discussion

To evaluate the social impact of AmI use, trust and privacy issues need to be understood. The framework used in this study to evaluate trust and privacy has revealed different contexts, stakeholders, device type, and actual users all need to be considered. This is important if we are to fully understand user interaction with AmI technologies.

As discussed earlier in this chapter, trust is not symmetrical, distributive, associative, or (at least strongly) transitive. The findings from this research support this view. Both privacy and trust are multidimensional constructs with underlying factors that dynamically change according to context. The findings support the view of Sillence et al. (2004) in that trust is multidimensional.

To establish trust and privacy, the following questions need to be addressed when related to information exchange: Who is receiving it? Who has access? Is the receiver credible, and predictable? Where is the information being sent and received? Does the user have choice and control? How does the device know who to communicate with, for example, through personalized agents? This raises interesting questions regarding permission setting within an AmI context: regarding the extent to which individuals should be allowed to make day to day decisions about who or what to trust on an ad hoc basis, or should employ agent technologies that represent their personal trust and privacy preferences and communicate these to other agents (Marsh,1994).

Disclosure of information in any form or society is a two-way process. Findings support, the Fair Information Practice-FIP (e.g., Federal Trade Commission of America, 2000) that suggests companies should give user: notice, choice, access, and security. We need to consider the following guidelines when considering adoption and use of AmI systems:

a.   **Choice:** The option to reveal or hide information.

b.   **Control:** The ability to manage, organize, and have power over all information exchanged and to be notified of information held about you.

c.   **Transparency:** The need for stakeholder's to be open to information held about a person, and for that person to have a right to access and change such information.

d.   **Global rules and regulations:** A global infrastructure of rules related to information exchange.

e.   **Obscurity:** The need for information exchange to be closed or made ambiguous dependent on the user's needs and desires at any one moment in time.

f.   **Trust and privacy preference:** The need for the user to set preferences that can be dynamic, temporary, and secure.

These guidelines are basic, and we need to consider the fact that humans are inherently social beings and their actions are always directly or indirectly linked to other people. Findings from this evaluation raise some interesting issues related to human values: Will people begin to rely to heavily on AmI technology? Will people be comfortable exchanging all types of information even when of a very personal nature? Will the way we socially interact change, and social norms along with it? Will our society become one where people feel more at home interacting with their fridge instead of other people? Will AmI technology blur the boundaries between home and workplace making society one of efficiency and productivity taking over from love and leisure time?

AmI systems do bring substantial benefits, including less time pressure, no queuing for goods, and memory enhancements. However, the disadvantages in our social world might be far greater, for example, less social interaction, reliance on machines, less privacy, and the potential erosion of trust. Distrust and suspicion of AmI systems appear key concepts that emerged from the group discussions in this study, and bear much further examination and understanding.

This book is dedicated to the concept of trust. However, if we begin to rely on systems to make decisions on our behalf by setting prior preferences, do we actually need to understand the concepts of privacy and trust? For AmI systems to work, societies need to be at least somewhat transparent. To be truly transparent then, we need complete trust and have no concern over privacy. The enigmatic nature of trust, privacy, and social values questions whether we can really understand this type of puzzle or even create a clear vision for future interactions with AmI systems.

Future Directions

Ambient intelligence is now an area intensely researched and undergoing rapid development already visible in advanced mobile, PDA, and notebook services. The vision of a future filled with smart and interacting everyday objects offers a whole range of possibilities. To some, the scenarios described in this chapter might appear somewhat "unrealistic." However, if Weiser's vision is to be realized, then we must acknowledge the advantages and disadvantages this transformation will have on society. For example, sensor and communication mechanisms in the environment will help people with disabilities lead a more independent life. We will be able to track everything from children, family, and friends to missing keys. However, we must question whether the transformation that will take place is ethical or even socially acceptable. Do we want or need to rely on embedded devices seamless exchanging information on our behalf?

Clear methodologies that allow in-depth investigation into how information exchange in an ambient world can be made trustworthy, secure, and private are needed. This requires cross-disciplinary approaches, where evaluation is based on both the technical and social aspects of such interactions.

The next stage in the research reported in this chapter is to develop a survey developed from the project findings. The survey will be a useful tool in measuring concepts related to trust, privacy, and social issues when considering ambient devices and information exchange. The findings will give further insight into how ambient devices can be designed to deliver specific services and information and therefore acceptance.

References

Abdul-Rahman, A. (2004). *A framework for decentralised trust reasoning.* PhD thesis, University of London.

Ahas, R., & Mark, Ü. (2005). Location based services—new challenges for planning and public administration? *Futures, 37*(6), 547-561.

Altman, I. (1975). *The environment and social behavior.* Belmont, CA: Wadsworth.

Altman, I., & Chemers, M. (1989). *Culture and environment.* Cambridge: Cambridge University Press.

Arndt, C. (2005). The loss of privacy and identity. *Biometric Technology Today, 13*(8), 6-7.

Beslay, L., & Punie, Y. (2002). *The virtual residence: Identity, privacy and security* (IPTS Report 67). Institute for Prospective Technological Studies. Special Issue on Identity and Privacy.

Bickmore T., & Cassell, J. (2001). Relational agents; A model and implementation of building user trust. In *Proceedings of CHI 2001* (pp. 396-403).

Bies, R. J. (2001). Interactional (in) justice: The sacred and the profane. In J. Greenberg & R. Cropanzano (Eds.), *Advances in organisational justice* (pp. 89-118). Stanford, CA: Stanford University Press.

Bødker, M. (2004). *Trust and the digital environment.* Retrieved March 2006, http://www.itu.dk/people/boedker/trustpaper.pdf

Bohn, J., Coroama, V., Langheinrich, M., Mattern, F., & Rohs, M. (2005). Social, economic, and ethical implications of ambient intelligence and ubiquitous computing. In W. Weber, J. Rabaey, & E. Aarts, *Ambient intelligence.* Berlin: Springer.

Bok, S. (1978). *Lying: Moral choice in public and private life.* New York: Pantheon Books.

Boon, S. D., & Holmes, J. (1991). The dynamics of interpersonal trust: Resolving uncertainty in the face of risk. In R. A. Hinde & J. Groebel (Eds.), *Cooperation and prosocial behaviour* (pp. 190-211). Cambridge: Cambridge University Press.

Brandies, L. D., & Warren, S. (1890). The right to privacy: The implicit made explicit. *Harvard Law Review, 4,* 193-220.

Brien, A. (1998). Professional ethics and the culture of trust. *Journal of Business Ethics, 17*(4), 391-409.

Briggs, P. (2004). *Key issues in the elicitation of disclosure preferences fro ambient intelligence—a view from a window.* Paper presented at Considering Trust in Ambient Societies Workshop (CHI 2004), Vienna, Austria.

Brin, D. (1998). *The transparent society: Will technology force us to choose between privacy and freedom.* UK: Perseus Press.

Boni, M., & Prigmore, M. (2002). Cultural aspects of Internet privacy. In *Proceedings of the UKAIS 2002 Conference*, Leeds, UK.

Burgoon, J. K. (1982). Privacy and communication. *Communication Yearbook, 6,* 206-249.

Chan, Y. (2000). Privacy in the family: Its hierarchical and asymmetric nature. *Journal of Comparative Family Studies, 31*(1), 1-23.

Chang, E., Thomson, P., Dillon, T., & Hussain, F. (2004). The fuzzy and dynamic nature of trust. In S. Katsikas, J. López, & G. Perum (Eds.), *TrustBus 2005* (LNCS 3592, pp. 161-174). Berlin: Springer.

Cheskin Research & Studio Archetype/Sapient. (1999). *eCommerce trust study.* Retrieved from http://www.cheskin.com/think/studies/ecomtrust.html

Cheskin Research. (2000). *Trust in the Wired Americas.* Retrieved from http://www.cheskin.com/p/ar.asp?mlid=7&arid=12&art=0

Clarke, R. (1999). *Introduction to dataveillance and information privacy, and definitions of terms*. Retrieved January 2004, from http://www.anu.edu.au/people/Roger.Clarke/DV/Intro.html

Consolvo, S., Smith, I. E., Matthews, T., LaMarca, A., Tabert, J., & Powledge, P. (2005, April). Location disclosure to social relations: Why, when, & what people want to share. In *Proceedings of the SIGCHI Conference on Human Factors in Computing Systems*, Portland, OR.

Corritore, C. L., Kracher, B., & Wiedenbeck, S. (2003). Online trust: Concepts, evolving themes, a model. *International Journal of Human Computer Studies, 58,* 737-758.

Cramer, L. (2002). *Web privacy with P3P*. O'Reilly & Associates.

Cranor, L. F., Reagle, J., & Ackerman, M. S. (1999). Beyond concern: Understanding net users' attitudes about online privacy. In I. Vogelsang & B. Compaine (Eds.), *The Internet upheaval: Raising questions, seeking answers in communications policy* (pp. 47-60). MIT Press.

Dawson, L., Minocha, S., & Petre, M. (2003). Social and cultural obstacles to the (B2C) e-commerce experience. In *People and computers XVII—designing for society* (pp. 225-241).

Dibben, M. R. (2000). *Exploring interpersonal trust in the entrepreneurial venture*. Hampshire: MacMillan Press.

Dritsas, S., Gritzalis, D., & Lambrinoudakis, C. (2005). Protecting privacy and anonymity in pervasive computing trends and perspectives. *Telematics and Information*. In press.

Egger, F N. (2000). Trust me, I'm an online vendor. In *CHI 2001 Proceedings Extended Abstracts* (pp. 101-102).

Egger, F. N. (2003). *From interactions to transactions: Designing the trust experience for business-to-consumer electronic commerce*. PhD thesis, Eindhoven University of Technology, The Netherlands.

Falcone, R., & Castelfranchi, C. (2001). The socio-cognitive dynamics of trust; Does trust create trust? In R. Falcone, M. Singh, & Y.-H. Tan, (Eds.), *Trust in cyber-societies* (LNAI 2246, pp. 55-72). Berlin: Springer.

Fiske, A. P., Kitayama, S., Markus, H. R., & Nisbett, R. E. (1998). The cultural matrix of social psychology. In D. T. Gilbert, S. T. Fiske, & G. Lindzey (Eds.), *The handbook of social psychology* (4th ed., Vol. 2, pp. 915-981). Boston: McGraw-Hill.

Friedman, B., Kahn, P. H., & Howe, D. C. (2000). Trust online. *Communications of the ACM, 43*(12), 34-40.

FTC Study. (2000, May). *Privacy online: Fair information practices in the electronic marketplace*. A report to Congress.

Fukuyama, F. (1996). *Trust: The social virtues and the creation of prosperity*. New York: Free Press.

Fung R. K. K., & Lee, M. K. O. (1999). EC-trust (Trust in Electronic Commerce): Exploring the antecedent factors. In *Proceedings of the American Conference on Information Systems* (pp. 517-519).

Gambetta, D. (2000). Can we trust trust. In D. Gambetta (Ed.), *Trust: Making and breaking cooperative relations* [electronic edition] (pp. 213-237). Department of Sociology, University of Oxford. Retrieved from http://www.sociology.ox.ac.uk/papers/gambetta213-237.pdf

Good, D. (2000). Individuals, interpersonal relations, and trust. In D. Gambetta (Ed.) *Trust: Making and breaking cooperative relations* [electronic edition] (pp. 31-48). Department of Sociology, University of Oxford. Retrieved from http://www.sociology.ox.ac.uk/papers/good31-48.pdf

Gotlieb, C.C. (1996). Privacy: A concept whose time has come and gone. In D. Lyon & E. Zureik (Eds.), *Computers, surveillance and privacy* (pp. 156-171). University of Minnesota Press.

Jackson, L., von Eye, A., Barbatsis, G., Biocca, F., Zhao, Y., & Fitzgerald, H. E. (2003). Internet attitudes and Internet use: Some surprising findings from the HomeNetToo project. *International Journal of Human-Computer Studies, 59*, 355-382.

Jarvenpaa, S., Tractinsky, N., & Saarinen, L.(1999). Consumer trust in an Internet store: A cross-cultural validation. *Journal of Computer Mediated Communication, 5*(2). Retrieved from http://jcmc.indiana.edu/vol5/issue2/jarvenpaa.html

Jessup, L., & Robey, D. (2002) The relevance of social issues in ubiquitous computing environments. *Communications of the ACM, 45*(12), 88-91.

Karvonen, K. (1999, November 1-2). Creating trust. In *Proceedings of the 4th Nordic Workshop on Secure IT Systems (NordSec 99)*, Kista, Sweden.

Kaya, N., & Weber, M. J. (2003). Cross-cultural differences in the perception of crowing and privacy regulation: American and Turkish students. *Journal of Environmental Psychology, 32,* 301-309.

Kostakos, V., Little, L., O'Neill, E. & Silence, E. (2005). The social implications of emerging technologies. *Interacting with Computers, 17,* 475-483.

Kozlov, S. (2004). *Achieving privacy in hyper-blogging communities: Privacy management for ambient technologies.* Retrieved June 2004, from http://www.sics.se/privacy/wholes2004/papers/kozlov.pdf

Lester, T. (2001). The reinvention of privacy. *The Atlantic Online.* Retrieved September 2001, from http://www.theatlantic.com/issues/2001/03/lester-pt.htm

Lewis, J. D., & Weigert, A. (1985). Trust as a social reality. *Social Forces, 63*(4), 967-985.

Little, L., Briggs, P., & Coventry, L. (2004, September). *Videotaped activity scenarios and the elicitation of social rules for public interactions.* BHCIG Conference, Leeds, UK.

Little, L., Briggs, P., & Coventry, L. (2005). Public space systems: Designing for privacy? *International Journal of Human Computer Studies, 63,* 254-268.

Luft, J. (1969). *Of human interaction.* Palo Alto, CA: National Press.

Luhmann, N. (1979). *Trust and power.* Chichester, UK: Wiley.

Luhmann, N. (2000). Familiarity, confidence, trust: Problems and alternatives. In D. Gambetta (Ed.), *Trust: Making and breaking cooperative relations* [electronic edition] (pp.

94-107). Department of Sociology, University of Oxford. Retrieved from http://www. sociology.ox.ac.uk/papers/luhmann94-107.pdf

Margulis, S. T. (2003). On the status and contribution of Westin's and Altman's theories of privacy. *Journal of Social issues, 59*(2), 411-429.

Marsh, S. (1994). *Formalising trust as a computational concept.* PhD thesis, University of Stirling, Scotland. Retrieved from http://www.stephenmarsh.ca

Marsh, S. (2005, October 4). *Artificial trust, regret, forgiveness, and boing.* Seminar given at University of St Andrews, Scotland. Retrieved from http://www.stephenmarsh.ca

Marsh, S., & Dibben, M. R. (2003). The role of trust in information science and technology. In B. Cronin (Ed.), *Annual Review of Information Science and Technology, 37,* 465-498.

Marshall, N. J. (1970). *Orientations towards privacy: Environmental and personality components* (University Microfilms No. 71-815). Unpublished doctoral dissertation, University of California, Berkley.

McCandlish, S. (2002). EFF's top 12 ways to protect your online privacy. *Electronic Frontier Technology.* Retrieved January 2004, from http://www.eff.org/Privacy/eff_privacy_top_12.html

Metzger, M. J. (2004). Exploring the barriers to electronic commerce: Privacy, trust, and disclosure online. *Journal of Computer-Mediated Communication, 9*(4). Retrieved from http://jcmc.indiana.edu/vol19/issue4/metzger.html

Misztal, B. (1996). *Trust in modern docieties.* Cambridge: Polity Press.

Moor, J. H. (1997) Towards a theory of privacy in the Information Age. *Computers and Society, 27*(3), 27-32.

Nguyen, D. H., & Truong, K. N. (2003). PHEmail: Designing a privacy honoring email system. In *Proceedings of CHI 2003 Extended Abstracts*, Ft. Lauderdale, FL.

Nijholt, A., Rist, T., & Tuinenbrejier, K. (2004). Lost in ambient intelligence? In *Proceedings of the ACM Conference on Computer Human Interaction (CHI 2004)*, Vienna, Austria.

Olsen, K., Grudin, J., & Horvitz, E. (2005). A study of preferences for sharing and privacy. In *Proceedings of the CHI 2005 Extended Abstracts on Human Factors in Computing Systems.*

Palen, L., & Dourish, P. (2003). Unpacking Privacy for a Networked World. In *Proceedings of the ACM, CHI 2003, 5*(1), 129- 135.

Patrick, A., Briggs, P., & Marsh, S. (2005*).* Designing systems that people will trust. In L. F. Cranor & S. Garfinkel, *Security and usability: Designing secure systems that people can use.* O'Reilly.

Pedersen, D. M. (1979). Dimensions of privacy. *Perceptual and Motor skills, 48,* 1291-1297.

Pedersen, D. M. (1997). Psychological functions of privacy. *Journal of Environmental Psychology, 17,* 147-156.

Pedersen, D. M. (1999). Model for types of privacy by privacy functions. *Journal of Environmental Psychology, 19,* 397-405.

Perry, M., O'Hara, K., Sellen, A., Brown, B., & Harper, R. (2001). Dealing with mobility: Understanding access anytime, anywhere. *ACM Transactions on Computer-Human Interaction, 8*(4), 323-347.

Price, B. A., Adam, K., & Nuseibeh, B. (2005). Keeping ubiquitous computing to yourself: A practical model for user control of privacy. *International Journal of Human-Computer Studies, 63*(1-2), 228-253.

Punie, Y. (2003). *A social and technological view of ambient intelligence in everyday life: What bends the trend?* Key delivered at The European Media and Technology in Everyday Life Network (EMTEL).

Riegelsberger, J., & Sasse, M. A. (2001). Trustbuilders and trustbusters. In Towards the e-society. In *Proceedings of the First IFIP Conference on E-Commerce, E-Society, and E-Government* (pp. 17-70). London: Kluwer.

Rousseau, D. M., Sitkin, S. B., Burt, R. S., & Camerer, C. (1998). Not so different after all: A cross-discipline view of trust. *Academy of Management Review, 23*(3), 393-404.

Siau, K., & Shen, Z. (2003). Building consumer trust in mobile commerce. *Communications of the ACM, 46*(4), 91-94.

Shneiderman, B. (2000). Designing trust into online experiences. In *Communications of the ACM, 4*,12.

Sillence, E., Briggs, P., Fishwick, L., & Harris, P. (2004, April 24-29). Trust and mistrust of online health sites. *Proceedings of CHI 2004, Vienna Austria* (pp. 663-670). ACM Press.

Streitz, N., & Nixon, P. (2005). The disappearing computer. *Communication of the ACM, 48*(3), 32-35.

Sztompka, F. (1999). *Trust: A sociological theory*. Cambridge University Press.

Teltzrow, M., & Kobsa, A. (2004). Impacts of user privacy perferences on personalized systems: A comparative study. In C.-M. Karat, J. Blom, & J. Karat (Eds.), *Designing personalized user experiences for e-commerce*. Dordrecht, The Netherlands: Kluwer Academic Publishers.

Thibaut, J. W., & Kelley, H. H. (1959) *The social psychology of groups*. New York: Wiley.

Viljanen, L. (2005). Towards an ontology of trust. In S. Katsikas, J. López, & G. Perum (Eds.), *TrustBus 2005* (LNCS 3592, pp. 175-194). Berlin: Springer.

Weiser, M. (1991). The computer for the 21st century. *Scientific American, 265*(3), 66-75.

Westin, A. (1967). *Privacy and freedom*. New York: Atheneum.

Chapter XII

User-Centric Identity, Trust and Privacy

Jean-Marc Seigneur, University of Geneva, Switzerland

Christian Damsgaard Jensen, Technical University of Denmark, Denmark

Abstract

This chapter introduces entification as a means of allowing the users of e-services to create and manage multiple pseudonyms in a decentralized way; thereby limiting the ability to link transactions and users, whilst mitigating attacks due to the ownership of multiple identities. The entification framework fills the gap between the identity and the computational trust/reputation layers. It is difficult to safely assess linked evidence about multiple virtual identities because there might be overcounting of overlapping trust pieces of evidence. The entification framework uses a new mechanism, called trust transfer, to mitigate this issue, and allows the users to trade privacy for trust. Such a framework is essential in a world where more and more e-services want to rely on user-centric identity management.

Introduction

During the past 3 decades, the computing environment has evolved from centralized stationary computers to potentially large, complex, and dynamic environments of distributed and mobile computers. This evolution has profound implications for the security models, policies, and mechanisms needed to protect users' information and resources in an increasingly global interconnected computing infrastructure. Security has evolved from "easy" (Gollmann, 1999) computer security in a single system with centralized security enforcement to systems that consist of a collection of computers linked via some network, that is, distributed systems. Security for systems connected to the Internet—the World Wide Web—is generally considered even more difficult, because the systems span a plethora of independent (possibly conflicting) administrative authorities. In traditional centralized stationary computer systems, security is typically based on the authenticated identity of the requesting principal. This is based on the assumption that known users are granted access to the system for specific purposes, so meaningful security policies can be specified in terms of the identity of a principal. Strong authentication mechanisms, such as Kerberos (Kohl & Neuman, 1993) or public key infrastructures (PKIs) support reliable authentication of users across networks, which allows this model to be extended to distributed systems that are contained within a single administrative domain or within a few closely collaborating domains. Identity-based security relies on the implicit assumption that real-world recourse mechanisms, such as contracts, insurance, or legislation, act as an effective deterrence against misbehaviour, that is, it is assumed that if the actions made by a computing entity can be bound to a real-world identity, the owner of a misbehaving computing entity can be brought to court and reparations will be possible. In open environment with no unique authority, such as the worldwide Internet, the feasibility of this approach is questionable. An example where prosecution is ineffective involves e-mail spammers who do not mind moving operations abroad-at the time of writing Brazil and China-to escape the risk of prosecution (Postini, 2004). This problem is exasperated by the fact that there are many legal jurisdictions on the Internet, and that the cost of prosecuting an entity in a foreign jurisdiction is often prohibitively high, so security based on the authenticated identity may be superfluous. Moreover, there is the underlying question of which authority may be put in charge of certifying the binding with the real-world identity, since there are no unique global authorities. "Who, after all, can authenticate US citizens abroad? The UN? Or thousands of pair wise national cross-certifications?" (Khare, 1999).

The problem of authentication in e-service environments creates problems with access control, because traditional identity-based security mechanism cannot authorize an operation without authenticating the requesting party. This means that no interaction can take place unless both parties are known to each other's authentication framework. This has profound implications for a global e-service environment, because seamless support for spontaneous interactions requires that a single, or a few trusted certificate authorities (CAs) emerge, which, based on the inability of a single global PKI to emerge over the past decade, seems highly unlikely in the foreseeable future. This state of the art is clearly unsatisfactory; instead, online users and devices need the ability to autonomously authenticate and authorize other parties that they encounter, without having to rely on a common authentication infrastructure.

In order to develop appropriate security abstractions for this global ubiquitous e-services environment, we have to realize that there is an inherent element of risk whenever a computing entity ventures into collaboration with a previously unknown party. One way to manage that risk is to develop models, policies, and mechanisms that allow an entity to assess the risk incurred by the proposed collaboration, and to explicitly reason about the trustworthiness of the other party in order to determine if the other party is trustworthy enough to mitigate the risk of collaboration. Formation of trust in other parties may be based on previous experience of interacting with that party, recommendations from reachable peers, or an assessment of the perceived reputation of the other party. One way to assess the reputation of the other party would be to use a reputation system such as the one used on eBay (Ebay). It is important to note that this formation of trust does not require the authenticated identity of the other party. It is sufficient that the authorizing entity is able to recognize the other party and that parties who exchange recommendations or opinions of reputation are able to decide on a common identifier for the concerned party. This means that local identifiers and weaker authentica- tion schemes may be employed, for example, self-proclaimed identities, local pseudonyms, physical cues, and so forth. The advantage of such weaker authentication systems is that it eliminates the need for a common trusted authentication infrastructure. Instead, authoriza- tion is primarily based on local information that may be enhanced with credentials from any trusted authentication infrastructure whenever they are available.

This model of *explicit trust management* promotes risk and trust to first-class citizens in the security model, which means that they can be used directly in the specification of security policies, and that they should be supported directly by the underlying security mechanism. Explicit trust management has additional advantages: it allows an entity to select the e-ser- vice provider that is most likely to provide the required service whenever it is faced with a number of previously unknown service providers. We therefore believe that a general trust management middleware will provide the enabling technology for secure and reliable col- laboration in e-services environments.

In such e-services environments, users need support to make decisions, especially about services that they are trying to use for the first time. Trust engines, based on computational models of the human notion of trust, have been proposed to facilitate (or even make) security decisions on behalf of their owner. For example, the SECURE project (SECURE; Seigneur, 2004) has built a generic and reusable trust engine. More generally, each computing entity would run a computational trust engine. A trust engine allows the entity to compute levels of trust in other entities based on the evidence provided by the sources of trust evidence relevant to the application domain, for example, knowledge given by an entity about other interacting entities: local observations of interaction outcomes or recommendations. Once a type of trust has been identified, sources of trust correspond to entities that provide this type of evidence. Other sources of trust may be found based on the application domain, but the main types of evidence have so far generally been related to knowledge about the interacting entities. An example of another type of trust evidence may be interest similarity between users as discussed in Ziegler and Golbeck (2006). Based on the computed trust value and given a trust policy, the trust engine may decide to grant or deny access to a requesting entity. Then, if access is given to an entity, the actions of the granted entity are monitored and the outcomes, positive or negative, are used to refine the trust value.

Application of explicit trust management raises the question of whether authentication of the real-world identity is really necessary to use the human notion of trust? This chapter focuses on this question. Indeed, a critical element for the use of trust is to collect and accumulate trust evidence about the interacting entities, but trust evidence does not necessarily consist of information about the real-world identity of the owner: trust evidence may simply be the count of positive interactions with a virtual identity. In order to retrieve trust evidence, in this chapter, we draw another parallel with human social networks, namely the notion of entity recognition. When a new person is introduced by a trustworthy recommender, the identity card of the recommended person is not used and it is subsequently sufficient to recognize this person, that is, formal authentication may never be required, and the recommended person may be known by a nickname rather than the real identity. This improves the spontaneity of the interactions, but it also highlights a potential benefit from a privacy point of view. As long as the interacting computing entities can be recognized, direct observations and recommendations can be exchanged in order to build trust, interaction after interaction. This level of trust can be used for trusting decisions. Thus, trust engines can provide dynamic protection without the assumption that real-world recourse mechanisms, such as legal recourse, are available in case of harm.

In this chapter, we first survey the previous work on trust management: why legacy security had to be revised with the advent of ubiquitous e-services environments. Then, we give an emphasis on how identity has been taken into account in this previous work to bring to light that there is no thorough integration of identity and evidence-based trust. This motivates why we have designed entification (Seigneur, 2005b), which is our own contribution to this field: entification fills the gap between identity and trust.

Background

In this section, we first examine legacy security abstractions in order to identify their shortcomings when applied to global, worldwide, e-services environments with different (possibly conflicting) jurisdictions. Then, we refine what we mean by implicit trust in traditional security and present the novel approach based on explicit computational trust.

Security and Trust in Pervasive Computing

Traditional security mechanisms used for e-services are generally confined to enforce security in a single administrative domain. Extending such mechanisms to the open dynamic and competitive environment of e-services is particularly difficult. Figure 1 depicts the scenario where legacy security mechanisms are applied to an environment with different e-services providers.

In Figure 1 (as well as in Figure 2), the security perimeters or domains of different parties (for example, two different e-services providers) are delimited by dashed lines; the flows of requests made by an entity are represented by large white arrows (from identification to authentication to authorization/reference monitor to the resource); and blue arrows are used to show where manual intervention is required, at some stage, to set some sort of trust relation. The blue colour of system administrators also indicates that they must be highly trusted. Figure 1 focuses on the e-services domain A, which has a security perimeter administered by an administrator. The basic scenario illustrated on Figure 1 shows an entity,

Figure 1. Security administration burden of legacy mechanisms

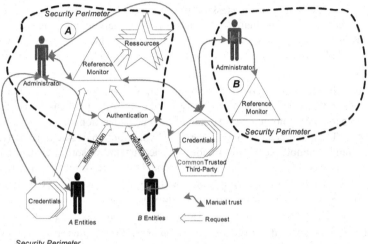

belonging to the security domain A, that wishes to access one or more protected resources in that domain. The entity first identifies itself as a known local entity of A's domain. After this initial identification, authentication is used to make sure that the entity really possesses the identity it claims to have. This authentication is usually possible because the trusted administrator of A's domain will have created an account (or related authentication material) for this entity. This usually involves manual tasks carried by the administrator to record information about the identity, which allows the system to authenticate the claimed identity. This process is known as enrolment, which is the first step of traditional authentication schemes. Enrolling new users may involve considerable work and resources: enrolment with smart tokens involves two separate activities: token programming and user management (Smith, 2001). There are already six steps needed for token programming. Once enrolment is complete, authentication normally consists of two steps: the requester claims an identity (a.k.a., identification), and the claimed identity is verified (a.k.a, verification). When the requesting entity has been authenticated, the reference monitor is consulted to find out whether that entity is allowed to access the requested resource. Again, this usually involves that, at least once in the past, the administrator manually decided that the entity is allowed access. A variant is when credentials are used directly instead of the identity. In this case, identity authentication is not needed. However, the credentials, which authorize access, still have to be manually configured at some stage, and the validity of these credentials must be verified by the reference monitor. To summarize, the access inside the security perimeter is restricted thanks to manual trust relationships set up by the administrator.

When collaboration between two e-services domains or two security perimeters (A and B in Figure 1) is required, the administrators of both domains must agree on how to merge their security domains. This can be facilitated by a common trusted third party, as illustrated by the pentagon in Figure 1, although manual tasks are still needed to associate the credentials of the third party to the entities in each domain. Due to the potential scale of the number of entities on the Internet, such an approach, where manual administrative tasks are constantly needed, would most likely overwhelm the people playing the role of administrators, or the price to pay for these administrative tasks to obtain the certification would be too high from the point of view of an individual. For example, in the e-mail domain, the cost of involving humans in security decisions concerning spam has underlined that even quick security decisions made by humans are very costly when they have to be made in a great number (Kantola, 2004).

Due to the global scale of the e-service environment shown in Figure 2, a foreign entity may have credentials from a trusted third party, but they are effectively useless because this trusted third party means nothing in the domain under consideration (that is, the domain A in our example). The authentication may be certified by the foreign trusted third party, but the reference monitor cannot take this information into account unless some translation between the two domains has been provided: this is represented by the red circle and question marks in Figure 2. Global PKI-based authentication would require a single or few commonly trusted CAs, which has not been viable on a global worldwide scale so far.

Instead of a global PKI, the main approach for identity management on the Internet has been based on decentralized creation and management of local logins and passwords. Consequently, different e-services providers have difficulty composing their services, as the same user may have set up a different login/password on the foreign provider side, or the login is already held by another user. Moreover, this lack of coordination prevents users from getting a single sign-on (SSO) experience. Federated identity management initiatives (LibertyAlliance; Microsoft) are designed to alleviate that problem. However, Microsoft has scaled down its federated identity management, called Passport (Microsoft), which seems to be an indicator that the overhead of a system-imposed federated identity management might remain too high. In addition, the Identity Gang task force (Castro & Muntz, 1999) has recently been set up to discuss whether or not the new Microsoft Identity Meta-system

Figure 2. Shortcoming of legacy security

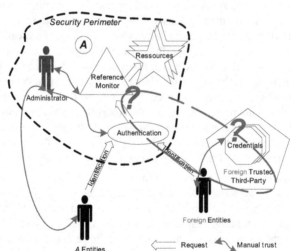

(Cameron) proposal is a sound basis for decentralized identity management. At the time of writing, the only viable solution seems to come from decentralized user-centric identity management (Seigneur, 2005a), where any user is free to choose how his or her identifiers and credentials are managed. The framework proposed in this chapter consists of such a user-centric identity management framework on top of which trust can be computed.

By trust, we do not mean the terms trust/trusted/trustworthy as they appear in the traditional computer security literature. The traditional use of these terms is not grounded in social science because they often correspond to an ill-defined and implicit element of trust. For example, the use of trusted third parties, called certification authorities (CAs), which are common in PKI infrastructures, implies that because the CA is trusted to certify crypto-graphic keys, some of this trust will be transferred to the holder of a certificate. Another example is the Trusted Computed Platform Alliance (TCPA), which makes it clear that we can speak of trust in technical components. Its goal is to create enhanced hardware by using cost-effective security hardware (more or less comparable to a smart card chip) that acts as the "root of trust." *They are trusted* means that they are assumed to make use of some (strong) security protection mechanisms. Therefore, they can/must implicitly be blindly trusted and cannot fail. This cannot address security when it is not known who or whether or not to blindly trust. On the Internet, where e-services may come and go, possibly due to market fluctuations, it is not sufficient to blindly trust a limited set of default e-services. It is necessary to be able to manage trust in newcomer e-services in spite of a lack of a priori trust, and trust management has been the first step to solve this problem.

Trust Management

The term "trust management" was first introduced in computer security by Blaze, Feigen-baum, and Lacy (1996) with the following definition: "specifying and interpreting security policies, credentials, and relationships that allows direct authorization of security-critical actions." Some of the trust management systems have been very effective in connected, ad-ministered, distributed, rather static environments; for example, Keynote (Blaze et al., 1996; Keromytis, 2004). Privileges can be delegated to nodes thanks to credentials or certificates. A chain of credentials may be created to represent the propagation of trust between nodes. Many extensions have been added, such as the possibility to negotiate credentials, and the specification of application security policies and credentials has been standardized. Thus, the policies can easily be distributed. Entities that, after identification, request the permission to carry out certain actions can do so if the compliance checker agrees, given the policy and the set of presented credentials. They differ from the previous system security approach, where trust policies are implicit, by using security credentials (or certificates) that must be held for authorization. The trust management system tries to prove that a request and a list of credentials comply with a specific policy. Others have argued that the model still relies on an implicit notion of trust because it only describes "a way of exploiting established trust relationships for distributed security policy management without determining how these relationships are formed" (Terzis, Wagealla, English, McGettrick, & Nixon, 2004). Automated trust negotiation (ATN) is proposed to improve trust management systems, such as Keynote, that all "support delegation of authority, but are not helpful for establishing trust between strangers using general-purpose credentials" (Winslett, Yu, Seamons, Hess,

Jacobson, & Jarvis, 2002). However, ATN "does not address the client's need for trust before it requests service" (Winsborough, Seamons, & Jones, 2000). Furthermore, because it is required to show credentials in order to start the collaboration, this type of system may have a bootstrapping problem when no credentials have already been obtained, or cannot be discovered, which may often be the case for new e-services. Moreover, ATN does not solve the problem when no third party is accepted as a common credential provider by both parties. This implies a need for trust formation mechanisms to establish trust from scratch between the two strangers. Credentials may be exchanged or accepted after this trust formation phase, but trust has to be present before it can be used in negotiations.

In order to be able to form trust from scratch, the use of an explicit notion of trust based on the human notion of trust has spawned a new class of trust management systems, called *evidence-based trust management*, where the level of trust is explicitly computed by a trust engine.

Computational Trust

There are many definitions of trust in a wide range of domains, as reviewed in Lo Presti, Cusack, and Booth (2003), and Terzis et al. (2004). In this chapter, we define the human notion of trust as Romano (2003) because it is a recent PhD thesis that has reviewed most previous work on trust in a very broad panel of disciplines in order to conceptually and operationally clarify the nature of trust.

Trust is a subjective assessment of another's influence in terms of the extent of one's perceptions about the quality and significance of another's impact over one's outcomes in a given situation, such that one's expectation of, openness to, and inclination toward such influence provide a sense of control over the potential outcomes of the situation. (Romano, 2003)

We call the trust in a given situation, the *trust context*. In social research, there are three main types of trust: interpersonal trust, based on past interactions with the trustee; dispositional trust, provided by the trustor's general disposition towards trust, independent of the trustee; and system trust, provided by external means such as insurance or laws (McKnight & Chervany, 2000; Rahman, 2005). Depending on the situation, a high level of trust in one of these types can become sufficient for the trustor to make the decision to trust. When there is insurance against a negative outcome, or when the legal system acts as a credible deterrent against undesirable behavior, it means that the level of system trust is high and the level of risk is negligible; therefore, the levels of interpersonal and dispositional trust are less important. It is usually assumed that by knowing the link to the real-world identity, there is insurance against harm that may be done by this entity: in essence, this is security based on authenticated identity and legal recourse. In this case, the level of system trust seems to be high, but one may argue that in practice, the legal system does not provide a credible deterrent against undesirable behavior, for example, it makes no sense to sue someone for a single spam e-mail, as the effort expended to gain redress outweighs the benefit. We have already emphasized that due to multiple jurisdictions, legal recourse on the Internet is questionable.

An interesting case might be to consider the real-world recourse mechanism as an entity, and then compute the level of trust explicitly based on the number of times the real-world recourse has successfully played its role (which is indeed evidence-based computation of the level of trust). This case brings to light that we may use the same approach for situational trust, where the current situation is approximated to previous similar situations considered as the same entity. Of course, scenarios where the level of system trust is low make inter-personal trust more important. Interpersonal trust is represented as:

a computed trust value, that is the digital representation of the trustworthiness or level of trust in the entity under consideration, that is seen as a non-enforceable estimate of the entity's future behaviour in a given context based on past evidence.

"Trust essentially is and should be based on knowledge" (Jøsang, 1996); knowledge is pro-vided by evidence. Evidence-based computational trust is a mechanism towards the prediction of behavior (Terzi, Chong, Bhargava, Pankaj, & Madria, 2003; Terzis et al., 2004).

Based on the trust value, security decisions can be made according to trust policies. For example, the resource is granted to any entities who are associated with a greater trust value than a threshold. The bootstrapping with unknown entities, strangers beyond the security perimeter, can now be carried out without a priori knowledge. The trust value can be formed after an interaction, and can be further refined during subsequent interactions. Previous direct interactions may not be obligatory if trustworthy recommenders recommend the newcomer.

Marsh's PhD thesis framework (Marsh, 1994) is one of the first computational models of trust based on social research. Each trust context is assigned an importance value in the range [0,1] and utility value in the range [-1,1]. Any trust value is in the range [-1,1]. In addition, each virtual identity is assigned a general trust value that is based on all the trust values with this virtual identity in all the trust contexts. Dispositional trust appears in the model as the basic trust value: it is the total trust values in all contexts in all virtual identities with whom the trustor has interacted so far. Risk is used in a threshold for trusting decision making.

Rahman's PhD thesis framework (Rahman, 2005) consists of a decentralized trust model based on social research. It focuses on the formation and evolution of trust values based on recommendations and direct observations, rather than the use of trust values for decision making. It is one of the reasons that no risk component is present in the framework. There are different levels of trust from very untrustworthy to very trustworthy. There are two main contexts for the trust values (Rahman, 2003): "direct," which is about the properties of the trustee; and "recommend," which is the equivalent to recommending trustworthiness. Trust contexts for direct trust values may be possible. Recommending trustworthiness is based on consistency on the "semantic distance" between the real outcomes and the recommendations that have been made. The default metric for consistency is the standard deviation based on the frequency of specific semantic distance values: the higher the consistency, the smaller the standard deviation and the higher the trust value in recommending trustworthiness. However, different rather arbitrary choices had to be made to map the consistency to trust values. In case of unknown virtual identities, the initial trust value may be based on other means, such as, related to dispositional. The "recommendation protocol" (Rahman & Hailes,

1997) is used by a trustor to find recommender chains about the trustee. The default recommendation search scheme is related to a depth-first search directed by the recommending trustworthiness of the recommenders if they do not know the subject.

Jøsang's framework (Jøsang, 1996, 2001) is called "subjective logic" and integrates the element of ignorance and uncertainty, which cannot be reflected by mere probabilities but is part of the human aspect of trust. In order to represent imperfect knowledge, an opinion is considered to be a triplet, whose elements are belief (b), disbelief (d), and uncertainty (u), such that:

$$b + d + u = 1 \qquad \{b, d, u\} \in [0,1]^3$$

The relation with trust evidence comes from the fact that an opinion about a binary event can be based on statistical evidence. Information on posterior probabilities of binary events is converted in the b, d, and u elements in a value in the range $[0,1]$. The trust value (w) in the virtual identity (S) of the virtual identity (T) concerning the trust context p is:

$$w^T_{p(S)} = \{b, d, u\}$$

The subjective logic provides more than 10 operators to combine opinions. For example, a conjunction ($\wedge$) of two opinions about two distinct propositions determines from the two opinions a new opinion reflecting the conjunctive truth of both propositions. The consensus of independent opinions is equivalent to two different virtual identities using the total of their independent direct observations to generate a new opinion. The recommendation ($\otimes$) operator corresponds to use the recommending trustworthiness (RT) to adjust his/her recommended opinion. If a recommender chain is used, Jøsang strengthens that opinion independence must be assumed, and transitivity is allowed only if the recommenders do not recommend different trust values about the same virtual identity, depending on the source of the request for recommendation. Noticeably, there is no risk component. Jøsang's approach can be used in many applications, since the trust context is open.

SECURE Trust Engine

In order to get a better understanding of a trust engine, we briefly present the SECURE trust engine. Figure 3 depicts the high-level view of the SECURE trust engine. The goal of the SECURE project (Cahill, Gray, Seigneur, Jensen, Chen, & Shand, 2003; SECURE; Seigneur, J.-M., Cahill, V., Jensen, C. D., Gray, E., & Chen, Y. ., 2004) was to achieve an advanced trust engine formally grounded and usable. The pentagonal decision-making component is called when a requested entity has to decide what action should be taken due to a request made by another entity, the requesting entity.

In order to take this decision, two subcomponents are used:

Figure 3. High-level view of the SECURE trust engine

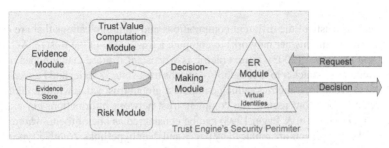

- One that can dynamically compute the trust value, that is, the trustworthiness of the requesting entity based on pieces of evidence (for example, direct observations or recommendations (Wagealla, Carbone, English, Terzis, & Nixon, 2003); by direct observations, we mean that the entity has directly interacted with the requesting entity and personally experienced the observation; another type of observation is when a third party observes an interaction between two parties and infers the type of outcome).

- A risk module that can dynamically evaluate the risk involved in the interaction (Dimmock, 2003; Dimmock, Bacon, Belokosztolszki, Eyers, Ingram, & Moody, 2004); risk evidence is also needed.

The chosen action should maintain the appropriate cost/benefit ratio (Dimmock, 2003; Dimmock et al., 2004). Depending on dispositional trust and system trust, the weight of the trust value in the final decision may be small. Dispositional trust of the owner may be reflected in the policies that are chosen by the owner of the trust engine. Risk evidence and the risk policy can be used to take into account system trust. In the background, another component is in charge of gathering evidence: recommendations, comparisons between expected outcomes of the chosen actions and real outcomes... This evidence is used to update risk and trust information. Thus, trust and risk follow a managed life-cycle (Terzis et al., 2004). A trust engine may be called a trust/risk-based security framework (TSF) due to the presence of this risk element.

The entity recognition (ER) module (Seigneur & Jensen, 2004a) deals with digital virtual identities and is in charge of dynamically recognizing them. In fact, this module is the first step to fill the gap between the notion of identities and trust, as we shall detail later in this chapter when entification is presented. We designed the ER module of the SECURE trust engine. Without this ER module, the SECURE trust engine would not address any identity or privacy attacks, but this ER module does not cover all aspects of entification as presented in this chapter. The ER module also participates in the population of risk data to be used by the risk analysis component. Information of interest corresponds to, on one hand, performance and overhead of ER schemes; on the other hand, an estimation of the security strength and threat context at the ER level.

Trust Metrics

A *trust metric* consists of the different computations and communications that are carried out by the trustor (and his/her network) to compute a trust value in the trustee. According to Twigg and Dimmock (2003), a trust metric is γ-resistant if more than γ nodes must be compromised for the attacker to successfully drive the trust value. Ziegler and Lausen (2004) discuss global group trust metrics, which compute a global trust value without taking into account personal bias, but require the complete trust network information. For example, Google's PageRank (Brin & Page, 1998) can be considered as one of them, where virtual identities and their contacts are replaced by pages and their hyperlinks. Another type of trust metric takes into account personal bias and is called local trust metric (Ziegler & Lausen, 2004). Local trust metrics have two subtypes (Ziegler & Lausen, 2004): local group metrics and local scalar metrics. The local group metrics, such as Appleseed (Ziegler & Lausen, 2004) or Levien's trust metric (Levien, 2004), return a subset of the most trustworthy peers from the point of view of the local trustor over a partial view of the trust network, given the amount of trustworthiness desired. Only Appleseed is surveyed since it appears to be more flexible with attack resistance similar to Levien's one, which in addition needs a number of virtual identities assumed to be trustworthy as an input to the trust metric. Local scalar metrics compute the trust value of a specific virtual identity from the point of view of the local trustor "tracking recommender chains from source to target" (Ziegler & Lausen, 2004). Finally, the computation may be centralized or distributed, meaning that the recommendation received is evaluated before being passed to the successor in the recommender chain.

Since some recommenders are more or less likely to produce good recommendations, even malicious ones, the notion of recommending trustworthiness has been added to advanced trust engines (Rahman & Hailes, 1997). Intuitively, recommendations must only be accepted from senders that the local entity trusts to make judgments close to those that it would have made about others. Assuming the user has a metric for measuring the accuracy of another sender's recommendations, Rahman and Hailes (1997) and Jøsang (1998) have suggested models for incorporating that information into the local trust computation. In many cases, the final trust value, which is used locally, may be different than the recommended one. For example, a recommender with trust value of 0.6 on a [0,1] scale giving a recommendation of 0.8 provides the adjusted trust value:

$$0.6 \times 0.8 = 0.48$$

However, different trust value formats are possible, and some formats are more suitable for evidence-based trust than others. For example, the previous format, a value on a [0,1] scale, may be intuitive for humans in order for them to manually set a value, but it does not give enough detail on the evidence used to choose this value. It is the reason that the standard SECURE trust value format (Nielsen, Carbone, & Krukow, 2004a) is a tree of (s,i,c)-triples, corresponding to a mathematical event structure (Nielsen, Carbone, & Krukow, 2004b; Nielsen, Plotkin, & Winskel, 1981): an event outcome count is represented as a (s,i,c)-triple, where s is the number of events that supports the outcome, i is the number of events that has no information or are inconclusive about the outcome, and c is the number of events that contradicts the expected outcome. This format takes into account the element of uncertainty via *i*.

To summarize this section, challenges to legacy approaches for computer security arise because the assumptions of the availability of mutually-trusted third parties may not be viable. Trust engines have been researched to facilitate the number of decisions that users have to take in large decentralized environments with user-centric identity management, which is the current viable approach for e-services on the Internet. Another advantage of trust engines is that trust can be built from scratch without the need of system trust and a priori knowledge–strangers beyond the security perimeter can slowly be granted more resources: interaction after interaction their trustworthiness is formed. An example of advanced trust engine is SECURE, and the ER module is crucial to bridge the gap between identity and trust.

Identity and Trust Framework Survey

In the previous section, when the ER module of the SECURE is presented, we mention that this module is only the first step to fill the gap between identity and trust. In order to clarify why we mention the presence of such a gap in previous work, this section presents a survey of previous frameworks dealing with identity and trust. This survey starts by frameworks that cannot be categorized as evidence-based trust management that rely on a clear count of observed evidence. For example, when users manually indicate a trust value of 82%, it is difficult to know why, because no clear count of pieces of evidence is provided. Then, we cover evidence-based trust management frameworks that rely on a clear count of pieces of evidence.

Identity and Trust in Frameworks without a Clear Count of Pieces of Evidence

First, we present how trust has been combined with identity and authentication in recent widespread frameworks supported by Java and the IETF. Then, we look at trust and identity in credential-based frameworks and ubiquitous computing frameworks. Finally, we present how identity has been dealt with in frameworks where users form social networks and manually set trust levels.

Java and IETF Approaches to Identity and Trust

The first two frameworks that we survey can be categorized as adaptable authentication and authorization frameworks, especially because they are based on standards describing how to plug different authentication schemes. Java Authentication and Authorization Service (JAAS) (Lai, Gong, Koved, Nadalin, & Schemers, 1999) is a framework and programming interface that enforces, in the Java platform, access control based on the identity of the user who runs the Java application code. The extensible authentication protocol (EAP) (Aboba, blunk, Vollbrecht, Carlson, & Levkowetz, 2004) is a peer-to-peer (P2P) authentication framework (described in an IETF RFC) that supports multiple authentication methods and takes into account their security strength according to a list of attacks at the authentication level and a static risk analysis. It underlines the first main category of attacks at the identity level, that is, the identity usurpation attacks. Usurpation attacks are more or less easy to be successfully carried out depending on the authentication scheme used. To have a static evaluation of the security strength of the authentication schemes is only a first step towards dynamic evidence-based trust management based on a clear count of pieces of evidence.

Credentials-Based Approaches to Identity and Trust

The next three frameworks are credentials-based authentication and authorization frameworks. The first one is the very influential identity-based framework, PGP (Zimmerman, 1995), which uses a web of trust to estimate the link between a user real-world identity and a public key. (Lampson, Abadi, Burrows, & Wobber, 1992; Wobber, Abadi, Burrows, & Lampson, 1994) use "speaks for" relations for a large panel of types of virtual identities (for example, even communication channels or roles). Their application programming interface (API) is depicted:

void send(Address dest, VirtualIdentity vI, Message m)

Channel getChannel(Address dest)

SubChannel getSubChannel(Channel c, VirtualIdentity vI)

VirtualIdentity getVirtualIdentity(SubChannel subC)

boolean grantAccess(ACL acl, VirtualIdentity vI)

Credential sign(Credential cred, VirtualIdentity vI)

The third advanced credentials-based framework is ATN (Winslett et al., 2002). In addition to what has been said, another interesting element of this framework is that it takes into account the privacy aspect of credentials released thanks to negotiation. In all these three credentials-based frameworks, there is no computation of the trustworthiness of the virtual identity itself based on a count of the actions carried out by this virtual identity.

Approaches to Identity and Trust in Ubiquitous Computing Frameworks

The survey continues with two ubiquitous computing frameworks. Al-Muhtadi, Anand, Mickunas, and Campbell's (2000) framework tackles the security issues, in a home equipped with enhanced computing appliances, thanks to the plug and play technology, based on Java, called Java Intelligent Network Infrastructure (JINI), and the Kerberos authentication framework (Kohl & Neuman, 1993). It provides a mechanism to authenticate and share temporary secret keys between cooperating processes. The second ubiquitous computing framework is Gaia. The environment of Gaia (Campbell, Al-Muhtadi, Naldurg, Sampermane, & Mickunas, 2002) goes beyond the previous environment of a single home, for example, a whole campus is enhanced thanks to ubiquitous computing. However, there is still the assumption that a managed infrastructure is present to provide these ubiquitous e-services, and that technology-aware and dedicated administrators manage this infrastructure. So, it is not yet Weiser's vision of calm ubiquitous computing (Weiser & Brown, 1996), where users are not interrupted by decision making due to computers. An interesting point is that the administrator must statistically set the "confidence" in the security protection given by the different possible authentication schemes. For example, active badge authentication is given 0.6 on a [0,1] scale. Depending on how many authentication means the user uses to authenticate his/her pseudonym, the final confidence p_n increases or decreases according to the following formula, where n authentication schemes are used and p_i is the confidence of a successfully passed authentication scheme:

$$p_{final} = 1 - (1-p_1) \ldots (1-p_n)$$

Another innovative element is to use this final confidence and other context information in the rules used for authorization decisions.

Approaches to Identity and Trust in E-Services Using Social Networks and Users' Ratings

The next related frameworks are based on real-world social networks, where users set manual trust values to other users. None of the frameworks explain how the manual trust value could be converted into a trust value based on a clear count of pieces of evidence.

For example, the friend-of-a-friend (FOAF) initiative can be described as a textual format for the online description of the profile of a user (identity, name, contact information, interests...), and links to the profiles of users that he/she knows. Generally, social networks bring interesting properties, since they exhibit the "small-world" phenomena (Gray, Seigneur, Chen, & Jensen, 2003; Travers & Milgram, 1969; Watts, Sheridan, & Newman, 2002), whereby the diameter (meaning the greatest number of hops between any two users) of the network increases logarithmically with the network size, and users can be reached in few hops. Milgram's experiment (Travers & Milgram, 1969), which ended up in the small-world theory or at maximum six degrees of separation between any two persons in the world, is wellknown.

In Golbeck's framework (Golbeck & Hendler, 2004a; Golbeck & Parsia, 2004), the FOAF schema has been extended to include "trust assertions," that is, manual trust values in the individuals targeted by these assertions. They use their network for a kind of antispam tool, called TrustMail, that is not supposed to be a spam filter but a layer used to "provide higher ratings to emails that come from non-spam senders" (Golbeck & Hendler, 2004b). E-mails from known, trustworthy senders are given higher priority in the user's inbox, whereas e-mails from unknown or disreputable senders are given lower priorities. E-mail senders are given a manual trust value in the range [1,10]; with 1 meaning that the recipient has little or no trust in the sender and 10 meaning that the recipient trusts the sender maximally.

In case an e-mail is received from an unknown sender, the recipient attempts to infer the equivalent of a manual trust value for the sender based on recommender chains starting with the recipient's known contacts. Using a breadth-first search in the whole network stored on the TrustMail centralized server, a path from the recipient to the sender is searched for, and manual trust values on the path are combined. Golbeck and Parsia (2004) notice that there are different layers of trust: "a security measure builds trust about the authenticity of data contained in the network, but does not describe trust between people in the network." The overall level of trust is the result of how much trust is found at each layer. However, they do not take into account trust about authenticity that we include in our entification section by means of *technical trust*.

In Ziegler and Lausen's (2004) trust metric, called Appleseed, the manual trust value ranges from 0 (lack of trust) to 1 (blind trust). Recommending trustworthiness does not explicitly appear, but it is reflected in the choice of the "spreading factor" (Ziegler & Lausen, 2004), which is recommended to be set to *0.85* and "may also be seen as the ratio between direct trust [...] and trust in the ability [...] to recommend others as trustworthy peers." Appleseed's spreading factor highlights that trustworthiness gained by a virtual identity may be passed to another virtual identity. However, this factor is not set by the recommender but by the computing trustor, and is similar for all virtual identities in the network. In fact, Appleseed is a local centralized group metric according to Ziegler and Lausen's (2004) taxonomy. They evaluate their work by simulations based on real social networks extracted from an online community Web site, and assume that all users make their manual trust values publicly available. This constitutes a threat to privacy, since a clear view of the network of acquaintances can be obtained, and one requirement of entification is to protect the user's privacy.

Evidence-Based Computational Trust with a Clear Count of Pieces of Evidence

As far as we know and at time of writing, the main frameworks that have tackled identity and trust based on a clear count of evidence are reviewed next. In addition to the identity usurpation attacks that we have introduced, this subsection also underlines other privacy issues and attacks on evidence-based trust engines due to the identity layer. Finally, this section discusses how P2P and social networks have been used to scale to the growing amount of evidence needed for trust and identity.

In Beth, Borcherding, and Klein's (1994) and Yahalom, Klein, and Beth's (1993) framework, entities communicate via channels, and have a unique identifier and a shared secret that can be used for authentication. Some of these entities are supposed to have the role of authentication servers. Each virtual identity is assigned several trust values based on probabilities, which are computed from a number of counters in different trust contexts. These counters are incremented or decremented each time there is an action and its associated outcome (positive or negative) related to the trust context.

One of Jøsang's applications of his subjective logic (1998, 2001) is especially relevant to this chapter focusing on trust and identity, since it deals with authentication using public keys in open environments. Jøsang argues that most of the previous related work based on trust values does not take into account the binding between the real-world identity and the public key and/or the element of uncertainty. Although recommender chains are possible, we only give the formula that he proposes to compute the trustworthiness of the binding between the real-world identity (*S*) and the public key based on a recommendation from a trustworthy recommender (*R*):

$$w^T_{Binding(S)} = \left(w^T_{BindingRT(R)} \wedge w^T_{Binding(R)}\right) \otimes w^R_{Binding(S)}$$

In the case of a recommender chain, a recommendation must specify the recommending trustworthiness and the binding trustworthiness. Only direct observations must be passed in order to avoid opinion dependence due to the overcounting of evidence. In case of multiple recommender chains, the consensus operator should be used.

Identity Multiplicity Attacks

Twigg and Dimmock (2003) explain that the consensus operator, which combines the opinions as if they were observed independently, allows the trust metric to be driven to a trust value chosen by an attacker due to an identity multiplicity attack. Douceur (2002) argues that in large scale networks where a centralized identity authority cannot be used to control the creation of virtual identities, a powerful real-world entity may create as many virtual identities as it wishes, and in doing so, challenge the use of a majority vote and flaw trust metrics. Sybil attack is the name given by Douceur to this type of attack. This is especially important in scenarios where the possibility to use many pseudonyms is facilitated and provided by the trust engine. In fact, a sole real-world entity can create many pseudonyms who blindly recommend one of these pseudonyms in order to fool the trust engine. The level of trust in the latter virtual identity increases and eventually passes above a threshold, which makes the decision to trust (the semantics of this depend on the application).

In Kinateder and Rothermel's (2003) framework, the trust value can be contextualized to the "trust category" (trust context) of concern of the current request (for example, with regard to book security expertise). Their recommendations can be considered as trust values contextualized to a particular trust context. A view rarely discussed in other frameworks, which is also argued in this chapter, is that "trust categories are not strictly independent but they are influencing each other" (Kinateder & Rothermel, 2003). Kinateder and Rothermel's (2003) framework is still prone to Douceur's Sybil attack, since a real-world identity could create an arbitrarily large number of faked virtual identities, then copy recommendations from recommenders with high trust values and present these as recommendations from the just created faked virtual identities. Their workarounds (Kinateder & Siani, 2003) involve system trust and are twofold. Firstly, some of the risks of pseudonymity are alleviated via TCPA-trusted hardware, including a trusted CA that would certify the pseudonym without disclosing the real-world identity until legal bodies want to retrieve the link. Secondly, the trust engine should be combined with electronic payment systems that allow the creation of an originality statement during the payment process that can be included in a recommendation. However, relying on real money turns the trust mechanism into a type of system trust that is high enough to make the use of interpersonal trust (that is, the trust value) almost superfluous. In the real world, tax authorities are likely to require traceability of money transfers, which would completely break privacy in a money-based system. Trusted third parties are likely to be needed if real-world identities must be bound to the keys, if trusted hardware is needed or when they introduce payment.

Further Privacy Aspects in Identity and Computational Trust Frameworks

Another view, taken in Kinateder and Rothermel's (2003) framework that has also been overlooked by other frameworks, is that privacy is generally required and users must be allowed to use virtual identities to minimize the risk of profiling based on the history of their transactions, which constitute the pieces of evidence required to compute their trust value. However, in Kinateder and in contrast to entification, one virtual identity should be used per trust context. Their approach works fine within their infrastructure, where management tools are provided, but they do not explain how authentication schemes different from key pairs would fit into their framework. There is no risk analysis in their trust model, especially with regard to the technical trustworthiness of their mechanism.

Sierra is the implementation of the OpenPrivacy computational trust management framework (Burton, 2002; OpenPrivacy, 2001). Sierra is composed of the "Nym Manager," which creates, manages, and authenticates the pseudonymous certificates; the "Reputation," which is signed by the current local virtual identity and used as recommendation or observation; the "Reputation Calculation Engine (RCE)," which implements the trust metric, computes, and maintains Reputations; the "Query" package to query and index data; the "Communication" interface for transparent communication with peers (the type of P2P network can be plugged with this interface); and the "Storage Manager." Any trust metric could be used as long as there is an RCE implementation of the trust metric. Noticeably, there is no risk component in their framework. The "Nym Manager" has many interesting features, although it is limited to public keys for authentication. According to the trust context, different virtual identities can be used. It is possible that a parent virtual identity generates different child virtual identities (Labalme & Burton, 2001). It is not clear how they would implement the automatic selection of the appropriate virtual identity according to the current context. Generally, the specifics of their framework are left undefined. They underline that long-lived virtual identities are preferable in order to be granted interactions requiring a great trust value. In entification, we introduce how to combine trust values of different virtual identities once a link has been proven between them. The final contribution of their framework is in the use of certificates of recommendations, called "gifts" (Burton, 2002), carried by the trustee. It is useful in scenarios where the recommender might become unreachable. It is supposed to work in a fully decentralized manner (but this will depend on the communication type chosen and the trust metrics).

P2P and Social Networks to Scale to the Growing Identity and Trust Evidence

The last type of frameworks covered are ones based on decentralised P2P techniques (Despotovic & Aberer, 2004b; Milojicic, Kalogeraki, Lukose, Nagaraja, Pruyne, & Richard, 2002) to deal with the increased amount of evidence. These frameworks can be built based on two P2P approaches. First, there are unstructured networks, where no index information is maintained, messages with search information, such as, time-to-live (TTL), message identifier or list of already contacted peers, flood the network. Their performance is roughly (Despotovic & Aberer, 2004a) search latency; storage and update costs low; good resilience to failures; and high messages bandwidth. Secondly, there are structured networks, where index information is distributed and maintained among the peers according to different solutions (for example, based on a distributed hash table or a binary search tree). Their performance is roughly (Despotovic & Aberer, 2004a) a logarithmic search but higher storage and update costs (for example, due to routing tables or replication). From a privacy point of view, the second approach is likely to imply that trust evidence of a user would be maintained by other users, who cannot be chosen by the user. When the network consists of a social network (as in these listed frameworks), a variant of the first P2P approach can be used. Thanks to the assumed small-world properties of the social network, the search may be optimized by directing the search according to properties of the target of the search and properties of the direct peers (Gray et al., 2003). For example, if an e-mail about movies has been sent by a previously unknown sender, the search for information about the sender would start with the contacts that are known to have an interest in movies. In this section, three peer-to-peer frameworks with adjunct computational trust are surveyed.

Damiani et al. (Damiani, Vimercati, Paraboschi, & Samarati, 2004) add a computational trust metric on top of a P2P unstructured network. The searching follows Gnutella's flooding technique (Frankel & Pepper, 2000), which consists of sending an identified search request message to a number of direct contacts with a TTL. Their first application domain is file sharing. The trust metric is used to choose the most-trustworthy peer among the peers who claim to have the sought-after file. In order to minimize the risk of Sybil attack, recommendations coming from a clique of IP addresses are discarded. Similarly, a number of recommenders are recontacted to check that they really meant the recommendation, and it is supposed to increase the cost of running faked virtual identities by the same real-world identity. The second application Damiani et al. (2004) reuses is their Gnutella-based computational trust to fight spam in e-mail settings. In order to protect the privacy of the users of a mail server, only the mail servers are considered to be peer in the unstructured network. The mail server aggregates direct observations of its e-mail users about spam e-mails. Since it is common that spam e-mails are slightly modified, a fuzzy hash mechanism is used to give the same hash for slightly different spam e-mails. The peers send an updated collection of hashes of spam e-mails, without reference to the involved e-mail users, to another type of peer, called super-peers. The super-peers maintain a distributed collection of spam hashes, and peers can query information about unknown e-mails. The result of the query is a number of recommendations that are used to compute the final trust value based on the recommenders trustworthiness and a trust metric, whose choice is left to the future users. However, there is no comprehensive generic identity layer in Damiani et al.'s (2004) frameworks.

The frameworks survey in this section underlines that to scale to evidence generated for trust and identity seems feasible thanks to P2P and social networks. However, this section also brings to light that there is no thorough integration of identity and evidence-based trust: legacy frameworks with a comprehensive identity layer where many authentication schemes can be used do not rely on evidence-based trust, and evidence-based trust frameworks do not comprehensively integrate user-centric identity management. In the next section, we describe the *entification* framework, which fills this gap between identity and computational trust.

Entification:
Safe User-Centric Identity and Trust Management

In this section, we present the entification framework, which is our contribution, and illustrate it in two application domains, namely, message antispam, and ubiquitous payment by means of e-services.

To entify, according to Merriam-Webster's online thesaurus, means to reify: "to regard something abstract as a material or concrete thing." Derived from entify, we introduce the term entification to allow us to regard a set of pieces of evidence as an entity on its own. Two main aspects have to be taken into account to compute the overall trust value of an entity defined by entification.

Beyond Static Isolated Technical Trust:
An Example at the Authentication Level

First, the technical trust must be computed. By technical trust, we mean that we explicitly take into account that different authentication schemes are more or less difficult to compromise. To obtain technical trust, we follow the ER process (Seigneur & Jensen, 2004a), for example, the process is carried out in the ER module of the SECURE trust engine:

1. **Triggering** of the recognition mechanism, for example, a user tries to log in to an e-service;

2. **Detective work** to recognize (initially distinguish) the entity using the available recognition scheme(s) and recognition clues; this provides the level of confidence (or technical trust) in recognition, which may be more fine grained than the binary yes or no decision in traditional authentication;

3. **Discriminative retention** of information relevant for possible recall or improved future recognition; this is the equivalent of enrolment and constitutes another main difference with authentication because it is moved down in the process;

4. **Upper-level action** based on the outcome of recognition, which includes technical trust; this constitutes a final main difference with authentication because the authentication result may not be binary.

As in the Gaia framework (surveyed previously), a level of confidence may be associated to the authentication scheme used. Instead of the static choice of a level of trust for a specific ER scheme, the ER scheme can be considered as an entity, and a trust value is explicitly computed based on direct observations and recommendations. For example, in a message-based e-service (e.g., e-mail or blog comments), in order to avoid spoofing of senders and spam (Seigneur, Cahill, Jensen, Gray, & Chen, 2004; Seigneur, Gray, & Jensen, 2005), we introduce a level of confidence in recognition, called *lcr*, with two components with regard to the technical trust of the ER scheme used to send messages (or post blog comments): one

Figure 4. lcr Event structure example (A → B means that event A is necessary for event B. We use the following representation: {eventname}:(s,i,c), *which corresponds to a standard SECURE triple).*

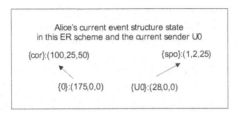

that is global to all senders and one that is related to the current sender. We use the SECURE trust value format with the event structure depicted in Figure 4. The event 0 is triggered each time the ER scheme is used, that is, if Bob or another sender sends a message, the counter is incremented. The event U0 is triggered each time the ER scheme is used for a specific sender, for example Bob. There is an event, called *cor*, that records that the ER outcome has been confirmed correct by a human. The confirmation can be implicit, for example, no complaint about a previously sent message and a potential sender's identity usurpation by a spammer is made after a timeout. Another event, called *spo*, records that this sender has been spoofed with this type of ER scheme. In Figure 4, this ER scheme has been used 175 times so far and 100 recognitions were confirmed right by Alice (the receiver), *25* messages have not been read by Alice yet, and 50 spoofings occurred due to this scheme. Then for the current sender, called Bob, Bob has been recognized 28 times by this ER scheme. Bob sent 25 e-mails that were correct, two unread messages from Bob have recently been received, and Bob has been spoofed one time with this ER scheme.

The final *lcr* consists of:

$$lcr = \frac{s_{cor}}{s_{cor} + i_{cor} + c_{cor}} \times \frac{c_{spo}}{s_{spo} + i_{spo} + c_{spo}}$$

The use of i_{cor} should become negligible over time compared to s and c because messages do not stay a very long time without human inspection: a user is likely to check his/her messages each week. However, this value can also be useful to detect denial-of-service attacks. Ideally, *cor* values should be global, which means that users should make their results regarding an ER scheme's strength publicly available. This can be done by recommendations distributed via the trust engines. In doing so, we obtain a dynamic evaluation of the technical trust of the ER schemes used. The trust engine manages at least two trust contexts: the trust value of the ER scheme, and the trust value of the interacting virtual identities.

Second, *fusionym* (Seigneur et al., 2005) is when two or more pseudonyms are linked together, so that they can be regarded as one pseudonym whose overall trust value is calculated based on the pieces of evidence of each composing pseudonym. A piece of evidence *ev* may be any statement about some entity(ies), especially: a transaction *tr*, a direct observation *obs* (i.e., evaluated outcome of a transaction (Jonker & Treur, 1999)), or a recommendation *rec*. The *link* (Seigneur & Jensen, 2004b) mechanism can be used to link different virtual identities if there is evidence that the virtual identities correspond to the same real-world identity. The linkage can be more or less strong. For example, if two e-mails are signed by the same public key, we generally assume that the linkage is stronger than if the e-mail only contains the same sender textual address, which is easy to spoof. Thus, we provide a mechanism that can link *n* pieces of evidence ev_i for $i=1,...,n$ and represented by:

$$link(ev_1, ev_2,...,ev_n)$$

From a privacy protection point of view, we argue for the use of multiple virtual identities, acting as pseudonyms, as a first technological line of defense. In Kobsa and Schreck's classification (2003), transaction pseudonyms (such as a pseudonym used for only one transaction), and anonymity cannot be effectively used because they do not allow linkability between transactions as required when building trust. Pseudonyms appear to be the appropriate solution for protecting privacy in trust-based systems and achieving some level of privacy and trust.

The minimum requirement is a local reference for the formation of trust, which is in turn managed by other components in the trust engine. According to the privacy protection principle of "collection limitation" (Langheinrich, 2001), data collection should be strictly restricted to mandatory required data for the purpose of the collection. Since trustworthiness estimation accuracy increases as information increases, it is not inbuilt for trust engines to minimize collection of personal information. Our requirement is to establish the trustworthiness of entities and not their real-world identity. This is why pseudonymity, the level of indirection between trust and the real-world entity, is sufficient. Giving users the option to conceal their identities seems a viable way to alleviate users' privacy concerns, whilst preserving the benefits of trusted interactions.

Although trust allows us to accept risk and engage in actions with potentially harmful outcome, a computational trust engine must take into account that humans need (or have the right to) privacy (Cooley, 1888; Maslow, 1954). However, depending on what benefits can be reaped through trustworthiness, people may be willing to trade part of their privacy for increased trustworthiness: hence, contextual privacy/trust trade is needed. Due to the division of trust evidence between many pseudonyms, it takes more time for the entities behind these pseudonyms to reach the same trustworthiness than for a unique virtual identity. Privacy expectations of a user vary across time and depend on contexts (Brunk, 2002). For example, users can get benefits from the knowledge of profiles, preferences, and identity information thanks to customized services (Kobsa & Schreck, 2003). Depending on what they can get, they may be willing to divulge some of their private data. Therefore, we introduce a model for privacy/trust trade based on linkability of pieces of evidence (Seigneur & Jensen, 2004b). If insufficient evidence is available under the chosen pseudonym, more evidence may be linked to this pseudonym in order to improve trustworthiness and grant the request. Based on the utility of the request, a threshold should be set concerning the acceptable evidence that should be disclosed.

Ubiquitous E-Services Example of Privacy/Trust Trade by Linkage

As an example, the following figure depicts the scenario where Alice plans to spend her holidays in SunnyVillage in a world where ubiquitous e-services are available. The dashed black arrow represents Alice flying to her holiday's location. The ovals indicate the different geographical regions covered by Alice's different public keys. The lines connecting the different symbols (for example, the blue line between hotel and baker) represent trust relationships, and indicate that recommendations are exchanged between the entities depicted by the symbols. Normally, Alice works and lives in RainyTown. She will take the plane and relax for 2 weeks in this village where she has never been, but that some of her friends recommended. She will have to pay to enjoy some of her leisure activities, which could be enhanced if collaboration with other local entities is allowed. We assume that Alice uses an e-purse. So, an e-purse is associated with public key (*Pub*)/private key (*Pri*) pairs: a public key becoming a pseudonym for Alice. An e-purse has also an embedded trust engine that takes care of trust decision-making and management. Similarly, a vendor's cashier-machine can be recognized with a public key and runs a trust engine. For example, exchange of Alice's trustworthiness in being a good payer in the neighbourhood would let her rent a large video display without being asked for real-world credentials (for example, a passport that she has forgotten at the hotel); credit may also become viable. Vendors would also benefit from computational trust adjunct. The video shop of SunnyVillage, having to deal with passing customers, would be reassured to take a lower risk if payment with electronic coins is combined with the level of trust in the customer. Nevertheless, Alice also wishes to protect her privacy and have different social profiles in different places. Alice has

Figure 5. Alice's smart world

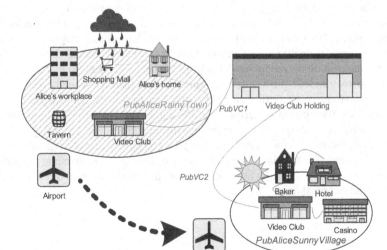

indeed two pseudonyms automatically selected according to location: one in RainyTown (*PubAliceRainyTown*) and one in SunnyVillage (*PubAliceSunnyVillage*). This offers better protection for her privacy than having one pseudonym. Even though the video club holding spans both domains, SunnyVillage's video club cannot obviously link *PubAliceRainyTown* and *PubAliceSunnyVillage* by comparing keys known by RainyTown's video club. The latter would not be true with a unique public key for Alice's e-purse.

Let us assume that the trustworthiness of people for being good payers is managed by the trust engine of the vendor's cashier-machine. Recalling the scenario in Figure 5, if Alice arrives in SunnyVillage's video club for the first time, her e-purse will exhibit *PubAlice-SunnyVillage* when she wants to pay for the large video display that she wants to rent. Since no direct observation, that is, a previous experience with *PubAliceSunnyVillage*, is available, *PubVC2* (the SunnyVillage video club cashier's public key) will ask for recommendations from its neighbours (for example, *PubBaker*). However, Alice's trust obtained through recommendations is not enough to commit the renting transaction because she has made too few transactions in SunnyVillage and cannot present her passport left at the hotel. Alice really wants the display, so she is now disposed to give up some of her privacy in order to exhibit enough trust. In fact, SunnyVillage's video club is held by a holding of video clubs that has a video club in RainyTown. The following example of contextual privacy/trust trade is started. The list of public keys owned by the holding is sent to Alice's e-purse, which finds that *PubVC1* of RainyTown's video club is a known virtual identity. Alice has noticed that she could link *PubAliceRainyTown* and *PubAliceSunnyVillage* in order to reach the necessary level of trust. Although Alice now knows that what she has done in RainyTown is potentially exposed to both areas, that is, RainyTown and SunnyVillage, she agrees to present herself as the owner of both keys/pseudonyms.

We emphasize that care should be taken when assessing linked evidence on multiple virtual identities: the main requirement is to avoid overcounting overlapping trust pieces of evidence. Safe fusionym is possible concerning direct observations and trust values based on the count of event outcomes (Seigneur et al., 2005). Due to the possibility of self-recommendations and attacks due to identity multiplicity, fusionym is more difficult when recommendations are used. The technique of *trust transfer* (Seigneur et al., 2005) mitigates these fusionym issues due to self-recommendations and identity multiplicity attacks, such as the Sybil attack. Trust transfer implies that recommendations cause trust on the trustor side to be transferred from the recommender to the subject of the recommendation. A second effect is that the trust on the recommender side for the subject is reduced by the amount of transferred trustworthiness. If it is a self-recommendation, then the second effect is moot, as it does not make sense for a real-world entity to reduce trust in his/her own pseudonyms. Trust transfer is still limited to scenarios where the number of interactions is important and transferring trust does not significantly undermine the recommenders. According to Ziegler and Lausen's (2004) trust metric classification, the trust transfer metric corresponds to a new type: a local decentralized scalar metric. The other main attacks occurring at the identity level based on identity usurpation are alleviated by the use of the level of confidence in recognition and technical trust.

Conclusion

To fill the gap between identities and their level of trust is one of the eight "major issues" (Damiani, Vimercati, & Samarati, 2003) in developing identity management for the next generation of distributed applications and use of e-services.

We propose a solution, called entification, based on the consumer's ability to create and manage multiple virtual identities (pseudonyms) and present different identities in different contexts, thereby limiting the ability to link transactions and users. Our approach corresponds to a user-centric identity management solution. Virtual identities are created by the customer alone, and the customer alone decides whether to reveal that two virtual identities belong to the same customer. This is also a solution for the identity composition issue (Damiani et al., 2003) that goes beyond traditional sequential identity lifecycles based on creation, use, and deletion of identities. Virtual identity management is used to allow the customer to decide which identity should be used in a specific context (Seigneur & Jensen, 2004b, 2004c), as well as to entify a new virtual identity when required. Evidence is linked along the time to form identities according to the user's will.

In the ER process, the enrolment phase is postponed. In doing so, more dynamic interactions are possible, but they may be less secure. The link with the real-world identity may be absent, but recognition is sufficient to build trust in a virtual identity based on pieces of evidence. The link with the real-world identity may bring greater system trust, but this is not mandatory. The fact that the link is not mandatory enhances the privacy of the users in the system. Furthermore, users may use multiple virtual identities, thus further enhancing the protection of their privacy. However, depending on the benefits that can be reaped through trustworthiness, people may be willing to trade part of their privacy to increase their trustworthiness: hence, we introduce a model for privacy/trust trade based on linkability of pieces of evidence.

It is difficult to safely assess linked evidence about multiple virtual identities because there might be overcounting of overlapping trust pieces of evidence. There is less risk with direct observations and trust values based on the count of event outcomes. Due to the possibility of self-recommendations and attacks due to identity multiplicity, it is more difficult when recommendations are used. Theoretically, the main attacks occurring at the identity level, based on identity usurpation, are alleviated by the use of the level of confidence in recognition and technical trust. The technique of trust transfer mitigates some of the issues due to self-recommendations and identity multiplicity attacks, such as the Sybil attack.

Future Trends

Practically, further work is needed to improve the attack resistance of e-services in the presence of entification, which will be the case if user-centric identity management becomes a popular approach for identity management in e-services.

References

Aboba, B., Blunk, L., Vollbrecht, J., Carlson, J., & Levkowetz, H. (2004). *Extensible authentication protocol (EAP)* (RFC 3748). Network Working Group.

Al-Muhtadi, J., Anand, M., Mickunas, M. D., & Campbell, R. (2000). *Secure smart homes using Jini and UIUC SESAME.*

Beth, T., Borcherding, M., & Klein, B. (1994). Valuation of trust in open networks. In *Proceedings of the 3rd European Symposium on Research in Computer Security.*

Blaze, M., Feigenbaum, J., & Lacy, J. (1996). Decentralized trust management In *Proceedings of the 17th IEEE Symposium on Security and Privacy* (pp. 164-173). IEEE Computer Society.

Brin, S., & Page, L. (1998). The anatomy of a large-scale hypertextual Web search engine. *Computer Networks, 30*(1-7).

Brunk, B. D. (2002). Understanding the privacy space. In *First Monday*. Chicago: Library of the University of Illinois.

Burton, K. A. (2002). *Design of the OpenPrivacy distributed reputation system: OpenPrivacy.org*. Retrieved from http://openprivacy.org

Cahill, V., Gray, E., Seigneur, J.-M., Jensen, C., Chen, Y., & Shand, B. (2003, July-September). Using trust for secure collaboration in uncertain environments. *Pervasive Computing, 2*(3), 52-61.

Cameron, K. *Microsoft's vision for an identity metasystem*. Retrieved November 29, 2005, from http://www.identityblog.com/stories/2005/07/05/IdentityMetasystem.htm

Campbell, R., Al-Muhtadi, J., Naldurg, P., Sampermane, G., & Mickunas, M. D. (2002, November 8). Towards security and privacy for pervasive computing. In *Proceedings of the International Symposium on Software Security*, Keio University, Tokyo, Japan.

Castro, P., & Muntz, R. (1999). Using context to assist in multimedia object retrieval. In *ACM Workshop on Multimedia Intelligent Storage and Retrieval Management*, Orlando, FL.

Cooley, T. M. (1888). *A treatise on the law of torts* (2nd ed.). Chicago: Callaghan.

Damiani, E., Vimercati, S. D. C. d., Paraboschi, S., & Samarati, P. (2003). Managing and sharing servants' reputations in P2P systems. In *Transactions on knowledge and data engineering* (pp. 840-854). IEEE.

Damiani, E., Vimercati, S. D. C. d., Paraboschi, S., & Samarati, P. (2004). P2P-based collaborative spam detection and filtering. In *Proceedings of the Fourth International Conference on Peer-to-Peer Computing (P2P'04).*

Damiani, E., Vimercati, S. D. C. d., & Samarati, P. (2003). Managing multiple and dependable identities. *IEEE Internet Computing, 7*(6), 29-37.

Despotovic, Z., & Aberer, K. (2004a). Maximum likelihood estimation of peers' performance in P2P networks. In *Proceedings of the Second Workshop on the Economics of Peer-to-Peer Systems.*

Despotovic, Z., & Aberer, K. (2004b). *Trust and reputation management in P2P networks.* CEC.

Dimmock, N. (2003). How much is 'enough'? Risk in trust-based access control. In *Proceedings of IEEE International Workshops on Enabling Technologies: Infrastructure for Collaborative Enterprises: Enterprise Security* (Special Session on Trust Management) (pp. 281-282).

Dimmock, N., Bacon, J., Belokosztolszki, A., Eyers, D., Ingram, D., & Moody, K. (2004). *Preliminary definition of a trust-based access control model.* SECURE Deliverable 3.2.

Douceur, J. R. (2002). The Sybil attack. In *Proceedings of the 1ˢᵗ International Workshop on Peer-to-Peer Systems.*

eBay. (n.d.). *Feedback Forum.* Retrieved November 29, 2005, from http://pages.ebay.com/services/forum/feedback.html

FOAF. *The Friend-of-a-Friend Project.* Retrieved April 8, 2006, from http://www.foaf-project.org/

Frankel, J., & Pepper, T. (2000). *Gnutella.* Nullsoft.

Golbeck, J., & Hendler, J. (2004a). *Accuracy of metrics for inferring trust and reputation in semantic Web-based social networks.*

Golbeck, J., & Hendler, J. (2004b). Reputation network analysis for email filtering. In *Proceedings of the First Conference on Email and Anti-Spam (CEAS).*

Golbeck, J., & Parsia, B. (2004). Trusting claims from trusted sources: Trust network based filtering of aggregated claims. In *Proceedings of the 3ʳᵈ International Semantic Web Conference (ISWC2004).*

Gollmann, D. (1999). *Computer security.* John Wiley & Sons.

Gray, E., Seigneur, J.-M., Chen, Y., & Jensen, C. D. (2003). Trust propagation in small worlds. In *Proceedings of the First International Conference on Trust Management* (LNCS 2693). Springer-Verlag.

Jonker, C. M., & Treur, J. (1999). Formal analysis of models for the dynamics of trust based on experiences. In *Proceedings of the 9ᵗʰ European Workshop on Modelling Autonomous Agents in a Multi-Agent World.* Multi-Agent System Engineering.

Jøsang, A. (1996). The right type of trust for distributed systems. In *Proceedings of the 1996 New Security Paradigms Workshop.* ACM.

Jøsang, A. (1998). A subjective metric of authentication. In J.- J. Quisquater, Y. Deswarte, C. Meadows, & D. Gollmann (Eds.), *ESORICS'98.* Louvain-la-Neuve, Belgium: Springer-Verlag.

Jøsang, A. (2001). A logic for uncertain probabilities. *Fuzziness and Knowledge-Based Systems, 9*(3).

Kantola, R.(2004). *Peer to peer and SPAM in the Internet.* Technical Report of the Helsinki University of Technology.

Keromytis, A. D. (2004). *The KeyNote trustmManagement system.*

Khare, R. (1999). *What's in a name? Trust*. 4K Associates.

Kinateder, M., & Rothermel, K. (2003). Architecture and algorithms for a distributed reputation system. In *Proceedings of the First Conference on Trust Management (LNCS)*.
Springer.

Kinateder, M. P., & Siani. (2003). A privacy-enhanced peer-to-peer reputation system. In
*Proceedings of the 4th International Conference on Electronic Commerce and Web
Technologies*.

Kobsa, A., & Schreck, J. (2003). Privacy through pseudonymity in user-adaptive systems.
In *ACM transactions on Internet technology* (pp. 149-183).

Kohl, J., & Neuman, B. C. (1993). *The Kerberos Network Authentication Service, Version
5*.

Labalme, F., & Burton, K. (2001). *Enhancing the Internet with reputations*.

Lai, C., Gong, L., Koved, L., Nadalin, A., & Schemers, R. (1999). User authentication and
authorization in the Java(TM) platform. In *Proceedings of the 15th Annual Computer
Security Application Conference*, Phoenix, AZ.

Lampson, B., Abadi, M., Burrows, M., & Wobber, E. (1992). Authentication in distributed
systems: Theory and practice. In *Transactions on computer systems*. ACM.

Langheinrich, M. (2001). Privacy by design—principles of privacy-aware ubiquitous systems. In *Proceedings of Ubicomp 2001: Ubiquitous Computing: Third International
Conference* (LNCS 2201, pp. 273-291). Heidelberg: Springer Verlag.

Levien, R. (2004). *Attack resistant trust metrics*. UC Berkeley.

LibertyAlliance. *Liberty Alliance Project*. Retrieved 29/11/2005, from http://www.project-
liberty.org/

Lo Presti, S., Cusack, M., & Booth, C. (2003). *Trust issues in pervasive environments*. Trusted
Software Agents and Services for Pervasive Information Environments project.

Marsh, S. (1994). *Formalising trust as a computational concept*. Department of Mathematics
and Computer Science, University of Stirling.

Maslow, A. H. (1954). *Motivation and personality*. Harper.

McKnight, D. H., & Chervany, N. L. (2000). What is trust? A conceptual analysis and an
interdisciplinary model. In *Proceedings of the Americas Conference on Information
Systems (AMCIS)*. AIS, Long Beach, CA.

Microsoft. (n.d.). *.NET Passport 2.5*. Retrieved November 29, 2005, from http://msdn.
microsoft.com/library/default.asp?url=/library/en-us/passport25/serviceguide/intro/
NET_Passport_SDK_Components.asp

Milojicic, D. S., Kalogeraki, V., Lukose, R., Nagaraja, K., Pruyne, J., & Richard, B. (2002).
Peer-to-peer computing.

Nielsen, M., Carbone, M., & Krukow, K. (2004a). *An operational model of trust*. SECURE
Deliverable 1.2.

Nielsen, M., Carbone, M., & Krukow, K. (2004b). *Revised computational trust model*.
SECURE Deliverable 1.3.

Nielsen, M., Plotkin, G., & Winskel, G. (1981). Petri nets, event structures and domains. *Theoritical Computer Science,* (13), 85-108.

OpenPrivacy. (2001). *Open Privacy project.* Retrieved November 11, 2005, from http://www. openprivacy.org/Postini.

Postini. (2004). *Worldwide map of origin of spam.* Retrieved November 11, 2005, from http://www.postini.com/SECURE.

Rahman, A. (2003). *Learning to rely on others' opinion on your own.* Computer Lab (Com Sci Dept), University of Cambridge.

Rahman, A. (2005). *A framework for decentralised trust reasoning.* University of London.

Rahman, A., & Hailes, S. (1997). *Using recommendations for managing trust in distributed systems.*

Romano, D. M. (2003). *The nature of trust: Conceptual and operational clarification.* Unpublished PhD thesis, Louisiana State University.

SECURE. *Secure environments for collaboration among ubiquitous roaming entities project.* Retrieved November 11, 2005, from http://secure.dsp.cs.tcd.ie/

Seigneur, J.-M. (2005a). Decentralized identity for the digital business ecosystem. *ERCIM News.*

Seigneur, J.-M. (2005b). Trust, security and privacy in global computing. *Trinity College Dublin PhD thesis, technical report TCD-CS-2006-02.* Retrieved from https://www. cs.tcd.ie/publications/tech-reports/reports.06/TCD-CS-2006-02.pdf

Seigneur, J.-M., Cahill, V., Jensen, C. D., Gray, E., & Chen, Y. (2004). *The SECURE framework architecture (Beta).* TCD Technical Report.

Seigneur, J.-M., Dimmock, N., Bryce, C., & Jensen, C. D. (2004). Combating spam with TEA (Trustworthy Email Addresses). In *Proceedings of the 2nd Conference on Privacy, Security and Trust.*

Seigneur, J.-M., Gray, A., & Jensen, C. D. (2005). Trust transfer: Encouraging self-recommendations without Sybil attack. In *Proceedings of the Third International Conference on Trust Management* (LNCS). Springer.

Seigneur, J.-M., & Jensen, C. D. (2004a). The claim tool kit for ad-hoc recognition of peer entities. *Journal of Science of Computer Programming.*

Seigneur, J.-M., & Jensen, C. D. (2004b). Trading privacy for trust. In *Proceedings of iTrust'04 the Second International Conference on Trust Management* (LNCS 2995). Springer-Verlag.

Seigneur, J.-M., & Jensen, C. D. (2004c). Trust enhanced ubiquitous payment without too much privacy loss. In *Proceedings of SAC 2004.* ACM.

Smith, R. E. (2001). *Authentication: From passwords to public keys.* Addison Wesley.

TCPA. Trusted Computing Platform Alliance. (2005). Retrieved from http://www.trusted-computing.org/

Terzi, E., Zhong, Y., Bhargava, B., Pankaj, & Madria, S. (2003). An algorithm for building user-role profiles in a trust environment. In *Proceedings of the International Conference on Data Warehousing and Knowledge Discovery*. Springer.

Terzis, S., Wagealla, W., English, C., McGettrick, A., & Nixon, P. (2004). *The SECURE collaboration model*. SECURE Deliverables D2.1, D.2.2 and D2.3.

Travers, J., & Milgram, S. (1969). An experimental study of the small world problem. *Sociometry, 32*(4), 425-443.

Twigg, A., & Dimmock, N. (2003). Attack-resistance of computational trust models. In *Proceedings of the Twelfth International Workshop on Enabling Technologies: Infrastructure for Collaborative Enterprises*. IEEE.

Wagealla, W., Carbone, M., English, C., Terzis, S., & Nixon, P. (2003). A formal model of trust lifecycle management. In *Proceedings of the Workshop on Formal Aspects of Security and Trust (FAST 2003)*.

Watts, D., Sheridan, D. P., & Newman, M. E. J. (2002). Identity and search in social networks. *Science 1*(1), 26-41.

Weiser, M., & Brown, J. S. (1996). Designing calm technology. *PowerGrid Journal, 1*(01).

Winsborough, W. H., Seamons, K. E., & Jones, V. E. (2000). Automated trust negotiation. In *DARPA Information Survivability Conference and Exposition*.

Winslett, M., Yu, T., Seamons, K. E., Hess, A., Jacobson, J., & Jarvis, R. (2002). *Negotiating trust on the Web* (pp. 30-37). IEEE.

Wobber, E., Abadi, M., Burrows, M., & Lampson, B. (1994). *Authentication in the Taos operating system*. ACM.

Yahalom, R., Klein, B., & Beth, T. (1993). Trust relationships in secure systems—a distributed authentication perspective. In *Proceedings of the Symposium on Security and Privacy* (pp. 150). IEEE.

Ziegler, C.-N., & Golbeck, J. (2006). Investigating correlations of trust and interest similarity—do birds of a feather really flock together? *Decision Support Systems 42*(3), 1111-1136.

Ziegler, C.-N., & Lausen, G. (2004). Spreading activation models for trust propagation. In *Proceedings of the International Conference on E-Technology, E-Commerce, and E-Service*. IEEE.

Zimmerman, P. R. (1995). *The pfficial PGP user's guide*. MIT Press.

About the Authors

About the Editors

Ronggong Song is an associate research officer in the Information Security Group, Institute for Information Technology, National Research Council Canada (NRC). He received his BSc (mathematics), MEng (computer science), and PhD (information security) from Beijing University of Posts and Telecommunications. Dr. Song was employed as network planning engineer at Telecommunication Planning Research Institute of MII, P.R.China, and postdoctoral fellow at the University of Ottawa, Canada. He joined NRC in the middle 2001, and involved several major R&D projects in the Information Security Group. He is a senior member of IEEE. His research interests include security, privacy protection, and trust management technologies for e-services, such as anonymous network, pseudonym system, and agent-based security and privacy applications.

Larry Korba is the group leader of the Information Security Group in the Institute for Information Technology of the National Research Council of Canada, Ottawa, ON. As a principal research officer with NRC, he is currently the research lead in a major R&D project involving the development of automated compliance technology for privacy. Recently, he has led several research privacy technology projects involving collaborators in the European

Union, Canada, and Taiwan. He has published over 130 research papers on various technologies. His research interests include network and application security, privacy protection, computer-supported collaborative work, and technologies for security intelligence.

George Yee (http://www.georgeyee.ca) is a Senior Information Scientist in the Information Security Group, Institute for Information Technology, National Research Council Canada (NRC). Prior to joining the NRC in late 2001, he spent over 20 years at Bell-Northern Research and Nortel Networks. George received his PhD (electrical engineering), MSc (systems and information science), and BSc (mathematics) from Carleton University, Ottawa, Canada, where he is currently an adjunct research professor. Dr. Yee is on the Editorial Review Board of several journals including *International Journal of Distance Education Technologies*, the *International Journal of E-Business Research*, and the *Journal of Autonomic and Trusted Computing*. He is a Senior Member of IEEE, and a member of ACM and Professional Engineers Ontario. His research interests include security and privacy for e-services; enhancing reliability, security, and privacy using software agents; and engineering software for reliability, security, and performance.

About the Authors

Carlisle Adams is an associate professor in the School of Information Technology and Engineering (SITE) at University of Ottawa. Prior to his academic appointment in 2003, he worked for 13 years in industry (Nortel, Entrust) in the design and standardization of a variety of cryptographic and security technologies for the Internet. His research and technical contributions include the CAST family of symmetric encryption algorithms, secure protocols for authentication and management in public key infrastructure (PKI) environments, a comprehensive architecture and policy language for access control in electronic networks, the design of efficient mechanisms to assess and constrain the trust that must be placed in unknown peers in a network, and the creation of effective techniques to preserve and enhance privacy on the Internet. Dr. Adams is coauthor of *Understanding PKI: Concepts, Standards, and Deployment Considerations* (2nd ed.) (Addison-Wesley, 2003).

K. Suzanne Barber is a professor in the Electrical and Computer Engineering Department at The University of Texas at Austin and director of The Center for Excellence in Distributed Global Environments (EDGE—http://www.edge.utexas.edu) bringing together multiple disciplines to revolutionize distributed engineering teams and distributed computation. She is also Director of The Laboratory for Intelligent Processes and Systems (http://www.lips.utexas.edu) where ongoing research projects address trust and coordination in distributed, autonomous, agent-based systems. Dr. Barber is a member of IEEE, AAAI, ACM, ASEE, Sigma Xi, Phi Kappa Phi, and Society of Women Engineers.

Morad Benyoucef is assistant professor at the University of Ottawa's School of Management since May 2003. He holds a PhD from Université de Montreal, specializes in management information systems, and dedicates his research to e-business issues and applications. He has published several peer-reviewed articles in journals and conference proceedings on areas such as e-negotiations, e-procurement, online marketplaces, and online trust. He is a reviewer for numerous scientific journals and is active in both the Canadian and international research communities. His research has attracted funding from NSERC, SSHRC, and ORNEC. Professor Benyoucef regularly sits on the program committees of international conferences.

Gregor von Bochmann is professor at the School of Information Technology and Engineering at the University of Ottawa since January 1998, after working during 25 years at the University of Montreal. He is a fellow of the IEEE and ACM and a member of the Royal Society of Canada. He did research on programming languages, compiler design, communication protocols, and software engineering, and published many papers in these areas. He was also actively involved in the standardization of formal description techniques for communication protocols and services. He had many research projects in collaboration with industry, and from 1989 to 1997, he held the Hewlett-Packard - NSERC - CITI industrial research chair on communication protocols at the University of Montreal. His present work is the area of software requirements engineering for distributed systems, quality of service and security management for distributed multimedia applications, and control procedures for optical networks.

Chris Booth received a BA in Mathematics in 1986 and an MSc in computation in 1987 from the University of Oxford. He has worked for QinetiQ and its precessors, DERA and DRA, since 1992 in a variety of research areas, including synchronization algorithms for parallel discrete event simulation, runtime reconfigurable FPGAs, and more recently in pervasive computing and trust.

Pamela Briggs completed her undergraduate and postgraduate studies at Nottingham University and was awarded a PhD in 1983. She then worked in Japan, steadying aspects of bilingual reading comprehension, before moving into the field of human computer interaction, firstly at Sheffield University and subsequently as chair in Applied Cognitive Psychology at Northumbria University. She is now dean of the School of Psychology and Sports Sciences at Northumbria, and is interested in how users' perceptions of trust, privacy, and security affect choice in the context of computer-mediated communication. She currently holds two ESRC awards, one an investigation of patient choices in the e-health domain, the other a study of trust and privacy issues for ambient intelligence.

George Bryan received his Bachor of Applied Science degree in applied mathematics and his Master of Applied Science degree in computer science from the Charles Sturt University, Bathurst in 1985 and 1998, respectively. A/Prof Bryan was the head of the School of Computing and Information Technology at University of Western Sydney from 2003 to 2006 and the director of the University's Centre for Advanced Data Engineering from 2000 to 2003. A/Prof Bryan research interests include parallel and distributed information systems, high performance graphics, and the virtual reality environments embodying autonomous agents.

Michael Butler received a BA in computer science from Trinity College, Dublin in 1988, an MSc and a DPhil in computation from the University of Oxford respectively in 1989 and 1992. His research interests include the application and combination of formal methods and their combination with semiformal design notations. He has worked on applying formal methods to several problems including security protocols and dependable systems. He was/is an investigator on three EU IST projects (MATISSE, PUSSEE, RODIN), he is on the PC of several formal methods conferences and on the editorial board of the *Formal Aspects of Computing Journal*.

Jennifer Chandler is an assistant professor at the Faculty of Law at the University of Ottawa. She has been a member of the Bar of Ontario since 1998. She holds an LLM from the Harvard Law School, an LLB from Queen's University, and a BSc from the University of Western Ontario. Before joining the Faculty of Law in 2002, she practiced law in Ottawa for several years, and was a law clerk for the Hon. Mr. Justice Sopinka at the Supreme Court of Canada. The overarching theme of her research is law, science, and technology, particularly with respect to the social and environmental effects of emerging technologies and the interaction of emerging technologies with law and regulation. In addition to work fitting within this broad theme, Professor Chandler has also written extensively in the areas of cybersecurity and cybertorts and speaks frequently in Canada, the U.S., and Europe on these topics.

Khalil el-Khatib is currently an assistant professor at the University of Western Ontario. He received a bachelor's degree in computer science from the American University of Beirut (AUB) in 1992, a master's degree in computer science from McGill University in 96, and a PhD degree from the University of Ottawa in 2005. Between the years of 1992 and 1994, he worked as a research assistant in the computer science Dept. at AUB. In 1996, he joined the High Capacity Division at Nortel Networks as a software designer. From February 2002, he worked as research officer in the Network Computing Group (lately renamed the Information Security Group) at the National Research Council of Canada for 2 years, and continued to be affiliated with the group for another 2 years. His research interest includes Parallel Discrete Event Simulation, QoS for multimedia applications, personal mobility, IP telephony, feature interaction for VoIP, ubiquitous computing environments, security and privacy issues for the Internet and for the mobile wireless ad hoc networks (MANET).

Lesley Fishwick is programme leader for the MA in Sports Development in the Division of Sport Sciences. Her discipline area is sociology of sport. Since completing her PhD in sociology at the University of Illinois at Champaign-Urbana, USA on occupational sex segregation in sport organizations, she has conducted a number of research projects focusing on using sociology critically to understand sport as part of people's lives. Recent articles focus on aspects of athletic identity and sociology of the body. Recent consultancy projects include an evaluation of Women Coaching in the Community programme. She is presently collaborating on an ESRC E-society project on the way people seek and evaluate health advice online.

Karen K. Fullam is a doctoral student and graduate research assistant in The Laboratory for Intelligent Processes and Systems at The University of Texas at Austin. She received her MS degree from The University of Texas at Austin in 2003 and her BS degree from The Colorado School of Mines in 1999. Her research concerns trustworthiness evaluation of information, as well as techniques for making trust-related decisions in complex systems. Ms. Fullam is the recipient of The University of Texas Micro-Electronics and Computer Development Fellowship and is a member of AAAI, Phi Kappa Phi, and Tau Beta Pi.

Tyrone Grandison manages the Data Disclosure Research team in the Intelligent Information Systems group at the IBM Almaden Research Center in San Jose, California. His research focuses on nonintrusive, high-performance, cell-level database security and privacy controls. His group develops novel technology (e.g., hippocratic databases) in response to real world problems in a myriad of application domains (e.g., healthcare, financial, retail, automotive, etc.). He received his doctorate from the Imperial College of Science, Technology and Medicine in the United Kingdom, and his master's and bachelor's degrees from the University of the West Indies in Jamaica.

Rolf Haenni is currently an assistant professor in computer science at the University of Berne, Switzerland. He has a diploma and a PhD degree in computer science from the University of Fribourg, Switzerland. As a post-doc researcher, he has formerly been involved in the following projects: "Defeasible Reasoning and Management of Uncertainty" (European Basic Research Activity, 1993-1996), "Symbolic and Probabilistic Argumentation Systems" (Swiss National Science Foundation, 1996-1998), "Inference and Deduction: An Integration of Logic and Probability" (Swiss National Science Foundation, 1998-2000), "Inference and Applications of Probabilistic Argumentation Systems" (University of California, Los Angeles, USA, 2001-2002), and "Philosophy, Probability, and Modeling" (University of Konstanz, Germany, 2002-2004). His main research interest is the integration of logical and probabilistic methods in the domain of uncertain reasoning and applications thereof.

Peter Harris completed his undergraduate and postgraduate studies at University College London. He has worked at the Universities of Nottingham, Hertfordshire, and Sussex (twice), and held visiting appointments at the Universities of Amsterdam, British Columbia, Oxford, and Pittsburgh. He is currently at the Department of Psychology at the University of Sheffield. His principal research interests and publications are in social and health psychology, particularly in the area of how people respond to health risk information.

Christian Damsgaard Jensen is an assistant professor at the Technical University of Denmark. His research interests include computer and network security, especially issues involving secure collaboration among mutually suspicious principals, and relaxed trust models in ad-hoc computing. He received his MSc in computer science from the University of Copenhagen and his PhD in computer science from Université Joseph Fourier in Grenoble, France.

Jacek Jonczy is a computer scientist and PhD student at the Institute of Computer Science and Applied Mathematics at the University of Berne, Switzerland. He received his BSc and MSc degrees in computer science from the University of Fribourg, Switzerland. His research interests include reasoning under uncertainty, trust and authenticity management, cryptography, and network reliability.

Reto Kohlas is currently a PhD student at the Institute of Computer Science and Applied Mathematics at the University of Berne, Switzerland. He received his MSc degree in computer science from the University of Fribourg, Switzerland. He is a former member of the Information Security and Cryptography Group at the Department of Computer Science, ETH Zürich, Switzerland. His main research interests are formal approaches to trust management and authentication, and reasoning under uncertainty.

Michael Leuschel is the head of the Software Engineering and Programming Languages group at the University of Düsseldorf. His main areas of research are automatic program analysis and optimisation (partial evaluation, abstract interpretation) and automated verification tools for high-level languages. He was awarded the IBM International Chair 1999 on Modelling and Optimisation. He has been program chair of several conferences, is head of the PEPM steering committee, and is on the editorial board for the journal *Theory and Practice of Logic Programming*. He was/is investigator in various EU IST projects. He has also developed several tools (ECCE, LOGEN, ProB).

Linda Little is a senior research associate and lecturer in social psychology at Northumbria University, UK. She completed her undergraduate and postgraduate studies at Northumbria and was awarded a PhD in 2004. She is currently working on a 2-year ESRC grant investigating trust and privacy permissions associated with ambient intelligence. Her main research areas are privacy, trust, technology use in public places, the impact of age and disability on technology use.

Stephane Lo Presti received an engineering diploma from the ENSIMAG School (Grenoble, France) in 1998 and a PhD from the INJPG University (Grenoble, France) in 2002. His research interests include trust, security, and formal methods that he has combined in the context of the UK EPSRC-funded T-SAS project at the University of Southampton and the EU IST OpenTC project at Royal Holloway, University of London. He has been the member of various programme committees of conferences and workshops related to trust.

Stephen Marsh is a research officer at in the National Research Council's Institute for Information Technology (NRC-IIT). While on leave in 2005, he was a research fellow in the Division of Psychology at Northumbria University, UK. His PhD, finished in 1994 at the University of Stirling, Scotland, introduced a formalisation of trust, applied to multiagent systems. His research interests include trust, HCI, ambient intelligence, and information sharing amongst autonomous agents. He has published in most of these areas, and has been an invited speaker on topics as diverse as collaboration between the arts and the sciences, trust, and multiagent systems. His Web site is at http://www.stephenmarsh.ca

Paolo Massa is a researcher at the Institute for Scientific and Technological Research (IRST) in Trento, Italy. He received his PhD from ICT International Graduate School of University of Trento in March 2006 defending a thesis titled "Trust-aware Decentralized Recommender Systems." He has a master's in computer science from Eastern Piedmont University, Italy. His research interests are trust and reputation, recommender systems and social software. Contact him at massa@itc.it

Jean-Marc Seigneur received a master's in electrical engineering from INSA Lyon, an MSc and a PhD in computer science from Trinity College Dublin (TCD). After his PhD, he became a TCD research fellow working on user-centric identity management for the EU-funded peer-to-peer digital business ecosystem. His publications cover pervasive computing security, trust and privacy. He administers the electronic technology transfer group on computational trust at http://www.trustcomp.org. He teaches peer-to-peer technologies in two universities, the University of Geneva and the University of Savoy. His main affiliation is with the CUI at the University of Geneva.

Elizabeth Sillence is a senior researcher at the University of Northumbria, UK. She has degrees in psychology and ergonomics and gained her PhD from Birmingham University in human-computer interaction. She is currently researching the use of the Internet in health advice, exploring issues of trust, risk, and social identity and examining the integration of different information resources. Her main research interests are trust factors in online advice, computer-mediated communication, digital communities, technology and personalisation, and the social aspects of mobile phone use.

Vijay Varadharajan is the Microsoft chair and professor of Computing at Macquarie University. He is also the director of Information and Networked System Security Research. He is also the technical board director of Computer Science, Australian Computer Society. He has published more than 250 papers in international journals and conferences, and has coauthored and edited 8 books. His current research interests are in distributed system security, network security, secure electronic commerce, mobile agent security, and trustworthy computing. He is on the editorial board of several journals and is a fellow of IEE, BCS, IEAust, ACS, and IMA.

Weiliang Zhao is currently a PhD candidate in School of Computing and Mathematics of University of Western Sydney. He received his Master of Honours - Computing and Information Technology from University of Western Sydney in 2003. He received his Bachelor of Science - Physics from Peking University in 1988. Weiliang Zhao was an application developer in ANZ bank from 2001 to 2003. His current areas of research interest include e-commerce security, security for Internet applications and Web services, and models and architectures of trust management.

Index

A

abstract trust model 142
access control 8, 32, 136, 151, 201, 210
access control management 201
accuracy 123
agent's transmission 20
ambient intelligence (AmI) 259, 270, 287
ambient society 261
ambient world, 260
AMEX-backed reward scheme 12
anonymity 141, 148, 266, 314
application programming interface (API)
    61, 79, 306
artificial trustee 271
audit trails 123
authentication 13, 29, 43, 105, 115,
    141, 148, 201, 294, 297
authentication management 201
authenticity problem 141
authorization 123, 201
automated trust negotiation (ATN) 299
availability 9, 62, 123, 129, 219, 305

B

badmouthing 229
ballot-stuffing 92
bans 61
Better Business Bureau (BBB) 229
binding 42
block list 60
blogosphere 56, 66
branding 219, 227
British Sign Language (BSL) 277
business/job networking sites 56, 62
business factor 12
business model 21

C

cash in 92
certificate 154, 299
certificate/certification authority (CA) 152,
    163, 202, 294, 299
certification trust 33
choice 283
Club Nexus 63